APPLIED MATHEMATICS-III

By

Dr. J.K. TYAGI
Professor & Head
Deptt. of Applied Science
Maharaja Agarsain Instt. of Tech.
Ghaziabad (U.P.)

Dr. S.K. TYAGI
Senior Lecturer
Amity School of Engg. & Tech.
Amity University,
NOIDA (U.P.)

KHANNA BOOK PUBLISHING CO. (P) LTD.

DELHI

Applied Mathematics-III

By Dr. J.K. Tyagi
Dr. S.K. Tyagi

Laser Typeset by : **PLUS COMPUTERS**, 696/1, Madhav Puram, Meerut. Ph. 0-9897079785.

Published by : Puneet Khanna
Khanna Book Publishing Co. (P) Ltd., 1695, Nai Sarak, Delhi-6.

Printed at : Polykam Printers, Delhi.

Dedicated

To

OUR PARENTS

Preface to the First Edition

The book is designed to meet all requirements of the students of B.Tech. third semester Applied Mathematics course of Amity University, Uttar Pradesh. Each chapter is well equipped with the concepts written in detail and a large number of solved and unsolved exercises from question papers of examinations held by various universities.

We express our profound and deep regards to our source of inspiration, respected Dr. Ashok K. Chauhan, Founder President, Ritnand Balved Education Foundation for his encouragement and blessing. Our thanks are due to our all time motivation Prof. Balvinder Shukla, Pro. Vice Chancellor AUUP, Director General, ASET, Noida for providing all necessary help. We are also thankful to Prof. A.L. Verma, Head, Department of Applied Science, ASET, Noida for his constructive suggestions to put the book present shape. The Director and Management of Maharaja Agarsain Institute of Technology, Ghaziabad are also thankfully acknowledged. Our sincere thanks are also due to all our colleagues for their critical and constructive suggestions.

The authors are very grateful to the numerous authors whose meticulous work has been consulted througout, to prepare this book.

We would like to extend our warm regards to our teachers for their blessing. We are also thankful to our family members for their patience and support during the preparation of this book.

We owe our gratitude to M/s Khanna Publishers and Printer for their full co-operation and utmost efficiency to bring out the boom in such a nice shape.

July, 2009 **AUTHORS**

SYLLABUS

APPLIED MATHEMATICS-III
(BTMT-20301)

UNIT-I : PARTIAL DIFFERENTIAL EQUATIONS *10 Lectures*

Formation of PDE, Equations sovable by Direct Integration, Linear Equations of the First Order, Non-linear Equations of the First Order, Charpit's Method, Homogeneous Linear Equations with Constant Coefficients, Non Homogeneosu Linear Equations.

UNIT-II : FOURIER SERIES *15 Lectures*

Periodic Functions, Fourier Series, Functions having points of discontinuity, Even or Odd Functions, Change of Interval, Half-range Series, Parseval's Formula, Complex form of Fourier Series, Practical Harmonic Analysis, Fourier Transforms, Sine and Cosine Transforms.

Unit-III : LAPLACE TRANSFORMATION *12 Lectures*

Definition, Transforms of Elementary Functions, Properties of Laplace Transforms, Existence Conditions, Transforms of Derivatives, Transforms of Integrals, Evaluation of Integrals by Laplace Transform, Inverse Transforms, Other Methods of finding Inverse Transforms, Convolution Theorem, Application to Differential Equations, Simultaneous Linear Equations with Constant Coefficients, Unit Step Functions, Periodic Functions.

Unit-IV : LINEAR PROGRAMMING *8 Lectures*

Formulation of the Problem, Graphical Method, Canonial and Standard Forms of L.P.P. Simplex Method, Artificial Variable Techniques Big-M-method, Two Phase Method, Degeneracy, Dual Simplex Method.

CONTENTS

CHAPTER 1 : PARTIAL DIFFERENTIAL EQUATIONS 1 - 46

CHAPTER 2 : FOURIER SERIES 47 - 119

1

Partial Differential Equations

1.1 INTRODUCTION

Differential equations both ordinary or partial arise as they represent one or the other phenomena which may be physical, chemical, geometrical, related with engineering or in any other field. The solutions of these equations give the solution of the problems dependent on them. Theoretically speaking, if we **eliminate the constant** m from relation $f(x, y, m) = 0$ between two variables, it results into an ordinary differential equation. If there be a relation having one **dependent variable** z and two **independent variables** x, y and some **constants** or **arbitrary functions** then the elimination of constants or the arbitrary functions result into a **partial differential equation**. In the study of partial differential equations, the problems may be :

(i) **Formation of differential equations by eliminating constants** or functions from a given relation,

(ii) **Finding the general solution of a given differential equation** and

(iii) **Determining that solution which satisfy the given the conditions.**

We consider these problems one by one.

1.1.1. Order of Partial Differential Equation

The order of the highest order partial differential coefficient represents the order of a partial differential equation.

1.1.2. Degree of Partial Differential Equation

The degree of partial differential equation is the largest power of the highest ordered derivative present in the partial differential equation provided no radial signs and fractional power should remain in the equation.

1.2 NOTATIONS

If $z = f(x, y)$ be a function of two independent variables x, y, expressed as $z = f(x, y)$

Then the first and second order partial derivatives are represented as

$$\frac{\partial z}{\partial x} = p, \quad \frac{\partial z}{\partial y} = q; \quad \frac{\partial^2 z}{\partial x^2} = r, \quad \frac{\partial^2 z}{\partial x \partial y} = \frac{\partial^2 z}{\partial y \partial x} = s, \quad \frac{\partial^2 z}{\partial y^2} = t.$$

1.3 FORMATION OF PARTIAL DIFFERENTIAL EQUATIONS

Partial differential equation may arise on elimination of arbitrary constants or arbitrary functions from a given relation involving two or more independent variables and the constants or functions. If the number of constants to be elimination be equal to the number of independent variables, the resulting partial differential equation, after elimination, becomes of first order but if the number of constants be more than the number of independent variables, the resulting equation becomes of second or higher order. If a relation involves arbitrary functions, the order of the partial differential equation after the elimination of those functions is generally equal to the number of functions to be eliminated.

Example 1.1. **Form the partial differential equation by eliminating the constant from the relations:**

(i) $z = ax + by + a^2 + b^2$ *(Madras 91)*

(ii) $(x - a)^2 + (y - b)^2 + z^2 = C^2$ *(Osmania 99S, 2003)*

Solution (i). Differentiating partially $z = px + qy + a^2 + b^2$, $\quad p = \frac{\partial z}{\partial x} = a, \quad q = \frac{\partial z}{\partial y} = b,$

Hence on elimination, we get $z = ap + bq + p^2 + q^2$.

(ii). Differentiating partially $(x - a)^2 + (y - b)^2 + z^2 = C^2$

partially w.r.t. x, $\quad 2(x - a) + 2z\frac{\partial z}{\partial x} = 0 \quad$ or $\quad x - u = p_z$

partially, w.r.t. y, $\quad 2(y - b) + 2z\frac{\partial z}{\partial y} = 0 \quad$ or $\quad y - b = -q_z$

Hence on eliminating $(x - a)^2$ and $(x - b)^2$, We get $z^2(p^2 + q^2 + 1) = C^2$.

Example 1.2. **Eliminate the arbitrary functions from**

(i) $z = f(x^2 - y^2)$

(ii) $z = f\left(\frac{xy}{z}\right)$ *(Andhra 91)*

(iii) $z = f_1(x)\, f_2(y)$ *(Madras 93)*

Solution. (i) Differentiating $z = f(x^2 - y^2)$, partially, we have

$$p = \frac{\partial z}{\partial x} = f'(x^2 - y^2) \cdot 2x, \quad q = \frac{\partial z}{\partial y} = f'(x^2 - y^2) \cdot (-2y)$$

Hence $\frac{p}{q} = \frac{2x\, f'(x^2 - y^2)}{-2y\, f'(x^2 - y^2)}$ or $py = qx = 0$ is the required equation

(ii) Differentiating $z = f\left(\frac{xy}{z}\right)$, partially

$$p = \frac{\partial z}{\partial x} = f'\left(\frac{xy}{z}\right) \cdot \frac{zy - xy\frac{\partial z}{\partial x}}{z^2} = \frac{y(z - px)}{z^2} f'\left(\frac{xy}{z}\right) \qquad ...(1)$$

and
$$q = \frac{\partial z}{\partial y} = f'\left(\frac{xy}{z}\right) \cdot \frac{xz - xy\frac{\partial z}{\partial y}}{z^2} = \frac{x(z - yq)}{z^2} f' \qquad ...(2)$$

On dividing (1) by (2) $\frac{p}{q} = \frac{y(z - px)}{x(z - qy)}$

or $px(z - qy) - qy(z - px) = 0$

or $z(px - qy) = 0$

So the required equation is $(px - qy) = 0$.

(iii) Differentiating $z = f_1(x)\, f_2(y)$ partially.

$$\boldsymbol{p} = \frac{\partial z}{\partial x} = f_1'(x)\, f_2(y) \qquad ...(1)$$

and
$$\boldsymbol{q} = \frac{\partial z}{\partial y} = f_1(x)\, f_2'(y) \qquad ...(2)$$

Differentiating (1) partially w.r.t. y, we have

$$\boldsymbol{s} = \frac{\partial^2 z}{\partial y \partial x} = f_1'(x)\, f_2'(y) = \left(\frac{p}{f_2(y)}\right)\left(\frac{q}{f_1(x)}\right) = \frac{pq}{z}$$

So the reqd. eq^n. is $zs = pq$.

Example 1.3. Form partial differential equations by eliminating the arbitrary functions form :

(i) $z = f(x + at) + g(x - at)$, *(Osmania 99)*

(ii) $f(x^2 + y^2, z - xy) = 0$ *(Assam 99, Madurai 99)*

Solution. (i) In $z = f(x + at) + g(x - at)$, there are two independent variables x and t, Differentiating partially,

$$\frac{\partial z}{\partial x} = f'(x + at) \cdot \frac{\partial (x + at)}{\partial x} + g'(x - at)\frac{\partial (x - at)}{\partial x}$$

$$= f'(x + at) + g'(x - at) \qquad ...(1)$$

and
$$\frac{\partial z}{\partial t} = f'(x + at) \cdot a - g'(x - at) \cdot a \qquad ...(2)$$

Differentiating (1) further partially w.r.t. x and (2) w.r.t. t, we have

$$\frac{\partial^2 z}{\partial x^2} = f'' + g'' \text{ and } \frac{\partial^2 z}{\partial t^2} = a^2 (f'' + g'')$$

Hence $\frac{\partial^2 z}{\partial t^2} = a^2 \frac{\partial^2 z}{\partial x^2}$ is the required differential equation

(ii) Let $x^2 + y^2 = u$ and $z - xy = v$ ...(1)

So we have $f(u, v) = 0$ ...(2)

and $$\frac{\partial u}{\partial x} = 2x, \frac{\partial u}{\partial y} = 2y \text{ and } \frac{\partial v}{\partial x} = p - y, \frac{\partial v}{\partial y} = q - x \quad \text{...(3)}$$

Taking total differential of (2)

$$df = \frac{\partial f}{\partial u} du + \frac{\partial f}{\partial v} dv = 0$$

So $$\frac{\partial f}{\partial x} = \frac{\partial f}{\partial u}\frac{\partial u}{\partial x} + \frac{\partial f}{\partial v}\frac{\partial v}{\partial x} = 0 \quad \text{...(4)}$$

and $$\frac{\partial f}{\partial y} = \frac{\partial f}{\partial u}\frac{\partial u}{\partial y} + \frac{\partial f}{\partial v}\frac{\partial v}{\partial y} = 0 \quad \text{...(5)}$$

Eliminating $\frac{\partial f}{\partial u}, \frac{\partial f}{\partial v}$ from (4) and (5)

$$\begin{vmatrix} \frac{\partial u}{\partial x} & \frac{\partial v}{\partial x} \\ \frac{\partial u}{\partial y} & \frac{\partial v}{\partial y} \end{vmatrix} = 0 \text{ or } \begin{vmatrix} 2x & p - y \\ 2y & q - x \end{vmatrix} = 0$$

So the required equation is $qx - x^2 - py + y^2 = 0$

or $$qx - yp = x^2 - y^2.$$

Example 1.4. **Form the partial differential equation, resulting on eliminating of *a, b, c* from**

$$\frac{x^2}{a^2} + \frac{y^2}{b^2} + \frac{z^2}{c^2} = 1$$

Solution. Differentiating partially, the given equation, we get

$$\frac{x}{a^2} + \frac{z}{c^2}\frac{\partial z}{\partial x} = 0 \text{ and } \frac{y}{b^2} + \frac{z}{c^2}\frac{\partial z}{\partial y} = 0$$

So $$\frac{z}{x}\frac{\partial z}{\partial x} = -\frac{c^2}{a^2} \text{ and } \frac{z}{y}\frac{\partial z}{\partial y} = -\frac{c^2}{b^2}$$

Hence on again differentiating partially

$$\frac{\partial}{\partial x}\left(\frac{pz}{x}\right) = 0 \quad \text{...(i)}$$

and $$\frac{\partial}{\partial y}\left(\frac{pz}{x}\right) = 0 \quad \text{...(ii)}$$

and $$\frac{\partial}{\partial x}\left(\frac{qz}{y}\right) = 0 \quad \text{...(iii)}$$

and $$\frac{\partial}{\partial y}\left(\frac{qz}{y}\right) = 0 \quad \text{...(iv)}$$

Any one of these may the required equations. From (i) we have

$$\frac{1}{x^2}\{x(pp + z.r) - pz\} = 0$$

or $$xzr + xp^2 - pz = 0 \quad \text{...(v)}$$

From (ii) We have $\frac{1}{x}\{sz + pq\} = 0$ or $sz + pq = 0$ ...(vi)

From (iii) $\frac{1}{y}\{sz + qp\} = 0$ or $sz + pq = 0$ ...(vii)

It is same as (vi) above.

From (iv) $$\frac{1}{y^2}\{y(tz + q\cdot q) - qz\} = 0$$

or $$yzt + yq^2 - qz = 0 \quad \text{...(viii)}$$

Any one of the above (v), (vii) or (viii) may be the answer.

Example 1.5. **Find the differential equations of the spheres :**

(i) whose centres lie on the z-axis, *(Osmania 95, Coimbatore 88)*

(ii) whose centres lie on the x–y plane and have a constant radius a. *(Bangalore 94)*

Solution. (i) Any sphere with centre $(0, 0, c)$ is $x^2 + y^2 + (z - c)^2 = r^2$

Differentiating partially, we have $2x + 2(z - c)p = 0$ and $2y + 2(z - c)q = 0$

Hence $\frac{x}{y} = \frac{p}{q}$ or $py - qx = 0$ is the required equation.

(ii) Any such sphere has centre $(\alpha, \beta, 0)$.

So the spheres have equations

$$(x - \alpha)^2 + (y - \beta)^2 + z^2 = a^2.$$

Differentiating partially, we have

$$2(x - \alpha) + 2zp = 0, (y - \beta) + zq = 0$$

So, on eliminating $x - \alpha$ and $y - \beta$, we get

$$(-pz)^2 + (-qz)^2 + z^2 = a^2$$

or $z^2(p^2 + q^2 + 1) = a^2$ is the required equation.

PROBLEM SET 1.1

1. Form the partial differential equations by eliminating the arbitrary constants from :

(i) $z = ax + a^2y^2 + b$,

(ii) $2z = \frac{x^2}{a^2} + \frac{y^2}{b^2}$ *(AUUP 2007; Osmania 88)*

(iii) $z = (x^2 + a)(y^2 + b)$

(iv) $z = ax + by + ab$.

Ans. (i) $q = 2p^2y$, (ii) $2z = px + qy$, (iii) $pq = 4xyz$ (iv) $x = px + qy + pq$

2. Form the partial differential equations by eliminating arbitrary functions from

(i) $z = yf(x) + xg(y)$ *(Karnataka 93, Madras 93)*

Ans. $xys = px + qy - z$

(ii) $xyz = \phi(x + y + z)$ *(Osmania 95, Calicut 94, Madras 93)*

Ans. $x(y - z)p + y(z - x)q = z(x - y)$

(iii) $z = f(x^2 - y^2)$ *(Kottayam 99)*

Ans. $py + qx = 0$

(iv) $z = y^2 + 2f\left(\frac{1}{x} \log y\right)$ *(Madras 2000PT V.T.U. 2000S)*

Ans. $px^2 + qy = 2y^2$

(v) $z = f(x) + e^y g(x)$ *(Madras 93)*

Ans. $t = q$, Diff. partially $\frac{\partial z}{\partial y} = e^y g(x)$

So $z = f(x) + q$ diff. partial w.r.t. y, $q = 0 + t$.

3. **Form the partial differential equation by eliminating the arbitrary functions from the following :**

(i) $z = xf1(x + t) + f2(x + t)$ *(Delhi 91)*

Ans. $\frac{\partial^2 z}{\partial x^2} - 2\frac{\partial^2 z}{\partial x\, \partial t} + \frac{\partial^2 z}{\partial t^2} = 0$

(ii) $f(x + y + z, x^2 + y^2 + z^2) = 0$ *(Ranchi 90)*

Ans. $(y - z)p + (z - x)q + (x - y)$

(iii) $z = f(x + i\lambda t) + \phi(x - i\lambda t)$ *(Bangalore 90, Karnataka 93)*

Ans. $\frac{\partial^2 z}{\partial x^2} + \frac{1}{\lambda^2}\frac{\partial^2 z}{\partial t^2} = 0.$

4. **Form the differential equation by eliminating arbitrary functions from :**

(i) $u = f(x^2 + 2yz, y^2 + 2zx)$

Ans. $(y^2 - zx)\frac{du}{\partial x} + (x^2 - yz)\frac{\partial y}{du} + (z^2 - xy)\frac{\partial u}{\partial z} = 0$ *(Guahati 99)*

(ii) $F(xy + z^2, x + y + z) = 0$ *(Madras 95, Kerala 90S)*

Ans. $p(x - 2z) + q(2z - y) = y - x$

5. **Find the differential equation of all planes which are at a constant distance from the origin.** *(Gulbarga 96; MOU 2004)*

Ans. Plane is $x \cos \alpha + y \cos \beta + z \sqrt{1 - \cos^2 \alpha - \cos^2 p} = p$ (a constant)

$z = px + qy + a\sqrt{1 + p^2 + q^2}$

6. **Find the differential equation resulting on eliminating the arbitrary functions from**

(i) $x = f_1(x + t) + f_2(x + t)$ *(Delhi 91)*

Ans. $\frac{\partial^2 z}{\partial x^2} - 2\frac{\partial^2 z}{\partial x\, \partial t} + \frac{\partial^2 z}{\partial t^2} = 0$

(ii) $z = xf1(y + 2x) + f2(y - 3x)$ *(S. Patel 97, Kuvempu 96)*

Ans. $\frac{\partial^2 z}{\partial x^2} + \frac{\partial^2 z}{\partial x\, \partial y} - 6\frac{\partial^2 z}{\partial y^2} = 0$

(iii) $vr = f(r - at) + \phi(r + at)$ *(S. Patel 97)*

Ans. $\frac{\partial^2 v}{\partial t^2} = \frac{a^2}{r^2}\frac{\partial}{\partial r}\left(r^2 \frac{\partial v}{\partial r}\right)$.

1.4 SOLUTIONS OF PARTIAL DIFFERENTIAL EQUATIONS

Definitions

Complete Integral

If $\phi((p, q; x, y, z) = 0$ be the differential equation resulting on elimination of two arbitrary constants a and b from $f(x, y, z, a, b) = 0$. Then $f(x, y, z, a, b) = 0$ is the solution of the partial differential equation $\phi((p, q; x, y, z) = 0$ This solution, which **contains two arbitrary constants**, is **called the complete integral of the given equation.**

Particular Integral

Giving particular values to a and b in the solution $f(x, y, z, a, b) = 0$, we have the solution called the **particular integral** of the given differential equation.

General Integral

If in the solution $f(x, y, z, a, b) = 0$, we let $b = \psi(a)$ and eliminate a between $f(x, y, z, a, \psi) = 0$ and equation $\dfrac{\partial f}{\partial a} = 0$, resulting on differentiating f w.r.t. a; the solution thus **obtained is called the general integral of** $\phi(x, y, z, a, b) = 0$.

Singular Integral

The result of eliminating a, b between the complete integral $f(x, y, z, a, b) = 0$, $\dfrac{\partial f}{\partial a} = 0$, $\dfrac{\partial f}{\partial b} = 0$, gives the solution called the envelope of the family represented by $f(x, y, z, a, b) = 0$. As the equation of envelope is also a solution of the differential equation, it is called its singular solution.

1.5 METHODS OF SOLUTION

The method of solution of a partial differential equation depends on the form of the differential equation itself. Some differential equations may be solvable by simple integration, some, which are of the form $p\,P(x, y, z) + q\,Q(x, y, z) = R\,(x, y, z)$, and are known as **Lagrange's linear equations**, (known after the persons, who first gave the method of their solution), are solved by Lagranges method and for other types of equations there are other methods. We consider them here one by one.

1.6 EQUATIONS SOLVABLE BY DIRECT INTEGRATION

Solution of such equations are best illustrated by examples.

Example 1.5. **Solve** $\dfrac{\partial^3 z}{\partial x^2\,\partial y} = \cos\,(2x + 3y)$ *(Mysore 1995)*

Solution. Integrating successively w.r.t. x then x, then y

$$\frac{\partial^2 z}{\partial x\,\partial y} = \int \cos\,(2x + 3y)\,dx = \frac{\sin\,(2x + 3y)}{2} + \phi_1(y)$$

$$\frac{\partial z}{\partial y} = \int \frac{\sin(2x+3y)}{2}\, dx + \phi_1(y) \int dx + \phi_2(y)$$

$$= -\frac{\cos(2x+3y)}{4} + x\phi_1(y) + \phi_2(y)$$

Now $\quad z = -\frac{1}{4}\int \cos(2x+3y)\, dy + x\int \phi_1(y)\, dy + \int \phi_2(y)\, dy + \phi_3(x)$

So the solution is $-\frac{\sin(2x+3y)}{12} + xF_1(y) + F_2(y) + \phi_3(x)$

Where $F_1(y), F_2(y)$ are another arbitrary functions of y.

Example 1.6. $\quad \frac{\partial^3 z}{\partial x^2\, \partial y} = 18xy^2 + \sin(2x - y) \quad$ ...(1)

Solution. Integrating partially w.r.t. x, we get

$$\frac{\partial^2 z}{\partial x\, \partial y} = \frac{18x^2y^2}{2} - \frac{\cos(2x-y)}{2} + \phi_1(y) \quad \text{...(2)}$$

Integrating (2) partially w.r.t. x, again

$$\frac{\partial z}{\partial y} = \frac{9x^3}{3}y^2 - \frac{\sin(2x-y)}{4} + \phi_1(y)\cdot x + \phi_2(y) \quad \text{...(3)}$$

Integrating (3) partially w.r.t. y

$$z = 3x^3\frac{y^3}{3} + \frac{\cos(2x-y)}{-4} + x\int \phi_1(y)dy + \int \phi_2(y)\, dy + \phi_3(x)$$

So $\quad z = x^3y^3 - \frac{1}{4}\cos(2x - y) + x\, F_1(y) + F_2(y) + \phi_3(x)$

Where F_1, F_2 are other arbitrary functions.

Example 1.7. Solve $\frac{\partial^2 z}{\partial x \partial y} = \sin x \sin y$, given $\frac{\partial z}{\partial y} = -2\sin y$, when $x = 0$; and $z = 0$, when y is an odd multiple of $\pi/2$. *(Mysore 97S; Madras 94S; V.T.U. 2004)*

Solution : Integrating the given equation partially w.r.t. x

$$\frac{\partial z}{\partial y} = -\cos x \sin y + \phi_1(y) \quad \text{...(2)}$$

Given $\frac{\partial z}{\partial y} = -2\sin y$, given when $x = 0$, so we have $\phi_1(y) = -\sin y$.

So $\quad \frac{\partial z}{\partial y} = -\sin y \cos x - \sin y \quad$ ...(3)

Integrating (3) partially w.r.t. y,

$$z = \cos y \cos x + \cos y + \phi_2(x)$$

given $z = 0$ when y is an odd multiple of $\pi/2$ as $y = \frac{\pi}{2}$,

So $\quad 0 = 0 + 0 + \phi_2(x) \quad$ so $\phi_2(x) = 0$

Hence the solution is

$$z = (1 + \cos x)\cos y$$

Example 1.8. **Solve $\frac{\partial^2 z}{\partial x^2} = a^2 z$, given that at $x = 0$, $\frac{\partial z}{\partial x} = a \sin y$ and $\frac{\partial z}{\partial y} = 0$.**

(Assam; Osmania 95)

Solution.

$$\frac{\partial^2 z}{\partial x^2} - a^2 z = 0 \qquad ...(1)$$

Let $z = e^{mx}$ then $m^2 - a^2 = 0$ or $m = \pm a$

Because the diferentiation is partial. So while integrating w.r.t. x, the arbitrary constants will be taken to be functions of y.

So let
$$z = \phi_1(y)\, e^{ax} + \phi_2(y)\, e^{-ax} \qquad ...(2)$$
be its solution

Differentiating (2),
$$\frac{\partial z}{\partial x} = a\, \{\phi_1(y)\, e^{ax} - \phi_2(y)\, e^{-ax}\}$$

Given, at $x = 0$, $\frac{\partial z}{\partial x} = a \sin y$

So
$$a \sin y = a\, \{\phi_1(y) - \phi_2(y)\} \qquad ...(3)$$

Differentiating (2) partially w.r.t. y

$$\frac{\partial z}{\partial y} = \phi_1'\, e^{ax} + \phi_2'\, e^{-ax}$$

at $x = 0$, $\frac{\partial z}{\partial y} = 0$

So
$$0 = \phi_1' + \phi_2' \qquad ...(4)$$

So
$$\phi_1 + \phi_2 = c \qquad ...(5)$$

From (3) and (4)
$$\phi_1 = \frac{\sin y + c}{2}, \quad \phi_2 = \frac{c - \sin y}{2}$$

Hence the solution is $z = \frac{c + \sin y}{2} e^{ax} + \frac{c - \sin y}{2} e^{-ax}$

or
$$z = c \cosh ax + \sin y \sinh ax.$$

Example 1.9. **Solve $\frac{\partial^2 z}{\partial x^2} + z = 0$, given that at $x = 0$, $z = e^y$ and $\frac{\partial z}{\partial x} = 1$.**

Solution. The solution of $\frac{d^2 z}{dx^2} + 1z = 0$ is $z = c_1 \cos x + c_2 \sin x$. Here the differentiation $\frac{\partial^2 z}{\partial x^2}$ is partial so c_1 and c_2 in the above solutions will be some functions of y.

So the solution is

$$z = \phi_1(y) \cos x + \phi_2(y) \sin x \qquad ...(1)$$

Differentiating (1) partially with subject to x

$$\frac{\partial z}{\partial x} = \phi_1(y)\,(-\sin x) + \phi_2\,(y) \cos x$$

$$\left(\frac{\partial z}{\partial x}\right)_{x=0} = 1 = 0 + \phi_2(y) \times 1$$

So $\qquad \phi_2(y) = 1$ ...(2)

From (1) at $x = 0$

$$e^y = (z)_{x=0} = \phi_1(y) + 0$$

So $\qquad \phi_1(y) = e^y$

Hence $z = e^y \cos x + 1 \sin x$ is the solution.

PROBLEM SET 1.2

Solve the following differential equations.

1. $\dfrac{\partial^2 z}{\partial x^2} = xy,$

Ans. $z = \dfrac{x^3 y}{6} + xf(y) + \phi(y)$

2. $\dfrac{\partial^2 z}{\partial x \partial y} = \dfrac{x}{y} + a,$

Ans. $z = \dfrac{x^2}{2} \log y + axy + \phi(x) + \psi(y)$

3. $\dfrac{\partial^2 z}{\partial y^2} = z$, given that when $y = 0, z = e^x$ and $\dfrac{\partial z}{\partial y} = e^{-x}$

Ans. $z = e^x \cosh y + e^{-x} \sinh y$

4. $\dfrac{\partial^2 u}{\partial x^2 y} = a \cos x$

Ans. $u = -ay \sin x + \phi_1(y) + \phi_2(x)$

5. $\dfrac{\partial^2 u}{\partial x \partial y} = e^{-y} \cos x$

Ans. $-e^{-y} \sin x + \phi_1(x) + \phi_2(y)$ ***(Madurai 88, Mysore 87)***

6. $\dfrac{\partial^2 z}{\partial x \partial y} = \dfrac{1}{xy}$

Ans. $z = \log x \log y + \phi_1(x) + \phi_2(y)$

7. $\dfrac{\partial^2 z}{\partial y^2} = \sin xy$

Ans. $z = -\dfrac{1}{x^2} \sin xy + y f(x) + \phi(x)$

8. $\dfrac{\partial^2 z}{\partial x\, \partial y} = e^{x+y}$

Ans. $z = e^{x+y} + \phi_1(x) + \phi_2(y)$

9. $\dfrac{\partial^2 z}{\partial x \partial y} = 2x + 2y$

Ans. $z = xy(x + y) + \phi_1(x) + \phi_2(y)$

10. $\dfrac{\partial^2 u}{\partial x \partial y} = x \sin(axy)$

Ans. $u = \dfrac{-\sin(axy)}{a^2 y} + \phi_1(x) + \phi_2(y)$

1.7 LINEAR PARTIAL DIFFERENTIAL EQUATIONS OF FIRST ORDER

Differential equations with only two independent variables x and y are called first order linear equatoins when they involve only the first order partial derivatives p, q and every term in it is at the most of one degree in p or q and so there be no term involving pq. The differential equation $pP + qQ = R$ is, of Lagrange's form where P, Q, R are same functions of x, y, z.

If $$u(x, y, z) = c_1,\ v(x, y, z) = c_2 \qquad ...(1)$$

be two functions of x, y, z,

Then $$du = u_x\,dx + u_y\,dy + u_z\,dz = 0,$$

and $$dv = v_x\,dx + v_y\,dy + v_z\,dz = 0.$$

On cross-multiplying

$$\frac{dx}{P} = \frac{dy}{Q} = \frac{dz}{R}.$$

But these are subsidiary equations of

$$pP + qQ = R \qquad ...(2)$$

where $$P = \frac{\partial(u, v)}{\partial(y, z)},\ Q = \frac{\partial(u, v)}{\partial(z, x)} \text{ and } R = \frac{\partial(u, v)}{\partial(x, y)} \qquad ...(3)$$

Thus $\phi(u, v) = 0$, where ϕ is an arbitrary function of $u = u(x, y)$ and $v = v(x, y)$, it also gives rise to the partial differential equation

$$pP + qQ = R \qquad ...(4)$$

Hence $\phi(u, v) = 0$, is a solution of (4).

1.8 SOLUTION OF LINEAR FIRST ORDER EQUATION

It is seen from above that the partial differential equation $pP + qQ = R$ resulted from $\phi(u, v) = 0$, which therefore its solution, where u and v are two independent solutions of $\dfrac{dx}{P} = \dfrac{dy}{Q} = \dfrac{dz}{R}$.

To establish the above preposition fully we have to prove that

(i) $u(x, y, z) = 0$, and $v(x, y, z) = c_2$ given rise to the subsidiary equations $\dfrac{dx}{P} = \dfrac{dy}{Q} = \dfrac{dz}{R}$,

(ii) and that the elimination of ϕ from $\phi(u, v) = 0$, gives rise to the differential equation $pP + qQ = R$.

Proof of (i) $u(x, y, z) = c_1$

So $$du = \frac{\partial u}{\partial x}dx + \frac{\partial u}{\partial y}dy + \frac{\partial u}{\partial z}dz = 0 \quad ...(6)$$

and from $v(x, y, z) = c_2$

$$dv = \frac{\partial v}{\partial x}dx + \frac{\partial v}{\partial y} + \frac{\partial v}{\partial z}dz = 0 \quad ...(7)$$

From (6) and (7) on cross-multiplicaton

$$\frac{dx}{\begin{vmatrix} \frac{\partial u}{\partial y} & \frac{\partial u}{\partial z} \\ \frac{\partial v}{\partial y} & \frac{\partial v}{\partial z} \end{vmatrix}} = \frac{dy}{\begin{vmatrix} \frac{\partial u}{\partial z} & \frac{\partial u}{\partial x} \\ \frac{\partial v}{\partial z} & \frac{\partial v}{\partial x} \end{vmatrix}} = \frac{dz}{\begin{vmatrix} \frac{\partial u}{\partial x} & \frac{\partial u}{\partial y} \\ \frac{\partial v}{\partial x} & \frac{\partial v}{\partial y} \end{vmatrix}}$$

or $$\frac{dx}{\frac{\partial(u, v)}{\partial(y, z)}} = \frac{dy}{\frac{\partial(u, v)}{\partial(z, x)}} = \frac{dz}{\frac{\partial(u, v)}{\partial(x, y)}}$$

or $$\frac{dx}{P} = \frac{dy}{Q} = \frac{dz}{R}$$

Proof of (ii)

Now from $\phi(u, v) = 0$

$$d\phi = \frac{\partial \phi}{\partial u}du + \frac{\partial \phi}{\partial v}dv = 0$$

Differentiating once partially w.r.t. x and second time w.r.t. y.

We have $$\frac{\partial \phi}{\partial u}\left\{\frac{\partial u}{\partial x} + \frac{\partial u}{\partial z}p\right\} + \frac{\partial \phi}{\partial v}\left\{\frac{\partial v}{\partial x} + \frac{\partial v}{\partial z}p\right\} = 0$$

and $$\frac{\partial \phi}{\partial u}\left\{\frac{\partial u}{\partial y} + \frac{\partial u}{\partial z}q\right\} + \frac{\partial \phi}{\partial v}\left\{\frac{\partial v}{\partial y} + \frac{\partial v}{\partial z}q\right\} = 0$$

Eliminating $\frac{\partial \phi}{\partial u}, \frac{\partial \phi}{\partial y}$, We have

$$\begin{vmatrix} \frac{\partial u}{\partial x} + \frac{\partial u}{\partial z}p & \frac{\partial v}{\partial x} + \frac{\partial v}{\partial z}p \\ \frac{\partial u}{\partial y} \quad \frac{\partial u}{\partial z}q & \frac{\partial v}{\partial y} \quad \frac{\partial v}{\partial z}q \end{vmatrix} = 0$$

Which gives

$$\begin{vmatrix} \frac{\partial u}{\partial x} & \frac{\partial v}{\partial x} \\ \frac{\partial u}{\partial y} & \frac{\partial v}{\partial y} \end{vmatrix} + \begin{vmatrix} \frac{\partial u}{\partial x} & \frac{\partial v}{\partial z}p \\ \frac{\partial u}{\partial y} & \frac{\partial v}{\partial z}q \end{vmatrix} + \begin{vmatrix} \frac{\partial u}{\partial z}p & \frac{\partial v}{\partial x} \\ \frac{\partial u}{\partial z}q & \frac{\partial v}{\partial y} \end{vmatrix} + pq\begin{vmatrix} \frac{\partial u}{\partial z} & \frac{\partial v}{\partial z} \\ \frac{\partial u}{\partial z} & \frac{\partial v}{\partial z} \end{vmatrix} = 0$$

or $$\frac{\partial(u, v)}{\partial(x, y)} + \frac{\partial u}{\partial x}\frac{\partial v}{\partial z}q - \frac{\partial v}{\partial z}\frac{\partial u}{\partial y}p + \frac{\partial u}{\partial z}\frac{\partial v}{\partial y}p - \frac{\partial v}{\partial x}\frac{\partial u}{\partial z}q + 0 = 0$$

or $$p\left\{\frac{\partial u}{\partial z}\frac{\partial v}{\partial y}-\frac{\partial u}{\partial y}\frac{\partial v}{\partial z}\right| + dq\left\{\frac{\partial u}{\partial x}\frac{\partial v}{\partial z}-\frac{\partial u}{\partial z}\frac{\partial v}{\partial x}\right\} + \frac{\partial(u, v)}{\partial(x, y)} = 0$$

$$-pP - qQ + R = 0 \qquad \text{Hence proved.}$$

1.9 METHOD OF SOLUTION

For solving the Lagrange's type equation $pP + qQ = R$, write the auxiliary equations $\frac{dx}{P} + \frac{dy}{Q} = \frac{dz}{R}$.

Solve these equations, using Componendo-dividendo or some other technique, depending on the terms of the equation and find two independent solutions $u(x, y, z) = c_1$ and $v(x, y, z) = c_2$, then $\phi(u, v) = 0$, is called the general solution of the given equation where ϕ is are arbitrary function.

Example 1.10. **Solve the following differential equations :**

(i) $(x^2 - yz)p + (y^2 - zx)q = (z^2 - xy)$

(A.M.I.E. 97, Madras 94S, 98, Ranchi 90, Karnataka 90)

(ii) $(mz - ny)p + (nx - lz)q = ly - mx$ *(V.T.U. 2004; A.M.I.E. 90, Madras 94S)*

(iii) $x^2(y - z)p + y^2(z - x)q = z^2(x - y)$ *(Madurai 90)*

(iv) $\frac{y^2 z}{x} p + xzq = y^2$ *(Madras 95, 97)*

Solution. (i) The auxiliary equations of the given equation are

$$\frac{dx}{x^2 - yz} = \frac{dy}{y^2 - zx} = \frac{dz}{z^2 - xy}$$

By Componendo-dividendo each of these fractions

$$= \frac{dx - dy}{(x - y)(x + y + z)} = \frac{dy - dz}{(y - z)(x + y + z)} = \frac{dz - dx}{(z - x)(x + y + z)}$$

So $\quad \log(x - y) = \log(y - z) + \log c_1$ and $\log(y - z) = \log(z - x) + \log c_2$

or $$\frac{x - y}{y - z} = c_1, \quad \frac{y - z}{z - x} = c_2$$

The solution is $\phi(c_1, c_2) = 0$

or $$\phi\left(\frac{x - y}{y - z}, \frac{y - z}{z - x}\right) = 0$$

Sol. (ii) The auxiilary equations of the given equation are

$$\frac{dx}{mz - ny} = \frac{dy}{nx - lz} = \frac{dz}{ly - mx}$$

By Componendo-dividendo, each of these fractions

$$= \frac{xdx + ydy + zdz}{\Sigma x(mz - xy) = 0} = \frac{ldx + mdy + ndz}{\Sigma l(mz - ny) = 0}$$

When denominator in zero, numerator should also be zero.

So $\quad xdx + ydy + zdz = 0$

or $\quad x^2 + y^2 + z^2 = c_1$

and $\quad lx + my + nz = c_2$

and also the solution is $\phi(x^2 + y^2 + z^2, lx + my + nz) = 0$

Sol. (iii) The auxiliary equations of the given equation are

$$\frac{dx}{x^2(y-z)} = \frac{dy}{y^2(z-x)} = \frac{dz}{z^2(x-y}$$

By Componendo dividendo, each of these fractions

$$= \frac{\frac{dx}{x} + \frac{dy}{y} + \frac{dz}{z}}{\Sigma\, x(y-z) = 0} = \frac{\frac{dx}{x^2} + \frac{dy}{y^2} + \frac{dz}{z^2}}{\Sigma\, (y-z) = 0}$$

When denominator is zero, the numerator should also be zero so

$$\frac{dx}{x} + \frac{dy}{y} + \frac{dz}{z} = 0$$

or $\quad \log xyz = \log c_1$

So one solution is $xyz = c_1$

and $\quad \frac{dx}{x^2} + \frac{dy}{y^2} + \frac{dz}{z^2} = 0$

So $\quad \frac{1}{x} + \frac{1}{y} + \frac{1}{z} = c_2.$

So the general solution is $\phi(xyz, x^{-1} + y^{-1} + z^{-1}) = 0$

Sol. (iv) The auxiliary equations are

$$\frac{xdx}{y^2z} = \frac{dy}{xz} = \frac{dz}{y^2}$$

Taking first and second fraction $x^2\,dx + y^2\,dz$ so $x^3 - y^3 = c_1$

Taking first and third $xdx = zdz$ or $x^2 - z^2 = c_2$

So the solution is $\phi(x^3 - y^3, x^2 - z^2) = 0$

Example 1.11. Solve the following differential equations :

(i) $x^2p + y^2q = (x+y)z,$

(ii) $y^2p - xy\,q = x\,(z - 2y)$

(iii) $(y^3x - 2x^4)p + (2y^4 - x^3y)q = 9z\,(x^3 - y^3)$

(iv) $(x^2 - y^2 - z^2)p + 2xyq = 2xz$ *(AUUP 2008)*

Solution. (i) The subsidiary equations of the given equation are

$$\frac{dx}{x^2} = \frac{dy}{y^2} = \frac{dz}{(x+y)z}$$

From first two fractions, one integration $\frac{1}{x} - \frac{1}{y} = c_1.$

By Componendo dividendo each of these fractions is also equal to

$$\frac{\frac{dx}{x} + \frac{dy}{y} - \frac{dz}{z}}{[(x+y) - (x+y)] = 0}$$

As the denominator is zero, so the numerator should also be zero.

Hence $$\int\left(\frac{dx}{x}+\frac{dy}{y}-\frac{dz}{z}\right)=\log c_2$$

or $$\log\frac{xy}{z}=\log c_2$$

Hence the solution is $$\phi\left(\frac{1}{x}-\frac{1}{y},\frac{xy}{z}\right)=0$$

Sol. (ii) The subsidiary equations are

$$\frac{dx}{y^2}=\frac{dy}{-xy}=\frac{dz}{x(z-2y)}$$

Taking first two fractions $xdx+ydy=0$ so $x^2+y^2=c_1$ is one solution. From second and third

$$\frac{dz}{dy}=\frac{z-2y}{-y}$$

or $$\frac{dz}{dy}+\frac{1}{y}z=2.$$

This is linear in z. Its I.F. $=e^{\int\frac{1}{y}dy}=y$

So the solution is $z\cdot y=2\int y\,dy=c_2$ or $yz-y^2=c_2$

So the general solution is $\phi(x^2+y^2,yz-y^2)=0$

Sol. (iii) The auxiliary equations of the given equation are

$$\frac{dx}{x(y^3-2x^3)}=\frac{dy}{y(2y^3-x^3)}=\frac{dz}{9z\,(x^3-y^3)}.$$

Each of the fractions by Componendo-dividendo is equal to

$$\frac{3\left(\frac{dx}{x}+\frac{dy}{y}\right)+\frac{dz}{z}}{\{3(-3)\,(x^3-y^3)+9(x^3-y^3)\}=0}$$

When the denominator is zero, the numerator should also be zero so

$$3\left(\frac{dx}{x}+\frac{dy}{y}\right)+\frac{dz}{z}=0 \text{ or } x^3y^3z=c_1$$

Taking the first two fractions $\frac{dy}{dx}=\frac{y(2y^3-x^3)}{x(y^3-2x^3)}$. It is a equation of homogeneous type. Let $y=vx$, so

$$\frac{dy}{dx}=v+x\frac{dv}{dx}=\frac{v(2v^3-1)}{v^3-2}$$

or $$x\frac{dv}{dx}=\frac{v\,\{2v^3-1-v^3+2\}}{v^3-2}$$

or $$\frac{(v^3-2)\,dv}{v(v^3+1)}=\frac{dx}{x}$$

Let $v^3=t$, $3v^2\,dv=dt$

So $$\frac{dx}{x} = \frac{1}{3}\frac{(t-2)}{t(t+1)}dt = \frac{1}{3}\left\{\frac{-2}{t} + \frac{3}{t+1}\right\}dt$$

So $$3\log x + 2\log t - 3\log(t+1) = \log c_2$$

or $$\frac{x^3 t^2}{(t+1)^3} = c_2^{-3} \text{ or } \left(\frac{x^2 y^2}{x^3 + y^3}\right)^3 = c_2^{-3}$$

So $$\frac{x^3 + y^3}{x^2 y^2} = c_2$$

So the general solution is

$$\phi\left(\frac{x^3 + y^3}{x^2 y^2}, x^3 y^3 z\right) = 0.$$

Sol. (iv) The auxiliary equations of the given partial differential equations are

$$\frac{dx}{x^2 - y^2 - z^2} = \frac{dy}{2xy} = \frac{dz}{2xz}$$

Taking the last two, we have

$$\frac{dy}{y} = \frac{dz}{z}$$

On integration,

$$\log y = \log z + \log c_1$$

$$\log\frac{y}{z} = \log c_1$$

$\Rightarrow$ $$\frac{y}{z} = c_1 \text{ or } y = c_1 z \qquad ...(1)$$

Using x, y, z as multipliers, we get

$$\text{each fraction} = \frac{xdx + ydy + zyz}{x(x^2 + y^2 + z^2)}$$

$$\therefore \frac{xdx + ydy + zyz}{x(x^2 + y^2 + z^2)} = \frac{dz}{2xz}$$

On integration, we get

$$\log(x^2 + y^2 + z^2) = \log z + \log c_2$$

or $$\log\frac{(x^2 + y^2 + z^2)}{z} = \log c_2$$

$\Rightarrow$ $$x^2 + y^2 + z^2 = zc_2 \qquad ...(2)$$

From equation (1) and (2), the general solution

$$\frac{x^2 + y^2 + z^2}{z} = f\left(\frac{y}{z}\right)$$

or $$x^2 + y^2 + z^2 = zf\left(\frac{y}{z}\right)$$

PROBLEM SET 1.3

Solve the following partial differential equations:

1. $pz - qz = z^2 + (x + y)^2$

Ans. $\phi\,[x + y, \log\{(x + y)^2 + z^2\} - 2x] = 0$

2. $px + qy = 3z$ *(A.U.U.P. 2007; A.M.I.E. 94)*

Ans. $\phi\left(\frac{x}{y}, \frac{x^3}{z}\right) = 0$

3. $p \tan x + q \tan y = \tan z$ *(Andhra 90, Kerala 87S)*

Ans. $\phi\left(\frac{\sin x}{\sin y}, \frac{\sin y}{\sin z}\right) = 0$

4. $p\sqrt{x} + q\sqrt{y} = \sqrt{z}$ *(Madurai 91)*

Ans. $\phi\,(\sqrt{x} - \sqrt{y}, \sqrt{x} - \sqrt{z}) = 0$

5. $z(px - qy) = y^2 - x^2$

Ans. $\phi\,(xy, x^2 + y^2 + z^2) = 0$

6. $x(z^2 - y^2)p + y(x^2 - z^2)q = z(y^2 - x^2)$ *(Madurai 2000; Coimbatore 88)*

Ans. $\phi\,(x^2 + y^2 + z^2, xyz) = 0$

7. $(x - y)p + (x - z)q = y - x$ *(Calicut 91)*

Ans. $\phi\,(x^2 + y^2 + z^2, x + y + z) = 0$

8. $(y + z)p + (z + x)q = (x + y)$ *(Madurai 88)*

Ans. $\phi\left(\frac{x - y}{y - z}, \frac{y - z}{z - x}\right) = 0$

9. $x(y - z)p + y(z - x)q = z(x - y)$ *(A.M.I.E. 97W; Calicut 94, Madras 93; Kerala 90)*

Ans. $\phi\,(x + y + z, xyz) = 0$

10. $yzp + zxq = xy$ *(Kerala 90)*

Ans. $\phi\,(x^2 - y^2, x^2 - z^2) = 0$

11. $(y - z)p + (x - y)q = z - x$ *(Punjabi 87S)*

Ans. $\phi\,(x + y + z, x^2 + 2yz) = 0$

12. $p \cos(x + y) + q \sin(x + y) = z$ *(Maradhwada 94)*

Ans. $\phi\,[(y - x) + \log\{\cos(x + y) + \sin(x + y)\}] = z^{\sqrt{2}} \tan\left(\frac{x + y}{2} + \frac{\pi}{8}\right)$

13. $p - q = \log(x + y)$

Ans. $x \log(x + y) - z = f(x + y)$

14. $px - qy = y^2 - x^2$ *(Madras 91)*

Ans. $\{x^2 + y^2 + 2z, \log(xy)\} = 0$

1.10 NON-LINEAR EQUATIONS OF THE FIRST ORDER

Those differential equations in which p and q occur in **non-linear form** (where the **sum of the degrees of p and q in some of the terms is two or more**) is called a first order non-linear partial differential equation. The complete solution of these equations is that which contains two arbitrary constants. Some partial differential equations can be solved easily if they are if some special forms, such equations have four standard forms. For those equations which do not come under any of these forms, there is a general method known as the **Charpit's method**, given by **Charpit**.

Standard Form—I

$$f(p, q) = 0$$

Such differential equations which have only p and q and none of x, y, z, come under this form. For the solution of such equations, **we assume $z = ax + by + c$** and differentiating it we have $\frac{\partial z}{\partial x} = p = a$ and $\frac{\partial z}{\partial y} = q = b$, putting these values of p and q in the given equation, we have $f(a, b) = 0$. From here let $b = \phi(a)$. So $z = ax + \phi(a)\, y + c$ is the required complete solution.

Example 1.12. **Solve $p^2 - q^2 = 1$**

Solution : The equation is of standard form I. Let $z = ax + by + c$

differentiating partially w.r.t. x and y respectively, we get $p = a, q = b$

Hence $a^2 - b^2 = 1$ or $b = \sqrt{a^2 - 1}$

So the solution is $$z = ax + y\sqrt{a^2 - 1} + c.$$

Example 1.13. **Solve $x^2p^2 + y^2q^2 = z^2$** *(Madras 93, 98, Calicut 91, Ranchi 90, Kerala 90S)*

Solution : The equation can be rewritten as $\left(\frac{x}{z}\frac{\partial z}{\partial x}\right)^2 + \left(\frac{y}{z}\frac{\partial z}{\partial y}\right)^2 = 1$. Let the variables be changed by the substitutions

$$\frac{dx}{x} = dX, \quad \frac{dy}{y} = dY, \quad \frac{dz}{dZ} = dZ$$

or $\log x = X$, $\log y = Y$, $\log z = Z$. The equation now becomes

$$\left(\frac{\partial Z}{\partial X}\right)^2 + \left(\frac{\partial Z}{\partial Y}\right)^2 = 1$$

or $$P^2 + Q^2 = 1$$

Which is of standard form one.

Let $$Z = aX + bY + C.$$

Differentiating partially w.r.t. X and Y, respectively, we get

$$P = a, \; Q = b$$

So $\quad a^2 + b^2 = 1$ or $b = \sqrt{1 - a^2}$

Hence the solution is $Z = aX + \sqrt{1 - a^2} + c$

or $\quad \log z = a \log x + \sqrt{1 - a^2} \log y + c.$

Example 1.14. **Solve $(x+y)(p+q)^2+(x-y)(p-q)^2=1$** *(A.U.U.P. 2008)*

Solution : Let $x+y=u$ and $x-y=v$ so $\frac{\partial u}{\partial x}=\frac{\partial u}{\partial y}=1$ and $\frac{\partial v}{\partial x}=-\frac{\partial v}{\partial y}=1$

$$p=\frac{\partial z}{\partial x}=\frac{\partial z}{\partial u}\frac{\partial u}{\partial x}+\frac{\partial z}{\partial v}\frac{\partial v}{\partial x}=P+Q \quad ...(2)$$

$$q=\frac{\partial z}{\partial y}=\frac{\partial z}{\partial u}\frac{\partial u}{\partial y}+\frac{\partial z}{\partial v}\frac{\partial v}{\partial y}=P-Q \quad ...(3)$$

So $\quad p+q=2P$ and $p-q=2Q$ ...(4)

So the equation changes to

$$u(2P)^2+v(2Q)^2=1$$

or

$$\left(\sqrt{u}\,\frac{\partial z}{\partial u}\right)^2+\left(\sqrt{v}\,\frac{\partial z}{\partial v}\right)^2=1/4 \quad ...(5)$$

Let

$$\frac{du}{\sqrt{u}}=dX \text{ and } \frac{dv}{\sqrt{v}}=dY \quad ...(6)$$

or $X=2\sqrt{u},\ V=2\sqrt{v}$

The equation (5) changes to

$$\left(\frac{\partial z}{\partial X}\right)^2+\left(\frac{\partial z}{\partial Y}\right)^2=1/4 \quad ...(7)$$

which is of standard *I*.

So the solution may be assumed as

$$z=aX+bY+c \quad ...(8)$$

Differentiating partially w.r.t. X, Y respectively

$$\frac{\partial z}{\partial X}=a,\ \frac{\partial z}{\partial Y}=b$$

So from (7) $\quad a^2+b^2=1$

Hence the solution (8) becomes

$$z=aX+\sqrt{\frac{1}{4}-a^2Y}+c$$

or

$$z=2a\sqrt{u}+2\sqrt{\frac{1}{4}-a^2}\sqrt{v}+c$$

$$=2a\sqrt{x+y}+2\sqrt{\frac{1}{4}-a^2}\sqrt{x-y}+c$$

Example 1.15. **Solve $(y-x)(qy-px)=(p-q)^2$** *(Bangalore 94)*

Solution : Let $\quad x+y=u$ ...(1)

and $\quad xy=v$ ...(2)

So

$$\frac{\partial u}{\partial x}=\frac{\partial u}{\partial y}=1$$

and

$$\frac{\partial v}{\partial x}=y,\ \frac{\partial v}{\partial y}=x \quad ...(3)$$

Now where $\frac{\partial z}{\partial u}=P$

$$p = \frac{\partial z}{\partial x} = \frac{\partial u}{\partial x}\frac{\partial z}{\partial u} + \frac{\partial v}{\partial x}\frac{\partial z}{\partial v} = 1P + yQ \quad ...(4)$$

$$\frac{\partial z}{\partial v} = Q$$

$$q = \frac{\partial z}{\partial y} = \frac{\partial u}{\partial y}\frac{\partial z}{\partial u} + \frac{\partial v}{\partial y}\frac{\partial z}{\partial v} = 1P + xQ \quad ...(5)$$

So $\quad p - q = (y - x)\,Q$

and $\quad qy - px = (P + xQ)\,y - (P + yQ)\,x = (y - x)\,P$

So the equation (1) becomes

$$(y - x)\,(y - x)\,P = (y - x)^2\,Q^2$$

or $\quad P = Q^2$, which is of standard I. ...(6)

So Let $\quad z = aU + bV + c$ ...(7)

Differentiating partially w.r.t. U and V,

$$\frac{\partial z}{\partial U} = P = a \text{ and } \frac{\partial z}{\partial V} = Q = b \quad ...(8)$$

So from (6) $a = b^2$

So the solution (7) becomes

$$z = aU + \sqrt{a}\,V + c$$

or $\quad \boldsymbol{z = a(x + y) + \sqrt{a}\,xy + c}$

Example 1.16. **Solve $z^2\,(p^2x^2 + q^2) = 1$** ***(Kerala 90, 93, Rewa 94, Ranchi 89, Bhopal 91, Madurai 90)***

Solution : The equation can be rewritten as

$$\left\{xz\frac{\partial z}{\partial x}\right\}^2 + \left(z\frac{\partial z}{\partial y}\right)^2 = 1$$

Let $z\,dz = dZ$, $\frac{dx}{x} = dX$, $dy = dY$

So we have

$$\left(\frac{\partial Z}{\partial X}\right)^2 + \left(\frac{\partial Z}{\partial Y}\right)^2 = 1$$

or $\quad P^2 + Q^2 = 1$ (standard form I)

Let $\quad Z = aX + bY + c$

Differentiating $\frac{\partial Z}{\partial Z} = P = a;\ \frac{\partial Z}{\partial Y} = Q = b$

as $\quad P^2 + Q^2 = 1$

So $\quad P = \sin\alpha = a,$

$\quad Q = \cos\alpha = b$

Hence the solution is $Z = \sin\alpha\,X + \cos\alpha\ + c$

or $$\frac{z^2}{2} = \sin\alpha\,\log x + \cos\alpha\,y + c$$

or $$\frac{z^2}{2} = \alpha\,\log x + \sqrt{1 - a^2}\;y + c.$$

Standard Form II

$$f(b, q, z) = 0$$

When the equation has the form $f(p, q, z) = 0$ (not containing x and y both) it is said to be of form II.

Method of solution of such equations

Let $X = x + ay$, we have $\frac{\partial X}{\partial x} = 1,\ \frac{\partial x}{\partial y} = a.$

Assuming z to be a function of X only, on differentiating z, partially,

$$p = \frac{\partial z}{\partial x} = \frac{\partial z}{\partial X}\frac{\partial X}{\partial x} = 1 \cdot \frac{\partial z}{\partial X}$$

and
$$q = \frac{\partial z}{\partial y} = \frac{\partial z}{\partial X}\frac{\partial X}{\partial y} = \frac{\partial z}{\partial X}$$

By these values of p and q, the given equation changes into an ordinary differential equation of the form $f\left(\frac{dz}{dx}, a\frac{dz}{dx}, z\right) = 0$, which can be solved for z as $z = \phi(X)$. So the solution will be $z = \phi\,(x + ay)$.

Example 1.17. **Solve $9(p^2 z + q^2) = 4$**

Solution : The equation is of standard II being of the form

$$f(p, q, z) = 0$$

So Let $X = x + ay$ and z only a function of X given as $z = f(X)$. There

$$p = \frac{dz}{dX},\ q = a\frac{dz}{dX}$$

So the given equation changes to $9\left\{\left(\frac{dz}{dX}\right)^2 z + a^2\left(\frac{dz}{dX}\right)^2\right\} = 4$

or
$$\left(\frac{dz}{dX}\right)^2 (z + a^2) = \frac{4}{9}$$

or
$$\int dz\,\sqrt{zY a^2} = 2/3\int dX$$

or
$$\frac{2}{3}(z + a^2)^{3/2} = \frac{2}{3}(X + c)$$

Hence the solution is $(z + a^2)^{3/2} = x + ay + c$

Example 1.18. **$q^2 = z^2 p^2 (1 - p^2)$.** *(Osmania 1999)*

Solution : The equation is of form $f(p, q, z) = 0$

So let $X = x + ay$ and $z = z(x)$ only then $p = \frac{dz}{dX},\ q = a\frac{dz}{dX}$.

So the given equation becomes

$$a^2\left(\frac{dz}{dX}\right)^2 = z^2\left(\frac{dz}{dX}\right)^2\left\{1 - \left(\frac{dz}{dX}\right)^2\right\}$$

Let $\frac{dz}{dX} \neq 0$ so $1 - \frac{a^2}{z^2} = \left(\frac{dz}{dX}\right)^2$

or $\displaystyle\int \frac{z\,dz}{\sqrt{z^2 - a^2}} = \int dX$ or $\sqrt{z^2 - a^2} = X + c$

So the solution is $\sqrt{z^2 - a^2} = x + ay + c$

or $$z^2 - a^2 = (x + ay + c)^2$$

Example 1.19. **Solve $z^2 (p^2 + q^2 + 1)\ a^2$** ***(Bangalore 90, Andhra 90)***

Solution : let $X = x + ay$ and z be a function of X alone replacing p by $\dfrac{dz}{dX}$, q by $a\,\dfrac{dz}{dX}$, the equation becomes

$$(1 + a^2)\left(\frac{dz}{dX}\right)^2 + 1 = \frac{a^2}{z^2}$$

$$\sqrt{1 + a^2}\,\frac{dz}{dX} = \sqrt{\frac{a^2 - z^2}{z^2}}$$

or $$\sqrt{1 + a^2}\,\frac{z\,dz}{\sqrt{a^2 - z^2}} = dX$$

or $$\sqrt{1 + a^2 (a^2 - z^2)} = X + b$$

So the solution is $(1 + a^2)(a^2 - z^2) = (x + ay + b)^2$

Standard III. The differential equation expressible as

$$f_1(p, x) = f_2(q, y)$$

When the given equation be of this form, the equation does not have z and the terms of p and x can all be taken on one side and those of q and y on the other. Then we let each side to be equal to **a constant *a***. Then from $f_1(p, x) = a$, we find the value of p and from $f_2(q, y) = a$, get the value of q in terms of y.

As $$dz = \frac{\partial z}{\partial x}dx + \frac{\partial z}{\partial y}dy = p\,dx + q\,dy$$

So integrating $z = \int p\,dx + \int q\,dy + c$ is the required solution.

Example 1.20. **Solve $py + qx + xy = 0$**

Solution : We have $py = -(q + y)\,x$ or $\dfrac{p}{x} = -\left(\dfrac{q + y}{y}\right) = a$ (say), a constant.

So $p = ax$ and $q = -ay - y$

Hence $\int dz = \int (p\,dx + q\,dy) = a\int x\,dx - (a + 1)\int y\,dy$

or $2z = ax^2 - (a + 1)\,y^2 + c$

Example 1.21. **Solve $y - p = (x - q)^2$**

Solution : Let $z = xy + u$

$$\frac{\partial z}{\partial x} = y + \frac{\partial u}{\partial x} \text{ and } \frac{\partial z}{\partial y} = x + \frac{\partial u}{\partial y}$$

So $-\dfrac{\partial u}{\partial x} = \left(-\dfrac{\partial u}{\partial y}\right)^2$ or $-P = Q^2$

Let $U = ax + by + c$ then $\frac{\partial U}{\partial x} = a = P$

$\frac{\partial U}{\partial y} = b = Q$ so $a = -b^2$

Hence the solution is $U = z - xy = -b^2x + by + c$

or $z = xy - b^2x + by + c$

Example 1.22. **Solve $\sqrt{p} + \sqrt{q} = 2x$**

Solution : We have $\sqrt{p} - 2x = -\sqrt{q} = a$ (say)

So $p = (a + 2x)^2,\ q = a^2$

Hence $dz = p\,dx + q\,dy = (a + 2x)^2 + a^2\,dy$

So $z = \frac{(a + 2x)^3}{6} + a^2y + c$ is the answer.

Example 1.23. **Solve $p^2 - q^2 = x - y$** *(Ranchi 87)*

Solution : We have $p^2 - x = q^2 - y = a$ (say)

So $p^2 = a + x,\ q^2 = a + y$

Hence from $dz = p\,dx + q\,dy = \sqrt{a + x}\,dx + \sqrt{a + y}\,dy$

So $\frac{2}{3}z = (a + x)^{3/2} + (a + y)^{3/2} + b$

Standard IV. Clairaut's form of equations

$$z = px + qy + f(p, q)$$

When the equation is in the form $z = px + qy + f(p, q)$
then the solution is $z = ax + by + f(z, b)$. ...(1)

Let $z = ax + by + c$ ...(2)

Differentiating $\frac{\partial z}{\partial x} = p = a,\quad \frac{\partial z}{\partial y} = q = b$

Putting these values in given equation (1) and comparing (1) and (2) we have $c = f(a, b)$.

Hence the solution is $Z = ax + by + f(a, b)$

Example 1.24. **(a) Solve $z = px + qy + \sqrt{1 + p^2 + q^2}$** *(Madras 93)*

(b) Solve $s(p + q)(z - px - qy) = 1$ *(A.U.U.P. 2007; PU 1999)*

Solution : (a) The equation is of clairaut's form. Let

$$z = ax + by + c \quad ...(1)$$

Differentiating we get $\frac{\partial z}{\partial x} = p = a,\ \frac{\partial z}{\partial y} = q = b$ putting these values of p and q in given equation

$$z = ax + by + \sqrt{1 + a^2 + b^2} \quad ...(2)$$

Comparing (1) and (2) $c = \sqrt{1 + a^2 + b^2}$

Hence the solute is $z = ax + by + \sqrt{1 + a^2 + b^2}$

(b) The given equation may be written as

$$z - px - qy = \frac{1}{p+q} \Rightarrow z = px + qy + \frac{1}{p+q}$$

$\because$ It is a clairaut's equation, the solution is given by

$$z = ax + by + \frac{1}{a+b}$$

Example 1.25. **Solve $q^2y^2 = z^2 - zpx$**

Solution : The equation on dividing by z^2, becomes

$$\left(\frac{y}{z}\frac{\partial z}{\partial y}\right)^2 = 1 - \left(\frac{x}{z}\frac{\partial z}{\partial x}\right) \quad ...(1)$$

Let $\frac{dx}{x} = dX$, $\frac{dy}{y} = dY$, $\frac{dz}{z} = dZ$. So the above equation becomes

$$\left(\frac{\partial Z}{\partial Y}\right)^2 = 1 - \left(\frac{\partial Z}{\partial X}\right)$$

or $$Q^2 = 1 - P \quad ...(2)$$

Let the solution be $Z = aX + bY + c$.

Differentiating $\frac{\partial Z}{\partial X} = P = a$, $\frac{\partial Z}{\partial Y} = Q = B$.

Putting in (2) $b^2 = 1 - a$.

Hence the solution is

$$Z = aX + \sqrt{1-a}\,Y + c$$

or $$\log z = a \log x + \sqrt{1-a}\,\log y + c$$

Example 1.26. **Solve $(x^2 + y^2)(p^2 + q^2) = 1$**

Solution : On changing to polars $r^2 = x^2 + y^2$

$$\frac{\partial r}{\partial x} = \frac{x}{r} = \cos\theta$$

$$\frac{\partial r}{\partial y} = \sin\theta$$

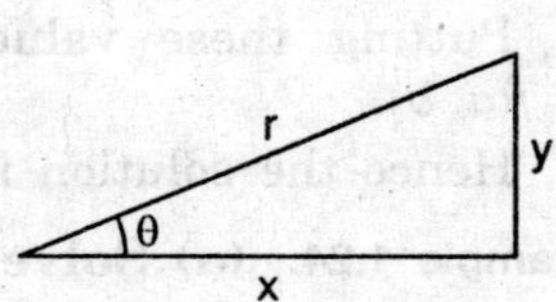

$$\theta = \tan^{-1}\frac{y}{x}$$

$$\frac{\partial \theta}{\partial x} = -\frac{\sin\theta}{r}$$

$$\frac{\partial \theta}{\partial y} = \frac{\cos\theta}{r}$$

$$\frac{\partial z}{\partial x} = \frac{\partial z}{\partial r}\cdot\frac{\partial r}{\partial x} + \frac{\partial z}{\partial \theta}\frac{\partial \theta}{\partial x}$$

$$p = \cos\theta\, P - \frac{\sin\theta}{r} Q$$

$$q = \sin\theta\, P + \frac{\cos\theta}{r} Q$$

$$p^2 + q^2 = P^2 + \frac{Q^2}{r^2}$$

So the given equation becomes

$$r^2\left[P^2 + \frac{Q^2}{r^2}\right] = 1$$

or $$\left(r\frac{\partial z}{\partial r}\right)^2 + \left(\frac{\partial z}{\partial \theta}\right)^2 = 1$$

Let $$\frac{dr}{r} = du,$$

So the equation becomes

$$\left(\frac{\partial z}{\partial u}\right)^2 + \left(\frac{\partial z}{\partial \theta}\right)^2 = 1, \text{ which is of standard form I.} \qquad ...(1)$$

Let its solution be

$$z = au + b\theta + c \qquad ...(2)$$

Differentiating $\frac{\partial z}{\partial u} = a, \frac{\partial z}{\partial \theta} = b.$

Hence from (1), $a^2 + b^2 = 1$

So the solution (2) becomes

$$z = a \log r + \sqrt{1 - a^2}\, \theta + c$$

or $$z = \frac{a}{2}\log(x^2 + y^2) + \sqrt{1 - a^2} \tan^{-1}\frac{y}{x} + c.$$

Example 127. **Solve $z^2(p^2 + q^2) = x^2 + y^2$** *(Madras 2000, Marathwada 1993)*

Solution : The equation can be written also as

$$\left(z\frac{\partial z}{\partial x}\right)^2 + \left(z\frac{\partial z}{\partial y}\right)^2 = x^2 + y^2 \qquad ...(1)$$

Let $z\,dz = dz$

So the equation (1) becomes

$$\left(\frac{\partial Z}{\partial x}\right)^2 + \left(\frac{\partial Z}{\partial y}\right)^2 = x^2 + y^2$$

or $$P^2 - x^2 + y^2 - Q^2 = a^2 \text{ (say)}$$

So $P = \sqrt{a^2 + x^2}$

and $Q = \sqrt{y^2 - a^2}$

As $dZ = P\,dx + Q\,dy = \sqrt{a^2 + x^2}\,dx + \sqrt{y^2 - a^2}\,dy$

So $Z = \int \sqrt{x^2 + a^2}\,dx + \int \sqrt{y^2 - a^2}\,dy$

or $$\frac{z^2}{2} = \frac{x}{2}\sqrt{x^2 + a^2} + \frac{a^2}{2}\log\{x + \sqrt{x^2 + a^2}\}$$

$$+ \frac{y\sqrt{y^2 - a^2}}{2} - \frac{a^2}{2}\log[y + \sqrt{y^2 - a^2}] + \frac{c}{2}$$

PROBLEM SET 1.4

Find the complete solution of the following equations :

1. $p^2 + q^2 = 1$ *(Osmania 2000)*

   Ans. $z = x \cos \alpha + y \sin \alpha + c$

2. $pq = 1$

   Ans. $z = ax + \frac{1}{a} y + c$

3. $p + q = pq$

   Ans. $z = ax + \frac{a}{a-1} y + c$

4. $pq + p + q = 0$

   Ans. $z = ax - \frac{a}{1+a} y + c$

5. $\sqrt{p} + \sqrt{q} = 1$ *(Karnataka 93, Gorakhpur 91)*

   Ans. $z = ax + (1 - \sqrt{a})^2 y + c$

6. $q = e^{-p/a}$

   Ans. $z = lx + e^{-l/a} y + c$

7. $\sqrt{p} + \sqrt{q} = 1$ *(Karnataka 93, Gorakhpur 91)*

8. $p^2z^2 + q^2 = 1$

   Ans. $z\sqrt{z^2 + a^2} + a^2 \log (z + \sqrt{z^2 + a^2}) = 2(x + ay + c)$

   Note. $\log \frac{z + \sqrt{z^2 + a^2}}{a} = \sinh^{-1} \frac{z}{a}$ also.

9. $p^2 = z^2 (1 - pq)$

   Ans. $x + ay + c = \sqrt{1 + az^2} + \log \left[\frac{\sqrt{1 + az^2} - 1}{\sqrt{a}\, z} \right]$

10. $qz = p^2$

    Ans. $\log z = a(x + ay) + b.$

11. $p(1 + q) = qz$

    Ans. $\log (az - 1) = x + ay + c$

12. $p^3 + q^3 = 27z$

    Ans. $(1 + a^3) z^2 = 8(x + ay + b)^3$

13. $p^3 + q^3 += 3pqz$

    Ans. $(1 + a^3) \log z = 3a(x + ay + c)$

14. $z^2 (p^2z^2 + q^2) = 1$

    Ans. $9(x + ay + b)^2 = (z^2 + a^2)^3.$

16. $p(1+q) = qz$ *(Madras 2000S, Kerala 1990S)*

Ans. $\log(az-1) = x + ay + b$

17. $z = p^2 + q^2$ *(Madras 97)*

Ans. $4z(1+a^2) = (x+ay+b)^2$

18. $z^2 = 1 + p^2 + q^2$ *(Madras 97)*

Ans. $z = \cosh\left(\dfrac{x+ay+b}{\sqrt{1+a^2}}\right)$

19. $px = qy$

Ans. $z = a \log xy + c$

20. $pe^y = qe^x$

Ans. $z = a(e^x + e^y) + c$

21. $py = qx$

Ans. $2z = a(x^2 + y^2) + b$

22. $p + q = 2x$

Ans. $z = ax + x^2 - ay + b$

23. $py + qx + pq = 0$ *(Marathwada 93)*

Ans. $2z = ay^2 - \dfrac{a}{a+1}x^2 + b$

24. $p + q = \sin x + \sin y$ *(Karnataka 93)*

Ans. $z = a(x-y) - (\cos x + \cos y) + b$

25. $z = px + qy - 2\sqrt{pq}$

Ans. $z = ax + by - 2\sqrt{ab}$

26. $(p^2 - q^2)z = x - y$ *(Calicut 91)*

Ans. $z^{3/2} = (x+a)^{3/2} + (y+a)^{3/2} + b$

27. $py = 2px + \log q$

Ans. $z = x^2 + ax + \dfrac{1}{a}e^{ay} + b.$

1.11 CHARPIT'S METHOD

Charpit's method of solution is a general method, applicable to both linear and non-linear partial differential equations.

Method

Let $f(x, y, z, p, q) = 0$ be the given partial differential equation.

Let
$$F(x, y, z, p, q) = 0 \quad \text{...(2)}$$
be one more relation between $x, > z, p, q$.

These equations can be used to solve for p and q. If these values of p and q be put in $dz = p\,dx + q\,dy$ and integrated, we get the solution required.

From (1) and (2) by total differentiation

$$df = \frac{\partial f}{\partial x} dx + \frac{\partial f}{\partial y} dy + \frac{\partial f}{\partial z} dz + \frac{\partial f}{\partial p} dp + \frac{\partial f}{\partial q} dq = 0 \quad ...(3)$$

and (here F and ϕ are same) $$dF = \frac{d\phi}{dx} dx + \frac{\partial \phi}{\partial y} dy + \frac{\partial \phi}{\partial z} dz + \frac{\partial \phi}{\partial p} dp + \frac{\partial \phi}{\partial q} dq = 0 \quad ...(4)$$

Taking partial differential of eq^n (3), w.r.t. x and y successively

$$0 = \frac{\partial f}{\partial x} + 0 + \frac{\partial f}{\partial z} p + \frac{\partial f}{\partial p}\frac{\partial p}{\partial x} + \frac{\partial f}{\partial q}\frac{\partial q}{\partial x} = 0 \quad ...(5)$$

$$\frac{\partial f}{\partial y} + \frac{\partial f}{\partial z} q + \frac{\partial f}{\partial p}\frac{\partial p}{\partial q} + \frac{\partial f}{\partial q}\frac{\partial q}{\partial y} = 0 \quad ...(6)$$

Similarly from (4)

$$\frac{\partial F}{\partial x} + \frac{\partial F}{\partial z} p + \frac{\partial F}{\partial p}\frac{\partial p}{\partial x} + \frac{\partial F}{\partial q}\frac{\partial q}{\partial x} = 0 \quad ...(7)$$

$$\frac{\partial F}{\partial y} + \frac{\partial F}{\partial z} q + \frac{\partial F}{\partial p}\frac{\partial p}{\partial y} + \frac{\partial F}{\partial q}\frac{\partial q}{\partial y} = 0 \quad ...(8)$$

Eliminating $\frac{\partial p}{\partial x}$ between (5) and (7) and $\frac{\partial q}{\partial y}$ between (6) and (8) we get

$$\left(\text{denoting } \frac{\partial f}{\partial x} = f_x \text{ etc.}\right)$$

$$(f_x + p\, f_z)\, F_p - (F_x + p\, F_z)\, f_p + q_x\, (f_q\, F_p - f_p\, F_q) = 0 \quad ...(9)$$

and $$(f_y + q\, f_z)\, F_q - (F_y + q\, F_z)\, f_q + p_y\, (f_p\, F_q - f_q\, F_p) = 0 \quad ...(10)$$

As $$q_x = p_y = \frac{\partial^2 z}{\partial x\, \partial y}$$

Adding (9) and (10) the last terms cancel out and we get

$$(f_x + pf_z)\, F_p + (f_y + q\, f_z)\, F_q + (-pf_p - qf_q)\, F_z + (-f_p)\, F_x + (-f_q)\, F_y = 0$$

This being Lagrange's form of linear equation in F_p, F_q, F_z, F_x, F_y, its auxiliary **equations are**

$$\frac{dp}{f_x + pf_z} = \frac{dq}{f_y + qf_y} = \frac{dx}{-f_p} = \frac{dy}{-f_q} = \frac{dz}{-(pf_p + qf_q)}$$

These are known as **Charpit's auxiliary equations. Solving these two of, we get one relation $F(x, p, z, p, q) = 0$ which when used with the given equation**, we get the values of p and q, required to be put in $dz = p\, dx + q\, dy$ and then on integration, we get the value of z.

Example 1.28. Solve $f(x, y, z, p, q) \equiv (p^2 + q^2)\, y - qz = 0$ *(Osmania 2000S, Bhopal 91; AUUP 2008)*

Solution : Differentiating the given equation, we may have

$$\frac{\partial f}{\partial x} = 0,\ \frac{\partial f}{\partial y} = (p^2 + q^2),\ \frac{\partial f}{\partial z} = -q_1,\ \frac{\partial f}{\partial p} = 2py$$

$\frac{\partial f}{\partial q} = 2qy - z$. Putting these values in charpit's equations, we have

$$\frac{dx}{-f_p} = \frac{dy}{-f_q} = \frac{dz}{-(pf_p + qf_q)} = \frac{dp}{f_x + pf_z} = \frac{dq}{f_y + qf_z}$$

$$\frac{dx}{-2py} = \frac{dy}{-(2qy - z)} = \frac{dz}{2p^2y + 2q^2y + qz} = \frac{dp}{0 - pq} = \frac{dq}{p^2 + q^2 - q^2}$$

From here $\frac{dp}{-q} = \frac{dq}{p}$ Hence $\boldsymbol{p^2 + q^2 = c^2}$

So from the given equation $q = \frac{c^2y}{z}$ and $p^2 = c^2 - q^2 = c^2 - \frac{c^4y^2}{z^2}$

Now $dz = p\,dx + q\,dy = \frac{c}{z}\sqrt{z^2 - c^2y^2}\,dx + \frac{c^2y}{z}dy$

or $dz - \frac{c^2y}{z}dy = \frac{c}{z}\sqrt{z^2 - c^2y^2}\,dx$

or $c\,dx = \int \frac{z\,dz - c^2y\,dy}{\sqrt{z^2 - c^2y^2}}$

so $cx = \sqrt{z^2 - c^2y^2} + b$

or $\boldsymbol{(cx - b)^2 = z^2 - c^2y^2}$ is the required solution.

Example 1.29. Solve by Charpit's method $f(x, y, z, p, q) = pq - z = 0$.

Solution : We have $\frac{\partial f}{\partial x} = f_x = 0,\ f_y = 0,\ f_z = -1,\ f_p = q,\ f_q = p$

The Charpits equations are

$$\frac{dx}{-f_p} = \frac{dy}{-f_q} = \frac{dz}{-(pf_p + qf_q)} = \frac{dq}{f_x + pf_z} = \frac{dq}{f_y + qf_z}.$$

There become $\frac{dz}{-q} = \frac{dq}{-p} = \frac{dz}{-(2pq)} = \frac{dp}{0 - p} = \frac{dq}{0 - q}$

Using, $\frac{dp}{p} = \frac{dq}{q}$ or $\log p = \log q + \log a$

So $\boldsymbol{p = aq}$.

Solving $p = aq$ and $pq = z$, $q = \sqrt{\frac{z}{a}}$ and $p = \sqrt{az}$

From $dz = p\,dx + q\,dy$

We have $\frac{dz}{\sqrt{z}} = \left(\sqrt{a}\,dx + \frac{1}{\sqrt{a}}dy\right)$

Integrating $2\sqrt{z} = \sqrt{a}\,x + \frac{1}{\sqrt{a}}y + c$, is the required solution.

Example 1.30. Solve $f(x, y, z, p, q) = pq\,xy - z^2 = 0$ *(Bhopal 91, Bangalore 94, Raj 2001)*

Solution : $\frac{\partial f}{\partial x} = f_x = pqy,\ f_y = pqx,\ f_z = -2z,\ f_p = q\,xy,\ f_q = pxy.$

The Charpit's equations are

$$\frac{dx}{-f_p} = \frac{dy}{-f_q} = \frac{dz}{-(pf_p + qf_q)} = \frac{dp}{f_x + pf_z} = \frac{dq}{f_y + qf_z}$$

becomes, $\frac{dx}{-qxy} = \frac{dp}{-pxy} = \frac{dz}{-2pqxy} = \frac{dp}{pqy - 2pz} = \frac{dq}{pqx - 2qz}$

By Componendo-dividendo each of these fractions is equal to

$$= \frac{p\,dx + x\,dp}{-pqxy + pqxy - 2pxz} = \frac{q\,dy + y\,dq}{-2qyz}$$

or
$$\frac{d\,(px)}{px} = \frac{d\,(qy)}{qy}.$$

Integrating $px = a^2\,qy$, giving equation is $pqxy = z^2$

So we have $p = \frac{az}{x},\ q = \frac{z}{ay}$.

From $\quad dz = p\,dx + q\,dy$

We have $\int \frac{dz}{z} = \int \frac{a}{x}\,dx + \frac{1}{a}\int \frac{dy}{y}$

$$\log z = a \log x + \frac{1}{a} \log y + \log c$$

or $\quad z = cx^a\,y^{1/a}$ is the complete solution.

Example 1.31. Solve $pxy + pq + qy - yz = 0 = f(x, y, z, p, q)$ ***(Punjab ME 90)***

Solution : $\frac{\partial f}{\partial x} \equiv f_x = p_y,\ f_y = py + q - z,\ f_z = -y$

$$f_p = xy + q,\ f_q = p + y$$

The Charpit's equations $\frac{dx}{-f_p} = \frac{dy}{-f_q} = \frac{dz}{-(pf_p + qf_q)} = \frac{dp}{f_x + pf_z} = \frac{dq}{f_y + qf_z}$

becomes

$$\frac{dx}{-(xy + q)} = \frac{dy}{-(p + y)} = \frac{dz}{-\{pxy + pq + pq + qy\}} = \frac{dp}{py - py} = \frac{dq}{f_y + qf_z}$$

So $\quad dp = 0$ or $\mathbf{p = c.}$

Hence $\quad c\,xy + cq + qy - yz = 0$

So
$$\boldsymbol{q = \frac{yz - cxy}{c + y}}$$

From $dz = p\,dx + q\,dy$, we have

$$dz = c\,dx + \frac{yz - c\,xy}{c + y}\,dy$$

$$dz - c\,dx = \frac{y}{c + y}\,(z - cx)\,dy$$

or
$$\int \frac{dz - c\,dx}{z - cx} = \int \frac{y}{c + y}\,dy$$

or
$$\boldsymbol{\log (z - cx) = y - c \log (c + y) + b}$$

is the solution.

Example 1.32. Solve $f(x, y, z, p, q) = q + px - p^2 = 0$ ***(Bhopal 91)***

Solution : $\frac{\partial f}{\partial x} = f_x = p,\ f_y = 0,\ f_z = 0,\ f_p = x - 2p,\ f_q = 1$

Charpit's equations $\frac{dx}{-f_p} = \frac{dy}{-f_q} = \frac{dz}{-(pf_p + qf_q)} = \frac{dp}{f_x + pf_z} = \frac{dq}{f_y + qf_z}$

becomes $\frac{dx}{-(x-2p)} = \frac{dy}{-1} = \frac{dz}{-(px-2p^2+q)} = \frac{dp}{p+0} = \frac{dq}{0+0}$

From $\frac{dy}{-1} = \frac{dp}{p}$

$\Rightarrow$ $\log p = -y$ or $p = e^{-y}$

So $q = p^2 - px = e^{-2y} - x\,e^{-y}$

As $dz = p\,dx + q\,dy$

So $dz = e^{-y}\,dx + (e^{-2y} - xe^{-y})\,dy$

$\int dz = \int (e^{-y}\,dx - x\,e^{-y}\,dy) + \int e^{-2y}\,dy$

or $z = x\,e^{-y} + \frac{e^{-2y}}{-2} + c$

PROBLEM SET 1.5

Solve by Charpit's method the following differential equations :

1. $2xz - px^2 - 2qxy + pq = 0$

   Ans. $z - cy = b(x^2 - c)$

2. $px + qy - pq = 0$ *(Raj 2001)*

   Ans. $2az = (y + ax)^2 + c$

3. $2xz - px^2 - 2qxy + pq = 0$ *(JNUV 94, MREC 2001)*

   Ans. $z - cy = b(x^2 - c)$

4. $pxy + pq + qy - yz = 0$ *(Raj 2001)*

   Ans. $(z - ax)(a + y)^a = ce^y$.

5. $2(z + pz + qy) - p^2 y = 0$ *(Raj 2001)*

   Ans. $yz = \frac{ax}{y} - \frac{a^2}{4y^2} + c$

6. $(x^2 - y^2)\,pq - xy\,(p^2 - q^2) - 1 = 0$ *(Raj 2003)*

   Ans. $z = \frac{a}{2}\log(x^2 + y^2) + \frac{1}{a}\tan^{-1}\frac{y}{x} + b$

7. $z = p^2 x + q^2 y$ *(Madurai 90)*

   Ans. $z = \frac{(\sqrt{ax} + \sqrt{b + y})^2}{1 + a}$

8. $1 + p^2 = qz$

   Ans. $\frac{z^2}{2} \pm \left\{\frac{z}{2}\sqrt{z^2 - 4a^2} - 2a^2 \log z + \sqrt{z^2 - 4a^2}\right\} = 2ax + 2y + b$

1.12 HOMOGENEOUS LINEAR PARTIAL DIFFERENTIAL EQUATIONS WITH CONSTANT COEFFICIENTS

Denoting $\frac{\partial}{\partial x} \equiv \boldsymbol{D}$, $\frac{\partial^2}{\partial x^2} = \boldsymbol{D^2}$ ... and $\frac{\partial}{\partial y} = \boldsymbol{D'}$ $\frac{\partial^2}{\partial y^2} = \boldsymbol{D'^2}$ ... etc., an equation of the form

$$\{\boldsymbol{D^n} + k_1 \boldsymbol{D^{n-1}} \boldsymbol{D'} + \dots k_n \boldsymbol{D'^n}\} z = f(x, y) \qquad \text{...(1)}$$

where the sum of the powers of D and D' is n in every term than the equation is called a homogeneous equation of order n ($k_0, k_1, \dots$ are here constants). On L.H.S. sum of powers of D and D' is always same $= n$ and where the coefficients of each term are constants so the equation is called a nth order **homogeneous linear equation with constant coefficients.** As like the case of ordinary differential equation, the solution will consist of two parts, the **complementary function (C.F.)** and the **particular integral (P.I.).** C.F. is the solution of $F(D, D') = 0$ with R.H.S. $= 0$, and involves arbitrary functions, whereas P.I. $= \phi(x, y)$ is a particular solution of full equation $F(D, D') = f(x, y)$.

1.13 METHODS OF FINDING THE COMPLEMENTARY FUNCTION

We consider a second order equation. The left hand member of (1) equated to zero will be the equation

$$\left(\frac{\partial^2}{\partial x^2} + k_1 \frac{\partial^2}{\partial x\, \partial y} + k_2 \frac{\partial^2}{\partial y^2}\right) z = 0 \qquad \text{...(2)}$$

Written symbolically as $(D^2 + k_1 DD' + k_2 D'^2) z = 0$. Let $z = \phi(y + mx)$ then

$$D = m\phi', \; D^2 = m^2 \phi''$$

$$D' = \phi', \; D'^2 = \phi''$$

Substituting these in (2) we get $m^2 + k_1 m + k = 0$ ...(3)

It is called the **auxiliary equation (A.E.).**

Case (I). Let the auxiliary equation (3) have roots m_1 and m_2 different.

So the equation is factoried as

$$(D - m_1 D')(D - m_2 D') z = 0$$

Consider the solution of

$$(D - m_1 D') z = 0 \;\text{ or }\; pz - m_1 qz = 0$$

Comparing it we get

$$pP + qQ = R$$

where $P = 1$, $Q = -m_1$, $R = 0$

So the auxiliary equation is $\frac{dx}{1} = \frac{dy}{-m_1} = \frac{dz}{0}$ its solution are $y + m_1 x = c_1$ and $z = c_2$.

The solution may be put in the form

$$c_2 = \phi(c_1) \;\text{ or }\; z = \phi(y + m_1 x)$$

Similarly the other solution is $z = \phi(y + m_2 x)$.

Hence the complete solution is

$$z = \phi_1 (y + m, n) + \phi_2 (y + m_2 x)$$

Case II. When the roots m_1 and m_2 of the A.E. are equal

So the equation reduce to $(D - m_1 D')(D - m_1 D') z = 0$

The solution of $(D - m_1 D') z$ is $u = \phi_1 (y + m_1 x)$

The solution of $(D - m_1 D') z = u = \phi_1 (y + m_1 x)$ has auxiliary equation

$$\frac{dx}{1} = \frac{dy}{-m_1} = \frac{dz}{\phi_1 (y + m_1 x)}$$

$$\frac{dx}{1} = \frac{dy}{-m_1} \text{ gives } y + m_1 x = c_1$$

and
$$\frac{dx}{1} = \frac{dz}{\phi_1 (c_1)} \text{ gives } z = \phi_1 (c_1) \cdot x + c_2$$

So
$$c_2 = \phi_2 (c_1) = \phi_2 (y + m_1 x)$$

Hence the complete solution is $\boldsymbol{z = x\phi_1 (y + m_1 x) + \phi_2 (y + m_1 x)}$

Example 1.33. **Solve** $\dfrac{\partial^2 z}{\partial x^2} - 3\dfrac{\partial^2 z}{\partial x\, \partial y} + 2\dfrac{\partial^2 z}{\partial y^2} = 0$

Solution : The equation can be written as $(D^2 - 3DD' + 2D'^2) z = 0$

The Auxiliary equation is $(D - D')(D - 2D') = 0$

Let $z = \phi(y + mx)$, then we have A.E. $(m - 1)(m - 2) = 0$ so the roots of A.E. are $m_1 = 1, m_2 = 2$.

Hence the solution is $z = \phi_1 (y + 1x) + \phi_2 (y + 2x)$.

Example 1.34. **Solve** $\dfrac{\partial^2 z}{\partial x^2} - 4\dfrac{\partial^2 z}{\partial x\, \partial y} + 4\dfrac{\partial^2 z}{\partial y^2} = 0$

Solution : The auxiliary equation is $D^2 - 4DD' + 4D'^2 = 0$

or $(D - 2D')^2 = 0$ so the roots are $\dfrac{D}{D'} = 2, 2$

The roots are repeated so the solution is $\boldsymbol{z = \phi_1 (y + 2x) + x\, \phi_2 (y + 2x)}$

PROBLEM SET 1.6

Solve the following equations :

1. $(D^2 + DD' - 6D'^2) z = 0$

   Ans. $z = \phi_1 (y + 2x) + \phi_2 (y - 3x)$

2. $(D^2 + 6DD' + 9D'^2) z = 0$

   Ans. $z = \phi_1 (y - 3x) + x\phi_2 (y - 3x)$

3. $(r - 6s + 9t) z = 0$

   Ans. $z = \phi_1 (y + 3x) + x\, \phi_2 (y + 3x)$

4. $(2D^2 + 5DD' + 2D'^2)\, z = 0$

Ans. $z = \phi_1 (y - 2x) + \phi_2 (2y - x)$

5. $(D^3 - 3D^2 D' + 3DD'^2 - D'^3)\, z = 0$

Ans. $z = \phi_1 (y + x) + x\, \phi_2 (y + x) + x^2\, \phi_3 (y + x)$

6. $(D^3 - D^2 D' - 7DD'^2 + 12D'^3)\, z = 0$

Ans. $z = \phi_1 (y + 2x) + x\phi_2 (y + 2x) + \phi_3 (y - 3x)$

1.14 PARTICULAR INTEGRAL

Consider the equation

$$\{D^2 - (m_1 + m_2)\, DD' + m_1 m_2 D'^2\}\, z = F(x, y)$$

One particular value of z satisfying this equation is denoted by

$$\text{P.I.} = \frac{1}{(D - m_1 D')\,(D - m_2 D')} F(x, y) = \frac{1}{f(D_1 D')} F(x, y)$$

Case I. $F(x, y) = e^{ax + by}$ **then** $\text{P.I.} = \frac{1}{F(D, D')} e^{ax + by} = \frac{1}{F(a, b)} e^{ax + by}$, **provided** $f(a, b) \neq 0$.

Case II. $F(x, y) = \sin (mx + ny)$ **or** $\cos (mx + ny)$

As
$$D^2 \sin (mx + ny) = -m^2 \sin (mx + ny)$$
$$DD' \sin (mx + ny) = -mn \sin (mx + ny)$$
$$D'^2 \sin (mx + ny) = -n^2 \sin mn + xy.$$
$$\text{P.I.} = \frac{1}{F(D^2, DD', D'^2)} \sin mx + ny = \frac{1}{F(-m^2, -mn, -n^2)} \sin (mx + ny).$$

Provided $f(-m^2, -mn, -n^2) \neq 0$

Case III. $F(x, y) = x^m y^n$.

To evaluate $\frac{1}{F(D, D')} x^m y^n$, $\frac{1}{F(D, D')}$ should be expanded by Binomial and then the terms D, D' etc are applied by differentiating the terms by term.

Case IV. When $F(x, y)$ **is any function of** x **and** y.

$$\text{P.I.} = \frac{1}{F(D, D')} F(x, y)$$

First $\frac{1}{F(D, D')}$ should be broken in partial functions. Take one,

Then for $\frac{1}{D - mD'} f(x, y)$, let the *P.I.* be $= \int f(x, c - mx)\, dx$, where c is replaced by $y + mx$ after the integration. Sum of all such terms will form the full P.I.

Summary

(1) For $(D - m_1 D')\,(D - m'_2)\, z = 0$ (where roots of A.E. are different)

Solution is $z = \phi_1 (y + m_1 x) + \phi_2 (y + m_2 x)$

(2) For $(D - mD')^2\, z = 0$ (Case of equal roots)

$$z = \phi_1 (y + mx) + x \phi_2 (y + mx)$$

(3) For $(D - mD')^2 (D - m_3D')z = 0$

$$z = \phi_1 (y + mx) + x \phi_2 (y + mx) + \phi_3 (y + m_3x)$$

(4) When the equation is $(D - m_1D') (D - m_2D')z = e^{ax + by}$

$$\text{P.I.} = \frac{1}{(a - m_1b)(a - m_2b)} e^{ax + by} \quad (D \text{ is replaced by } a \text{ and } D' \text{ by } b)$$

Provided $(a - m_1, b) \neq 0$, $(a - m_2b) \neq 0$. It can also be stated as

For a second order equation with $(F(a, b) \neq 0)$

$$\frac{1}{F(D, D')} \psi(ax + by) = \frac{1}{F(a, b)} \iint \psi(u)\,(du)^2$$

Put $u = ax + by$ after integration.

If equation be of order n, then integration on R.H.S. will be n times, when $F(a, b) = 0$.

$$\frac{1}{bD - aD'} \psi(ax + by) = x \frac{1}{b} \psi(ax + by)$$

or

$$\frac{1}{(bD - aD')^2} \psi(ax + by) = \frac{x^2}{2b^2} \psi(ax + by)$$

(5) $\dfrac{1}{f(D^2, D, D', D'^2)} \sin (mx + ny)$ or $\cos (mx + ny)$

$$\text{P.I.} = \frac{1}{f(-m^2, -mn, -n^2)} \sin (mx + ny) \text{ or } \cos (mx + ny) \text{ as the case } b$$

(6) For $\dfrac{1}{F(D, D')} x^m y^m$, expand $\{F(D, D')\}^{-1}$ and then apply D and D' operates term by term.

1.15 METHOD FOR FINDING THE P.I. IN THE GENERAL CASE

Let $F(x, y)$ be any function of x and y then

Let $$\frac{1}{(D - mD')} F(x, y) = \phi(x, y)$$

then $$(D - mD')\, \phi(x, y) = F(x, y)$$

The subsidiary equation is

$$\frac{dx}{1} = \frac{dy}{-m} = \frac{dz}{F(x,y)}$$

From $\dfrac{dx}{1} = \dfrac{dy}{-m}$ we have $y + mx = c_1$

From $$\frac{dx}{1} = \frac{dz}{F(x, y)} = \frac{dz}{F(x, c_1 - mx)}$$

$$z = \int F(x, c_1 - mx)\, dx = \text{P.I.}$$

After integration $(c_1 - mx)$ should be replaced y.

Example 1.35. Solve $\dfrac{\partial^3 z}{\partial x^3} - 3\dfrac{\partial^3 z}{\partial x^2 \partial y} + 4\dfrac{\partial^3 z}{\partial y^3} = e^{x+2y}$ *(AMIE 90, Gorakhpur 91)*

Solution : The auxiliary equation is $D^3 - 3D^2 D' + 4D'^3 = 0$

or $(D + D')(D^2 - 4D'D + 4D'^2) = 0$

or $(D + D')(D - 2D')^2 = 0$

So C.F. $= \phi_1(y - x) + \phi_2(y + 2x) + x\,\phi_3(y + 2x)$

$$\text{P.I.} = \frac{e^{x+2y}}{1^3 - 3(1^2)(2) + 4(2^3)} = \frac{e^{x+2y}}{27}y$$

Complete solution is

$$z = \phi_1(y - x) + \phi_2(y + 2x) + x\,\phi_3(y + 2x) + \frac{e^{x+2y}}{27}$$

Example 1.36. Solve $(D^3 - 4D^2 D' + 4DD'^2)\, z = \cos(2x + 3y)$ *(Gorakhpur)*

Solution : The Auxiliary equation is $m^3 - 4m^2 + 4m = 0$

$$m(m - 2)^2 = 0$$

So C.F. $= \phi_1(x + 0y) + \phi_2(x + 2y) + x\,\phi_3(x + 2y)$

$$\text{C.F.} = \frac{1}{D}\frac{1}{(D^2 - 4DD' + 4D'^2)}\cos(2x + 3y)$$

$$= \frac{1}{D}\left\{\frac{1}{-2^2 - 4(-2 \times 3) - 4(3^2)}\cos(2x + 3y)\right.$$

$$= \frac{1}{-16}\int \cos(2x + 3y)\,dx = \frac{\sin(2x + 3y)}{-32}$$

Hence the general solution is

$$z = \phi_1(x) + \phi_2(x + 2y) + x\,\phi_3(x + 2y) - \frac{1}{32}\sin(2x + 3y)$$

Example 1.37. Solve $\dfrac{\partial^2 z}{\partial x^2} - \dfrac{\partial^2 z}{\partial x\,\partial y} = \cos x \cos 2y$

Solution : A.E. is $D^2 - DD' = 0$ $D(D - D') = 0$

$\dfrac{D}{D'} = 0$ or $\dfrac{D}{D'} = 1$ So C.F. $= \phi_1(x) + \phi_2(x + y)$

$$\text{P.I.} = \frac{1}{(D^2 - D'D)}\frac{1}{2}\{\cos(x + 2y) + \cos(x - 2y)\}$$

$$= \frac{1}{2}\left\{\frac{1}{-1 + 2}\cos(x + 2y) + \frac{1}{-1 - 2}\cos(x - 2y)\right\}$$

$$= \frac{1}{2}\cos(x + 2y) - \frac{1}{6}\cos(x - 2y)$$

Hence the complete solution is

$$z = \phi_1(x) + \phi_2(x + y) + \frac{1}{2}\cos(x + 2y) - \frac{1}{6}\cos(x - 2y)$$

Example 1.38. **Solve $(D^2 - 2DD' + D'^2)\, z = 12xy$**

Solution : A.E. is $(D - D')^2 = 0$

So C.F. is $\phi_1 (x + y) + x\, \phi_2 (x + y)$

$$\text{P.I.} = \frac{1}{D^2}\left(1 - \frac{D'}{D}\right)^{-2} 12xy = \frac{1}{D^2}\left(1 + \frac{2D'}{D} \ldots\right) 12xy$$

$$= \frac{1}{D^2} 12xy - \frac{2}{D^3} 12x = \frac{12x^3}{6} y + \frac{2 \times 12\, x^4}{24} = 2x^3 y + x^4$$

Hence the solution is $z = \phi_1 (x + y) + x\, \phi_2 (x + y) + 2x^3 y + x^4$

Example 1.39. **Solve $\left(\frac{\partial^2 z}{\partial x^2} - 4\frac{\partial^2 z}{\partial x\, \partial y} + 4\frac{\partial^2 z}{\partial y^2}\right) = e^{2x + y}$** *(Madurai 90)*

Solution : The A.E. in $D^2 - 4DD' + 4D^2 = 0$ or $(D' - 2D)^2 = 0$

So C.F. $= \phi_1 (x + 2y) + x\, \phi_2 (x + 2y)$

$$\text{P.I.} = \frac{1}{(D - 2D')^2} e^{2x + y}.$$

On putting $D = 2, D' = 1,\ D - 2D' = 0$

So the general method has to be used Let $y + 2x = c$

We apply $\frac{1}{(D - 2D')^2}$ in two stages

$$y = c - 2x$$

Stage I $\frac{1}{D - 2D'} e^{2x + y} = \int f(x, c - 2x)\, dx$

Stage 2 $\frac{1}{D - 2D'} \frac{1}{D - 2D'} e^{2x + y} = \frac{1}{D - 2D'} x\, e^{2x + y}$

$$= \int x\, e^c\, dx = \frac{x^2}{2} e^c = \frac{x^2}{2} e^{y + 2x}$$

Hence the complete solution is

$$y = \phi_1 (x + 2y) + x\, \phi_2 (x + 2y) + \frac{x^2}{2} e^{2x + y}$$

Example 1.40. **Solve $(D^2 - 4DD' + 3D'^2)\, z = \sqrt{x + 3y}$** *(Nagpur 97)*

Solution : A.E. is $(D - D')\,(D - 3D') = 0$ so $\frac{D}{D'} = 1$ or 3

C.F. $= \phi_1 (y + x) + \phi_2 (y + 3x)$

$$\text{P.I.} = \frac{1}{(D - D')\,(D - 3D')} (x + 3y)^{\frac{1}{2}}$$

$$= \frac{1}{D - D'} \int \{x + 3(c - 3x)\}^{\frac{1}{2}}\, dx$$

$y + 3x = c$

$$y = c - 3x = \frac{1}{D - D'} \int (3c - 8x)^{\frac{1}{2}}\, dx$$

$$= \frac{1}{D-D'} \frac{2(3c-8x)^{3/2}}{3(-8)} = -\frac{1}{12}\frac{1}{D-D'}(x+3y)^{3/2}$$

$$= -\frac{1}{12}\int \{x+3(c_2-x)\}^{3/2}\,dx \quad x+y=c_2$$

$$= -\frac{1}{12}\int (3c_2-2x)^{3/2}\,dx = -\frac{1}{12}\frac{(3c_2-2x)^{5/2}}{-2}\times\frac{2}{5} = -\frac{1}{60}(x+3y)^{5/2}$$

$$z = \phi_1(y+x)+\phi_2(y+3x)-\frac{1}{60}(x+3y)^{5/2} \quad \textbf{Ans.}$$

Example 1.41. $(D^2 - DD' - 2D'^2)\,z = (y-1)\,e^x$ *(Rewa 94)*

Solution : A.E. in $(D-2D')(D+D') = 0$ so $\frac{D}{D'} = -1, 2$

$$\text{C.F.} = \phi_1(y-x)+\phi_2(y+2x)$$

$$\text{P.I.} = \frac{1}{(D+D')(D-2D')}(y-1)\,e^x$$

$y + 2x = c_1$

$$= \frac{1}{D+D'}\int (c_1-2x-1)\,e^x\,dx = \frac{1}{D+D'}\{c_1-1-2(x-1)\}\,e^x$$

$$= \frac{1}{D+D'}(y+1)\,e^x = \int (c_2+x+1)\,e^x\,dx$$

$y - x = c_2$

$$= (c_2+1)\,e^x+(x-1)\,e^x = (c_2+x)\,e^x = y\,e^x$$

Hence the solution is $z = \phi_1(y-x)+\phi_2(y+2x)+y\,e^x$.

Example 1.42. Solve $\{D^3 + D^2D' - DD'^2 - D'^3\}\,z = e^x \cos 2y$ *(Bhopal 91)*

Solution :

$$\text{A.E.} = D^3 + D^2D' - DD'^2 - D'^3 = 0$$

$$(D-D')(D^2+2DD'+D'^2) = 0$$

$$(D-D')(D+D')^2 = 0$$

$$\frac{D}{D'} = 1, -1, -1$$

So

$$\text{C.F.} = \phi_1(y+x)+\phi_2(y-x)+x\,\phi_3(y-x)$$

$$\text{P.I.} = \text{Real part}\ \frac{1}{(D-D')\{D+D'\}^2}e^{x+2iy}$$

$$= R\,\frac{1}{(1+2i)5}e^{x+2i} = R\,\frac{(1-2i)}{25}e^{x+2i}$$

$$= R\,\frac{e^x(1-2i)(\cos 2y + i\sin 2y)}{25}$$

$$= \frac{e^x(\cos 2y + 2\sin 2y)}{25}$$

Hence the complete solution is

$$z = \phi_1 (y + x) + \phi_2 (y - x) + x\, \phi_3 (y - x) + \frac{e^x}{25} (\cos 2y + 2 \sin 2y)$$

Example 1.43. **Solve $(D^2 + 2DD' + D'^2)\, z = 2 \cos y - x \sin y$** *(AUUP 2007)*

Solution : A.E. is $(D + D')^2 = 0$ roots of C.F. are $\frac{D}{D'} = -1, -1$

So $\quad$ C.F. $= \phi_1 (y - x) + x\, \phi_2 (y - x)$

Ist term (P.I.)

$$T_1 = 2 \frac{1}{D^2 + 2DD' + D'^2} \cos (0x + y) = \frac{2 \cos y}{0 + 0 + (-1^2)} = -2 \cos y$$

2nd term (P.I.)

$$y - x = c_1$$

$$T_2 = -\frac{1}{D + D'} \int x \sin (c_1 + x)\, dx$$

$$= -\frac{1}{D + D'} \{-x \cos (c_1 + x) + \sin (c_1 + x)\}\, dx$$

$$= -\int \{-x \cos (c_1 + x) + \sin (c_1 + x)\}\, dx$$

$$= x \sin (c_1 + x) + \cos (c_1 + x) + \cos (c_1 + x)$$

So $\quad$ (P.I.) $= (T_1 + T_2) = -2 \cos y + (x \sin y + 2 \cos y) = x \sin y$

Hence the complete solution is

$$z = \phi_1 (y - x) + x\, \phi_2 (y - x) + x \sin y.$$

PROBLEM SET 1.7

Solve the following :

1. $(D^2 + 2DD' + D'^2)\, z - e^{2x + 3y}$

   Ans. $z = \phi_1 (y - x) + x\, \phi_2 (y - x) + \frac{1}{25} e^{2x + 3y}$

2. $(D^2 - 5DD' + 6D'^2)\, z = e^{x + y}$

   Ans. $z = \phi_1 (y + 2x) + \phi_2 (y + 3x) + \frac{e^{x + y}}{2}.$

3. $(r - 2s + t) = \sin (2x + 3y)$

   Ans. $z = \phi_1 (y + x) + x\, \phi_2 (y + x) - \sin (2x + 3y)$

4. $(D^2 - a^2 D'^2)\, z = x^2$

   Ans. $z = \phi_1 (y + ax) + \phi_2 (y - ax) + \frac{x^4}{12}$

5. $(D^2 + 3DD' + 2D'^2)\, z = x + y$

Ans. $z = f_1\,(y - 2x) + f_2\,(y - x) + \frac{1}{2} xy^2 - \frac{1}{3} x^3.$

6. $(2D^2 - 5DD' + 2D'^2)\, z = 24(y - x)$

Ans. $z = f_1\,(y + 2x) + f(2y + x) + 6yx^2 + 3x^3$

7. $(D^2 - DD' - 6D'^2)\, z = xy$

Ans. $z = f_1\,(y + 3x) + f_2\,(y - 2x) + \frac{1}{6} x^3 y + \frac{1}{24} x^4$

8. $(D^3 - 2D^2D')\, z = 2e^{2x} + 3x^2 y$ *(Madras 99, Marathwada 94)*

Ans. $z = f_1(y) + x f_2(y) + f_3(y + 2x) + \frac{e^{2x}}{4} + \frac{x^5 y}{20} + \frac{x^6}{60}.$

9. $(D^2 + DD' - 6D'^2)\, z = \cos\,(2x + y)$ *(Madras 94)*

Ans. $z = f_1(y - 3x) + f_2\,(y + 2x) + \frac{x}{5} \sin\,(2x + y) + \frac{1}{25} \cos\,(2x + y).$

10. $(D^2 + DD' - 6D^2)\, z = y \cos x$ *(Madras 2000S, Assam 99, AMIE 97, Osmania 99, AUUP 2008)*

Ans. $z = f_1\,(y - 3x) + f_2\,(y + 2x) + \sin x - y \cos x$

11. $\frac{\partial^2 z}{\partial x^2} - 2\frac{\partial^2 z}{\partial x\, \partial y} + \frac{\partial^2 z}{\partial y^2} = \sin x$ *(UPTU 2004, Punjab 1990)*

Ans. $z = f_1\,(y + x) + x\, f_2(y + x) - \sin x$

12. $\frac{\partial^2 z}{\partial x^2} - \frac{\partial^2 z}{\partial x\, \partial y} = \sin x \cos 2y$ *(Madras 94S, Madurai 90)*

Ans. $z = f_1(y) + f_2(y + x) + \frac{1}{3} \{\sin x \cos 2y + 2 \cos x \sin 2y\}$

13. $\frac{\partial^2 z}{\partial x^2} - \frac{\partial^2 z}{\partial y^2} = \cos 2x \cos 3y$

Ans. $z = \phi_1\,(y + x) + f_2\,(y - x) + \frac{1}{5} \cos 2x \cos 3y$

14. $\frac{\partial^3 z}{\partial x^3} - \frac{\partial^3 z}{\partial y^3} = x^3 y^3$ *(AUUP 2008)*

Ans. $f_1(y + x) + f_2(y + wx) + f_3(y + w^2 x) + \frac{x^6 y^3}{120} + \frac{x^9}{10080}$

1.16 NON-HOMOGENEOUS LINEAR EQUATIONS

When in the equation $f(D, D')z = 0$, $f(D, D')$ contains not only the second order partial derivatives but also of first order and a constant term, the equation becomes a non-homogeneous type equation. Example of such an equation is $(D - mD' - a)\, z = 0$. If it is a linear partial differential equation of order one whose auxiliary equations are $\frac{dx}{1} = \frac{dy}{-m} = \frac{dz}{az}$

Its one solution is $y = mx = c_1$.

The other solution is

$$\log \frac{z}{c_2} = ax$$

If $c_2 = \phi(c_1)$, then $z = \phi(y + mx)\, e^{ax}$

If we have the equation

$$(D - mD' - a)(D - nD' - b)\, z = 0$$

Its general solution is

$$z = e^{ax}\, \phi\, (y + mx) + e^{bx}\, \phi\, (y + nx)$$

Case when the two roots of the auxiliary equation are equal

Consider the equation $(D - mD' - a)^2 z = 0$.

The solution in this case is

$$z = e^{ax}\, \phi_1\, (y + mx) + x\, e^{ax}\, \phi_2\, (y + mx)$$

Example 1.44. Solve $DD'(D - 2D' - 3)\, z = 0$.

Solution : The roots of auxiliary equation are $\frac{D}{D'} = 0, \infty, 2$

So $\quad$ C.F. $= \phi_1\, (y) = \phi_2(x) + e^{3x}\, \phi_3\, (y + 2x)$

Example 1.45. Solve $\{D^2 + 2DD' + D'^2 + 2D + 2D' + 1\}\, z = 0$

Solution : The A.E. equation can be written as

$$(D + D')^2 + 2(D + D') + 1 = 0$$

or $\quad (D + D' + 1)^2 = 0$

So the solution is $e^{-x}\, \{\phi_1\, (y - x) + x\, \phi_2\, (y - x)\}$

Example 1.46. Solve $(D^2 - D'^2 + D - D')z = 0$

Solution : The A.E. is $(D - D')(D + D' + 1) = 0$

So the solution is $z = \phi_1\, (y + x) + e^{-x}\, \phi_1\, (y - x)$.

Particular Integrals.

Consider the equation $f(D, D')\, z = F(x, y)$

Case (i). $F(x, y) = e^{ax + by}$

the $\quad$ P.I. $= \dfrac{1}{f(D, D')}\, e^{ax + by} = \dfrac{e^{ax + by}}{f(a, b)}$ provided $f(a, b) \neq 0$

Case (ii). $F(x, y) = \sin(ax + by)$ **or** $\cos(ax + by)$

$$\frac{1}{F(D, D')} \sin(ax + by) = \frac{1}{f(-a^2, -ab, -b^2)} \sin ax + by$$

where D^2 is replaced by $-a^2$, DD' by $-ab$ and D'^2 by $-b^2$.

Case (iii). $F(x, y) = x^m y^n$, for $\dfrac{1}{f(D, D')} x^m y^m$, expand $\{f(D, D')\}^{-1}$ by binomial and apply the resulting operators term by term.

Case (iv). $\dfrac{1}{f(D, D')} e^{ax+by} V = e^{ax+by} \dfrac{1}{f(D+a, D'+b)} V$

Example 1.47. **Solve** $(D^2 - 3DD' + 2D'^2 + D' - 1)\, z = e^{4x+5y}$

Solution : The equation is

$$\{(D - 2D')(D - D') + (D - D') - (D - 2D') - 1\}\, z = e^{4x+5y}$$

or
$$(D - 2D' + 1)(D - D' - 1)\, z = e^{4x+5y}$$

$$\text{C.F.} = e^{-x} \phi_1 (y + 2x) + e^{x} \phi_2 (y + x)$$

$$\text{P.I.} = \frac{1}{(4 - 10 + 1)(4 - 5 - 1)} e^{4x+5y}$$

$$= \frac{e^{4x+5y}}{10}$$

Example 1.48. **Solve** $(D + D' - 1)(D + 2D' - 3)\, z = 2x + 3y$

Solution :
$$\text{C.F.} = e^{x} \phi_1 (y - x) + e^{3x} \phi_1 (y - 2x)$$

$$\text{P.I.} = \frac{1}{(-1)(-3)} \{1 - (D + D')\}^{-1} \left\{1 - \frac{D + 2D'}{3}\right\}^{-1} (2x + 3y)$$

$$= \frac{1}{3} [\{1 + (D + D') + \ldots\} \left\{1 + \frac{D + 2D'}{3} + \ldots\right\} (2x + 3y)$$

$$= \frac{1}{3}\left[1 + \frac{4}{3} D + \frac{5}{3} D' + \ldots\right] 2x + 3y$$

$$= \frac{1}{3}\left\{2x + 3y + \frac{8}{3} + 5\right\} = \frac{2x + 3y}{3} + \frac{23}{9}$$

Hence the complete solution is

$$z = e^{x} \phi_1 (y - x) + e^{2x} \phi_1 (y - 2x) + \frac{2}{3} x + y + \frac{23}{9}.$$

Example 1.49. **Solve** $(D^2 - DD' - 2D)\, z = \sin (3x + 4y)$

Solution :
$$\text{C.F.} = \phi_1 (y) = e^{2x} \phi_2 (y + x)$$

$$\text{P.I.} = \frac{1}{D^2 - DD' - 2D} \sin (3x + 4y)$$

$$= \frac{1}{-3^2 - (-3 \times 4) - 2D} \sin (3x + 4y)$$

$$= \frac{(3 + 2D)}{(3 - 2D)(3 + 2D)} \sin (3x + 4y)$$

$$= (3 + 2D) \frac{1}{9 - 4(-9)} \sin (3x + 4y)$$

$$= \frac{1}{45}\{(3\sin(3x+4y)+6\cos(3x+4y)\}$$
$$= \frac{1}{15}\sin(3x+4y)+\frac{2}{15}\cos(3x+4y)$$
$$z = \text{C.F.} + \text{P.I.}$$

PROBLEM SET 1.8

Solve the following equations

1. $(D-D'-1)(D-D'-2)z = e^{2x-y}$ *(A.M.I.E. 90)*

Ans. $z = e^x\,\phi_1(y+x)+e^{2x}\,\phi_2(y+x)+\frac{e^{2x-y}}{2}$

2. $(D-D'-1)(D-D'-2)z = x$

Ans. $z = e^x\,\phi_1(y+x)+e^{2x}\,\phi_2(y+x)+\frac{x}{2}+\frac{3}{4}$

3. $(D^2-D'^2-3D+3D')z = e^{x+2y}$

Ans. $z = f_1(x+y)+e^{3x}\,f_2(y-x)-y\,e^{x+2y}$

4. $(DD'+D+D')z = xy$

Ans. $z = e^x\,f_1y+e^{-y}\,f_2(x)+1+x-y-xy.$

5. $(D^2+DD'+D-1)z = e^{-x}$

Ans. $z = e^{-x}\,\phi_1(y)+e^x\,\phi_2(y-x)-\frac{x\,e^{-x}}{2}$

6. $(D^2-DD'+D'-1)\cos(x+2y)$

Ans. $z = e^x\,\phi_1(y)+e^{-x}\,\phi_2(x+y)+\frac{1}{2}\sin(x+2y)$

7. $(D^2-DD'+D)z = x^2+y^2$ *(Madras 2000S)*

Ans. $z = f_1(y)+e^{-x}\,f_2(y+x)+\frac{1}{3}x^3+xy^2-x^2+2xy+4x.$

8. $(2DD'+D'^2-3D')\,z = 3\cos(3x-2y)$ *(Bhopal 91)*

Ans. $z = f_1(x)+e^{3y}\,\phi_2(x+y)+\frac{3}{50}\{4\cos(3x-2y)+3\sin(3x-2y)\}$

9. $(D+D'-1)(D+2D'-3)z = 4+3x+6y$

Ans. $z = e^x\,\phi_1(y-x)+e^{3x}\,\phi_2(y-2x)+x+2y+6.$

10. $(D-3D'-2)^2z = 2e^{2x}\tan(y+3x)$ *(AUUP 2008)*

Ans. $z = e^{2x}\,f_1(y+3x)+xe^{2x}\,f_2(y+3x)+x^2e^{2x}\,f_3(y+3x)+x^3e^{2x}\sin(3x+y)$

1.17 EQUATIONS REDUCIBLE TO PARTIAL DIFFERENTIAL EQUATIONS WITH CONSTANT COEFFICIENT

A partial differential equation having coefficient of partial derivative of order k as x^k, can be reduced to the partial differential equation with constant coefficient.

By making the assumption $x = e^X$, $y = e^Y$, *i.e.*, $X = \log x$, $Y = \log y$.

We get

$$\frac{\partial z}{\partial x} = \frac{\partial z}{\partial X} \cdot \frac{\partial X}{\partial x} = \frac{1}{x}\frac{\partial z}{\partial X}$$

i.e.,
$$x\frac{\partial z}{\partial x} = \frac{\partial z}{\partial X}$$

or
$$x\frac{\partial z}{\partial x} = Dz, \qquad \text{where } D \equiv \frac{\partial}{\partial X} = x\frac{\partial}{\partial x}$$

In a similar manner one can get

$$x^2\frac{\partial^2 z}{\partial x^2} = (D-1)Dz$$

$$x^3\frac{\partial^3 z}{\partial x^3} = D(D-1)(D-2)z, \text{ and so on.}$$

Also we can obtain $y\dfrac{\partial z}{\partial y} = D'z$, where $D' = \dfrac{\partial}{\partial Y} = y\dfrac{\partial}{\partial y}$

$$y^2\frac{\partial^2 z}{\partial y^2} = D'(D'-1)z$$

$$y^3\frac{\partial^3 z}{\partial y^3} = D'(D'-1)(D'-2)z, \text{ and so on.}$$

Also
$$xy\frac{\partial^2 z}{\partial x \partial y} = DD'z$$

On substituting all these in the given partial differential equation, we get a partial differential equation with constant coefficient.

Example 1.50. Solve the partial differential equation

$$x^2\frac{\partial^2 z}{\partial x^2} - y^2\frac{\partial^2 z}{\partial y^2} + x\frac{\partial z}{\partial x} - y\frac{\partial z}{\partial y} = \log x$$

Solution : Let $x = e^X$ and $y = e^Y$, *i.e.*, $X = \log x$ and $Y = \log y$

The given equation reduces to

$$[D(D-1) - D'(D'-1) + D - D']z = X$$

$$\Rightarrow \quad [D^2 - D'^2]z = X$$

This is homogeneous partial differential equation with constant coefficents.

$$\therefore \quad \text{C.F.} = f_1(Y+X) + f_2(Y-X) = f_1(\log y + \log x) + f_2(\log y - \log z)$$

and
$$\text{P.I.} = \frac{1}{(D^2 - D'^2)}X \equiv \frac{1}{D'^2\left[1 - \dfrac{D^2}{D'^2}\right]}$$

$$= -\frac{1}{D'^2}\left[1-\left(\frac{D}{D'}\right)\right]^{-1} X$$

$$= -\frac{1}{D'^2}\left[1+\left(\frac{D}{D'}\right)^2+\left(\frac{D}{D'}\right)^4+\ldots\right]X$$

$$= \frac{-1}{D'^2}[X+0+\ldots] = -\frac{1}{D'^2}X$$

$$-X\frac{Y^2}{2} = -\frac{XY^2}{2} = -\frac{(\log x)(\log y)^2}{2}$$

Hence, the complete solution is

$$z = f_1(\log y + \log x) + f_2(\log y - \log x) - \frac{(\log x)(\log y)^2}{2}$$

$$= f_1(\log xy) + f_2\left(\log\frac{y}{x}\right) - \frac{(\log x)(\log y)^2}{2}$$

Example 1.51. Solve the partial differential equation

$$x^2\frac{\partial^2 z}{\partial x^2} + 2y^2\frac{\partial^2 z}{\partial y^2} + x\frac{\partial z}{\partial x} - 3xy\frac{\partial^2 z}{\partial x \partial y} + 2y\frac{\partial z}{\partial y} = x + 2y$$

Solution : **Let** $x = e^X$ and $y = e^Y$, *i.e.*, $X = \log x$, $Y = \log y$

The given partial differential equation is

$$[D(D-1) + 2D'(D'-1) + D - 3DD' + 2D']z = e^X + 2e^Y$$

where $D \equiv \frac{\partial}{\partial X}$, $D' = \frac{\partial}{\partial y}$, $DD' \equiv \frac{\partial^2}{\partial X \partial Y}$

$\Rightarrow \quad [D^2 - D + 2D'^2 - 2D' + D - 3DD' + 2D']z = e^X + 2e^Y$

$\Rightarrow \quad (D^2 - 3DD' + 2D'^2)z = e^X + 2e^Y$

$\Rightarrow \quad (D - D')(D - 2D')z = e^X + 2e^Y$

$\therefore \quad$ C.F. $= f_1(Y + X) + f_2(Y + 2X) = f_1(\log y + \log x) + f_2(\log y + 2\log x)$

$$= f_1(\log xy) + f_2(\log x^2 y)$$

and

$$\text{P.I.} = \frac{1}{(D^2 - 3DD' + 2D'^2)}(e^X + 2e^Y)$$

$$= \frac{1}{(D^2 - 3DD' + 2D'^2)}e^X + 2\frac{1}{(D^2 - 3DD' + 2D'^2)}e^Y$$

$$= \frac{e^X}{(1-0+0)} + 2\frac{e^Y}{(0-0+2)}$$

$$= e^X + e^Y = x + y$$

Hence the complete solution is

$$z = f_1(\log xy) + f_2(\log x^2 y) + x + y$$

PROBLEM SET 1.9

Solve the following partial differential equations :

1. $x^2 \dfrac{\partial^2 z}{\partial x^2} + 2xy \dfrac{\partial^2 z}{\partial x \partial y} + y^2 \dfrac{\partial^2 z}{\partial yz} = 0$

   Ans. $z = f_1\left(\dfrac{y}{x}\right) + x\, f_2\left(\dfrac{y}{x}\right)$

2. $x^2 \dfrac{\partial^2 z}{\partial x^2} - y^2 \dfrac{\partial^2 z}{\partial y^2} = xy$

   Ans. $z = f_1\,(\log xy) + x\, f_2\left(\log \dfrac{y}{x}\right) + xy \log x$

3. $(x^2 D^2 + 2xyDD' + y^2 D'^2)z = x^m y^n$

   Ans. $z = f_1\left(\log \dfrac{y}{x}\right) + x\, f_2\left(\log \dfrac{y}{x}\right) + \dfrac{x^m y^n}{(m+n)\,(m+n-1)}$

4. $(x^2 D^2 - y^2 D'^2)z = x^2 y$

   Ans. $z = f_1\,(xy) + x f_2\left(\dfrac{y}{x}\right) + \dfrac{1}{2} x^2 y$

5. $x^2 \dfrac{\partial^2 z}{\partial x^2} + 2xy \dfrac{\partial^2 z}{\partial x \partial y} - x \dfrac{\partial z}{\partial x} = \dfrac{x^3}{y^2}$

   Ans. $z = f_1(y) + x^2 f_2\left(\dfrac{y}{x^2}\right) - \dfrac{x^3}{9y^2}$

2

Fourier Series

Before coming to the main topic of **Fourier series**, we give a brief idea of what we mean by **eigen values**, **eigen functions**, **orthogonality** of a set of functions and a **complete set of orthonormal functions**, in order to understand, motivation for the expansion of a function as series of sines and cosines of multiples of angles.

2.1 EIGEN VALUES AND EIGEN FUNCTIONS

Consider a set of two simultaneous equations

$$(1 - \lambda)x + 2y = 0$$

$$2x + (1 - \lambda)\, y = 0$$

For a non-trivial solution of these questions to exist (other than $x = 0, y = 0$) the condition on the parameter λ, is

$$\begin{vmatrix} 1-\lambda & 2 \\ 2 & 1-\lambda \end{vmatrix} = 0$$

or

$$(1 - \lambda)^2 - 2 = 0$$

The values $\lambda = \lambda_1 = -1$ and $\lambda = \lambda_2 = +3$ are called the **eigen values**, for the set of equations to have a non trivial solution. The corresponding solutions for $\lambda_1 = 1$, is $x_1 = k, y_1 = -k$ and for $\lambda_2 = +3$, it is $x_2 = k, y_2 = k$ **are called the eigen functions**.

An another example for the equation $x^2 = \lambda$, to have a real solution the eigen values are those which satisfy $\lambda > 0$, and the correspondingly there may be two sets of eigen functions :

(i) $x = +\sqrt{\lambda}$ and

(ii) $x = -\sqrt{\lambda}$.

2.2 VIBRATING STRING

Consider a string fastened between two points $x = 0$ and $x = l$ and bearing a constant tension T. It is given some initial displacement and is made to vibrate, the dislacement U at any time t and distance x from one end A satisfy the partial differential equation

$$\rho \frac{\partial^2 U}{\partial t^2} = T \frac{\partial^2 U}{\partial x^2},$$

ρ being the density per unit length of the string.

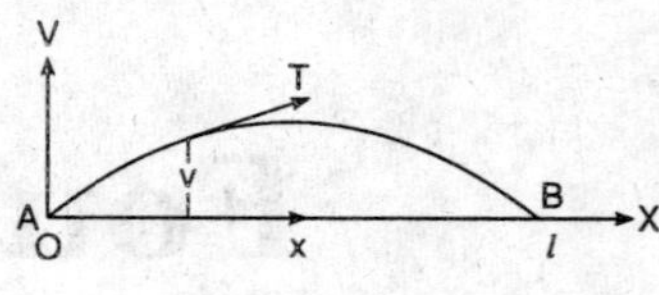

Fig. 2.1

If the string vibrate with angular frequency $\omega = 2\pi \sqrt{\frac{T}{\rho}}$, the solution may be assumed to be of the form $U = S(x) \sin \omega t$

or $U = S(x) \cos \omega t$. S then satisfy

$$\frac{\partial^2 S}{\partial x^2} + k^2 S = 0 \text{ where } k^2 = \frac{\omega^2 \rho}{T^2}.$$

The solution $S = A \sin kx + B \cos kx$ has to satisfy the boundary conditions $S(0) = S(l) = 0$

So $B = 0$ and $\sin kl = 0 = \sin n\pi$ where n is an integer, the values $k = k_n = \frac{n\pi}{l}$, are its eigen values and $A_n \sin \frac{n\pi x}{l}$ are the corresponding eigen functions. Giving to n, the values 1, 2, 3, ... we have an infinite set of eigen functions. These eigen functions have two important properties

(i) They are orthogonal, and (ii) form a complete set.

2.3 ORTHOGONALITY OF EIGEN FUNCTIONS

Arranging the eigen functions $S_n = A_n \sin \frac{n\pi x}{l}$ in the order of corresponding eigen values

$$k_n = \frac{n\pi}{l}, \; n = 1, 2, \ldots n, \text{ we have}$$

$$\int_0^l S_n(x) \, S_m(x) \, dx = 0, \text{ when } n \neq m.$$

For $$I = \frac{A_n^2}{2} \int_0^l \left\{ \cos (n - m) \frac{\pi x}{l} - \cos (n + m) \frac{\pi x}{l} \right\} dx$$

$$= \frac{A_n^2}{2}\left[\frac{l \sin (n-m)\,\pi x/l}{(n-m)\,\pi} - \frac{l}{(n+m)\,\pi} \sin (n+m)\,\pi l\right]_0^l = 0$$

and for $n = m$ $\displaystyle\int_0^l A_n^2 \sin^2 \frac{n\pi x}{l} = C_n.$

In C_n be equal to 1 then the set of functions is called an orthogonal set. So

$$\frac{A_n^2}{2}\int_0^l \left(1 - \frac{\cos 2n\pi x}{l}\right) dx = 1$$

or

$$\frac{A_n^2}{2}\left[x - \frac{l}{2n\pi} \sin \frac{2n\pi x}{l}\right]_0^l = 1$$

$$\frac{A_n^2}{2}[l - 0] = 1 \text{ so } A_n = \sqrt{\frac{2}{l}}$$

Hence the set of functions $\left\{\sqrt{\dfrac{2}{x}} \sin \dfrac{n\pi x}{l}, n \in N\right\}$ is an orthogonal set.

2.4 COMPLETENESS OF AN ORTHOGONAL SET OF FUNCTIONS

A set of functions is said to be complete, if any arbitrary function $f(x)$, satisfying the same boundary conditions as the functions of the set, can be expressed in a series of these functions in the form

$$f(x) = \sum_1^\infty a_n S_n(x) \qquad ...(1)$$

In the present case—if l be taken equal to π

$$f(x) = \sum_1^\infty a_n \sin nx. \qquad ...(2)$$

Using the orthogonal property on them, the coefficients a_n are given by

$$a_n = \frac{2}{\pi}\int_0^\pi f(\xi) \sin n\xi \, d\xi \qquad ...(2)$$

Hence the solution of the problem of vibrating string is

$$U = \sum_{n=1}^\infty a_n S_n(x) \cos \omega_n t,$$

$$\omega_n = k_n \sqrt{\frac{I_m}{m}} \qquad ...(3)$$

With $k_n = \frac{n\pi}{l}$, The initial solution for $t = 0$ is

$$U = \sum_{1}^{\infty} a_n S_n(x) \qquad ...(4)$$

Corresponding to the initial configuration of the string with boundary conditions $S(0) = 0$, $S(l) = 0$, the constants are given by (2). Equation (3) gives the complete solution of the wave equation.

Equations (2) and (3) are equivalent to the Fourier theorem, which states that a functions $f(x)$ vanishing at $x = 0$ and $x = \pi$ may be expressed as

$$f(x) = \sum_{n=1}^{\infty} a_n \sin nx$$

Where a_n is given by $a_n = \frac{2}{\pi}\int_0^{\pi} f(\xi) \sin n\xi \, d\xi$.

A function $f(x)$ defined between $x = 0$ and $x = \pi$, may also be expanded as a cosine series

$$f(x) = \frac{1}{2} b_0 + \sum_{1}^{\infty} b_n \cos nx$$

where $$b_n = \frac{2}{\pi}\int_0^{\pi} f(\xi) \cos n\xi \, d\xi.$$

having different values at the end points $x = 0$ and $x = l$.

2.5 PERIODIC FUNCTION

If $f(x)$ be a periodic function with period T, then

$$f(x) = f(x + T) = f(x + 2T) \ldots = f(x + nt) \ldots n \in N.$$

The fourier series of a periodic function represents the function not only for $0 \le x \le T$ but for every interval $\alpha + (n-1)T \le x \le \alpha + nT$, where the width of the interval = the period of $\sin x$ or $\cos x$ which are periodic with period 2π.

If the width of the interval is 2π, the terms of the series are

$$\frac{a_0}{2} + \sum a_n \cos nx + \sum b_n \sin nx.$$

If the width is $2l$, the terms of the fourier series will have

$$\sin \frac{n\pi x}{l} \text{ and } \cos \frac{n\pi x}{l}$$

and then $$f(x) = \frac{a_0}{2} + \sum_{1}^{\infty}\left(a_n \cos \frac{n\pi x}{l} + b_n \sin \frac{n\pi x}{l}\right)$$

because width of $\frac{\pi x}{l}$ is 2π.

2.6 FOURIER SERIES

Let a function $f(x)$ be defined in the interval $-\pi$ to π. Then it can be represented as a series of sines and cosines of the multiples of the angles in the form

$$f(x) = \frac{1}{2} a_0 + a_1 \cos x + a_2 \cos 2x + \ldots + b_1 \sin x + b_2 \sin 2x + \ldots$$

If $f(x)$ be periodic with period 2π, then the series represent the function for all x, as $f(x + 2npi) = f(x)$, for all integral values of n.

$$= \frac{1}{2} a_0 + \sum_1^{\infty} a_n \cos nx + \sum_1^{\infty} b \sin nx. \qquad \ldots(1)$$

which is called the **Fourier Series** for the given function $f(x)$.

The coefficients a_0, a_n, b_n are given by

$$a_0 = \frac{1}{\pi} \int_{-\pi}^{\pi} f(x)\, dx \qquad \ldots(2)$$

$$a_n = \frac{1}{\pi} \int_{-\pi}^{\pi} f(\xi) \cos n\xi \, d\xi \qquad \ldots(3)$$

$$b_n = \frac{1}{\pi} \int_{-\pi}^{\pi} f(\xi) \sin n\xi \, d\xi \qquad \ldots(4)$$

For establishing these results, the following formulae should be remembered :

(i) $\int_{\pi}^{\pi} \sin mx \, dx = 0, \qquad \int_{-\pi}^{\pi} \cos mx \, dx = 0$

odd function

(ii) $\int_{-\pi}^{\pi} \cos nx \sin mx \, dx \; (n \neq m) = 0$

odd function

(iii) $\int_{-\pi}^{\pi} \sin nx \sin mx \, dx, \; (n \neq m) = \frac{1}{2} \int_{-\pi}^{\pi} \{\cos (m - x)x - \cos (m + x)x\} \, dx = 0$

(iv) $\int_{-\pi}^{\pi} \cos^2 mx \, dx = 2 \int_0^{\pi} \frac{1 + \cos 2mx}{2} dx = \left[\pi + \frac{\sin 2m\pi}{2m}\right]_0^{\pi} = \pi$ and $\int_{-\pi}^{\pi} \sin^2 mx \, dx = \pi$

(v) $\int_{-\pi}^{\pi} \cos nx \sin mx \, dx = 0, \; m \neq n.$

odd function

Since $\sin x$ and $\cos x$ and periodic with period 2π denoting them by $f(x)$

$$\int_{-\pi}^{\pi} f(x)\,dx = \int_{0}^{2\pi} f(x)\,dx = \int_{\alpha}^{2\pi+\alpha} f(x)\,dx.$$

Proof. Multiplying both sides of (1) by 1 and integrating from $-\pi$ to π, we have

$$\int_{-\pi}^{\pi} f(x)\,dx = \frac{1}{2}a_0 \int_{-\pi}^{\pi} dx + \int_{-\pi}^{\pi} \{\Sigma\, a_n \cos nx + \Sigma\, b_n \sin nx\}\,dx$$

$$= \frac{a_0}{2}\, 2\pi + 0 + 0$$

So we get (2).

Multiplying both the sides of (1) by $\cos mx$ and integrating from $-\pi$ to $+\pi$, we get

$$\int_{-\pi}^{\pi} f(x)\cos mx\,dx = \frac{a_0}{2}\left[\frac{\sin mx}{m}\right]_{-\pi}^{\pi} + a_m \int_{-\pi}^{\pi} \cos^2 mx\,dx$$

$$+ \sum_{n \neq m} a_n \int_{-\pi}^{\pi} \cos nx \cos mx + \Sigma\, b_n \int_{-\pi}^{\pi} \sin nx \cos mx\,dx$$

$$= 0 + \frac{a_m\, 2\pi}{2} + 0 + 0$$

So $$a_m = \frac{1}{\pi}\int_{-\pi}^{\pi} f(x)\cos mx\,dx, \text{ which is (3)}$$

Multiplying both sides of (1) by $\sin mx$ and integrating from $-\pi$ to π, we get

$$\int_{-\pi}^{\pi} f(x)\sin mx\,dx = \frac{a_0}{2}\left[\frac{\cos mx}{-m}\right]_{0}^{\pi} + \sum a_n \int_{-\pi}^{\pi} \cos nx \sin mx\,dx$$

$$+ b_m \int_{-\pi}^{\pi} \cos^2 mx\,dx + \sum_{n \neq m} b_n \int_{-\pi}^{\pi} \cos nx \cos mx\,dx$$

$= 0 + 0 + b_m\,\pi + 0$ so we get ...(4)

2.7 SUM OF SERIES AT POINTS OF DISCONTINUITY OF $f(x)$ AND AT END POINTS

If x be a point of discontinuity, the average of the left hand right hand limits of $f(x)$ at the point

= the sum of the series.

So $$S = \lim \frac{1}{2}\{f(x-0) + f(x+0)\}$$

At either end point the sum of the series $= \frac{1}{2}[f(-\pi+0) + f(\pi-0)]$ where $f(-\pi+0)$ is the limit of functions at left end and $f(\pi-0)$ the limit at the right end point.

Example 2.1. **Find the Fourier series to represent $f(x) = x - x^2$ for $-\pi < x < \pi$**
Hence deduce $\frac{1}{1^2} - \frac{1}{2^2} + \frac{1}{3^2} - \frac{1}{4^2} + \ldots = \frac{\pi^2}{12}$

(Calicut 94, Coimbatore 94, Osmania 95, Bhopal 91, Kerala 90S, Mysore 97, Guahati 99, VTU 2001)

Solution : Let $x - x^2 = \frac{1}{2} a_0 + \sum_{1}^{\infty} a_n \cos nx + \sum_{1}^{\infty} b_n \sin nx.$

$$\frac{1}{2} a_0 = \frac{1}{2\pi}\left[\int_{-\pi}^{\pi} x - \int_{-\pi}^{\pi} x^2\,dx\right] = \frac{1}{2\pi}\left[0 - 2\int_{0}^{\pi} x^2\,dx\right]$$

as x is odd and x^2 an even function for $-\pi < x < \pi$.

$$= -\left[\frac{x^3}{3}\right]_0^{\pi} = -\frac{\pi^2}{3} \qquad \ldots(1)$$

$$a_n = \frac{1}{\pi}\left[\int_{-\pi}^{\pi} \underset{\text{odd}}{x \cos nx\,dx} - \int_{-\pi}^{\pi} \underset{\text{even}}{x^2 \cos nx\,dx}\right] = \frac{1}{\pi}\left[0 - 2\int_{0}^{\pi} \underset{\text{I}}{x^2} \underset{\text{II}}{\cos nx}\,dx\right]$$

$$= -\frac{2}{\pi}\left[\frac{x^2 \sin nx}{n} - \frac{2}{n}\int \underset{\text{I}}{x} \underset{\text{II}}{\sin nx}\,dx\right]_0^{\pi}$$

$$= -\frac{2}{\pi}\left[\frac{x^2 \sin nx}{n} + \frac{2x}{n^2}\cos nx - \frac{2 \sin nx}{n^3}\right]_0^{\pi}$$

$$= -\frac{4\pi}{\pi n^2}(-1)^n = \frac{4(-1)^{n+1}}{n^2} \qquad \ldots(2)$$

$$b_n = \frac{1}{\pi}\left[\int_{-\pi}^{\pi} \underset{\text{even}}{x \sin nx\,dx} - \int_{-\pi}^{\pi} \underset{\text{odd}}{x^2 \sin nx\,dx}\right] = \frac{1}{\pi}\left[2\int_{0}^{\pi} \underset{\text{I}}{x} \underset{\text{II}}{\sin nx}\,dx - 0\right]$$

$$= \frac{2}{\pi}\left[-x\frac{\cos nx}{n} + \frac{\sin nx}{n^2}\right]_0^{\pi} = -\frac{2\pi}{n\pi}(-1)^n = \frac{2(-1)^{n+1}}{n} \qquad \ldots(3)$$

Hence

$$f(x) = x - x^2 = -\frac{\pi^2}{3} + 4\left\{\frac{\cos x}{1^2} - \frac{\cos 2x}{2^2} + \frac{\cos 3x}{3^2} + \ldots\right\}$$
$$+ 2\left\{\frac{\sin x}{1} - \frac{\sin 2x}{2} + \frac{\sin 3x}{3} + \ldots\right\} \qquad \ldots(4)$$

Putting $x = 0$ in (4),

$$0 = -\frac{\pi^2}{3} + 4\left\{\frac{1}{1^2} - \frac{1}{2^2} + \frac{1}{3^2} + \ldots\right\}$$

Hence the result.

Example 2.2. **Expand $f(x) = x \sin x, 0 < x < 2\pi$, as a Fourier series.**

(UPTU 2003, MUO 2005; Madras 91, 97)

Solution : Let $f(x) = \frac{1}{2} a_0 + \sum_1^\infty a_n \cos nx + \sum_1^\infty b_n \sin nx$ where

$$\frac{a_0}{2} = \frac{1}{2\pi}\int_0^{2\pi} x \sin x \, dx = \frac{1}{2\pi}[-x\cos x + \sin x]_0^{2\pi} = -\frac{2\pi}{2\pi} = -1 \quad ...(1)$$

$$a_n = \frac{1}{\pi}\int_0^{2\pi} x \sin x \cos nx \, dx = \frac{1}{2\pi}\int_0^{2\pi} x\{\sin(n+1)x - \sin(n-1)x\}dx$$

$$= \frac{1}{2\pi}\left[\frac{-x\cos(n+1)x}{n+1} + \frac{\sin(n+1)x}{(n+1)^2} + \frac{x\cos(n-1)x}{(n-1)} - \frac{\cos(n-1)x}{(n-1)^2}\right]_0^{2\pi}$$

$n = \neq 1$

$$= \frac{1}{2\pi}\left[\frac{-2\pi}{n+1} + 0 + \frac{2\pi}{n-1}\right] = \frac{2}{n^2-1} (n \neq 1) \quad ...(2)$$

For $n = 1$,

$$a_1 = \frac{1}{\pi}\int_0^{2\pi} x \sin x \cos x \, dx = \int_0^{2\pi} \frac{x}{2\pi} \sin 2x \, dx$$

$$= \frac{1}{2\pi}\left[\frac{-x\cos 2x}{2} + \frac{\sin 2x}{4}\right]_0^{2\pi} = -\frac{2\pi}{4\pi} = -\frac{1}{2} \quad ...(3)$$

$$b_n = \frac{1}{\pi}\int_0^{2\pi} x \sin x \sin nx \, dx$$

$$= \frac{1}{2\pi}\int_0^{2\pi} \underset{\text{I}}{x}\, \underset{\text{II}}{\{\cos(n-1)x - \cos(n+1)x\}} \, dx$$

$$= \frac{1}{2\pi}\left[\frac{x\sin(n-1)x}{n-1} + \frac{\cos(n-1)x}{(n-1)^2} - \frac{x\sin(n+1)x}{n+1} - \frac{\cos(n+1)x}{(n+1)^2}\right]_0^{2\pi}$$

$n \neq 1$

$$= \frac{1}{2\pi}\left[\frac{1-1}{(n-1)^2} - \frac{1-1}{(n+1)^2}\right], n \neq 1, = 0 \quad ...(4)$$

For $n = 1$

$$b_1 = \frac{1}{\pi}\int_0^{2\pi} x \sin^2 x \, dx = \frac{1}{2\pi}\int_0^{2\pi} (x - x\cos 2x) \, dx$$

$$= \frac{1}{2\pi}\left[\frac{x^2}{2} - \frac{x\sin 2x}{2} + \frac{\cos 2x}{4}\right]_0^{2\pi}$$

$$= \frac{4\pi^2}{4\pi} = \pi \qquad ...(5)$$

Hence $f(x) = -1 - \frac{1}{2}\cos x + 2\sum_1^\infty \frac{1}{n^2-1}\cos nx + \pi \sin x + 0$

$$= -1 + \pi \sin x - \frac{1}{2}\cos x + \frac{2}{2^2-1}\cos 2x + \frac{2}{3^2-1}\cos 3x + \ldots$$

Example 2.3. **Find the Fourier series to represent $f(x) = e^{ax}$ in $-\pi < x < \pi$.** *(Bhopal 91)*

Solution : Let $f(x) = \frac{a_0}{2} + \sum_1^\infty a_n \cos nx + \sum_1^\infty b_n \sin nx$

where $\frac{a_0}{2} = \frac{1}{2\pi}\int_{-\pi}^{\pi} e^{ax}\, dx = \frac{1}{2\pi}\frac{[e^{ax}]_{-\pi}^{\pi}}{a} = \frac{1}{a\pi}\frac{e^{a\pi} - e^{-\pi a}}{2} = \frac{1}{a\pi}\sinh a\pi \qquad ...(1)$

$$a_n = \frac{1}{\pi}\int_{-\pi}^{\pi} e^{ax}\cos nx\, dx = \frac{1}{\pi(a^2+n^2)} e^x \{a \cos nx + n \sin nx\}_{-\pi}^{\pi}$$

$$= \frac{1}{\pi(a^2+n^2)}\left[a(e^{a\pi} - e^{-a\pi})(-1)^n + 0\right] = \frac{2a(-1)^n \sinh a\pi}{\pi(a^2+n^2)} \qquad ...(2)$$

$$b_n = \frac{1}{\pi}\int_{-\pi}^{\pi} e^{ax}\sin nx\, dx = \frac{1}{\pi(a^2+n^2)} e^{ax}[a \sin nx - n \cos nx]_{-\pi}^{\pi}$$

$$= \frac{1}{\pi(a^2+n^2)}(-n)(-1)^n\left\{e^{a\pi} - e^{-a\pi}\right\} = -\frac{2n(-1)^n \sinh a\pi}{\pi(a^2+n^2)} \qquad ...(3)$$

Hence $e^{ax} = \frac{\sinh a\pi}{\pi}\left[\frac{1}{a} + 2a\sum_1^\infty \frac{(-1)^n \cos nx}{a^2+n^2} - 2\sum_1^\infty \frac{(-1)^n n \sin nx}{a^2+n^2}\right]$

or $\frac{e^{ax}}{\sinh a\pi} = \frac{1}{\pi}\left[\frac{1}{a} - 2a\left\{\frac{\cos x}{a^2+1} - \frac{\cos 2x}{a^2+2^2} + \frac{\cos 3x}{a^2+3^2} + \ldots\right\}\right.$

$$\left. + 2\left\{\frac{\sin x}{a^2+1} - \frac{2\sin 2x}{a^2+2^2} + \frac{3\sin 3x}{a^2+3^2} + \ldots\right\}\right]$$

Example 2.4. **Expand $f(x) = x \sin x$ as a Fourier series in the interval $-\pi \le x \le \pi$ and deduce**

$$\frac{1}{1\cdot 3} - \frac{1}{3\cdot 5} + \frac{1}{5\cdot 7} - \frac{1}{7\cdot 9} + \ldots = \frac{\pi - 2}{4}$$

(Delhi 1991)

Solution : Let $f(x) = \frac{a_0}{2} + \sum_1^\infty (a_n \cos nx + b_n \sin nx)$

$$\frac{a_0}{2} = \frac{1}{2\pi}\int_{-\pi}^{\pi} \underset{\text{even}}{x \sin x}\, dx = \frac{2}{2\pi}\int_0^{\pi} x \sin x\, dx = \frac{1}{\pi}[-x\cos x + \sin x]_0^{\pi} = \frac{\pi}{\pi} = 1 \qquad ...(1)$$

$$a_n = \frac{1}{\pi}\int_{-\pi}^{\pi} \underset{\text{even}}{x \sin x \cos nx}\, dx = \frac{2}{\pi}\int_0^{\pi} x\left\{\frac{\sin (n+1)x - \sin (n-1)x}{2}\right\} dx$$

$$= \frac{1}{\pi}\left[x\left\{\frac{\cos (n+1)x}{-(n+1)} - \frac{\cos (n-1)x}{-(n-1)}\right\} + \left\{\frac{\sin (n+1)x}{(n+1)^2} - \frac{\sin (n-1)x}{(n-1)^2}\right\}\right]_0^{\pi}, n \neq 1$$

$$= \frac{1}{\pi}\left[\pi(-1)^n\left\{\frac{1}{n+1} - \frac{1}{n-1}\right\} + 0\right]; (n \neq 1)$$

$$= \frac{2(-1)^{n+1}}{n^2-1}, n \neq 1 \qquad \text{...(2)}$$

for $n = 1$

$$a_1 = \frac{1}{\pi}\int_{-\pi}^{\pi} x \sin x \cos x\, dx = \frac{2}{\pi}\int_0^{\pi} \frac{x \sin 2x}{2} dx = \frac{1}{\pi}\left[-x\frac{\cos 2x}{2} + \frac{\sin 2x}{4}\right]_0^{\pi}$$

$$= -\frac{1}{2} \qquad \text{...(3)}$$

$$b_n = \frac{1}{\pi}\int_{-\pi}^{\pi} \underset{\text{odd}}{x \sin x \sin nx}\, dx = 0 \qquad \text{...(4)}$$

Hence $x \sin x = 1 - \frac{1}{2}\cos x + 2\sum_2^{\infty} \frac{(-1)^{n+1}}{n^2-1} \cos nx$

$$= 1 - \frac{1}{2}\cos x + 2\left\{\frac{-\cos 2x}{2^2-1} + \frac{\cos 3x}{3^2-1} - \frac{\cos 4x}{4^2-1} + \ldots\right\}$$

Taking $x = \pi/2$

$$\frac{\pi}{2} - 1 = 0 + 2\left\{\frac{1}{1\cdot 3} - \frac{1\times 0}{2\cdot 4} - \frac{1}{3\cdot 5} + \ldots\right\}$$

or
$$\frac{\pi-2}{4} = \frac{1}{1\cdot 3} - \frac{1}{3\cdot 5} + \frac{1}{5\cdot 7} + \ldots$$

PROBLEM 2.1

1. Expand $f(x) = x$, in a Fourier series for the interval $0 < x < 2\pi$.

Ans. $f(x) = \pi - 2\sum_1^{\infty} \frac{\sin nx}{n}$.

2. Prove that for $-\pi < x < \pi$,

$$x = 2\left\{\frac{\sin x}{1} - \frac{\sin 2x}{2} + \frac{\sin 3x}{3} + \ldots\right\}$$

3. Expand $f(x) = \pi - x$, in a Fourier series for x lying in the interval $-\pi < x < \pi$.

Ans. $f(x) = 2\sum_1^{\infty} \frac{\sin nx}{n}$.

4. If $f(x) = \left(\frac{\pi - x}{2}\right)^2$, $0 < x < 2\pi$, show that

$$f(x) = \frac{\pi^2}{1^2} + \sum_1^\infty \frac{\cos nx}{n^2}$$

(Madras 2000PT, Madras 98)

5. Find the Fourier series for $f(x) = e^{-x}$, $0 < x < 2\pi$.

$$e^{-x} = \frac{1 - e^{-2x}}{\pi}\left[\frac{1}{2} + \left(\frac{\cos x}{1 + 1^2} + \frac{\cos 2x}{1 + 2^2} + \ldots\right) + \left(\frac{\sin x}{1 + 1^2} + \frac{2 \sin 2x}{1 + 2^2} + \frac{3 \sin 3x}{1 + 3^2} + \ldots\right)\right]$$ ***(Nagpur 97)***

6. Obtain a Fourier expansion for $f(x) = e^{-ax}$ for $-\pi < x < \pi$. Hence derive a series for $\frac{\pi}{\sinh \pi}$.

Ans. $$e^{-ax} = \frac{\sinh a\pi}{\pi}\left[\frac{1}{a} + 2a \sum_1^\infty \frac{(-1)^n \cos nx}{a^2 + n^2} + 2\sum_1^\infty \frac{(-1)^n\, n \sin nx}{a^2 + n^2}\right]$$

$$\frac{\pi}{\sinh a\pi} = 2\, e^{ax}\left[\frac{1}{2^a} + a\sum_1^\infty \frac{(-1)^n \cos nx}{a^2 + n^2} + \sum_1^\infty \frac{(-1)^n\, n \sin nx}{a^2 + n^2}\right]$$

7. (i) Prove that for $0 < x < 2\pi$

$$x \sin x = -1 - \frac{1}{2}\cos x + \pi \sin x + 2\left[\frac{\cos 2x}{2^2 - 1} + \frac{\cos 3x}{3^2 - 1} \ldots + \frac{\cos nx}{n^2 - 1}\right].$$

(Mysore 95, Madras 91, 97)

(ii) Prove that for $-\pi \le x \le \pi$

$$x - x^2 = -\frac{\pi^2}{3} + 4\left\{\frac{\cos x}{1^2} - \frac{\cos 2x}{2^2} + \frac{\cos 3x}{3^2} + \ldots\right\} + 2\left\{\frac{\sin x}{1} - \frac{\sin 2x}{2} + \frac{\sin 3x}{3} + \ldots\right\}$$

(UPTU 2003, Agra 2001, Mysore 97, Osmania 95)

8. Prove that for $-\pi < x < \pi$, with a being a fraction,

$$\frac{\sin ax}{\sin a\pi} = \frac{2}{\pi}\left\{\frac{\sin x}{1^2 - a^2} - \frac{2 \sin 2x}{2^2 - a^2} + \frac{3 \sin 3x}{3^2 - a^2} + \ldots\right\}$$

9. Prove that for $-\pi < x < \pi$

$$x + x = \frac{\pi^2}{3} + 4\sum_1^\infty \frac{(-1)^n \cos nx}{n^2} - 2\sum_1^\infty (-1)^n \frac{\sin nx}{n}.$$

10. Find a series of sines and cosines of multiples of x to represent $f(x) = \frac{\pi}{2 \sinh \pi} e^x$ for $-\pi < x < \pi$

$$f(x) = \frac{1}{2} + \sum_1^\infty \frac{(-1)^n \cos nx}{n^2 + 1} - \sum_1^\infty (-1)^n \frac{n \sin nx}{n^2 + 1}$$

11. Find the Fourier series for $f(x) = \pi - x$, in the interval $0 < x < 2\pi$. ***(Raj 2001)***

Ans. $$\pi - x = 2\left[\frac{\sin x}{1} + \frac{\sin 2x}{2} + \frac{\sin 3x}{3} + \ldots\right]$$

12. Prove that for $-\pi < x < \pi$

$$\cosh ax = \frac{2a}{\pi} \sinh a\pi \left[\frac{1}{2a^2} + 2 \sum_{1}^{\infty} (-1)^2 \frac{\cos nx}{n^2 + a^2} \right]$$

13. Prove that for $-\pi < x < \pi$

$$x^2 = \frac{\pi^2}{3} - 4\left(\frac{\cos x}{1^2} - \frac{\cos 2x}{2^2} + \frac{\cos 3x}{3^2} - \ldots \right)$$

Hence show (i) $\sum_{1}^{\infty} \frac{1}{n^2} = \frac{\pi^2}{6}$ (ii) $\sum_{1}^{\infty} \frac{(-1)^{n+1}}{n^2} = \frac{\pi^2}{12}$, (iii) $\sum_{1}^{\infty} \frac{1}{(2n-1)^2} = \frac{\pi^2}{8}$ ***(Mysore 94S)***

14. Obtain Fourier series for

$$f(x) = \begin{cases} 1 + \frac{2x}{\pi}, & -\pi \le x \le \\ 1 - \frac{2x}{\pi}, & 0 \le x \le \pi \end{cases}$$

(AUUP 2007, Mangalore' 97, Delhi 91)

Hence deduce $\frac{1}{1^2} + \frac{1}{3^2} + \frac{1}{5^2} + \ldots = \frac{\pi^2}{8}$

(Kerala 90S)

15. Expand $f(x) = |\sin x|$, in a Fourier series for $-\pi < x < \pi$ ***(AUUP 2007, Andhra 90S)***

$$|\sin x| = \frac{2}{\pi} - \frac{4}{\pi}\left[\frac{\cos 2x}{3} + \frac{\cos 4x}{15} + \ldots + \frac{\cos 2nx}{4n^2 - 1} \right]$$

16. Expand $|\cos x|$ in a Fourier series for $-\pi < x < \pi$. ***(Delhi 92)***

Ans. $|\cos x| = \frac{2}{\pi} + \frac{4}{\pi}\left[\frac{\cos 2x}{3} - \frac{\cos 4x}{15} + \ldots \right]$

17. prove that for $-\pi < x < \pi$

$$x(\pi^2 - x^2) = 12\left[\frac{\sin x}{1^3} - \frac{\sin 2x}{2^3} + \frac{\sin 3x}{3^3} - \frac{\sin 4x}{4^3} \ldots \right]$$

18. Find a Fourier series for $f(x)$ $-\pi < x < \pi$, when

$$f(x) = \begin{cases} \pi + x, & -\pi < x < 0 \\ \pi - x, & 0 < x < \pi \end{cases}$$

Ans. $f(x) = \frac{\pi}{2} + \frac{4}{\pi}\left(\frac{\cos x}{1^2} + \frac{\cos 3x}{3^2} + \frac{\cos 5x}{5^2} + \ldots \right)$

19. Find a Fourier series for the function $f(x) = x + x^2$, $-\pi < x < \pi$. Hence show that

(i) $\frac{\pi^2}{6} = 1 + \frac{1}{2^2} + \frac{1}{3^2} + \frac{1}{4^2} + \ldots$

(AUUP 2008)

(ii) $\frac{\pi}{12} = \frac{1}{1^2} \frac{-1}{2^2} + \frac{1}{3^2} - \frac{1}{4^2} + \ldots$

2.8 DIRICHLET'S CONDITIONS FOR FOURIER EXPANSION OF A FUNCTION

Without discussing the conditions of convergence of a Fourier expansion for a function, we only state the conditions which $f(x)$ must satisfy for its expansion in a Fourier series. The conditions known as Dirichlet's condition are

A function $f(x)$ has the expansion as a Fourier series

$$\frac{a_0}{2} + \sum_{1}^{\infty} (a_n \cos nx + b_n \sin nx), \text{ subject to the conditions :}$$

(i) $f(x)$ is periodic, finite and single valued,

(ii) it is either continuous or atmost only a finite number of finite discontinuities in one period,

(iii) it has only a finite number of extremas (maxima or minima) × minima in one period.

So function as $f(x) = \operatorname{cosec} x$, which is not finite or $f(x) = \sin \frac{1}{x}$, which makes infinite oscillations as $x \to 0$, cannot have a fourier expansion.

2.9 FOURIER EXPANSION FOR DISCONTINUOUS FUNCTIONS

Let $\qquad f(x) = \phi(x), \; 0 < x < c$

$\qquad\qquad = \psi(x), \text{ for } c < x < 2\pi$

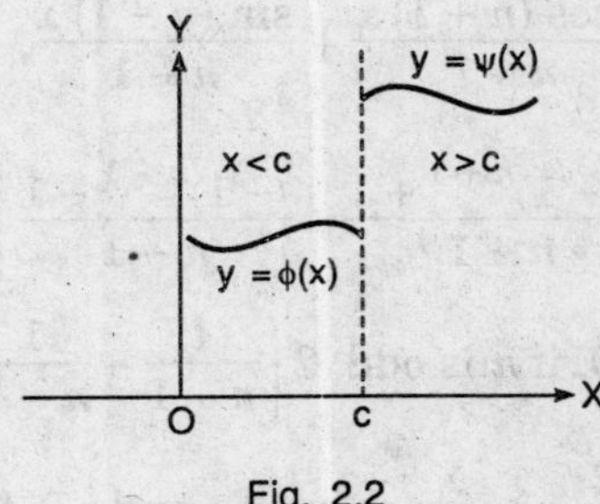

Fig. 2.2

The constants are evaluated separately for parts of the interval at the point of discontinuity. Thus

$$\frac{a_0}{2} = \frac{1}{\pi}\left[\int_0^c \phi(x)\,dx + \int_c^{2\pi} \psi(x)\,dx\right]$$

$$a_n = \frac{1}{\pi}\left[\int_0^c \phi(x)\cos nx\,dx + \int_0^{2\pi} \psi(x)\cos nx\,dx\right]$$

$$b_n = \frac{1}{\pi}\left[\int_0^c \phi(x)\sin nx\,dx + \int_c^{2\pi} \psi(x)\sin nx\,dx\right]$$

The sum of the series at the point of discontinuity equals to $= \frac{1}{2}[f(c-0)+f(c+0)]$.

Example 2.5. **Find Fourier expansion for $f(x) = 0, \quad -\pi \le x \le 0$**

$= \sin x, \quad 0 \le x \le \pi$

and prove that (i) $\frac{1}{1\cdot 3} + \frac{1}{3\cdot 5} + \ldots = \frac{1}{2}$ *(Bhopal 91; Madras 98)*

(ii) $\frac{1}{1\cdot 3} - \frac{1}{3\cdot 5} + \frac{1}{5\cdot 7} \ldots = \frac{\pi-2}{4}$ *(Madurai 90)*

Solution : Let $f(x) = \frac{a_0}{2} = \sum_1^\infty a_n \cos nx + \sum_1^\infty b_n \sin nx$

$$\frac{a_0}{2} = \frac{1}{2\pi}\left[\int_{-\pi}^0 0\,dx + \int_0^\pi \sin x\,dx\right] = \frac{1}{2\pi}[-\cos x]_0^\pi = \frac{1}{\pi}$$

$$a_n = \frac{1}{\pi}\left[0 + \int_0^\pi \sin x \cos nx\,dx\right] = \frac{1}{2\pi}\int_0^\pi \{\sin(n+1)x - \sin(n-1)x\}\,dx$$

$$= \frac{1}{2\pi}\left[\frac{-\cos(n+1)x}{n+1} + \frac{\sin(n-1)x}{n-1},\right]_0^\pi \quad \text{for } n \ne 1$$

$$= \frac{1}{2\pi}\left[\frac{-(-1)^{n+1}+1}{n+1} + \frac{(-1)^{n-1}-1}{n-1}\right], (n \ne 1)$$

$$= \frac{1}{2\pi}\left[= 0, \text{ if } n \text{ is odd}, 2\left(\frac{1}{n+1} - \frac{1}{n-1}\right) \text{ when } n = \text{even}\right]$$

$$= -\frac{2}{\pi(n^2-1)} \text{ for } n \text{ even and } 0 \text{ for } n \text{ odd}$$

For $n = 1$

$$a_1 = \frac{1}{\pi}\int_0^\pi \sin x \cos x\,dx = \frac{1}{\pi}\left[\frac{\sin^2 x}{2}\right]_0^\pi = 0$$

$$b_n = \frac{1}{\pi}\int_0^\pi \sin x \sin nx\,dx = \frac{1}{2\pi}\int_0^\pi \{\cos(n-1)x - \cos(n+1)x\}\,dx$$

$$= \frac{1}{2\pi}\left[\frac{\sin(n-1)x}{n-1} - \frac{\sin(n+1)x}{n+1}, n \ne -1\right]_0^\pi = 0$$

for $n = 1$

$$b_1 = \frac{1}{\pi}\int_0^{\pi} \sin^2 x\, dx = \frac{1}{2\pi}\int_0^{\pi} (1 - \cos 2x)\, dx$$

$$= \frac{1}{2\pi}\left[x - \frac{\sin 2x}{2}\right]_0^{\pi} = \frac{1}{2}$$

Hence $f(x) = \sin x = \frac{1}{\pi} + \frac{2}{\pi}\left\{-\frac{\cos 2x}{2^2 - 1} - \frac{\cos 4x}{4^2 - 1} - \frac{\cos 6x}{6^2 - 1} - \ldots\right\} + \frac{1}{2}\sin x + 0$ ...(1)

when $(0 < x < \pi)$

Taking $x = 0$,

$$0 = \frac{1}{\pi}\left[1 - 2\left(\frac{1}{1\cdot 3} + \frac{1}{3\cdot 5} + \frac{1}{5\cdot 7}\ldots\right)\right]$$

So $\frac{1}{2} = \frac{1}{1\cdot 3} + \frac{1}{3\cdot 5} + \frac{1}{5\cdot 7}\ldots$ ...(2)

Putting $x = \pi/2$ in (1)

$$1 = \frac{1}{\pi} - \frac{2}{\pi}\left(\frac{-1}{1\cdot 3} + \frac{1}{3\cdot 5} - \frac{1}{5\cdot 7}\ldots\right) + \frac{1}{2}\sin\frac{\pi}{2}$$

So $\left(\frac{1}{2} - \frac{1}{\pi}\right)\frac{\pi}{2} = \frac{1}{1\cdot 3} - \frac{1}{3\cdot 5} - \frac{1}{5\cdot 7}\ldots$ ...(3)

or $\frac{\pi - 2}{4} = \frac{1}{1\cdot 3} - \frac{1}{3\cdot 5} - \frac{1}{5\cdot 7} + \ldots$ ...(4)

Example 2.6. Find the Fourier expansion for $f(x)$, if

$$f(x) = -\pi, \quad -\pi < x < 0$$
$$= x, \quad 0 < x < \pi.$$

and deduce that $\frac{1}{2^2} + \frac{1}{3^2} + \frac{1}{5^2} + \ldots = \frac{\pi^2}{8}$.

(MOU 2004, Triputi 98S)

Solution : Let $f(x) = \frac{1}{2}a_0 + \sum_1^{\infty} a_n \cos nx + \sum_1^{\infty} b_n \sin nx$

then $\frac{a_0}{2} = \frac{1}{2\pi}\left[\int_{-\pi}^{0} -\pi\, dx + \int_0^{\pi} x\, dx\right] = \frac{1}{2\pi}\left[-\pi\,\{x\}_{-\pi}^{0} + \left\{\frac{x^2}{2}\right\}_0^{\pi}\right]$

$$= \frac{1}{2\pi}\left[-\pi(0 + \pi) + \frac{\pi^2}{2}\right] = -\frac{\pi^2}{2\pi \times 2} = -\frac{\pi}{4} \quad \ldots(1)$$

$$a_n = \frac{1}{\pi}\left[\int_{-\pi}^{0} -\pi \cos nx\, dx + \int_0^{\pi} x \cos nx\, dx\right]$$

$$= \frac{1}{\pi}\left[\left[-\pi\frac{\sin nx}{x}\right]_{-\pi}^{0} + \left\{\frac{x \sin nx}{n} + \frac{\cos nx}{n^2}\right\}_0^{\pi}\right]$$

$$= 0 \text{ for } n \text{ even } 2, 4, 6, \ldots$$

$$= \frac{1}{\pi}\left[0 + 0 + \frac{(-1)^n - 1}{n^2}\right] = -\frac{2}{\pi n^2} \text{ for } n = \text{odd} = 1, 3, 5 \ldots$$

$$b_n = \frac{1}{\pi}\left[\int_{-\pi}^{0} -\pi \sin nx\, dx + \int_0^{\pi} x \sin nx\, dx\right]$$

$$= \frac{1}{\pi}\left[\frac{\pi \cos nx}{x}\right]_{-\pi}^{0} + \frac{1}{\pi}\left[\frac{-x\cos nx}{n} + \frac{\sin nx}{n^2}\right]_0^{\pi}$$

$$= \frac{1-(-1)^n}{n} + \frac{-(-1)^n}{n} = \frac{1-2(-1)^n}{n}$$

So $\quad b_1 = \frac{+3}{1}, b_2 = \frac{-1}{2}, b_3 = \frac{3}{3}, b_4 = -\frac{1}{4}$ etc.

Hence $\quad f(x) = -\frac{\pi}{4} - \frac{2}{\pi}\left\{\frac{\cos x}{1^2} + \frac{\cos 3x}{3^2} + \frac{\cos 5x}{5^2} + \ldots\right\}$

$$+ \left\{3 \sin x - \frac{1}{2} \sin 2x + \sin 3x - \frac{1}{4} \sin 4x \ldots\right\}$$

where $\quad f(x) = -\pi, \text{ for } -\pi < x < 0,$

$\quad = x \text{ for } \quad 0 < x < \pi.$

For point of discontinuity $x = 0$, sum of the series $= \frac{1}{2}$ [$f(0-0) + f(0+0$]

$$= \frac{1}{2}[-\pi + 0] = -\frac{\pi}{2}$$

Sum of the series at $x = 0$, $= -\frac{\pi}{4} - \frac{2}{\pi}\left(1 + \frac{1}{3^2} + \frac{1}{5^2} + \ldots\right)$

Hence $\quad -\frac{\pi}{2} = -\frac{\pi}{4} - \frac{2}{\pi}\left(1 + \frac{1}{3^2} + \frac{1}{5^2} + \ldots\right)$

or $\quad \frac{\pi^2}{8} = 1 + \frac{1}{3^2} + \frac{1}{5^2} + \ldots$

PROBLEM SET 2.2

1. Find the Fourier series to represent $f(x)$, given by $f(x) = x$, for $0 \le x \le \pi = 2\pi - x$, for $\pi \le x \le 2\pi$ and deduce that $\frac{1}{1^2} + \frac{1}{3^2} + \frac{1}{5^2} + \ldots = \frac{\pi^2}{8}$.

(Andhra 94, Rewa 94, Madras 2000S, VTU 2000S)

Ans. $f(x) = \left.\begin{matrix} x, & 0 \le x \le \pi \\ 2\pi - x, & \pi \le x \le 2\pi \end{matrix}\right\} = \frac{\pi}{2} - \frac{4}{\pi}\left\{\frac{\cos x}{1^2} + \frac{\cos 3x}{3^2} + \ldots\right\}$

At $x = 0$, $0 = \frac{\pi}{2} - \frac{4}{\pi}\left\{\frac{1}{1^2} + \frac{1}{3^2} + \frac{1}{5^2} \ldots\right\}$ Hence the result.

2. Find the Fourier expansion for the function

$$f(x) = \begin{cases} x^2, & 0 \le x \le \pi \\ -x^2, & -\pi \le x \le 0 \end{cases}$$

(Karnataka 90)

Ans. $f(x) = 2\left(\pi - \frac{4}{\pi}\right)\sin x - \pi \sin 2x + \frac{2}{3}\left(\pi - \frac{4}{9\pi}\right)\sin 3x - \frac{\pi}{2}\sin 4x + \ldots$

3. Find The Fourier series to represent $f(x) = -k$, for $-\pi < x < 0 = +k$ for $0 < x < \pi$ and deduce that $\frac{\pi}{4} = 1 - \frac{1}{3} + \frac{1}{5} - \frac{1}{7} + \ldots$

Ans. $f(x) = \frac{4k}{\pi}\left(\sin x + \frac{\sin 3x}{3} + \frac{\sin 5x}{5} \ldots\right)$

4. Find Fourier series for $f(x) = 0,\ -\pi < x < 0 = x^2,\ 0 < x < \pi$.

Ans. $f(x) = \frac{\pi^2}{6} - 2\left\{\cos x - \frac{\cos 2x}{2^2} + \frac{\cos 3x}{3^2} + \ldots\right\} - \frac{1}{\pi}\left\{\left(\frac{2}{1^3} - \frac{\pi^2}{1}\right)\sin x - \left(\frac{2}{2^3} - \frac{\pi^2}{2}\right)\sin 2x \ldots\right\}$

5. An alternating current after passing through a rectifier has the form

$$i = \begin{cases} I_0 \sin x, & \text{for } 0 \le x \le \pi \\ 0 & \pi < x \le 2\pi \end{cases}$$

where $I_0 = i_{\max}$. Express I as a Fourier series. *(Delhi 97, Coimbatore 90)*

Ans. $I = \frac{I_0}{\pi} + \frac{1}{2} I_0 \sin x - \frac{2I_0}{\pi} \sum_1^{\infty} \frac{\cos 2nx}{4n^2 - 1}$

6. Show that for

$$f(x) = \begin{cases} 0 & \text{for } -\pi < x < 0 \\ 0 \sin x & \text{for } 0 < x < \pi \end{cases}$$

$$f(x) = \frac{1}{\pi} + \frac{1}{2}\sin x - \frac{2}{\pi}\sum_1^{\infty} \frac{\cos 2nx}{4n^2 - 1}$$

(Madras 98)

7. Find the Fourier expansion for $f(x) = \begin{cases} 1 & \text{for } 0 < x < \pi \\ 2 & \text{for } \pi < x < 2\pi \end{cases}$ and deduce that

$$\frac{\pi}{4} = 1 - \frac{1}{3} + \frac{1}{5} - \frac{1}{7} + \ldots$$

(Punjab 1994)

Ans. $f(x) = \frac{3}{2} - \frac{2}{\pi}\left\{\sin x + \frac{\sin 3x}{3} + \frac{\sin 5x}{5} + \ldots\right\}$

2.10 CHANGE OF INTERVAL

Let $f(x)$ be defined in $-l \le x \le l$.

So $$-\pi \le \frac{\pi x}{l} \le \pi$$

Let $$\frac{\pi x}{l} = y,\ f(x) = f\left(\frac{l}{\pi} y\right)$$

So $f\left(\frac{l}{\pi} y\right)$, $-\pi < y < \pi$ should be expanded.

$$f\left(\frac{l}{\pi} y\right) = \frac{a_0}{2} + \sum_1^{\infty} (a_n \cos ny + b_n \sin ny)$$

After evaluating a_0, a_n, b_n, after replacing y by $\frac{\pi x}{l}$

We would have $$f\left(\frac{l}{\pi}\frac{\pi}{l}x\right) = f(x) = \frac{a_0}{2} + \sum_1^{\infty}\left\{a_n \cos\frac{n\pi x}{l} + b_n \sin\frac{n\pi x}{l}\right\}$$

or we write directly as $$f(x) = \frac{a_0}{2} + \Sigma\left(a_n \cos\frac{n\pi x}{l} + b_n \sin\frac{n\pi x}{l}\right), -l < x < l$$

where $$\frac{a_0}{2} = \frac{1}{2l}\int_{-l}^{l} f(x)\,dx,$$

$$a_n = \frac{1}{l}\int_{-l}^{l} f(x)\cos\frac{n\pi x}{l}\,dx$$

and $$b_n = \frac{1}{l}\int_{-l}^{l} f(x)\sin\frac{n\pi x}{l}.$$

Example 2.7. Expand $f(x) = x^2$, for $-l < x < l$. *(Tirupati 98S, Nagpur 97)*

Solution : Let $$f(x) = x^2 = \frac{a_0}{2} + \sum_{n=1}^{\infty}\left(a_n \cos\frac{n\pi x}{l} + b_n \sin\frac{n\pi x}{l}\right).$$

Then $$\frac{a_0}{2} = \frac{1}{2l}\int_{-l}^{l} \underset{\text{even}}{x^2}\,dx = \frac{2}{2l}\int_0^l x^2\,dx = \frac{l^2}{3} \quad ...(1)$$

$$a_n = \frac{1}{l}\int_{-l}^{l} x^2 \cos\frac{n\pi x}{l}\,dx$$

Let $\frac{\pi x}{l} = y$

$$a_n = \frac{1}{l}\int_{-\pi}^{\pi} \frac{l^2}{\pi^2}y^2 \cos ny \,\frac{l}{\pi}\,dy$$

$$= \frac{l^2}{\pi^3} \times 2\int_0^{\pi} y^2 \cos ny\,dy$$

$$= \frac{2l^2}{\pi^3}\left[\frac{y^2 \sin ny}{n} - \frac{2}{n}\int y \sin ny\,dy\right]_0^{\pi}$$

$$= \frac{2l^2}{\pi^3}\left[\frac{y^2 \sin ny}{n} + \frac{2}{n^2}y\cos ny - \frac{2}{n^3}\sin ny\right]_0^{\pi} = \frac{4l^2}{\pi^3}\frac{\pi(-1)^n}{n^2}$$

$$= \frac{4l^2}{\pi^2}\frac{(-1)^n}{n^2} \quad ...(2)$$

$b_n = 0$ as $f(x)$ is an even function.

Hence $$x^2 = \frac{l^2}{3} - \frac{4l^2}{\pi^2}\left\{\frac{\cos\frac{\pi x}{l}}{1^2} - \frac{\cos\frac{2\pi x}{l}}{2^2} - \frac{\cos\frac{3\pi x}{l}}{3^2} + \ldots\right\}$$

Example 2.8. **Expand $f(x) = e^{-x}$ as a Fourier series for $-l < x < l$.**

(Hamirpur 96, Mysore 94)

Solution : Let $$f(x) = \frac{a_0}{2} + \Sigma\left(a_n \cos\frac{n\pi x}{l} + b_n \sin\frac{n\pi x}{l}\right)$$

then $$\frac{a_0}{2} = \frac{1}{2l}\int_{-l}^{l} e^{-x}\,dx = \frac{1}{2l}[-e^{-x}]_{-l}^{l} = \frac{1}{l}\sinh l \qquad \ldots(1)$$

$$a_n = \frac{1}{l}\int_{-l}^{l} e^{-x}\cos\frac{n\pi x}{l}\,dx\,dy\left[\int e^{-ax}\cos bx\,dx = e^{-ax}\frac{(-a\cos bx + b\sin bx}{a^2+b^2}\right]$$

$$= \frac{1}{l}\frac{1}{1+\frac{n^2\pi^2}{l^2}}\left[e^{-l}\left(-\cos\frac{n\pi l}{l} + \frac{n\pi}{l}\sin n\pi\right) - e^{l}(-1\cos n\pi + 0)\right]$$

$$= \frac{l}{l^2+n^2\pi^2}(-1)^n\,2\sinh l \qquad \ldots(2)$$

So $$a_1 = \frac{-2l\sinh l}{l^2+\pi^2},\ a_2 = \frac{2l\sinh l}{l^2+2^2\pi^2}\ \text{etc.}$$

and $$b_n = \frac{1}{l}\int_{-l}^{l} e^{-x}\sin\frac{n\pi x}{l}\,dx$$

$$= \frac{1}{l}\frac{1}{1+\frac{n^2\pi^2}{l^2}}\left[e^{-l}\left(-\sin\frac{n\pi l}{l} - \frac{n\pi}{l}\cos n\pi\right) - e^{l}\left(\sin\frac{n\pi l}{l} - \frac{n\pi}{l}\cos n\pi\right)\right]$$

$$= \frac{l}{l^2+n^2\pi^2}\left[\frac{n\pi}{l}\cos n\pi\,2\sinh l\right] \qquad \ldots(3)$$

So $$b_1 = \frac{-2\pi\sinh l}{l^2+\pi^2},\ b_2 = \frac{2\cdot 2\pi\sinh l}{l^2+2^2\pi^2}\ \text{etc.}$$

Hence $$f(x) = e^{-x} = \sinh l\left[\frac{1}{l} - 2l\left\{\frac{1}{l^2+\pi^2}\frac{\cos\pi x}{l} - \frac{1}{l^2+2^2\pi^2}\frac{\cos 2\pi x}{l}\ldots\right\}\right.$$

$$\left. - 2\pi\left\{\frac{1}{l^2+\pi^2}\frac{\sin\pi x}{l} - \frac{1}{l^2+2^2\pi^2}\frac{\sin 2\pi x}{l}\ldots\right\}\right]$$

Example 2.9. **Find Fourier expansion of $f(x) = x - x^2$ for $-1 < x < 1$.**

Solution : Let $$f(x) = \frac{a_0}{2} + \Sigma \left\{ a_n \cos \frac{n\pi x}{1} + b_n \sin n\pi x \right\}$$

So, $$\frac{a_0}{2} = \frac{1}{2}\int_{-1}^{1} (x - x^2)\, dx + 0 - \frac{1}{2} \times 2 \int_0^1 x^2\, dx = -\frac{1}{3} \qquad \text{...(1)}$$

$$a_n = \frac{1}{1}\int_{-1}^{1} (x - x^2) \cos nx\pi\, dx = 0 - 2\int_0^1 x^2 \cos nx\,\pi\, dx$$

$$= -2\left[\frac{x^2 \sin nx\,\pi}{n\pi} - \frac{2}{n\pi}\int x \sin nx\pi\right]_{-1}^{1}$$

$$= -2\left[\frac{x^2 \sin n\pi x}{n\pi} + \frac{2}{n^2\pi^2} x \cos n\pi x - 2 \sin \frac{n\pi x}{\pi^3 n^3}\right]_0^1$$

$$= -2\left[0 + \frac{2}{n^2\pi^2}(-1)^n\right] = -\frac{4}{n^2\pi^2}(-1)^n \qquad \text{...(2)}$$

$$b_n = \frac{1}{1}\int_{-1}^{1} (x - x^2) \sin nx\pi\, dx = 2\int_0^1 \underset{\text{I}}{x} \underset{\text{II}}{\sin n\pi x}\, dx + 0$$

$$= 2\left[\frac{-x \cos n\pi x}{n\pi} + \frac{\sin n\pi x}{n^2\pi^2}\right]_0^1 = -\frac{2}{n\pi}(-1)^n \qquad \text{...(3)}$$

Hence $$f(x) = x - x^2 = -\frac{1}{3} + \frac{4}{\pi^2}\left\{\frac{\cos \pi x}{1^2} - \frac{\cos 2\pi x}{2^2} + \frac{\cos 3\pi x}{3^2} + \ldots\right\} + \frac{2}{\pi}\left(\frac{\sin \pi x}{1} - \frac{\sin 2\pi x}{2} + \frac{\sin 3\pi x}{3} - \ldots\right)$$

Example 2.10. **Obtain Fourier expansion of**

$$f(x) = \pi x,\quad 0 \le x \le 1$$
$$= \pi(2 - x),\quad 1 \le x \le 2.$$

(Kuvempu 96, Andhra 2000, VTU 2001)

Solution : Let $$f(x) = \frac{a_0}{2} + \sum_1^{\infty} \{a_n \cos n\pi x + b_n \sin n\pi x\}$$

$$\frac{a_0}{2} = \frac{1}{2} \times \left[\pi\int_0^1 x\, dx + \pi\int_1^2 (2 - x)\, dx\right] = \frac{\pi}{2}\left[\left[\frac{x^2}{2}\right]_0^1 + \left[2x - \frac{x^2}{2}\right]_1^2\right]$$

$$= \frac{\pi}{2}\left[\frac{1}{2} + (4 - 2) - \left(2 - \frac{1}{2}\right)\right] = \frac{\pi}{2} \qquad \text{...(1)}$$

$$a_n = \frac{1}{1}\pi\left[\int_0^1 \underset{\text{I}}{x} \underset{\text{II}}{\cos n\pi}\, dx + \int_1^2 \underset{\text{I}}{(2 - x)} \underset{\text{II}}{\sin n\pi}\, dx\right]$$

$$= \pi\left[\frac{x \sin n\pi}{n\pi} + \frac{\cos n\pi}{n^2\pi^2}\right]_0^1 + \pi\left[\frac{(2 - x)\sin n\pi}{n\pi} - \frac{\cos n\pi}{n^2\pi^2}\right]_1^2$$

$$= \pi \frac{\cos n\pi - 1}{n^2\pi^2} + \pi \frac{(-1 + \cos n\pi)}{n^2\pi^2} = \frac{2}{n^2\pi}\{(-1)^n - 1\} \qquad ...(2)$$

$= 0$ if n is even $(= 2, 4$ etc.) and

$= -\dfrac{4}{n^2\pi^2}$ if n is odd $(= 1, 3, 5 \ldots)$

$$b_n = \int_0^2 f(x) \sin n\pi x \, dx$$

$$= \int_0^1 \pi x \sin n\pi x \, dx + \int_1^2 \pi (2 - x) \sin n\pi x \, dx$$

$$= \pi \left[\frac{x \cos n\pi x}{-n\pi} + \frac{\sin n\pi x}{n^2\pi^2} \right]_0^1 + \pi \left[\frac{(2-x)\cos n\pi x}{-n\pi} - \frac{\sin n\pi x}{n^2\pi^2} \right]_1^2$$

$$= \pi \left(\frac{-\cos n\pi}{n\pi} \right) + \pi \left[0 + \frac{\cos n\pi}{n\pi} \right] = 0$$

Hence $f(x) = \dfrac{\pi}{2} - \dfrac{4}{\pi}\left[\dfrac{\cos \pi x}{1^2} + \dfrac{\cos 3\pi x}{3^2} + \dfrac{\cos 5\pi x}{5^2} + \ldots \right]$

PROBLEM SET 2.3

1. Find a Fourier series for $f(x) = 1 - t^2, \; -1 < t < 1,$ ***(Calicut)***

Ans. $1 - t^2 = \dfrac{2}{3} + \dfrac{4}{\pi^2}\left[\cos \pi t - \dfrac{\cos 2\pi t}{2^2} + \dfrac{\cos 3\pi t}{3^2} + \ldots \right]$

2. Obtain the Fourier series for $f(x) = \pi x, \; 0 \le x \le 2.$

$$f(x) = -\frac{2}{\pi} \sum_1^\infty \frac{\sin n\pi x}{n}.$$

3. Develop $f(x) = \begin{cases} 0, & -2 < x < 0, \\ 1, & 0 < x < 2 \end{cases}$, in a Fourier series in $(-2, 2)$

Ans. $f(x) = \dfrac{1}{2} + \dfrac{2}{\pi}\left[\dfrac{\sin \pi x}{2} + \dfrac{\sin 3\pi x/2}{3} + \dfrac{\sin 5\pi x/2}{5} + \ldots \right]$

4. If $f(x) \begin{cases} \pi x, & 0 \le x \le 1 \\ \pi(2 - x), & 1 \le x \le 2 \end{cases}$. Show that in the interval $(0, 2)$

$$f(x) = \frac{\pi}{2} - \frac{\pi}{4}\left[\frac{\cos \pi x}{1^2} + \frac{\cos 3\pi x}{3^2} + \frac{\cos 5\pi x}{5^2} + \ldots \right]$$

Hence deduce $\dfrac{1}{1^2} + \dfrac{1}{3^2} + \dfrac{1}{5^2} + \ldots \; \dfrac{\pi^2}{8}$ ***(Assam 99)***

5. Find the Fourier series for

$$f(x) = \begin{cases} 0, & -2 < x < -1 \\ k, & -1 < x < 1 \\ 0, & 1 < x < 2 \end{cases}$$

Ans. $f(x) = \frac{k}{2} + \frac{2k}{\pi}\left[\frac{\cos \pi x}{2} - \frac{1}{3}\frac{\cos 3\pi x}{2} + \frac{1}{5}\frac{\cos 5\pi x}{2} \cdots\right]$

6. Find the Fourier series for $f(x) = x^2 - 2, -2 < x < 2$.

Ans. $x^2 - 2 = -\frac{2}{3} - \frac{16}{\pi^2}\left[\frac{\cos \pi x}{2} - \frac{1}{4}\cos \pi x + \frac{1}{9}\frac{\cos 3\pi x}{2} + \ldots\right]$

7. A sinusoidal voltage $E \sin \omega t$ is passed through a half-wave rectifier which clips the negative portion of the wave. Expand the resulting periodic function

$$u(t) = \begin{cases} 0, & -\frac{T}{2} < t < 0 \\ E \sin \omega t, & 0 < t < T/2 \end{cases}$$

where $T = \frac{2\pi}{\omega}$, is a Fourier series

$$u(t) = \frac{E}{\pi} + \frac{E}{2}\sin \omega t - \frac{2E}{\pi}\left[\frac{\cos 2\omega t}{1 \cdot 3} + \frac{\cos 4\omega t}{3 \cdot 5} + \frac{\cos 6\omega t}{5 \cdot 7} + \ldots\right]$$

8. Find the Fourier series for

$$f(t) = \begin{cases} t, & 0 < t < 1 \\ 1 - t, & 1 < t < 2 \end{cases}$$

Ans. $f(t) = -\frac{4}{\pi^2}\left[\cos \pi t + \frac{\cos 3\pi t}{3^2} + \frac{\cos 5\pi t}{5^2} + \ldots\right] + \frac{2}{\pi}\left(\sin \pi t + \frac{\sin 3\pi t}{3} + \ldots\right)$

2.11 EVEN AND ODD FUNCTIONS

2.11.1 Odd Functions

Let $F(x) = \begin{cases} f_1(x), & x > 0 \\ f_2(x) & x < 0 \end{cases}$ and if $\boldsymbol{f_2(-x) = -f_1(x)}$

The function $F(x)$ is called an odd function.

$$F(x) \begin{cases} x^3, & x > 0 \\ x^3, & x < 0 \end{cases}$$

Satisfy $f_2(x) = x^3,\ f_1(x) = x^3$

$$f_2(-x) = (-x)^3 = -x^3 = -f_1(x)$$

So, $F(x)$ is an odd Function etc.

Also $\sin x$, $\tan x$ are odd functions.

2.11.2 Even Functions

$F(x) = \begin{cases} f_1(x), & x > 0 \\ f_2(x) & x < 0 \end{cases}$ and if $f_2(-x) = f_1(x)$,

$F(x)$ is called an even function

$$F(x) = \begin{cases} x^2, & x > 0 \\ x^2, & x < 0 \end{cases} \text{ satisfy } f_2(x) = x^2,\ f_1(x) = x^2$$

$$f_2(-x) = (-x)^2 = x^2 = f_1(x)$$

So, $F(x)$ is an even function.

Also $\cos x$ is an even function.

A sine series is equivalent to an odd function for the whole interval $-\pi$ to π and a cosine series represents an even function for the whole interval $(-\pi, \pi)$ since any function can be expressed as sum of two functions one even and other odd, the most general representation for $f(x)$ in $(-\pi$ to $\pi)$ is

$$f(x) = \frac{a_0}{2} + \sum_1^\infty a_n \cos nx + \sum_1^\infty b_n \sin nx.$$

If $f(x)$ be assumed $= a_0^1 + \Sigma\,(a_n \cos nx + b_n \sin nx)$, the values of a_0 and a_0^1 will be related by $\frac{a_0}{2} = a_0^1$. So both the forms may be used.

Function $f_1(x) = x,\ f_2(x) = x^3,\ f_3(x) = \sin x$

$f_4(x) = \tan x$, satisfy the conditions $f(-x) = -f(x)$

Their graphs have symmetry in first and third quadrants or second and 4th quadrants i.e. they are symmetrical about the x axis. Such a function is called an odd functions.They may be called symmetrical about origin

$$\int_{-c}^{c} f(x)\,dx = 0$$

General Graph of An Odd Function

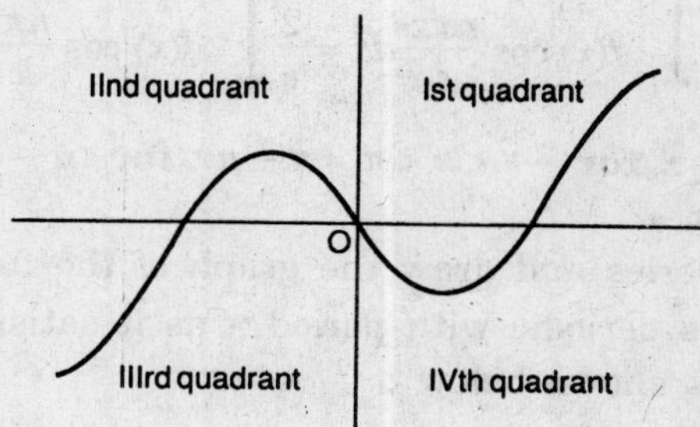

Fig. 2.3

Functions $g_1(x) = x^2,\ g_2(x) = \cos x$

Satisfy the condition $g(-x) = g(x)$

Their graphs are symmetrical about the y-axis. Such fucntions are called even functions

General graph of an even function

$$\int_{-c}^{c} f(x)\,dx = 2\int_0^c f(x)\,dx.$$

General Graph of An Even Function

Its graph is symmetrical about y-axis.

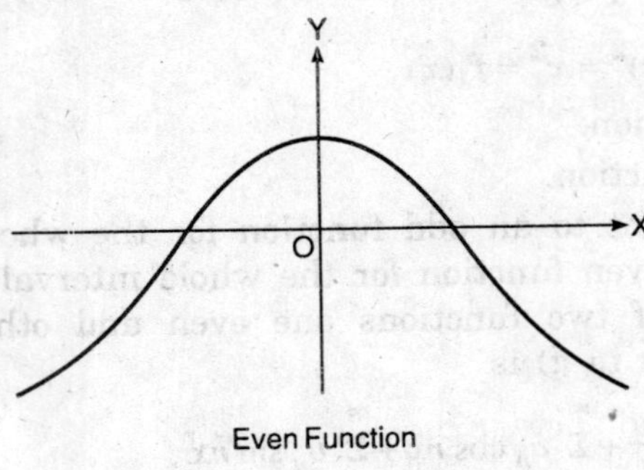

Even Function

Fig. 2.4

Fourier Series of an odd fucntion has only the sine term because

Graph of odd function is symmetrical about y-axis with sign changed

$a_0 = 0$, because $a_n = 0$

$$b_n = \frac{1}{c}\int_{-c}^{c} f(x) \sin x \frac{x\pi}{c}\, dx = \frac{2}{c}\int_{0}^{c} f(x) \sin \frac{n\pi x}{c}\, dx.$$

Fourier series of an even function has only the cosine term because $b_n = 0$.

So for even function ($b_n = 0$)

and
$$\frac{a_0}{2} = \frac{1}{2c}\int_{-c}^{c} f(x)\, dx = \frac{1}{c}\int_{0}^{c} f(x)\, dx$$

$$a_n = \frac{1}{c}\int_{-c}^{c} f(x) \cos \frac{n\pi x}{c}\, dx = \frac{2}{c}\int_{0}^{c} f(x) \cos \frac{n\pi x}{c}\, dx$$

Example 2.11. **Express $f(x) = x$ for $-\pi < x < \pi$ $= x - n\pi$ for $(n-1)\pi < x < n\pi$**
$n \in \pi$

as a Fourier series and draw the graph of the function.

Solution : The function is periodic with period π as it satisfy $f(\pi + x) = f(x)$.

Its graph is as shown below :

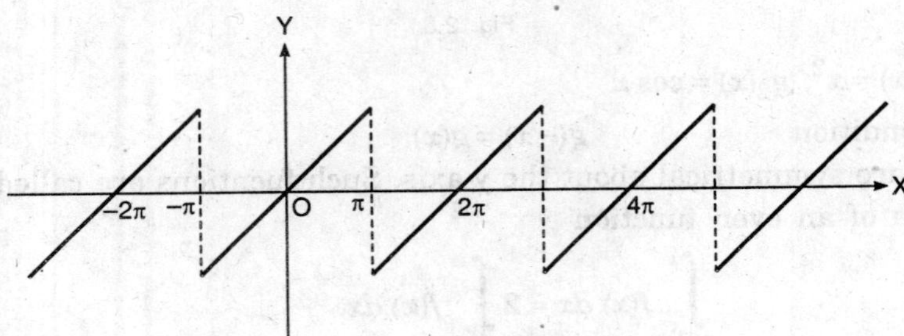

Fig. 2.5

2.12 FOURIER SERIES OF ODD AND EVEN FUNCTION

$f(x)$ is an odd function, so $a_0 = 0$, $a_n = 0$

and $$b_n = \frac{1}{\pi}\int_{-\pi}^{\pi} x \sin nx\, dx = \frac{2}{\pi}\int_0^{\pi} x \sin nx\, dx$$

$$= \frac{2}{\pi}\left[-x\frac{\cos nx}{n} + \frac{\sin nx}{n^2}\right]_0^{\pi} = -\frac{2}{n}(-1)^n.$$

Hence $f(x) = x = 2\left(\sin x - \frac{1}{2}\sin 2x + \frac{1}{3}\sin 3x - \frac{1}{4}\sin 4x \ldots\right)$

Example 2.12. Obtain Fourier series for the function $f(x)$, given by

$$f(x) = 1 + \frac{2x}{\pi},\ -\pi \le x \le 0$$

$$= 1 - \frac{2x}{\pi},\ 0 \le x \le \pi$$

(AUUP 2007; Madras 2000)

Deduce that $\frac{1}{1^2} + \frac{1}{3^2} + \frac{1}{5^2} + \ldots = \frac{\pi^2}{8}$. Draw graph also.

(i) for $-\pi < x < 0$, $y = 1 + \frac{2x}{y}$

x	0	π
y	1	–1

(ii) for $0 < x < y$, $y = 1 - \frac{2x}{\pi}$

x	1	π
y	0	–1

Soluton. The graph has symmetry about y axis. So it is an even function. In its Fourier series we will have $b_n = 0$

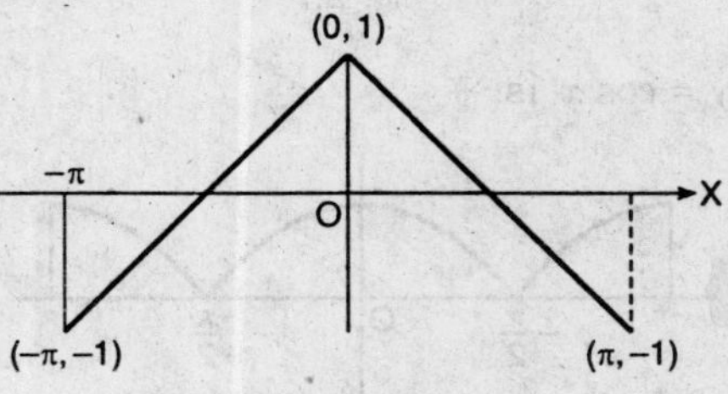

Fig. 2.6

If $$f(x) = a_0 + \sum_1^{\infty} a_n \cos nx + \sum_1^{\infty} b_n \sin nx$$

$$a_0 = \frac{1}{2\pi}\int_0^{\pi} 2\left(1 - \frac{2x}{\pi}\right)dx = \frac{1}{\pi}\left[x - \frac{x^2}{\pi}\right]_0^{\pi} = 0$$

$$a_n = \frac{1}{\pi}\cdot 2\int_0^{\pi}\left(1-\frac{2}{\pi}x\right)\cos nx\,dx$$

$$= \frac{2}{\pi}\left[\frac{\sin nx}{n} - \frac{2}{\pi}\left(-x\frac{\sin nx}{n} + \frac{\cos nx}{n^2}\right)\right]_0^{\pi}$$

$$= -\frac{4}{\pi^2}\frac{(-1)^n - 1}{n^2} = \frac{4}{\pi^2}\left\{\frac{1-(-1)^n}{n^2}\right\} = 0$$

If n is even $= \frac{8}{\pi^2 n^2}$ if n is odd $= 1, 3, 5$

Hence $f(x) = \frac{8}{\pi^2}\left[\frac{\cos x}{1^2} + \frac{\cos 3x}{3^2} + \frac{\cos 5x}{5^2} + \ldots\right]$

at $x = 0$, $f(x) = 1$

So $\quad 1 = \frac{8}{\pi^2}\left[\frac{1}{1^2} + \frac{1}{3^2} + \frac{1}{5^2} + \ldots\right]$

or $\quad \frac{1}{1^2} + \frac{1}{3^2} + \frac{1}{5^2} + \ldots = \frac{\pi^2}{8}$

Example 2.13. If $f(x) = |\cos x|$, expand $f(x)$ as a fourier series in $(-\pi, \pi)$ so graph of $y = \cos x$ is

Solution : The graph of $y = \cos x$ is

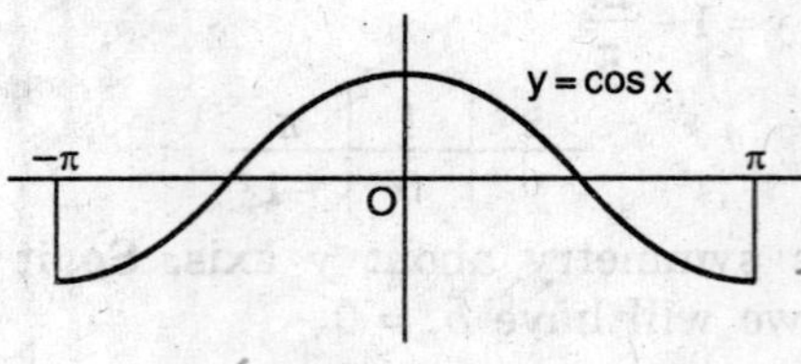

Fig. 2.7

The graph of $y = \cos x$ is

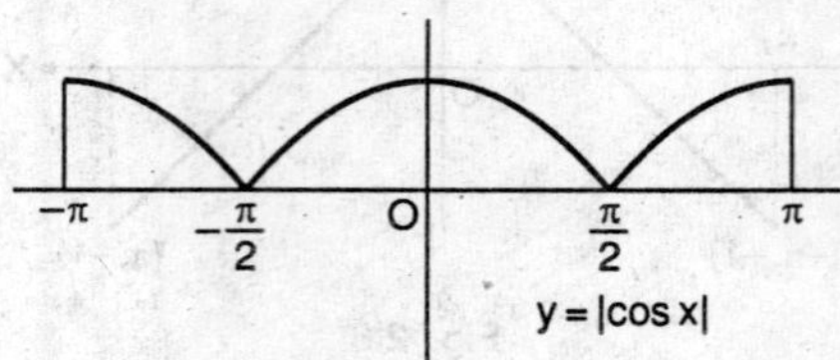

Fig. 2.8

The graph of $y = |\cos x|$ is symmetrical about y axis. So it is an even function with $y > 0$ for all x.

By symmetry $b_n = 0$ in $f(x) = a_0 + \sum_1^{\infty} a_n \cos nx + \sum_1^{\infty} b_n \sin nx$

$$a_0 = \frac{1}{2\pi}\int_{-\pi}^{\pi} (\cos x)\, dx = \frac{2}{2\pi}\left[\int_0^{\pi/2} \cos x\, dx + \int_{\pi/2}^{\pi} -\cos x\, dx\right]$$

$$= \frac{1}{\pi}\left[[\sin x]_0^{\pi/2} - [\sin x]_{\pi/2}^{\pi}\right] = \frac{1}{\pi}[1 - 0 - (0 - 1)] = \frac{2}{\pi}$$

$$a_n = \frac{2}{\pi}\left[\int_0^{\pi/2} \cos x \cos nx\, dx - \int_{\pi/2}^{\pi} \cos x \cos nx\, dx\right]$$

$$= \frac{1}{\pi}\left[\int_0^{\pi/2} [\cos (n+1) x + \cos (n-1) x]\, dx - \int_{\pi/2}^{\pi} [\cos (n+1) x + \cos (n-1) x]\, dx\right]$$

$$= \frac{1}{\pi}\left[\left\{\frac{\sin (n+1) x}{n+1} + \frac{\sin (n-1) x}{n-1}\right\}_0^{\pi/2} - \left\{\frac{\sin (n+1) x}{n+1} + \frac{\sin (n-1) x}{n-1}\right\}_{\pi/2}^{\pi}\right]$$

$$= \frac{2}{\pi}\cos\frac{n\pi}{2}\left[\frac{1}{n+1} - \frac{1}{n-1}\right] = \frac{-4\cos\frac{n\pi}{2}}{\pi(n^2-1)},\ n \neq 1$$

$$a_1 = \frac{2}{\pi}\left[\int_0^{\pi/2} \cos^2 x\, dx - \int_{\pi/2}^{\pi} \cos^2 x\, dx\right]$$

$$= \frac{1}{\pi}\left[\int_0^{\pi/2} (1 + \cos 2x) - \int_{\pi/2}^{\pi} (1 + \cos 2x)\, dx\right]$$

$$= \frac{1}{\pi}\left[\left[x + \frac{\sin 2x}{2}\right]_0^{\pi/2} - \left[x + \frac{\sin 2x}{2}\right]_{\pi/2}^{\pi}\right]$$

$$= \frac{1}{\pi}\left[\frac{\pi}{2} - \left(\pi - \frac{\pi}{2}\right)\right] = 0$$

Hence $f(x) = |\cos x| = \frac{4}{\pi}\sum_{n=2}^{\infty} -\frac{\cos\frac{nx}{2}}{n^2-1}$

$$= \frac{4}{\pi}\left[\frac{1}{1\cdot 3}\cos 2x - \frac{1}{3\cdot 5}\cos 4x + \ldots\right]$$

PROBLEM SET 2.4

1. Expand $f(x) = x \sin x$ as a Fourier series in $-\pi \leq x \leq \pi$ and deduce

$$\frac{1}{1\cdot 3} - \frac{1}{3\cdot 5} + \frac{1}{5\cdot 7} - \ldots = \frac{1}{4}(\pi - 2)$$

Ans. $f(x) = 1 - \frac{1}{2}\cos x - \frac{2}{1\cdot 3}\cos 2x + \frac{2}{2\cdot 4}\cos 3x - \frac{2}{3\cdot 5}\cos 4x \ldots$

2. Show that for $-\pi < x < \pi$, $\sin ax = \dfrac{2 \sin a\pi}{\pi}$

$$\left\{\frac{\sin x}{1^2 - a^2} - \frac{2 \sin 2x}{2^2 - a^2} + \frac{3 \sin 3x}{3^2 - a^2} + \ldots\right\}$$

3. For $f(x) = |x|$, $-\pi < x < \pi$, obtain the Fourier series and deduce that

$$\frac{\pi^2}{8} = \frac{1}{1^2} + \frac{1}{3^2} + \frac{1}{5^2} + \frac{1}{7^2} + \ldots$$

(Assam 99, Jammu 98, Madras 99)

4. Prove that $x \cos x = -\dfrac{1}{2} \sin x + 2 \sum\limits_{n=2}^{\infty} \dfrac{n(-1)^n}{n^2 - 1} \sin nx$, for $-\pi < x < \pi$. ***(VTU 2000S)***

5. If $f(x) = -x$ for $-\pi < x < 0$
$= +x$, $\quad 0 < x < \pi$

Show that $f(x) = \dfrac{\pi}{2} - \dfrac{\pi}{4}\left[\dfrac{1}{1^2} \cos x + \dfrac{1}{3^2} \cos 3x + \dfrac{1}{5^2} \cos 5x + \ldots\right]$

6. For $f(x) = \begin{cases} -x + 1, & \text{for } -\pi < x < 0 \\ x + 1 & \phantom{\text{for }} 0 < x < \pi \end{cases}$.

Find the Fourier series and deduce

$$\frac{1}{1^2} + \frac{1}{3^2} + \frac{1}{5^2} = \frac{\pi^2}{8}$$

$$f(x) = \frac{\pi}{2} + 1 - \frac{4}{\pi}\left(\cos x + \frac{1}{3^2} \cos 3x + \frac{1}{5^2} \cos 5x + \ldots\right)$$

(Bhopal 91)

7. Find the Foruier series to represent
$f(x) = |\sin x|$, $-\pi < x < \pi$.

$$f(x) = \frac{2}{\pi} - \frac{4}{\pi}\left\{\frac{\cos 2x}{3} + \frac{\cos 4x}{15} + \ldots + \frac{\cos 2nx}{4n^2 - 1} + \ldots\right\}$$

(Madras 2000S)

8. Find Fourier series of $f(x) = \begin{cases} -k, & -\pi < x < 0 \\ +k, & 0 < x < \pi \end{cases}$, and draw graph given that $f(x + 2\pi) = f(x)$.

Deduce that $\qquad \dfrac{\pi}{4} = \sum\limits_{1}^{\infty} \dfrac{(-1)^{n+1}}{2^{n-1}}$

$$f(x) = \frac{4k}{\pi}\left\{\sin x + \frac{\sin 3x}{3} + \frac{\sin 5x}{5} + \ldots \infty\right\}.$$

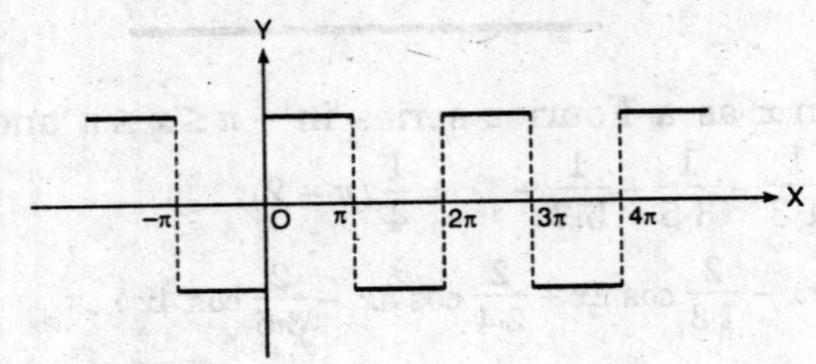

2.13 HALF RANGE SERIES

If $f(x)$ is defined only for $0 < x < c$

Then the function $F_{\text{odd}}(x)$, defined as

$$F_{\text{odd}}(x) = \begin{cases} f(x), & 0 < x < c \\ \phi(x), & -c < x < 0 \end{cases} \text{ where } \phi(-x) = -f(x)$$

is odd and will **have only the sine series and Function F_{even},**

$$F_{\text{even}} = \begin{cases} f(x), & 0 < x < c \\ \psi(x), & -c < x < 0 \end{cases}, \text{ where } \psi(-x) = f(x)$$

is **even and will have only the cosine terms in its Fourier expansion.**

Function $F_{\text{odd}} = F_{\text{even}}$, for $0 < x < c$

they differ only in the other half range $-c < x < 0$.

2.14 SINE AND COSINE SERIES

If a function is defined only for half range $0 \le x \le \pi$, it can have its Fourier expansion both as a sine series and a cosine series if assumption be made for form of $f(x)$ in the interval $-\pi < x < 0$. If $f(x)$ is expanded as a sine series in $0 \le x \le \pi$ then for the other half interval $-\pi < x < 0$, it represents an odd function satisfying $f(-x) = -f(x)$, but if $f(x)$ is expanded as a cosine series then in the other half interval $-\pi < x < 0$, it represent $f(x)$, which is even and satisfy $f(-x) = +f(x)$. For half range $0 \le x \le \pi$ both for sine and cosine series the values of $a_0\ a_n$ or b_n gets doubled of those for the full interval $-\pi \le x \le \pi$. Thus if $f(x)$ is asked to have a half range **sine series** for $0 \le x \le \pi$,

$$f(x) = \sum_{1}^{\infty} b_n \sin nx$$

where $$b_n = \frac{2}{\pi}\int_0^{\pi} f(x) \sin nx\, dx \text{ and } \boldsymbol{a_n} \text{ is not required.}$$

If some function $f(x)$ be asked to have a half range cosine series for $0 \le x \le \pi$ then

$$f(x) = \frac{a_0}{2} + \sum_{1}^{\infty} a_n \cos nx \text{ where } a_0 = \frac{2}{\pi}\int_0^{\pi} f(x)\, dx \text{ and } a_n = \frac{2}{\pi}\int_0^{\pi} f(x) \cos nx\, dx \text{ and } b_n \text{ is not}$$

to be calculated.

Example 2.14. Find a series of sines and cosines of multiples of x which represent $f(x) = x$, in the interval $-\pi \le x \le \pi$.

Solution : Here full range is given so full range series is required where $f(x) = x = $ odd so a_n will be $= 0$

Let $$f(x) = \frac{1}{2}a_0 + \sum_{1}^{\infty} a_n \cos nx + \sum_{1}^{\infty} b_n \sin nx$$

$$a_0 = \frac{1}{\pi}\int_{-\pi}^{\pi} x\, dx = 0, \textbf{ as } x \textbf{ is an odd function}$$

$$a_n = \frac{1}{\pi}\int_{-\pi}^{\pi} (x \cos nx)\, dx = 0, \text{ as } x \cos nx \text{ is odd.}$$

$$b_n = \frac{1}{\pi}\int_{-\pi}^{\pi} x \sin nx\, dx = \frac{2}{\pi}\int_0^{\pi} \underset{I}{x} \underset{II}{\sin nx}\, dx, \text{ as } x \sin nx \text{ is even}$$

$$= \frac{2}{\pi}\left[\frac{x \cos nx}{-n} + \frac{\sin nx}{n^2}\right]_0^{\pi} = -\frac{2}{n}(-1)^n$$

So $$x = 2\left[\sin x - \frac{1}{2}\sin 2x + \frac{1}{3}\sin 3x + \ldots\right]$$

Example 2.15. Find the half range cosines series for $f(x) = x$ in $0 \le x \le \pi$ and show that $1 + \frac{1}{3^2} + \frac{1}{5^2} \to \ldots = \pi^2/8$.

Solution :

$$x = \frac{1}{2}a_0 + \sum_1^{\infty} a_n \cos nx$$

where $$a_0 = \frac{2}{\pi}\int_0^{\pi} x\, dx = \frac{2}{\pi}\frac{\pi^2}{2} = \pi \qquad \ldots(1)$$

$$a_n = \frac{2}{\pi}\int_0^{\pi} \underset{I}{x} \underset{II}{\cos nx}\, dx = \frac{2}{\pi}\left\{\left[x\frac{\sin nx}{n}\right]_0^{\pi} - \left[-\frac{\cos nx}{n^2}\right]_0^{\pi}\right\}$$

$$= \frac{2}{\pi}\left\{0 + \frac{(-1)^n - 1}{n^2}\right\} = 0 \text{ for } n \text{ even} = 2, 4, 6 \ldots$$

$$= -\frac{4}{\pi n^2} \text{ for } n \text{ odd} = 1, 3, 5, \ldots$$

Hence $$f(x) = x = \frac{\pi}{2} - \frac{4}{\pi}\left\{\frac{\cos x}{1^2} + \frac{\cos 3x}{3^2} + \frac{\cos 5x}{5^2} + \ldots\right\}$$

When $x = 0$, in particular, we have

$$f(x) = x = \frac{\pi}{2} - \frac{4}{\pi}\left\{\frac{1}{1^2} + \frac{1}{3^2} + \frac{1}{5^2} + \ldots\right\}$$

$$\therefore \quad 1 + \frac{1}{3^2} + \frac{1}{5^2} + \ldots = \frac{\pi^2}{8}.$$

Example 2.16. Obtain the Fourier series for $f(x) = x^2$, $-\pi < x < \pi$. and deduce

(i) $\frac{\pi^2}{6} = 1 + \frac{1}{2^2} + \frac{1}{3^2} + \ldots$

(ii) $\frac{\pi^2}{1^2} = 1 - \frac{1}{2^2} + \frac{1}{3^2} - \frac{1}{4^2} + \ldots$

(Raj 2001, .95)

(iii) $\dfrac{\pi^2}{8} = 1 + \dfrac{1}{3^2} + \dfrac{1}{5^2} + \ldots$

(Mysore 94S, Mangalore 97)

Solution : Let $f(x) = \frac{1}{2} a_0 + \Sigma a_n \cos nx + \Sigma b_n \sin nx$

then $$\frac{a_0}{2} = \frac{1}{2\pi}\int_{-\pi}^{\pi} x^2\,dx = \frac{2}{2\pi}\int_0^{\pi} x^2\,dx = \frac{1}{\pi}\left[\frac{x^3}{3}\right]_0^{\pi} = \frac{\pi^2}{3} \qquad ...(1)$$

$$a_n = \frac{1}{\pi}\int_{-\pi}^{\pi} \underset{\text{I}}{x^2} \underset{\text{II}}{\cos nx}\,dx = \frac{2}{\pi}\int_0^{\pi} x^2 \cos nx\,dx, \quad \text{as } x^2 \cos nx \text{ is even}$$

$$= \frac{2}{\pi}\left[\frac{x^2 \sin nx}{n} - \frac{2}{n}\int x \sin nx\,dx\right]_0^{\pi}$$

$$= \frac{2}{\pi}\left[\frac{x^2 \sin nx}{n} + \frac{2x}{n}\frac{\cos nx}{n} - \frac{2 \sin nx}{n^3}\right]_0^{\pi} = \frac{4\pi(-1)^n}{\pi n^2} \qquad ...(2)$$

$$b_n = \frac{1}{\pi}\int_{-\pi}^{\pi} x^2 \sin nx\,dx = 0 \text{ as } x^2 \sin nx \text{ is an odd function of } x$$

Hence $$f(x) = x^2 = \frac{\pi^2}{3} - 4\left[\frac{\cos x}{1^2} - \frac{\cos 2x}{2^2} + \frac{\cos 3x}{3^2} - \frac{\cos 4x}{4^2}\right] \qquad ...(3)$$

Taking $x = 0$ in (3)

$$0 = \frac{\pi^2}{4} - 4\left(\frac{1}{1^2} - \frac{1}{2^2} + \frac{1}{3^2} \ldots\right)$$

So $$\frac{1}{1^2} - \frac{1}{2^2} + \frac{1}{3^2} - \frac{1}{4^2} + \ldots = \frac{\pi^2}{12} \qquad ...(4)$$

Taking $x = \pi$ in (3),

$$f(x) = \lim_{\varepsilon \to 0} \frac{f(-\pi + \varepsilon) + f(\pi - \varepsilon)}{2} = \lim_{\varepsilon \to 0} \frac{(-\pi + \varepsilon)^2 + (\pi - \varepsilon)^2}{2} = \pi^2$$

$$\pi^2 = \frac{\pi^2}{3} - 4\left\{\frac{-1}{1^2} - \frac{1}{2^2} - \frac{1}{3^2} \ldots\right\}$$

So $$\frac{1}{1^2} + \frac{1}{2^2} + \frac{1}{3^2} + \frac{1}{4^2} \ldots = \frac{1}{4}\left(\pi^2 - \frac{\pi^2}{3}\right) = \frac{\pi^2}{6} \qquad ...(5)$$

Adding (4) and (5)

$$\frac{\pi^2}{6} + \frac{\pi^2}{12} = 2\left\{\frac{1}{12} + \frac{1}{3^2} + \frac{1}{5^2} + \ldots\right\}$$

So $$\frac{1}{1^2} + \frac{1}{3^2} + \frac{1}{5^2} = \frac{\pi^2}{8} \qquad ...(6)$$

Example 2.17. **Draw the graph of**

$$f(x) = \begin{cases} x, & 0 < x < \pi/2 \\ \pi - x, & \dfrac{\pi}{2} \le x < \pi \end{cases} \quad ...(1)$$

Extend it in the interval $-\pi$ to 0 so that it may have :

(i) a half range sine series only,

(ii) a half range cosine series only. *(Madras 98, Mysore 97)*

Solution : (i) **Function $f(x)$ having a half range sine series.** It will be an odd function so it graph will have symmetry in first and third quadrant and second and 4th quadrant.

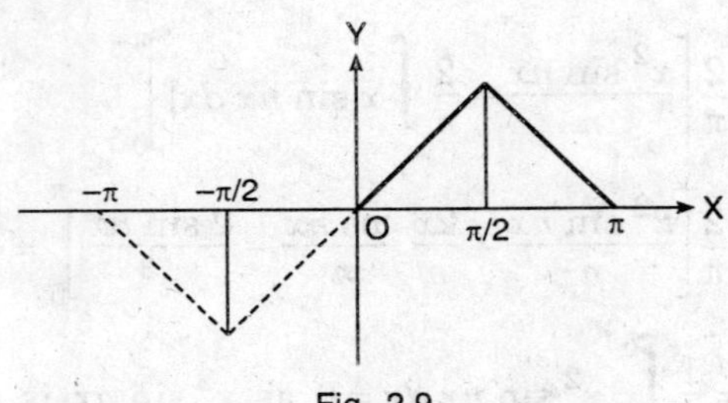

Fig. 2.9

$$f(x) = \sum_{0}^{\infty} b_n \sin nx$$

where $b_n = \dfrac{2}{\pi}\displaystyle\int_0^{\pi} f(x) \sin nx \, dx$

$$= \frac{2}{\pi}\left[\int_0^{\pi/2} x \sin nx \, dx + \int_{\pi/2}^{\pi} (\pi - x) \sin nx \, dx\right]$$

$$= \frac{2}{\pi}\left[-\frac{x \cos nx}{n} + \frac{\sin nx}{n^2}\right]_0^{\pi/2} + \frac{2}{\pi}\left[(\pi - x)\frac{\cos nx}{n} - \frac{\sin nx}{n^2}\right]_{\pi/2}^{\pi}$$

$$= \frac{2}{\pi}\left[\frac{-\frac{\pi}{2}\cos n\pi/2}{n} + \frac{\sin n\pi/2}{n^2} + \frac{\frac{\pi}{2}\cos\frac{n\pi}{2}}{n} + \frac{\sin\frac{n\pi}{2}}{n^2}\right]$$

$$b_n = \frac{4}{\pi}\frac{\sin n\pi/2}{n^2}$$

So $f(x) = \displaystyle\sum_{0}^{\infty} b_n \sin nx$

$$= \frac{4}{\pi}\left[\frac{\sin x}{1^2} - \frac{\sin 3x}{3^2} + \frac{\sin 5x}{5^2} + \ldots\right]$$

(ii) **Function $f(x)$ having a half range cosine series**

It will be an even function so its graph will have symmetry about y-axis. Graph of even function corresponding to (1).

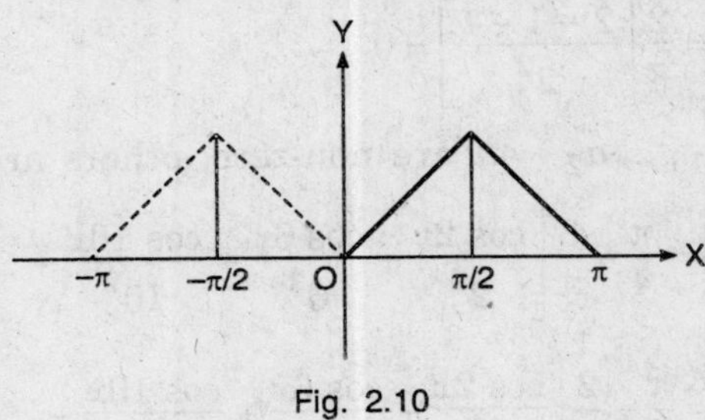

Fig. 2.10

$$f(x) = a_0 + \sum_1^{\infty} a_n \cos nx$$

$$a_0 = \frac{2}{2\pi}\int_0^{\pi} f(x)\,dx = \frac{1}{\pi}\left[\int_0^{\pi/2} x\,dx + \int_{\pi/2}^{\pi} (\pi - x)\,dx\right]$$

$$= \frac{1}{\pi}\left[\frac{\pi^2}{2\times 4}\right] - \frac{1}{\pi}\left[\frac{(\pi - x)^2}{2}\right]_{\pi/2}^{\pi}$$

$$= \frac{1}{2\pi}\left[\frac{\pi^2}{4} - 0 + \frac{\pi^2}{4}\right] = \frac{\pi}{4}$$

$$a_n = \frac{2}{\pi}\int_0^{\pi} f(x)\cos nx\,dx$$

$$= \frac{2}{\pi}\left[\int_0^{\pi/2} x\cos nx\,dx + \int_{\pi/2}^{\pi} (\pi - x)\cos nx\,dx\right]$$

$$= \frac{2}{\pi}\left[\left\{\frac{x\sin nx}{n} + \frac{\cos nx}{n^2}\right\}_0^{\pi/2} + \left[\frac{(\pi - x)\sin nx}{n} - \frac{\cos nx}{n^2}\right]_{\pi/2}^{\pi}\right]$$

$$= \frac{2}{\pi}\left[\frac{\frac{\pi}{2}\sin\frac{n\pi}{2}}{n} + \frac{(\cos n\pi/2 - 1)}{n^2} - \frac{\frac{\pi}{2}\sin\frac{n\pi}{2}}{n} - \frac{(-1)^n - \cos\frac{n\pi}{2}}{n^2}\right]$$

$$= \frac{2}{\pi n^2}\left[2\cos\frac{n\pi}{2} - 1 - (-1)^n\right]$$

$$a_1 = \frac{2}{\pi}\left[\frac{0 - 1 + 1}{1^2}\right] = 0,$$

$$a_2 = \frac{2}{\pi}\left[\frac{-2 - 1 - 1}{2^2}\right] = -\frac{8}{\pi\times 2^2}$$

$$a_3 = \frac{2}{\pi}\left[\frac{0 - 1 + 1}{3^2}\right] = 0,$$

$$a_4 = \frac{2}{\pi}\left[\frac{2 - 1 - 1}{2^2}\right] = 0$$

So $a_2, a_6, a_{10} \ldots a_2 + 4n$ are non-zero, others are zero. Hence

$$f(x) = \frac{\pi}{4} - \frac{8}{\pi}\left[\frac{\cos 2x}{2^2} + \frac{\cos 6x}{6^2} + \frac{\cos 10x}{10^2} + \ldots\right]$$

$$= \frac{\pi}{4} - \frac{2}{\pi}\left[\frac{\cos 2x}{1^2} + \frac{\cos 6x}{3^2} + \frac{\cos 10x}{5^2} + \ldots\right]$$

Example 2.18. **Express $f(x) = x$, $0 < x < 2$ as a :** *(VTU 2001, Delhi 97S)*
(i) half range sine series,
(ii) a half range cosine series.
Draw graphs from $(-2, 2)$

Solution : (i) **Half range sine series.** The graph of the function will be symmetrical in first and third quadrant

$$f(x) = \sum_{1}^{\infty} b_n \sin \frac{n\pi x}{2}$$

where $$b_n = \frac{2}{2}\int_0^2 x \sin \frac{n\pi x}{2}\, dx$$

$$= \frac{2}{2}\left[\frac{-2x}{n\pi}\cos\frac{n\pi x}{2} + \frac{4}{n^2\pi^2}\sin\frac{n\pi x}{2}\right]_0^2$$

$$= -\frac{4}{\pi}\frac{(-1)^n}{n}$$

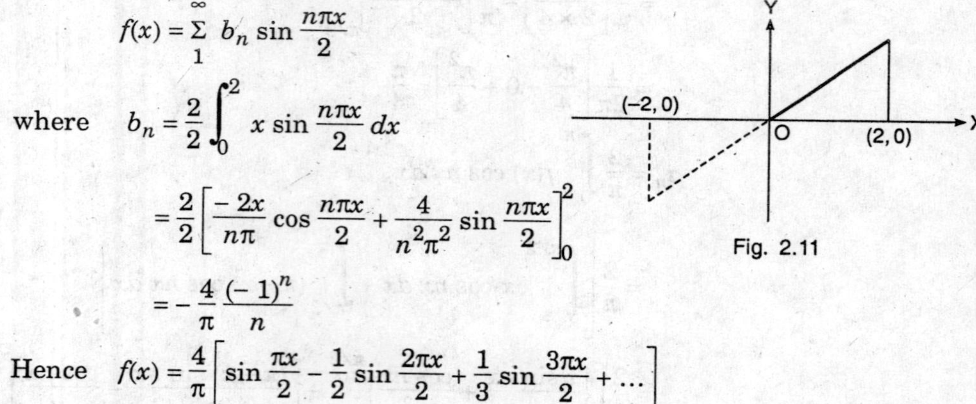

Fig. 2.11

Hence $$f(x) = \frac{4}{\pi}\left[\sin\frac{\pi x}{2} - \frac{1}{2}\sin\frac{2\pi x}{2} + \frac{1}{3}\sin\frac{3\pi x}{2} + \ldots\right]$$

(ii) **Half range cosine series.** The graph of the function will be symmetrical about y-axis

$$f(x) = a_0 + \sum_{1}^{\infty} a_n \cos\frac{n\pi x}{2}$$

$$a_0 = \frac{2}{2\times 2}\int_0^2 x\, dx = \frac{1}{2}\frac{(2)^2}{2} = 1$$

$$a_n = \frac{2}{2}\int_0^2 x \cos\frac{n\pi x}{2}\, dx$$

Fig. 2.12

$$= \left[\frac{2}{n\pi} x \sin\frac{n\pi x}{2} + \frac{4}{n^2\pi^2}\cos\frac{n\pi x}{2}\right]_0^2$$

$$= 0 + \frac{4}{n^2\pi^2}[(-1)^n - 1]$$

$$a_1 = \frac{-4\times 2}{\pi^2 \times 1^2},\ a_2 = 0,$$

$$a_3 = +\frac{-4}{\pi^2\times 3^2} \text{ etc.}$$

So $$f(x) = 1 - \frac{8}{\pi^2}\left[\frac{\cos\frac{\pi x}{2}}{1^2} + \frac{\cos\frac{3\pi x}{2}}{3^2} + \frac{\cos\frac{5\pi x}{2}}{5^2} + \ldots\right]$$

PROBLEM SET 2.5

1. Express $f(x) = x$ as a half range sine series in $0 < x < 2$. *(Assam 99, Karnataka 94)*

   Ans. $f(x) = \frac{4}{\pi}\left[\sin\frac{\pi x}{2} - \frac{1}{2}\sin\frac{2\pi x}{2} + \frac{1}{3}\sin\frac{3\pi x}{2} - \frac{1}{4}\sin\frac{4\pi x}{2}\right]$

2. Expand

   $$f(x) = \begin{cases} \frac{1}{4} - x, \text{ if } 0 < x < l/2, \\ x - \frac{3}{4}, \frac{l}{2} < x < l \end{cases}$$, as the Fourier sine series.

   (Andhra 2000, Mangalore 97, Madras 95)

   Ans. $f(x) = \left(\frac{1}{\pi} - \frac{4}{\pi^2}\right)\sin\pi x + \left(\frac{1}{3\pi} + \frac{4}{3^2\pi^2}\right)\sin 3\pi x + \left(\frac{1}{5\pi} - \frac{4}{5^2 x^2}\right)\sin 5\pi x + \ldots$

3. Obtain cosine andsine series for $f(x) = x$, in the interval $0 < x < \pi$. Hence show that

   $$\frac{1}{1^2} + \frac{1}{3^2} + \frac{1}{5^2} + \ldots = \frac{\pi^2}{8}$$

   (Coimbatore 94)

   Ans. (i) $\frac{\pi}{2} - \frac{4}{\pi}\left[\cos x + \frac{1}{3^2}\cos 3x + \frac{1}{5^2}\cos 5x + \ldots\right]$; (ii) $2\left[\sin x - \frac{1}{2}\sin 2x + \frac{1}{3}\sin 3x - \ldots\right]$

4. Obtain a half range cosine series for

   $$f(x) = \begin{cases} kx \text{ for } 0 \le n \le l/2 \\ k(l - x) \text{ for } l/2 \le x \le l \end{cases}$$

   (VTU 2000; Tirupati 98S, Calicut 94)

   also deduce sum of the series $\frac{1}{1^2} + \frac{1}{3^2} + \frac{1}{5^2} + \ldots$

   Ans. $f(x) = \frac{kl}{3} - \frac{8kl}{\pi^2}\left[\frac{1}{2^2}\cos\frac{2\pi x}{l} + \frac{1}{6^2}\cos\frac{6\pi x}{l} + \frac{1}{10^2}\cos\frac{10\pi x}{l} + \ldots\right]; \frac{\pi^2}{8}$

5. Show that a cosntant c can be expanded in a infinite series

   $$\frac{4c}{\pi}\left\{\sin x + \frac{\sin 3x}{3} + \frac{\sin 5x}{5} + \ldots\right\}$$ in the range $0 < x < \pi$.

6. If $f(x) = \sin x$ for $0 \le x \le \pi/4$
$= \cos x$, for $\pi/4 \le x \le \pi/2$,
expand $f(x)$ in a series of sines.

$$\frac{8}{\pi} \cos \frac{\pi}{4} \left[\frac{\sin 2x}{1 \cdot 3} - \frac{\sin 6x}{5 \cdot 7} + \frac{\sin 10x}{9 \cdot 11} + \ldots \right]$$

7. Find the half range cosine series for $f(x) = x^2$ inthe range $0 \le x \le \pi$. ***(Karnataka 93)***

Ans. $\frac{\pi^2}{3} - 4 \left[\cos x - \frac{\cos 2x}{2^2} + \frac{\cos 3x}{3^2} - \frac{\cos 4x}{4^2} \ldots \right]$

8. For the function $f(x) = \frac{h}{a} x, \quad 0 < x < a$

$= \frac{h}{(l-a)} (l - x), \quad a < x < l$

Find the half range sine series.

$$f(x) = \frac{2l^2 h}{a(l-a)\pi^2} \left[\sin \frac{\pi a}{l} \sin \frac{\pi x}{l} + \frac{1}{2^2} \sin \frac{2\pi a}{l} \sin \frac{2\pi x}{l} + \frac{1}{3^2} \sin \frac{3\pi a}{l} \sin \frac{3\pi x}{l} \right]$$

9. Obtain the half range sine series for $f(x) = e^x$, for $0 < x < 1$. ***(Madras 99, Mangalore 99)***

Ans. $f(x) = \sum_1^\infty \frac{2n\pi}{1 + n^2\pi^2} (1 - e \cos n\pi) \sin n\pi x.$

10. Find the half range cosine series for $f(x) = (x - 1)^2$ in the interval $0 < x < 1$. ***(Andhra 2000, Mysore 95)***

Ans. $f(x) = \frac{1}{3} + \frac{4}{\pi^2} \sum_1^\infty \frac{\cos n\pi x}{n^2}$

11. Find the half range sine series for $f(x) = x - x^2$, $0 < x < 1$. ***(Andhra 98, S. Palel 97)***

Ans. $f(x) = \frac{8}{\pi^3} \left[\frac{\sin \pi x}{1^3} + \frac{\sin 3\pi x}{3^3} + \frac{\sin 5\pi x}{5^3} + \ldots \right]$

12. Obtain the Fourier expansion of $x \sin x$ as a cosine series in $(0, \pi)$. ***(Andhra 98)***

Ans. $1 - \frac{1}{2} \cos x - \frac{2 \cos 2x}{1 \cdot 3} + \frac{2 \cos 3x}{2 \cdot 4} - \frac{2 \cos 4x}{3 \cdot 5} + \ldots$

2.15 PARSEVAL'S THEOREM ON FOURIER CONSTANTS

If a function $f(x)$ has a Fourier expansion for the interval $(-l, l)$ and if the series be convergent uniformly in this interval then

$$\frac{1}{2l} \int_{-l}^{l} [f(x)]^2 dx = \left(\frac{a_0}{2} \right)^2 + \frac{1}{2} \sum_1^\infty (a_n^2 + b_n^2) \qquad \ldots(1)$$

where

$$f(x) = \frac{1}{2} a_0 + \sum_1^\infty \left(a_n \cos \frac{n\pi x}{l} + b_n \sin \frac{n\pi x}{l} \right) \qquad \ldots(2)$$

is its fourier expansion where $a_0 = \frac{1}{l}\int_{-l}^{l} f(x)\,dx,$

PROOF. $a_n = \frac{1}{l}\int_{-l}^{l} f(x)\cos\frac{n x \pi}{l}\,dx$ and $b_n = \frac{1}{l}\int_{-l}^{l} f(x)\sin\frac{n\pi x}{l}\,dx$

Multiplying both sides of (2) by $f(x)$

$$[f(x)]^2 = \frac{1}{2}a_0 f(x) + \sum_1^\infty a_n f(x)\cos\frac{n\pi x}{l} + \sum_1^\infty b_n f(x)\sin\frac{n\pi x}{l} \quad ...(3)$$

Integrating (3) from $-l$ to l

$$\int_{-l}^{l} f^2(x)\,dx = \frac{1}{2}a_0\int_{-l}^{l} f(x)\,dx + \sum_1^\infty a_n\int_{-l}^{l} f(x)\cos\frac{n\pi x}{l}\,dx + \sum_1^\infty b_n\int_{-l}^{l} f(x)\sin\frac{n\pi x}{l}\,dx$$

or $$\int_{-l}^{l} f^2\,dx = \frac{1}{2}a_0\, l\, a_0 + \sum_1^\infty a_n\, a_n\, l + \sum_1^\infty b_n\,(l\, b_n)$$

$$\frac{1}{2l}\int_{-l}^{l} f^2\,dx = \left(\frac{a_0}{2}\right)^2 + \frac{1}{2}\sum_1^\infty (a_n^2 + b_n^2) \quad ...(4)$$

Hence proved.

If $f(x)$ be defined for $0 < x < 2l$, then (4) changes to $\frac{1}{2l}\int_0^{2l} f^2\,dx = \left(\frac{a_0}{2}\right)^2 + \frac{1}{2}\sum_1^\infty (a_n^2 + b_n^2)$, with corresponding changes in the limits for values of a_0, a_n and b_n.

For the half range series for formula changes to

(i) for half range cosine series $\frac{1}{l}\int_0^{l} [f(x)]^2\,dx = \left(\frac{a_0}{2}\right)^2 + \frac{1}{2}\sum_1^\infty a_n^2$

and (ii) for half range sine series $\frac{1}{l}\int_0^{l} [f(x)]^2 = \frac{1}{2}\sum_0^\infty b_n^2.$

2.16 ROOT MEAN SQUARE (rms) VALUE

The root mean square value of a function $f(x)$ integrated over the interval (a, b) = square root of mean of the integral of $f^2(x)$

$$\text{Mean} = \overline{f^2(x)} = \frac{1}{b-a}\int_a^b f^2(x)\,dx$$

$$\text{Root mean} = \sqrt{(\overline{f^2(x)})} = \sqrt{\frac{1}{b-a}\int_a^b f^2(x)\,dx}\,.$$

In alternating current phenomena where the mean current is zero the rms values are calculated. Wherever period functions are used, in electric circuit theorem or in mechanical vibrations, root mean square values are used. The r.m.s. value of the periodic function over its whole period is also known as its effective value.

Example 2.19 **Use Fourier's expansion of x^2 in $-\pi$ and π and the Parceval's identity to prove**

$$\frac{\pi^4}{90} = \Sigma\, 1 + \frac{1}{2^4} + \frac{1}{3^4} + \ldots$$

(Madras 95)

Solution : $f(x) = x^2$ is an even function. So in its fourier expansion $b_n = 0$, and we have

$$f(x) = \frac{a_0}{2} + \sum_1^{\infty} a_n \cos nx$$

$$a_0 = \frac{1}{\pi}\int_{-\pi}^{\pi} x^2\, dx = \frac{1}{\pi}\, 2\, \frac{\pi^3}{3} = \frac{2}{3}\pi^2 \qquad \ldots(1)$$

$$a_n = \frac{1}{\pi}\int_{-\pi}^{\pi} x^2 \cos nx\, dx$$

$$= \frac{2}{\pi}\left[\frac{x^2 \sin nx}{n} + \frac{2x\cos nx}{n^2} - \frac{2\sin nx}{n^3}\right]_0^{\pi}$$

$$= \frac{2}{\pi}\left[\frac{2}{n^2}(-1)^n\right]$$

So $$f(x) = \frac{\pi^2}{3} + \Sigma\, 4\,(-1)^n \frac{\cos nx}{n^2} \qquad \ldots(2)$$

Parcevel's identify is

$$\frac{1}{2\pi}\int_{-\pi}^{\pi} f^2(x)\, dx = \left(\frac{a_0}{2}\right)^2 + \frac{\Sigma\,(a_n^2 + b_n^2)}{2}$$

$$\text{L.H.S.} = \frac{1}{2\pi}\int_{-\pi}^{\pi} x^4\, dx = \frac{1}{2\pi}\, 2\int_0^{\pi} x^4\, dx = \frac{1}{\pi}\left[\frac{x^5}{5}\right]_0^{\pi} = \frac{\pi^4}{5} \qquad \ldots(3)$$

$$\left(\frac{a_0}{2}\right)^2 = \left(\frac{2}{3}\frac{\pi^2}{2}\right)^2 = \frac{\pi^4}{9} \qquad \ldots(4)$$

$$\frac{\Sigma\, a_n^2 + 0^2}{2} = \frac{1}{2}\sum_1^{\infty}\left\{\frac{4\,(-1)^n}{n^2}\right\}^2 = 8\sum_1^{\infty}\frac{1}{n^4} \qquad \ldots(5)$$

Hence $$\frac{\pi^4}{5} = \frac{\pi^4}{9} + 8\sum_1^{\infty}\frac{1}{n^4}$$

or $$\frac{\pi^4}{90} = \sum_1^{\infty}\frac{1}{n^4} = \left(\frac{1}{1^4} + \frac{1}{2^4} + \frac{1}{3^4} + \ldots\right)$$

Hence proved.

PROBLEM SET 2.6

1. If $f(x)$ has the Fourier expansion for $f(x)$ is $\alpha \le x \le \alpha + 2l$

Show $\frac{1}{2l}\int_{\alpha}^{\alpha+2l} [f(x)]^2\, dx = \left(\frac{a_0}{2}\right)^2 + \frac{1}{2}\sum_{1}^{\infty} (a_n^2 + b_n^2),$

where $f(x) = \frac{a_0}{2} + \sum_{1}^{\infty}\left(a_n \cos\frac{nx\pi}{l} + b_n \sin\frac{n\pi x}{l}\right)$

With $a_0 = \frac{1}{l}\int_{\alpha}^{\alpha+2l} f(x)\, dx,\quad a_n = \frac{1}{l}\int_{\alpha}^{\alpha+2l} f(x)\cos\frac{n\pi x}{l}\, dx$ and

$$b_n = \frac{1}{l}\int_{\alpha}^{\alpha+2l} f(x)\sin\frac{n\pi x}{l}\, dx$$

2. If $f(x) = \frac{a_0}{2} + \sum_{1}^{\infty} a_n \cos\frac{n\pi x}{l}$, $0 < x < l$ be the half range cosine series of $f(x) = x$, prove

$$\frac{1}{l}\int_0^l [f(x)]^2\, dx = \left(\frac{a_0}{2}\right)^2 + \frac{1}{2}\sum_{1}^{\infty} a_n^2$$

(Madras 86, 93)

3. If $f(x) = \sum_{1}^{\infty} b_n \sin\frac{n\pi x}{l}$ be the Fourier half range sine series for $f(x)$ in $(0, l)$, show that

$$\frac{1}{l}\int_0^l [f(x)]^2\, dx = \frac{1}{2}\sum_{1}^{\infty} b_n^2.$$

4. Prove that for $0 < x < l$,

$$x = \frac{l}{2} - \frac{4l}{\pi^2}\left(\cos\frac{\pi x}{l} + \frac{1}{3^2}\cos\frac{3\pi x}{l} + \frac{1}{5^2}\cos\frac{5\pi x}{l} + \ldots\right)$$

and deduce that $\frac{1}{1^4} + \frac{1}{3^4} + \frac{1}{5^4} + \ldots = \frac{\pi^4}{96}.$

5. By using $f(x) = 1$ in $0 < x < \pi$, show that

$$\frac{\pi^2}{8} = \frac{1}{1^2} + \frac{1}{3^2} + \frac{1}{5^2} + \ldots$$

(Hamirpur 96)

2.17 TYPICAL WAVEFORMS

For the various waveforms met within communication engineering, we give their functions to be used in their Fourier expansions :

(i) Square waveform $f(x) = -k,\ -\pi < x < 0$

$= +k \quad 0 < x < \pi$

$f(x + 2\pi) = f(x)$

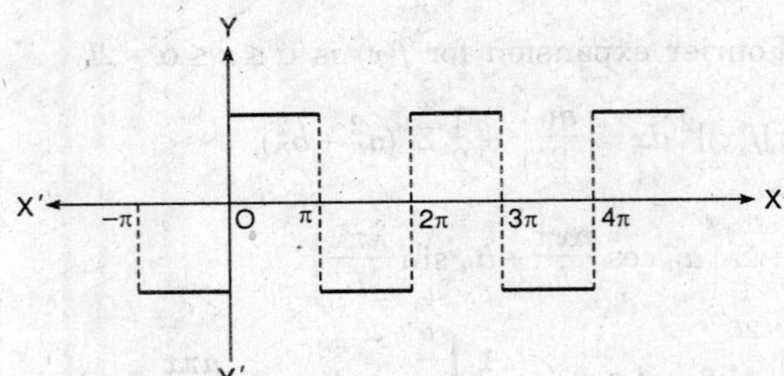

Fig. 2.13

(ii) Saw toothed waveform

$$f(x) = x, \; -\pi < x < \pi$$

$$f(2\pi + x) = f(x).$$

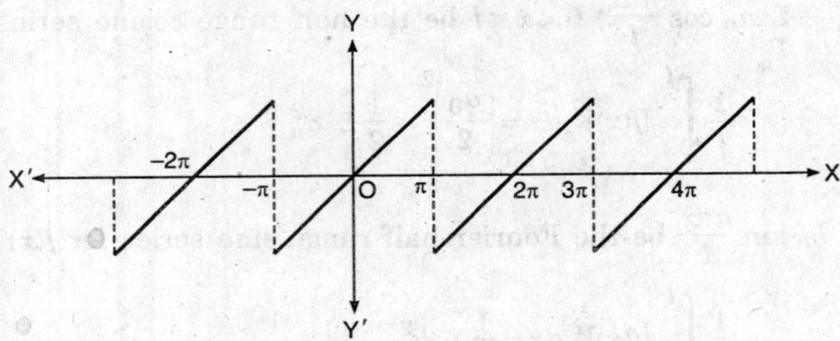

Fig. 2.14

(iii) Triangular waveform

$$f(x) = |x|, \qquad -\frac{l}{2} < x < l/2$$

$$= |l - x|, \qquad \frac{l}{2} < x < l.$$

$$f(\pi + x) = f(x)$$

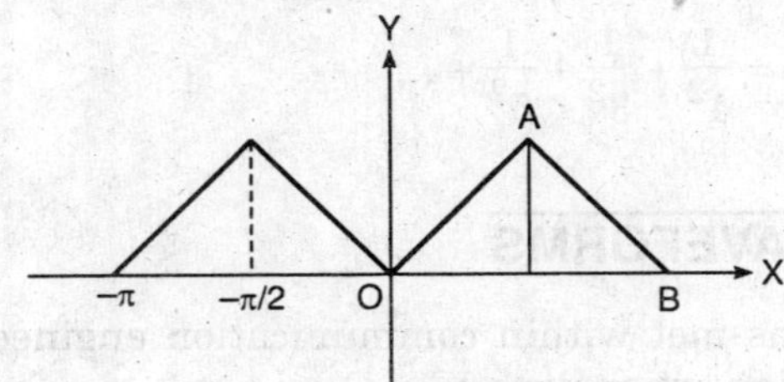

Fig. 2.15

(iv) Half wave rectifier

$$I_0 = I \sin x, \; 0 \le x \le \pi$$
$$= 0 \qquad \pi \le x \le 2\pi$$

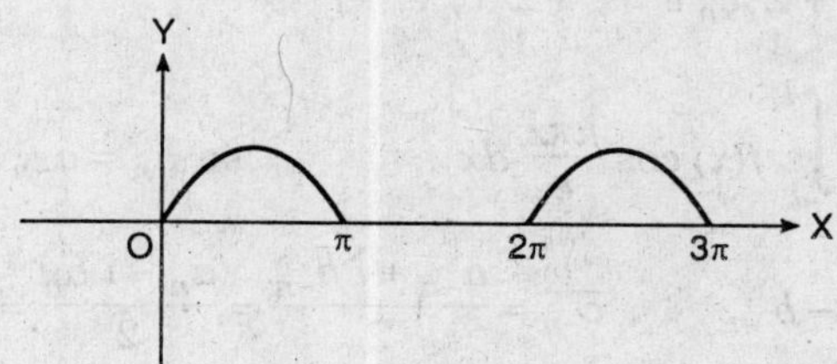

Fig. 2.16

(v) Full wave rectifier

$$I = I_0 \, |\sin x| \; -\pi \le x \le \pi$$

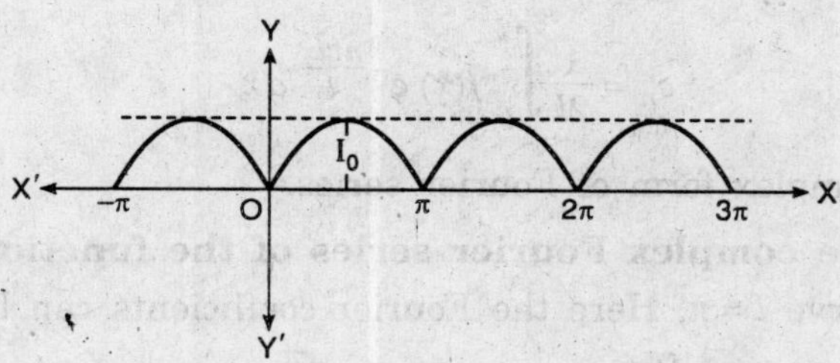

Fig. 2.17

2.18 COMPLEX FORM OF FOURIER SERIES

Using the exponential values of sin θ and cos θ, as given by

$$\sin\theta = \frac{e^{i\theta} - e^{-i\theta}}{2} \text{ and } \cos\theta = \frac{e^{i\theta} + e^{-i\theta}}{2},$$

the Fourier series can be expressed in terms of exponential functions, which is called the Complex form of Fourier series.

If $f(x) = \dfrac{a_0}{2} + \sum_1^{\infty} \left(a_n \cos \dfrac{n\pi x}{l} + b_n \sin \dfrac{n\pi x}{l} \right)$ be the Fourier series of $f(x)$ for $-l < x < l$.

then
$$\left(a_n \cos \frac{n\pi x}{l} + b_n \sin \frac{n\pi x}{l} \right) = a_n \left(\frac{e^{\frac{n\pi xi}{l}} + e^{\frac{-n\pi xi}{l}}}{2} \right) + b_n \left(\frac{e^{\frac{n\pi xi}{l}} - e^{\frac{-n\pi xi}{l}}}{2i} \right)$$
$$= \left(\frac{a_n - i\,b_n}{2} \right) e^{\frac{n\pi ix}{l}} + \left(\frac{a_n + i\,b_n}{2} \right) e^{-\frac{n\pi ix}{l}}$$
$$= c_n e^{\frac{n\pi ix}{l}} + \overline{c_n}\, e^{-\frac{n\pi ix}{l}}$$

where $\overline{c_n} = \dfrac{a_n + i\,b_n}{2}$ is the conjugate of $c_n = \dfrac{a_n - i\,b_n}{2}$

and with $\frac{a_0}{2} = c_0$,

$$f(x) = c_0 + \sum_1^{\infty} c_n e^{\frac{n\pi i x}{l}} + \sum_1^{\infty} \overline{c_n} e^{-\frac{n\pi i x}{l}} \quad ...(1)$$

Further $a_n = \frac{1}{l}\int_{-l}^{l} f(x) \cos\frac{n\pi x}{e} dx$ so $a_n = a_{-n}$

and $b_n = -b_{-n}$ $\overline{c_{-n}} = \frac{a_{-n} + i b_{-n}}{2} = \frac{a_n - i b_n}{2} = c_n$

Hence $\sum_1^{\infty} \overline{c_n} e^{-\frac{n\pi i x}{l}} = \sum_{-\infty}^{-1} \overline{c_{-n}} e^{\frac{n\pi i x}{l}} = \sum_{-\infty}^{-1} c_n \frac{e^{n\pi i x}}{l}$ ...(2)

So (1) can be written as $f(x) = \sum_{-\infty}^{+\infty} c_n e^{\frac{n\pi i x}{l}}$ ...(3)

where $c_n = \frac{1}{2l}\int_{-l}^{l} f(x) e^{-\frac{n\pi i x}{l}} dx$ ...(4)

(3) is called the complex form of Fourier series.

Example 2.20. Find the complex Fourier series of the function $f(x) = e^{-x}$, $-\pi < x < \pi$.

Solution : We observe $l = \pi$, Here the Fourier coefficients can be given as follows :

$$C_n = \frac{1}{2\pi}\int_{-\pi}^{\pi} e^{-x} e^{-inx} dx = \frac{1}{2\pi}\int_{-\pi}^{\pi} e^{-(1+in)x} dx$$

$$= \frac{-1}{2\pi(1+in)}[e^{-(1+in)x}]_{-\pi}^{\pi} = \frac{-1}{2\pi(1+in)}[e^{-(1+in)\pi} - e^{(1+in)\pi}]$$

$$= -\frac{(1-in)}{2\pi(1+n^2)}[e^{-\pi}(\cos n\pi - i\sin n\pi) - e^{\pi}(\cos n\pi + i\sin n\pi)]$$

$$= -\frac{(1-in)}{2\pi(1+n^2)}[-\cos n\pi\,(e^{\pi} - e^{-\pi})] = \frac{\sin h\pi}{\pi(1+n^2)}(1-in)\cos n\pi$$

Thus, the complex form of the Fourier series is

$$f(x) = \frac{\sin h\pi}{\pi}\sum_{n=-\infty}^{\infty} (-1)^n \left(\frac{1-in}{1+n^2}\right) e^{inx}$$

Example 2.21. Find the complex form of the Fourier series for the function $f(x) = e^{ax}$, $-\pi < x < \pi$ where a is a real constant and deduce

(i) $\cos ax = \frac{\sin \pi a}{\pi}\sum_{-\infty}^{\infty} (-1)^n \frac{a}{a^2 - n^2} e^{inx}$, $-\pi < x < \pi$

(ii) $\frac{\pi}{a \sinh a\pi} = \sum_{-\infty}^{\infty} \frac{(-1)^n}{n^2 + a^2}$ *(Madras 91, 92)*

Solution : The complex form of Fourier series of $f(x)$ in $-\pi < x < \pi$

is $$f(x) = \sum_{-\infty}^{\infty} c_n e^{inx} \text{ where } c_n = \frac{1}{2\pi}\int_{-\pi}^{\pi} f(x)\, e^{-nix}\, dx$$

$$c_n = \frac{1}{2\pi}\int_{-\pi}^{\pi} e^{(a-ni)x}\, dx = \frac{1}{2\pi}\left[\frac{e^{(a-ni)\,x}}{a-ni}\right]_{-\pi}^{\pi}$$

$$= \frac{1}{2\pi} \cdot \frac{1}{a-ni}\left(e^{a\pi - ni\pi} - e^{-a\pi + ni\pi}\right)$$

$$= \frac{1}{2\pi}\,\frac{1}{(a-ni)}\left[e^{a\pi}(\cos n\pi i - i\sin n\pi i) - e^{-a\pi}(\cos n\pi i + i \sin n\pi i)\right]$$

$$= \frac{1}{2\pi\,(a-ni)}\,[(-1)^n\, 2\sinh a\pi + 0i] = \frac{(a+ni)\,(-1)^n \sinh a\pi}{\pi\,(a^2+n^2)}$$

Hence $$f(x) = \sum_{-\infty}^{\infty} \frac{(-1)^n \sinh a\pi}{\pi}\,\frac{(a+ni)\,e^{nix}}{(a^2+n^2)} = (e^{+ax} + 0i) \qquad \text{...(1)}$$

PROBLEM 2.7

1. Find the complex form of Fourier series of $f(x)$ on the given interval.

(i) $f(x) = \begin{cases} 1, & -2 \le x < 1 \\ 0, & 1 \le x < 2 \end{cases}$

Ans. $\frac{3}{4} + \frac{1}{2\pi i} \sum_{\substack{n=-\infty \\ n \ne 0}}^{\infty} \left[\frac{1}{n}\,(e^{in\pi} - e^{-in\pi/2})\, e^{in\,x/2}\right]$

(ii) $f(x) = \begin{cases} x, & -\pi < x \le 0 \\ 0, & 0 < x \le \pi \end{cases}$

Ans. $-\frac{\pi}{4} + \frac{1}{2\pi} \sum_{\substack{n=-\infty \\ n \ne 0}}^{\infty} \left[\frac{1}{n^2}\,(1 - e^{in\pi}) + \frac{i\pi}{n}\, e^{in\pi}\right] e^{inx}$

2. Find the complex form of Fourier series of the function $f(x) = e^{-|x|}$, $-2 < x < 2$.

Ans. $\sum_{n=-\infty}^{\infty} \frac{2}{4 + n^2\pi^2}\left[\{1 - (-1)^n e^{-2}\}\right] e^{in\pi\,x/2}$

3. Find the complex form of Fourier series of the function $f(x) = \cos x$, $-\pi < x < \pi$.

Ans. $\frac{a}{\pi} \sin a\pi \sum_{-\infty}^{\infty} \frac{(-1)^n e^{inx}}{a^2 - x^2}$

4. Obtain the complex form of the fourier series of the function $f(x) = \begin{cases} 0, & -\pi \le x < 0 \\ 1, & 0 \le x \le \pi \end{cases}$

Ans. $\frac{1}{2} - \frac{1}{i\pi}\left[(e^{ix} - e^{-ix})\,\frac{1}{3}\,(e^{3ix} - e^{-3ix}) + \frac{1}{5}\,(e^{5ix} - e^{-5ix}) + \ldots\right]$

5. Find the complex form of the Fourier series of the function $f(x) = x + x^2, \ -\pi < x < \pi$.

Ans. $\sum_{n=-\infty}^{\infty} \frac{(-1)^n}{n}\left(\frac{2}{n} + i\right)e^{inx}$

6. Find the complex form of the Fourier series of the function $f(x) = \sin x, \ 0 < x < \pi$.

Ans. $f(x) = \frac{2}{\pi}\left[1 - \left(\frac{e^{2ix} + e^{-2ix}}{1.3}\right) - \left(\frac{e^{4ix} + e^{-4ix}}{3.5}\right) - \ldots\right]$

2.19 PRACTICAL HARMONIC ANALYSIS

If $f(x)$ is defined continuously on $0 \le x \le 2\pi$ the Fourier series of $f(x)$ is given as

$$f(x) = a_0 + \sum_1^{\infty} a_n \cos nx + \sum_1^{\infty} b_n \sin nx$$

$$= a_0 + (a_1 \cos x + b_1 \sin x) + (a_2 \cos 2x + b_2 \sin 2x) + (a_3 \cos 3x + b_3 \sin 3x) + \ldots$$

where the coefficients are given to be

$$a_0 = \frac{1}{2\pi}\int_0^{2\pi} f(x)\, dx = \text{Mean of } f(x) \text{ over the interval } (0, 2\pi),$$

$$a_n = \frac{1}{2\pi}\int_0^{2\pi} 2 f(x) \cos nx\, dx = \text{Mean of } \{2f(x) \cos nx\} \text{ over, the interval } (0, 2\pi)$$

$$b_n = \frac{1}{2\pi}\int_0^{2\pi} 2f(x) \sin nx\, dx = \text{Mean of } \{2f(x) \sin nx\}; \text{ over, the interval } (0, 2\pi)$$

If $f(x)$ is not given continuously but only at certain points over the interval 0 to 2π, for its Fourier series a_0, a_n, b_n are to be calculated by the interpretation as given above.

If we have a graph or a table from which the values of $f(x)$, $f(x) \cos nx$, $f(x) \sin nx$, can be read for $n = 1, 2, \ldots$ for the complete interval 0 to 2π, after finding $a_0, a_n\ b_n$, we get the Fourier series.

The term $(a_1 \cos x + b_1 \sin x)$ of the series is called **the fundamental** or **the first harmonic.**

The **second term** $(a_2 \cos 2x + b_2 \sin 2x)$ is **called the second harmonic and so on.**

Example 2.22. The following table gives the variations of periodic current over a period *T*.

Time *t* is rise	**0**	$\frac{T}{6}$	$\frac{2T}{6}$	$\frac{3T}{6}$	$\frac{4T}{6}$	$\frac{5T}{6}$	$\frac{6T}{6}$
Current *i* in amps	**1.98**	**1.30**	**1.05**	**1.30**	**−0.88**	**−0.25**	**1.98**

Show that there is a direct current part of .75 amp in the variable current and obtain the amplitude of the first harmonic.

Solution : If current $A = a_0 + \left(a \cos \frac{2\pi}{T} t + b_1 \sin \frac{2\pi}{T} t\right) + \ldots$

The constant a_0 will be the direct current part, as it remains constant for all time T.

No.	t	$\frac{2\pi t}{T}$	$\cos\frac{2\pi t}{T}$	$\sin\frac{2\pi t}{T}$	A	$A\frac{\cos 2\pi t}{T}$	$A\frac{\sin 2\pi t}{T}$
1.	0	0	1	0	1.98	1.98	0.00
2.	$\frac{T}{6}$	$\frac{2\pi}{6}=60°$	.5	0.866	1.30	0.65	1.126
3.	$\frac{2T}{6}$	$\frac{4\pi}{6}=120°$	−0.5	0.866	1.05	−0.525	0.909
4.	$\frac{3T}{6}$	$\frac{6\pi}{6}=180°$	−1.0	0.000	1.30	−1.30	0.000
5.	$\frac{4T}{6}$	$\frac{8\pi}{6}=240°$	−0.5	−0.866	−0.88	+0.44	0.762
6.	$\frac{5T}{6}$	$\frac{10\pi}{6}=300°$	+0.5	−0.866	−0.25	−0.125	0.217
(Last value $t = T$ is same as $t = 0$. Only one of them is to be considered)							
	$0=\frac{6T}{6}$	$\frac{12\pi}{6}=360°$	+1.0	0.000	$\Sigma A = 4.5$	$\Sigma A\frac{\cos 2\pi t}{T} = 1.12$	$\Sigma A\frac{\sin 2\pi t}{T} = 3.014$

$$a_0 = \frac{\Sigma A}{6} = \frac{4{\cdot}5}{6} = {\cdot}75$$

$$a_1 = \frac{2\,\Sigma A\cos 2\pi t/6}{6} = \frac{1}{3}(1{\cdot}12) = {\cdot}373,$$

$$b_1 = \frac{1}{3}\,3{\cdot}014 = 1{\cdot}004$$

Direct part of current $= a_0 = {\cdot}75$ amp.

Amplitude of first harmonic

$$= \sqrt{a_1^2 + a_2^2} = \sqrt{({\cdot}373)^2 + (1{\cdot}005)^2} = 1{\cdot}072.$$

Example 2.23. Obtain the first three coefficients in the Fourier Cosine series for *y*, where *y* is given by the following table

x:	0	1	2	3	4	5
y:	4	8	15	7	6	2

(Andhra 99, Mysore 97, Kanpur 96, AUUP 2008)

Solution : Fourier Cosines series in the interval $0, 2\pi$ is

$$y = a_0 + (a_1\cos\theta + a_2\cos 2\theta + a_3\cos 3\theta \ldots),\ \theta = \frac{2\pi x}{6}.$$

$\theta =$	0°	60°	120°	180°	240°	300°
x	0	1	2	3	4	5
y	4	8	15	7	6	2

x	θ	$\cos\theta$	$\cos 2\theta$	$\cos 3\theta$	y	$y\cos\theta$	$y\cos 2\theta$	$y\cos 3\theta$
0	0°	1	1	1	4	4	4	4
1	60°	0.5	cos 120° = –.5	cos 180° = –1	8	4	–4	–8
2	120°	–0.5	cos 240° = –.5	cos 360° = 1	15	–7.5	–7.5	15
3	180°	–1.0	cos 360° = 1	cos 540° = –1	7	–7	7	–7
4	240°	–0.5	cos 480° = –.5	cos 720° = +1	6	–3	–3	6
5	300°	+0.5	cos 600° = –.5	cos 900° = –1	2	1	–1	–2
					$\Sigma y = 42$	$\Sigma y \cos\theta = -8{\cdot}5$	$\Sigma y \cos 2\theta = -4{\cdot}58$	$\Sigma y \cos 3\theta = 8$

Hence $a_0 = \frac{42}{6} = 7,$ $\qquad a_1 = \frac{2(-8\cdot5)}{6} = -2{\cdot}8,$

$a_2 = \frac{2(-4{\cdot}5)}{6} = -1{\cdot}5,$ $\qquad a_3 = 2(8/6) = 2{\cdot}7$

$$f(x) = a_0 + a_1 \cos\theta + a_2 \cos 2\theta + a_3 \cos 3\theta$$

where $\theta = \frac{2\pi x}{6}$.

$$= 7 + (-2{\cdot}8)\cos\theta + (-1{\cdot}5)\cos 2\theta + (2{\cdot}7)\cos 3\theta$$

Example 2.24. Obtain the constant term and the coefficients of the first sine and cosine terms in the Fourier expansion of y as given by the following table :

x:	0	1	2	3	4	5
y:	0	18	24	28	26	20

(Karnataka 94, Punjab 90, Kerala 96, Madras 92)

Solution : Let $y = a_0 + \left(a_1 \cos\frac{\pi}{3}x + b_1 \sin\frac{\pi x}{3}\right) + \left(a_2 \cos\frac{2\pi x}{3} + b_2 \sin\frac{2\pi x}{3}\right) + \ldots$

x	$\cos\frac{\pi x}{3}$	$\sin\frac{\pi x}{3}$	y	$y\cos\frac{\pi x}{3}$	$y\sin\frac{\pi x}{3}$
0	cos 0° = 1	sin 0° = 0	9	9	0
1	cos 60° = .5	sin 60° = .866	18	9	18 × .866
2	cos 120° = –.5	sin 120° = .866	24	–12	24 × .866
3	cos 180° = –1	sin 180° = 0	28	–28	0
4	cos 240° = –.5	sin 240° = –.866	26	–13	–26 × .866
5	cos 300° = +.5	sin 300° = –.866	20	10	–20 × .866
			$\Sigma y = 125$	$\Sigma y \cos \frac{\pi x}{3} = -25$	$\Sigma y \sin\left(\frac{\pi x}{3}\right) = -4 \times 8{\cdot}66$

$$a_0 = \frac{\Sigma y}{6} = \frac{125}{6} = 20{\cdot}83;$$

$$a_1 = \frac{2\Sigma y \cos\left(\frac{\pi x}{3}\right)}{6} = -\frac{25}{3} = -8{\cdot}33$$

$$b_1 = \frac{2}{6}\Sigma y \sin\frac{\pi x}{3} = -\frac{4}{3}\times{\cdot}866 = -1{\cdot}15$$

Hence $y = 20{\cdot}83 + \left(-8{\cdot}33\cos\frac{\pi x}{3} - 1{\cdot}15\sin\frac{\pi x}{3}\right) + \ldots$

Example 2.25. The turning moment T units of the crank shaft of a steam engine is given for a sreis of values of the crank angle θ in degrees

θ:	0°	30°	60°	90°	120°	150°	180°
T:	0	5224	8097	7850	5499	2626	0.

Find the first four terms in a series of series to represent T. Also calculate T for $\theta = 75°$. *(Rewa 94, Delhi 92)*

Solution : Example Let the half range sine series to represent T be

$$T = b_1 \sin\theta + b_2 \sin 2\theta + b_3 \sin 3\theta + b_4 \sin 4\theta, \quad \theta \text{ is in radians.}$$

θ	$\sin\theta$	$\sin 2\theta$	$\sin 3\theta$	$\sin 4\theta$	T	$T\sin\theta$	$T\sin 2\theta$	$T\sin 3\theta$	$T\sin 4\theta$
0°	0	0	0	0	0	0	0	0	0
30°	.5	.866	1	.866	5224	$\frac{1}{2}\times 5224$	$\frac{\sqrt{3}}{2}\times .5224$	.5224	$\frac{\sqrt{3}}{2}\times 5224$
60°	.866	.866	0	–.866	8097	$\frac{\sqrt{3}}{2}\times 8097$	$\frac{\sqrt{3}}{2}\times 8097$	0	$\frac{\sqrt{3}}{2}\times 8097$
90°	1.0	0	–1	0	7850	1×7850	0	–7850	0
120°	.866	–.866	0	.866	5499	$\frac{\sqrt{3}}{2}\times 5499$	$-\frac{\sqrt{3}}{2}\times 5499$	0	$\frac{\sqrt{3}}{2}\times 5499$
150°	.5	–.866	1	–.866	2626	$\frac{1}{2}\times 2626$	$-\frac{\sqrt{3}}{2}\times 2626$	2626	$-\frac{\sqrt{3}}{2}\times 2626$

$$b_1 = \frac{2}{6}\Sigma T\sin\theta$$

$$= \frac{1}{3}\left[\frac{1}{2}(5224 + 2626) + {\cdot}866(8097 + 5499) + 7850\right] = \frac{23549}{3} = 7850$$

$$b_2 = \frac{1}{3}\left[\frac{\sqrt{3}}{2}(5224 + 8097 - 5499 - 2626)\right] = \frac{1}{3}\times 0{\cdot}866\times 5197 = 1500$$

$$b_3 = \frac{1}{3}[5224 - 7850 + 2626] = 0$$

$$b_4 = \frac{1}{3}\left[\frac{\sqrt{3}}{2}(5224 + 8097 + 5499 - 2626)\right] = 0$$

Hence $T = b_1\sin\theta + b_2\sin 2\theta + 0 + 0$

$$= 7850\sin\theta + 1500\sin 2\theta$$

$$T \text{ for } \theta = 75 = 7850 \sin 75° + 1500 \times \frac{1}{2} = 7850 \times \cdot 9659 + 750$$

$$= 8332.$$

Example 2.26. Analyse harmonically the data given below and express y is Fourier series upto the third harmonic.

x:	0	$\pi/3$	$2\pi/3$	π	$45\pi/3$	$5\pi/3$	2π
y:	1·0	1·4	1·9	1·7	1·5	1·2	1·0

(Madras 91, 93, 94)

Solution : The value for $\theta = 2\pi$ and $\theta = 0$ are the same so $\theta = 2\pi$ is not to be taken into account.

Let $y = a_0 + (a_1 \cos x + b_1 \sin x) + (a_2 \cos 2x + b_2 \sin 2x) + (a_3 \cos 3x + b_3 \sin 3x)$.

The values of $x, y, y \cos x, y \cos 2x, y \cos 3x, y \sin x$ etc. are as tabulated below :

x	$\cos x$	$\cos 2x$	$\cos 3x$	y	$y \cos x$	$y \cos 2x$	$y \cos 3x$
0	1	1	1	1	1	1	1
$\pi/3$	$\frac{1}{2}$	$-\frac{1}{2}$	–1	1.4	.7	–.7	–1.4
$2\pi/3$	$-\frac{1}{2}$	$-\frac{1}{2}$	1	1.9	–.95	–.95	1.9
π	–1	1	–1	1.7	–1.7	1.7	–1.7
$4\pi/3$	$-\frac{1}{2}$	$-\frac{1}{2}$	1	1.5	–.75	–.75	1.5
$5\pi/3$	$\frac{1}{2}$	$-\frac{1}{2}$	–1	1.2	+.60	–.60	–1.2
				$\Sigma y = 8.7$	$\Sigma y \cos x = -1.1$	$\Sigma y \cos 2x = -.3$	$\Sigma y \cos 3x = -.1$

$$a_0 = \frac{8 \cdot 7}{6} = 1 \cdot 45, \qquad a_1 = -\frac{1 \cdot 1 \times 2}{6} = - \cdot 37$$

$$a_2 = -\frac{\cdot 3 \times 2}{6} = - \cdot 1, \qquad a_3 = -\frac{\cdot 1 \times 2}{3} = - 0 \cdot 033$$

x	$\sin x$	$\sin 2x$	$\sin 3x$	y	$y \sin x$	$y \sin 2x$	$y \sin 3x$
0	0	0	0	1	0	0	0
$\pi/3$	$\frac{\sqrt{3}}{2}$	$\frac{\sqrt{3}}{2}$	0	1.4	$\frac{\sqrt{3}}{2} \times 1.4$	$\frac{\sqrt{3}}{2} \times 1.4$	0
$2\pi/3$	$\frac{\sqrt{3}}{2}$	$-\frac{\sqrt{3}}{2}$	0	1.9	$\frac{\sqrt{3}}{2} \times 1.9$	$-\frac{\sqrt{3}}{2} \times 1.9$	0
π	0	0	0	1.7	0	0	0
$4\pi/3$	$-\frac{\sqrt{3}}{2}$	$\frac{\sqrt{3}}{2}$	0	1.5	$-\frac{\sqrt{3}}{2} \times 1.5$	$\frac{\sqrt{3}}{2} \times 1.5$	0
$5\pi/3$	$-\frac{\sqrt{3}}{2}$	$-\frac{\sqrt{3}}{2}$	0	1.2	$-\frac{\sqrt{3}}{2} \times 1.2$	$-\frac{\sqrt{3}}{2} \times 1.2$	0
					$\Sigma y \sin x = .866 \times .6$	$\Sigma y \sin 2x = -.2$	$\Sigma = 0$

$$b_1 = \frac{2\,\Sigma\, y \sin x}{6} = \frac{1}{3} \times \cdot 866 \times \cdot 6 = \cdot 17$$

$$b_2 = \frac{2\,\Sigma\, y \sin 2x}{6} = \frac{1}{3}(-\cdot 2) = -\cdot 06$$

$$b_3 = 0$$

Hence $y = 1{\cdot}45 + (-\cdot 37 \cos x + \cdot 17 \sin x) - (\cdot 1 \cos 2x + \cdot 06 \sin 2x) + (\cdot 03 \cos 3x + 0 \sin 3x)$

Example 2.27. **The following values of y give the displacement in inches of a machine part for rotation x of the flywheel. Expand y in the form of a Fourier series :**

x :	0	$\pi/6$	$\frac{2\pi}{6}$	$\frac{3\pi}{6}$	$\frac{4\pi}{6}$	$\frac{5\pi}{6}$
y :	0	9.2	14.4	17.8	17.3	11.7

(Madurai 90, Bangalore 94, Calicut 96)

Let $x' = 2x$	$\cos x' = \cos 2x$	$\cos 2x'$ $\cos 4x$	$\sin x'$ $\sin 2x$	$\sin 2x'$ $\sin 4x$	y	$y \cos x' = y \cos 2x$
0	1	1	0	0	0	0
$x' = \pi/3$	$\frac{1}{2}$	$-\frac{1}{2}$	$\frac{\sqrt{3}}{2}$	$\frac{\sqrt{3}}{2}$	9.2	$\frac{1}{2} \times 9.2$
$x' = 2\pi/3$	$-\frac{1}{2}$	$-\frac{1}{2}$	$+\frac{\sqrt{3}}{2}$	$-\frac{\sqrt{3}}{2}$	14.4	$-\frac{1}{2} \times 9.2$
$x' = \pi$	-1	$+1$	0	0	17.8	-17.8
$x' = \frac{4\pi}{3}$	$-\frac{1}{2}$	$-\frac{1}{2}$	$\frac{\sqrt{3}}{2}$	$\frac{\sqrt{3}}{2}$	17.3	$-\frac{1}{2} \times 17.3$
$x' = \frac{5\pi}{3}$	$\frac{1}{2}$	$-\frac{1}{2}$	$-\frac{\sqrt{3}}{2}$	$-\frac{\sqrt{3}}{2}$	11.7	$\frac{1}{2}$ 11.7

Solution : We get $a_0 = \frac{1}{6}\Sigma y = \frac{1}{6} 70{\cdot}4 = 11{\cdot}73$

$$a_1 = \frac{2}{6}\Sigma y \cos 2x = \frac{1}{3}[\cdot 5\,(9{\cdot}2 - 14{\cdot}4 - 17{\cdot}3 + 11{\cdot}7) - 17{\cdot}8]$$

$$= \frac{1}{3}(-23{\cdot}2) = -7{\cdot}73$$

$$a_2 = \frac{2}{6}\Sigma y \cos 4x = \frac{1}{3}[-\cdot 5\,(9{\cdot}2 + 14{\cdot}4 + 17{\cdot}3 + 11{\cdot}7) + 17{\cdot}8]$$

$$= \frac{1}{3}(-8{\cdot}5) = -2{\cdot}83$$

$$b_1 = \frac{1}{3}[\cdot 87\,(9{\cdot}2 + 14{\cdot}4 - 17{\cdot}3 - 11{\cdot}7)] = \frac{\cdot 87}{3}(-5{\cdot}4) = -1{\cdot}566$$

$$b_2 = \frac{1}{6}[\cdot 87\,(9{\cdot}2 - 14{\cdot}4 + 17{\cdot}3 - 11{\cdot}7)] = \frac{1}{3} \times \cdot 87 \times 4 = \cdot 116$$

Hence $y = a_0 + (a_1 \cos 2x + b_1 \sin 2x) + (a_2 \cos 4x + b_2 \sin 4x)$

$$= 11{\cdot}73 + (-7{\cdot}73 \cos 2x - 1{\cdot}56 \sin 2x) + (-2{\cdot}83 \cos 4x + \cdot 116 \sin 4x)$$

PROBLEM SET 2.8

1. Obtain the first thre coefficients in the Fourier cosine series for y, where y is given as follows :

x :	0	1	2	3	4	5
y :	4	8	15	7	6	2

(Mysore 95, 97S, Ranchi 87)

Ans. $y = 7 - 2{\cdot}8 \cos \theta - 1{\cdot}5 \cos 2\theta + 2{\cdot}7 \cos 3\theta$.

2. The following values of y give the displacement of a certain machine part for the rotation x of the flywheel

x :	0°	60°	120°	180°	240°	300°
y :	1·98	2·15	2·77	– ·22	– ·31	1·43

Express y in Fourier series upto the third harmonic.

$y = 1{\cdot}3 + ({\cdot}92 \cos x + 1{\cdot}097 \sin x) - ({\cdot}42 \cos 2x + {\cdot}681 \sin 2x) + {\cdot}36 \cos 3x$.

3. Determine the first two harmonic of the fourier series for the following series

$x°$:	0°	30°	60°	90°	120°	150°	180°	210°	240°	270°	300°	330°
y :	1.64	2.34	3.01	3.68	4.5	3.69	2.20	0.83	0.51	0.88	1.09	1.19

$y = 2{\cdot}102 - {\cdot}283 \cos x + 1{\cdot}6 \sin x - {\cdot}18 \cos 2x - {\cdot}49 \sin 2x$

4. In a machine the displacement y of a given point is given for a certain angle θ as follows:

$\theta° =$	0	30°	60°	90°	120°	150°	180°	210°	240°	270°	300°	330°
$y =$	7·9	8·0	7·2	5·6	3·6	1·7	0·5	0·2	0·9	2·5	4·7	6·8

Find the coefficient of sin 2θ in the Fourier series representing the above variations.

$\theta = -0{\cdot}072$.

5. The turning moment T on the crank of a steam engine for the crank angle θ degress is as given below :

θ :	0	15°	30°	45°	60°	75°	90°	105°	120°	135°	150°	165°
T :	0	2.7	5.2	7.0	8.1	8.3	7.9	6.8	5.5	4.1	2.6	1.2

Expand T in a series of sines upto third harmonic

$T = 7{\cdot}8 \sin \theta + 1{\cdot}5 \sin 2\theta - {\cdot}03 \sin 3\theta$

6. The displacements y of a part of a machine for angular movement $\theta°$ of the crank angle are as follows.

$x°$	0	30°	60°	90°	120°	155°	180°	210°	240°	270°	300°	330°
T :	1.80	1.10	0.30	0.16	0.50	1.30	2.16	1.25	1.30	1.52	1.76	2.0

(S. Patel 1996S, Coimbatore 88)

Express y as a Fourier series upto third harmonic.

Ans. $y = 1{\cdot}26 + ({\cdot}04 \cos x - {\cdot}63 \sin x) + ({\cdot}53 \cos 2x - {\cdot}23 \sin 2x) + (-{\cdot}1 \cos 3x + {\cdot}085 \sin 3x)$.

2.20 FOURIER TRANSFORM : AN INTRODUCTION

Oliver Haeviside (1850—1925), an **English engineer**, used transform techniques, also known as **operational calculus** in solving the boundary value problems of differential equations arising in electrical engineering. Starting with Laplace transform, many more integral transforms, are now defined, wherever formula for their inverse could be possible. On taking integral transform of a partial differential equation, for one variable, the number of independent variables in the differential equation is reduced by one. The choice of a transform used for solving a partial differential equation depends on the equation and the boundary conditions, given.

2.21 DEFINITIONS

For a function $f(x)$, the integral

$$\bar{f}(s) = \int_{x_1}^{x_2} f(x)\, k(s, x)\, dx,$$

is called the **integral transform of $f(x)$**, with respect to the **kernel $k(s, x)$**. The integral transform is well defined only when there exists another kernel $k_2(s, x)$ such that

$$f(x) = \int_{s_1}^{s_2} \bar{f}(s)\, k_2(s, x)\, dx.$$

2.22 IMPORTANT TRANSFORMS

(i) **Laplace Transform** for which the kernel is $k(s, x) = e^{-kx}$ for $-\infty < x < \infty$ is a two sided transform

$$L\, f(x) = \bar{f}(s) = \int_{-\infty}^{\infty} f(x)\, e^{-sx}\, dx.$$

If x lies only in $0 < x < \infty$, then **one sided Laplace transform** is defined as

$$L\,\{f(x)\} = \int_{0}^{\infty} f(x)\, e^{-sx}\, dx$$

(ii) **Fourier Transform**

Kernel $k(s, x) = e^{-isx}$, $(-\infty < x < \infty)$

$$F\,\{f(x)\} = \int_{-\infty}^{\infty} f(x)\, e^{-isx}\, dx$$ is called the **Fourier transform** of $f(x)$.

(iii) **Hankel Transform,**

For kernel $k(s, x) = J_n(st)$, $0 < x < \infty$

$$H\,\{f(x)\} = \bar{f}(s) = \int_{0}^{\infty} f(x)\, x\, J_n(sx)\, dx$$ is known as **Hankel's transform** of $f(x)$.

(iv) **Mellin Transform,**

$k(s, t) = t^{s-1}, \ 0 < t < \infty$

$M\{f(x)\} = \bar{f}(s) = \int_0^{\infty} f(t)\, t^{s-1}\, dt$, is called the Mellin transform of $f(x)$.

Fourier sine and cosine transform are special forms of the Fourier transform, which will be considered in this chapter.

2.23 FOURIER TRANSFORM

The **French mathematician J.B.J. Fourier** (1768—1830) showed that any periodic signal or a function can be represented by an infinite series of sinusoids (a series of sines and cosine terms of frequencies $\frac{2\pi}{T}, 2\left(\frac{2\pi}{T}\right) \ldots$.

If a function is non periodic, it may be regarded as periodic with its period $T \to \infty$. In that case the frequencies of successive terms become infinitely close and the series change into an integral related to the Fourier transform.

For a function $f(t)$, the integral

$$\boldsymbol{F\{f(t)\} = S(i\omega)} = \int_{-\infty}^{\infty} f(t)\, e^{-i\omega t}\, dt \qquad \ldots(1)$$

is called the **Fourier Transform** of $f(t)$ and its inverse fourier transform $F^{-1}\{S(i\omega)\}$ is given by

$$F^{-1}\{S(i\omega)\} = \frac{1}{2\pi}\int_{-\infty}^{\infty} S(i\omega)\, e^{i\omega t}\, d\omega \qquad \ldots(2)$$

Some authors associate $\frac{1}{\sqrt{2}\,\pi}$ with F transform and $\frac{1}{\sqrt{2}\,\pi}$ also with inverse transform F^{-1}. Ultimately the product of coefficients becomes $= \frac{1}{2\pi}$ as in (2) above. It is to be noted that the sign of i is opposite in the kernels of F transform and its inverse. If it is $e^{i\omega t}$ in one, it is $e^{-\omega t}$ in its inverse or vice-versa.

2.23.1 Fourier Sine Transform $\bar{F}_S\{f(x)\}$ or $F_S(s)$

It is defined as

$$\bar{F}_S(s) = \sqrt{\frac{2}{\pi}}\int_0^{\infty} f(t)\sin st\, dt$$

Inverse sine transform. It is defined by

$$f(t) = \sqrt{\frac{2}{\pi}}\int_0^{\infty} \bar{F}_S(s)\sin st\, ds.$$

2.23.2 Fourier Cosine Transform

$$\overline{F}_C\,[f(x)] \quad \text{or} \quad = \overline{F}_C(s) = \sqrt{\frac{2}{\pi}} \int f(t) \cos st\, dt$$

and its **inverse transform is**

$$f(t) = \sqrt{\frac{2}{\pi}} \int_0^{\infty} \overline{F}_C(s) \cos st\, ds.$$

2.24 FOURIER INTEGRAL THEOREM

If a function satisfies the Dirichlet's conditions (It is single valued, periodic and is either continuous or has only a finite number of finite discontinuities in every finite interval $-l$ to $+l$) then it can be represented as a series of sines and cosines of multiples of $\frac{\pi x}{l}$ as

$$f(x) = \frac{1}{2} a_0 + \sum_1^{\infty} a_n \cos \frac{n\pi}{l} x + \sum_1^{\infty} b_n \sin \frac{n\pi}{l} x \qquad \text{...(1)}$$

where the coefficients on integration after multiplying with 1, $\cos \frac{n\pi x}{l}$, $\sin \frac{n\pi x}{l}$ respectively are given by

$$\boldsymbol{a_0} = \frac{1}{l} \int_{-l}^{l} f(\xi)\, d\xi;$$

$$\boldsymbol{a_n} = \frac{1}{l} \int_{-l}^{l} f(\xi) \cos n \frac{\pi}{l} \xi\, d\xi$$

and

$$\boldsymbol{b_n} = \frac{1}{l} \int_{-l}^{l} f(\xi) \sin \frac{n\pi}{l} \xi\, d\xi \qquad \text{...(2)}$$

On putting the values of these constants in (1), it takes the form

$$f(x) = \frac{1}{2l} \int_{-l}^{l} f(\xi)\, d\xi + \sum_{n=1}^{\infty} \frac{1}{l} \int_{-l}^{l} f(\xi) \cos \frac{n\pi}{l} (\xi - x)\, d\xi \qquad \text{...(3)}$$

Here if we allow l to tend to ∞, then as $\int_{-l}^{l} f(\xi)\, d\xi$ is finite,

so
$$\lim_{l \to \infty} \frac{1}{2l} \int_{-l}^{l} f(\xi)\, d\xi \to 0$$

and replacing $\frac{\pi}{l}$ by $d\lambda_1$, $\frac{n\pi}{l}$ by λ, the sum (3) change into the integral

$$f(x) = \frac{1}{\pi} \int_{-\infty}^{\infty} \int_0^{\infty} f(\xi) \cos \lambda (\xi - x)\, d\xi\, d\lambda \qquad \text{...(4)}$$

As **cos** $\lambda\,(\xi - \boldsymbol{x})$ is an even function so

$$\int_0^{\infty} \cos \lambda\,(\xi - x)\, d\lambda = \frac{1}{2}\int_{-\infty}^{\infty} \cos \lambda\,(\xi - x)\, d\lambda$$

Hence $$f(x) = \frac{1}{2\pi}\int_{-\infty}^{\infty}\int_{-\infty}^{\infty} f(\xi) \cos \lambda\,(\xi - x)\, d\xi\, d\lambda \qquad ...(5)$$

(Madurai 90)

It is called the **Fourier integral formula** for $f(x)$. The integral on R,H.S. represents $f(x)$ at all the points of continuity of $f(x)$. At a point of discontinuity, of $f(x)$, the integral equals to $\frac{1}{2}\{f(x-0) + f(x+0)\}$ where $f(x-0)$ is the left limit and $f(x+0)$, the right limit of $f(x)$ at the point of discontinuity x.

2.25 FOURIER COMPLEX INTEGRAL

Replacing $\cos \lambda\,(\zeta - x)$ by $e^{i\lambda(\zeta - x)}$ the representation

$$\boldsymbol{f(x) = \frac{1}{2\pi}\int_{-\infty}^{\infty}\int_{-\infty}^{\infty} f(\xi)\, e^{i\lambda(\xi - x)}\, d\lambda\, d\xi}$$

is called **the complex Fourier integral.**

2.26 FOURIER SINE AND COSINE INTEGRALS

If $f(x)$ is defined only for $0 \le x \le \infty$ then the integral representation

$$\boldsymbol{f(x) = \frac{2}{\pi}\int_0^{\infty} \sin \lambda x \int_0^{\infty} f(\xi) \sin \lambda \xi\, d\xi\, d\lambda}$$

is called **the Fourier sine integral of** $\boldsymbol{f(x)}$.

The integral representation

$$\boldsymbol{f(x) = \frac{2}{\pi}\int_0^{\infty} \cos \lambda x \int_0^{\infty} f(\xi) \cos \lambda \xi\, d\xi\, d\lambda}$$

is called the **Fourier cosine integral of** $f(x)$.

It should be noted that the sine integral and cosine integral represent the same function $f(x)$ in $\boldsymbol{0 < x} < \infty$, but not in $-\infty < x < 0$.

The sine integral represents an odd function in $-\infty < x < 0$. While the cosine integral represents an even function in $-\infty < x < 0$. However if a function be neither completely even nor completely odd as $f(x) = x^2 + x$, it can be expressed as $f(x) = \phi(x) + \psi(x)$ where $\phi(x) = \dfrac{f(x) + f(-x)}{2}$ is even and $\psi(x) = \dfrac{f(x) - f(-x)}{2}$ is odd. A sine integral or a cosine integral both represent $f(x)$ in the common region $0 < x < \infty$, but in the region $-\infty < x < 0$, they represent different functions. The sine integral represents $\psi(x)$ in $-\infty < x < 0$ and the cosine integral represents $\phi(x)$ in $-\infty < x < 0$.

Example 2.28. **Express $f(x) = \begin{cases} 1, & \text{for } 0 \le x \le \pi \\ 0, & \text{for } x > \pi \end{cases}$ as a Fourier sine integral and hence evaluate**

$$\int_0^\infty \frac{1 - \cos \pi \lambda}{\lambda} \sin \lambda x \, d\lambda.$$

(Mangalore 99, Kerala 90, Madurai 90)

Solution : By using the Fourier sine integral, for the given function,

$$f(x) = \frac{2}{\pi} \int_0^\infty \sin \lambda x \, d\lambda \int_0^\infty f(\xi) \sin (\lambda \xi) \, d\xi$$

$$= \frac{2}{\pi} \int_0^\infty \sin \lambda x \, d\lambda \left\{ \int_0^\pi 1 \sin \lambda \xi \, d\xi + 0 \right\} = \frac{2}{\pi} \int_0^\infty \sin \lambda x \left[\frac{\cos \lambda \xi}{-\lambda} \right]_0^\pi d\lambda$$

$$f(x) = \frac{2}{\pi} \int_0^\infty \sin \lambda x \left\{ \frac{-\cos \pi \lambda + 1}{\lambda} \right\} d\lambda$$

Hence $\displaystyle\int_0^\infty \frac{1 - \cos \pi \lambda}{\lambda} \sin \lambda x \, d\lambda = \frac{\pi}{2} f(x) = \frac{\pi}{2} \begin{cases} 1 & \text{for } 0 \le x \le \pi \\ = 1 & \text{for } x > \pi \end{cases}$

At the point of discontinuity $x = \pi$, the integral equals to

$$\frac{f(\pi - 0) + f(\pi + 0)}{2} = \frac{\pi/2 + 0}{2} = \frac{\pi}{4}.$$

Example 2.29. **Find the Fourier transform of $f(x) = \begin{cases} 1 - x^2, & -1 < x < 1 \\ 0, & |x| > 1 \end{cases}$ and use it to evaluate**

$$\int_0^\infty \frac{x \cos x - \sin x}{x^3} \cos \frac{x}{2} \, dx.$$

(Mysore 97S, Madras 91, 93, 96, 97)

Solution : Taking Fourier transform, $f\{f(x)\} = \dfrac{1}{\sqrt{2\pi}} \displaystyle\int_{-\infty}^\infty f(x) \, e^{isx} \, dx = F_f(s)$ or $= \bar{f}(s)$ of the given function,

$$\bar{f}(s) = \frac{1}{\sqrt{2\pi}} \int_{-1}^1 (1 - x^2) \, e^{isx} \, dx + 0 = \frac{1}{\sqrt{2\pi}} \left[\int_{-1}^0 (1 - x^2) \, e^{isx} \, dx + \int_0^1 (1 - x^2) \, e^{isx} \, dx \right]$$

Let $x = -t$

$$= \frac{1}{\sqrt{2\pi}} \left[\int_1^0 (1 - t^2) \, e^{-ist} \, (-dt) = \int_0^1 (1 - x^2) \, e^{-isx} \, dx \right] + \frac{1}{\sqrt{2\pi}} \int_0^1 (1 - x^2) \, e^{isx} \, dx$$

$$= \frac{1}{\sqrt{2\pi}} \int_0^1 (1 - x^2) \, 2 \cos sx \, dx, \text{ integrating by parts,}$$

$$\bar{f}(s) = \frac{2}{\sqrt{2\pi}}\left[\left\{(1-x^2)\frac{\sin sx}{s}\right\}_0^1 + \frac{2}{s}\int_0^1 x \sin sx\, dx\right] = 0\ 0$$

$$= \frac{4}{s\sqrt{2\pi}}\left[0 + \frac{x\cos sx}{-s} + \frac{\sin sx}{s^2}\right]_0^1$$

$$= \frac{4}{\sqrt{2\pi}}\frac{1}{s^3}(\sin s - s\cos s) \qquad \ldots(1)$$

By the inversion formula for Fourier transform

$$f(x) = \frac{1}{\sqrt{2\pi}}\int_{-\infty}^{\infty} \bar{f}(s)\, e^{-isx}\, dx$$

$$f(x) = \sqrt{2\pi}\,\frac{4}{\sqrt{2\pi}}\left[\int_{-\infty}^{0} \frac{\sin s - s\cos s}{s^3}\, e^{-isx}\, ds + \int_0^{\infty} \frac{\sin s - s\cos s}{s^3}\, e^{-isx}\, dx\right]$$

Let $s = -t$ in first integral,

$$= \frac{4}{2\pi}\left[\int_{\infty}^{0} -\frac{\sin t - t\cos t}{-(t^3)}\, e^{itx}(-dt) = \int_0^{\infty} \frac{\sin t - t\cos t}{t^3}\right] + \frac{4}{2\pi} I_2$$

$$= \frac{4}{2\pi}\int_0^{\infty} \frac{\sin t - t\cos t}{t^3}\,(e^{itx} + e^{-itx})\, dt$$

$$f(x) = -\frac{4}{\pi}\int_0^{\infty} \frac{t\cos t - \sin t}{t^3}\cos tx\, dt$$

Hence $\displaystyle\int_0^{\infty} \frac{x\cos x - \sin x}{x^3}\cos xt\, dx = -\frac{\pi}{4} f(t) = -\frac{\pi}{4}\begin{cases}(1-t^2), & |t| < 1\\ 0, & |t| > 1\end{cases}$

Taking $t = .5$, $|t| < 1$ so

$$\int_0^{\infty} \frac{x\cos x - \sin x}{x^3}\cos\frac{x}{2}\, dx = -\frac{\pi}{4}\left(\frac{3}{4}\right) = -\frac{3\pi}{16},$$

Example 2.30. Find the Fourier transform of $f(x)\begin{cases}1 & \text{for } |x| < 1\\ 0 & \text{for } |x| > 1\end{cases}$

Hence evaluate $\displaystyle\int_0^{\infty} \frac{\sin x}{x}\, dx$

(Andhra 2000; V.T.U. 2000S)

Solution : Taking Fourier transform of $f(x)$

$F\{f(x)\} = \dfrac{1}{\sqrt{2\pi}}\displaystyle\int_{-\infty}^{\infty} f(x)\, e^{isx}\, dx = \dfrac{1}{\sqrt{2\pi}}\int_{-1}^{1} e^{isx}\, dx$, as x is non-zero only from -1 to $+1$

$$= \frac{1}{\sqrt{2\pi}} \frac{[e^{-sx}]_{-1}^{1}}{is} = \frac{2i \sin s}{\sqrt{2\pi}\, is} = \frac{2}{\sqrt{2\pi}} \frac{\sin s}{s}.$$

Taking the inverse Fourier transform of above,

$$f(x) = \frac{1}{\sqrt{2\pi}} \frac{2}{\sqrt{2\pi}} \int_{-\infty}^{\infty} e^{-isx} \frac{\sin s}{s} ds$$

So $$\int_{-\infty}^{\infty} e^{-isx} \frac{\sin s}{s} ds = \pi f(x) = \pi \text{ if } |x| < 1$$

$$= 0 \text{ if } |x| > 1$$

taking limit as $x \to 0$

$$\int_{-\infty}^{\infty} \frac{\sin s}{s} ds = \pi$$

or $$\int_{0}^{\infty} \frac{\sin x}{x} dx = \frac{\pi}{2}.$$

Example 2.31. Find the Fourier transform of $f(x) = \begin{cases} 1, & |x| \le a \\ 0, & |x| > a \end{cases}$ and evaluate $\int_{-\infty}^{\infty} \frac{\sin \lambda a \cos \lambda x}{\lambda} d\lambda$. Hence deduce the value of the integral $\int_{0}^{\infty} \frac{\sin x}{x} dx$

(Raj 2001)

Solution : Taking Fourier transform of $f(x)$

$$F f(x) = \bar{f}(s) = \frac{1}{\sqrt{2\pi}} \left[\int_{-a}^{a} 1\, e^{isx} dx + 0 \right]$$

$$= \frac{1}{\sqrt{2\pi}} \frac{[e^{isx}]_{-a}^{a}}{is} = \frac{1}{\sqrt{2\pi}} \frac{2i \sin as}{is} = \frac{2}{\sqrt{2\pi}} \frac{\sin as}{s} \quad ...(1)$$

Taking the inverse transform of (1)

$$f(x) = \frac{1}{\sqrt{2\pi}} \frac{2}{\sqrt{2\pi}} \int_{-\infty}^{\infty} \frac{\sin as}{s} e^{-isx} ds$$

$$f(x) = \frac{1}{\pi} \int_{-\infty}^{\infty} \frac{\sin as}{s} \{\cos sx - i \sin sx\} ds$$

Separating the real parts

$$\int_{-\infty}^{\infty} \frac{\sin as \cos sx}{s} ds = \pi f(x) = \begin{cases} \pi, & |a| \le 1 \\ 0, & |a| > 1 \end{cases}$$

Taking limit as $x \to 0$

$$\int_{-\infty}^{\infty} \frac{\sin as}{s}\, ds = \pi$$

or
$$\int_0^{\infty} \frac{\sin ax}{x}\, dx = \frac{\pi}{2} \text{ where } |a| < 1$$

Example 2.32. Find the Fourier sine transform of $e^{-|x|}$. Hence show that $\int_0^{\infty} \frac{x \sin mx}{1+x^2}\, dx = \frac{\pi e^{-m}}{2}$, $m > 0$. *(V.T.U. 2000, Kanpur 95)*

Solution : When $0 < x < \infty$, $|x| = x$

Fourier sine transform $e^{-|x|} = F_s\{f(x)\} = \int_0^{\infty} e^{-x} \sin sx\, dx$

$$= \left[e^{-x} \frac{(-\sin sx - s\cos sx)}{1+s^2} \right]_0^{\infty} = 0 - (-)\frac{s}{1+s^2} \qquad ...(1)$$

Taking the inverse transform, we have

$$e^{-|x|} = \frac{2}{\pi}\int_0^{\infty} \frac{s}{1+s^2} \sin sx\, ds.$$ Replacing x by m and s by x,

Hence
$$\int_0^{\infty} \frac{x \sin mx}{1+x^2} = \frac{\pi}{2} e^{-m}$$

Example 2.33. Find the Fourier Cosine transform of $f(x) = \frac{1}{1+x^2}$ *(Bhopal 98)*

Solution :
$$F_c\{f(x)\} = \int_0^{\infty} \frac{\cos sx}{1+x^2}\, dx = I, \text{ (say)} \qquad ...(1)$$

Differentiating w.r.t. s

So
$$\frac{dI}{ds} = \int_0^{\infty} -\frac{x}{1+x^2} \sin sx\, dx = \int_0^{\infty} \frac{1}{x}\left\{\frac{1}{1+x^2} - \frac{1}{1}\right\} \sin sx\, dx$$

$$= \int_0^{\infty} \frac{\sin sx}{x(1+x^2)} - \pi/2, \text{ as } \int_0^{\infty} \frac{\sin sx}{x}\, dx = \frac{\pi}{2} \qquad ...(2)$$

Again differentiating, from above,

$$\frac{d^2 I}{ds} = \int_0^{\infty} \frac{x\cos sx}{x(1+x^2)}\, dx.$$ It is again $= I$ so $(D^2 - 1)I = 0$

where $D = \frac{d}{ds}$

or $$I = C_1 e^s + C_2 e^{-s} \quad ...(3)$$

So $$\frac{dI}{ds} = C_1 e^s - C_2 e^{-s} \quad ...(4)$$

From (1)

$$(I)_{s=0} = \int_0^\infty \frac{1}{1+x^2} dx = [\tan^{-1} x]_0^\infty = \pi/2$$

From (2) $$\left(\frac{dI}{ds}\right)_{s=0} = 0 - \pi/2$$

Hence from (3) and (4)

$$\frac{\pi}{2} = C_1 + C_2 \text{ and } -\frac{\pi}{2} = C_1 - C_2$$

So $C_1 = 0$, $C_2 = \pi/2$ and $I = \frac{\pi}{2} e^{-s}$ from (3)

Example 2.34. Solve the integral equation $\int_0^\infty f(x) \cos \lambda x \, dx = e^{-\lambda}$; $\lambda > 0$

Solution : As cosine transform of any function $f(x)$ is defined by

$$F_C \{f(x)\} = \int_0^\infty f(x) \cos sx \, dx. \quad \text{So, we are to find} \quad ...(1)$$

$f(x)$, whose cosine transform $= e^{-s}$

then by definition of inverse cosine transform

$$f(x) = \frac{2}{\pi} \int_0^\infty e^{-s} \cos sx \, ds$$

So $$f(x) = \frac{2}{\pi} \frac{1}{1+x^2} \{e^{-s} [-\cos sx + s \sin sx]\}_{s=0}^\infty = \frac{0-(-1)}{1+x^2}$$

$$= \frac{2}{\pi}\left(\frac{1}{1+x^2}\right).$$ This is the solution of the given integral equation, ...(2)

Hence from the given equation, $\int_0^\infty \frac{\cos \lambda x}{1+x^2} dx = \frac{\pi}{2} e^{-\lambda}$, (replacing s by λ)

Example 2.35. Prove that $\int_0^\infty \frac{\sin \pi\lambda \cos \lambda x}{1-\lambda^2} d\lambda = \begin{cases} \frac{1}{2}\pi \sin x & 0 < x < \pi \\ 0 & x > \pi \end{cases}$ *(Madras 99)*

Solution : Let $f(x) = \begin{cases} \sin x, & x < \pi \\ 0, & x > \pi \end{cases}$ then its Fourier sine transform is given by

$$F_s \{f(x)\} = -\int_0^\pi \sin x \sin sx \, dx = 0 = \frac{1}{2} \int_0^\pi \{\cos (1-x) x - \cos (1+sx) x\} dx$$

$$= \frac{1}{2}\left[\frac{\sin(1-s)x}{1-s} - \frac{\sin(1+s)x}{1+s}\right]_0^{\pi}$$

$$= \frac{1}{2}\left\{\frac{\sin \pi s}{1-s} - \frac{-\sin \pi s}{1+s}\right\} = \frac{\sin \pi s}{1-s^2}$$

Taking its inverse sine transform

$$f(x) = \frac{2}{\pi}\int_0^{\infty} \frac{\sin \pi s}{1-s^2} \sin sx \, ds, \text{ replacing } s \text{ by } \lambda,$$

or
$$\int_0^{\infty} \frac{\sin \pi\lambda \sin \lambda x}{1-\lambda^2} d\lambda = \frac{\pi}{2}\begin{cases} \sin x, & 0 < x \le \pi \\ 0, & x > \pi \end{cases}$$

Example 2.36. Using Fourier Cosine transform prove

$$\int_0^{\infty} \frac{s^2+2}{s^4+4} \cos sx \, ds = e^{-x} \cos x \;\; x \ge 0$$

Solution : Let $f(x) = e^{-x} \cos x$. Taking cosine transform of $f(x)$

$$F_C\{f(x)\} = \int_0^{\infty} e^{-x} \cos x \cos sx \, dx = \frac{1}{2}\int_0^{\infty} e^{-x} \{\cos(s+1)x + \cos(s-1)x\} \, dx$$

$$= \frac{1}{2}\left[e^{-x}\left\{-\frac{\cos(s+1)x - \sin(s+1)x}{1+(s+1)^2}\right\}\right]_0^{\infty} + \frac{1}{2}\left[\frac{e^{-x}\{-\cos(s-1)x - \sin(s-1)x\}}{1+(s-1)^2}\right]_0^{\infty}$$

$$= \frac{1}{2}\left\{\frac{0-(-1)}{s^2-2+2s} + \frac{-(-1)}{s^2+2-2s}\right\} = \frac{s^2+2}{s^4+4} \quad ...(1)$$

Taking inverse transform of (1)

$$f(x) = \frac{2}{\pi}\int_0^{\infty} \frac{s^2+2}{s^4+4} \cos sx \, ds$$

Hence
$$\int_0^{\infty} \frac{s^2+2}{s^4+4} \cos sx \, ds \; \frac{\pi}{2} f(x) = \frac{\pi}{2} e^{-x} \cos x.$$

Example 2.37. Find the Fourier sine transform of $f(x) = \frac{e^{-ax}}{x}$. *(Bangalore 94)*

Solution :
$$F_s\{f(x)\} = \int_0^{\infty} \frac{e^{-ax}}{x} \sin sx \, dx = I \text{ say}$$

$$\frac{dI}{ds} = \int_0^{\infty} \frac{x}{x} e^{-ax} \cos sx \, dx$$

$$= \left[e^{-ax} \frac{\{-a \cos sx + s \sin sx\}}{s^2 + a^2} \right]_0^\infty = \frac{a}{s^2 + a^2}$$

Hence $\quad I = \int \frac{a}{s^2 + a^2} ds = \tan^{-1} \frac{s}{a} + C$

When $s = 0, I = 0$ so $C = 0$

Hence $\quad F_s \left\{ \frac{e^{-ax}}{x} \right\} = \tan^{-1} \frac{x}{a}$

Example 2.38. Solve the integral equation

$$\int_0^\infty \phi(s) \cos sx \, ds = \begin{cases} 1 - x, & 0 \le x \le 1 \\ 0, & x > 1 \end{cases}$$

(Madras 99; Gorakhpur 91)

Solution : Let $f(x) = 1 - x, 0 < x < 1$, taking Fourier Cosine transform of $f(x)$.

$$= 0, x > 1 \qquad ...(1)$$

$$F_C \{f(x)\} = \int_0^1 (1 - x) \cos sx \, dx = \left[(1 - x) \frac{\sin sx}{s} - \frac{\cos sx}{s^2} \right]_0^1$$

$$= \frac{1 - \cos s}{s^2} \qquad ...(2)$$

Taking inverse transform of (2)

$$f(x) = \frac{2}{\pi} \int_0^\infty \frac{1 - \cos s}{s^2} \cos sx \, ds$$

Hence
$$\frac{2}{\pi} \int_0^\infty \frac{(1 - \cos s)}{s^2} \cos sx \, ds = \begin{cases} 1 - x, & 0 \le x \le 1 \\ 0, & x > 1 \end{cases}$$

Hence
$$\phi(x) = \frac{2}{\pi} \frac{1 - \cos s}{s^2} = \frac{4 \sin^2 s/2}{\pi s^2}$$

Further from

$$\frac{2}{\pi} \int_0^\infty \frac{1 - \cos s}{s^2} \cos sx \, dx = \begin{cases} 1 - x, & x < 1 \\ 0, & x > 1 \end{cases}$$

Taking limit as $x \to 0$

$$\frac{2}{\pi} \cdot 2 \int_0^\infty \frac{\sin^2 s/2}{s^2} ds = 1$$

Let $s/2 = t$

$$\int_0^\infty \frac{\sin^2 t}{t^2} dt = \frac{\pi}{2}$$

Example 2.39. **Find the Fourier cosine transform of $f(x) = e^{-x^2}$.** *(Calicut 94)*

Solution : $F_C\{f(x)\} = \int_0^\infty e^{-x^2} \cos sx \, dx = I$ (say)

So $\frac{dI}{ds} = -\int_0^\infty x\, e^{-x^2} \sin sx \, dx$, integrating by parts.

$$\frac{dI}{ds} = -\left[\frac{e^{-x^2}}{-2} \sin sx\right]_0^\infty + \frac{1}{2} s \int_0^\infty e^{-x^2} \cos sx \, dx = -\frac{s}{2} I$$

So $\frac{dI}{I} = -\int \frac{s}{2} ds$ or $\log \frac{I}{C_0} = -\frac{s^2}{4}$.

So $I = C_0 e^{-s^2/4}$

So $I = \int_0^\infty e^{-x^2} \cos sx \, dx = C_0 e^{-s^2/4}$

When $s \to 0$ $\int_0^\infty e^{-x^2} dx = \frac{\sqrt{\pi}}{2} = C_0$

Hence $I = \frac{\sqrt{\pi}}{2} = e^{-s^2/4}$.

Note : When $F_C\{f(x)\}$ is defined to have the factor

$$\sqrt{\frac{2}{\pi}} \int_0^\infty f(x) \cos sx \, dx = I \text{ then}$$

$$I = \sqrt{\frac{2}{\pi}} \frac{\sqrt{\pi}}{2} e^{-s^2/4} = \frac{1}{\sqrt{2}} e^{-s^2/4}$$

PROBLEM SET 2.9

1. Obtain the Fourier transform of

$$f(x) \begin{cases} x^2, & \text{for } |x| \le a \\ 0, & |x| > a \end{cases}$$

Ans. $= \frac{2}{\sqrt{2\pi}} \left[\frac{a^2 s^2 - 2s}{s^3} \sin as + \frac{2a \cos as}{s^2}\right]$

2. Express $f(x) \begin{cases} 1, & |x| \le 1 \\ 0, & |x| > 1 \end{cases}$ as a Fourier integral.

Ans. $f(x) = \frac{2}{\pi} \int_0^\infty \frac{\sin s \cos sx}{s} dx$

3. Find $f(x)$, whose Fourier cosine transform is $\frac{\sin as}{s}$.

Ans. $f(x) = \begin{cases} 1, & x \le a \\ 0, & x > a \end{cases}$

4. If $f(x)$ be such that

$$\int_0^\infty f(x) \cos sx \, dx + \begin{cases} 1 - s, & 0 < s < 1 \\ 0, & s > 1 \end{cases}$$

Ans. $f(x) = \frac{2}{\pi}\left(\frac{1 - \cos x}{x^2}\right)$.

5. Find $f(x)$ such that

$$\int_0^\infty f(x) \sin sx \, dx = \begin{cases} 1, & 0 \le s < 1 \\ 2, & 1 \le s < 2 \\ 0, & s \ge 2 \end{cases}$$

(Gulbarga 96)

Ans. $f(x) = \frac{2}{\pi} \frac{1 + \cos x - 2\cos 2x}{x}$

6. Find the sine transform of $\frac{x}{1 + x^2}$.

Ans. $\sqrt{\frac{2}{\pi}} \frac{\pi}{2} e^{-s}$

7. Find the cosine transform of $\frac{1}{1 + x^2}$.

Ans. $\sqrt{\frac{\pi}{2}}\, e^{-s}$

8. Find Fourier sine transform of $f(x) = \frac{1}{x}$.

Ans. $\sqrt{\frac{2}{\pi}} \cdot \frac{\pi}{2}$

9. Find sine and cosine transforms of $e^{-x}, x > 0$

Ans. $\sqrt{\frac{2}{\pi}} \frac{s}{s^2 + 1}, \sqrt{\frac{2}{\pi}} \frac{1}{1 + s^2}$

10. Find Fourier transform of $f(x) = \begin{cases} e^{0\omega x}, & a < x < b \\ 0, & x > b \end{cases}$

Ans. $\frac{i}{s + \omega} [e^{i(s+\omega)a} - e^{i(s+\omega)b}]$

11. Find Fourier sine transform of $f(x)$, given by

$$f(x) \begin{cases} 0, & 0 < x < a \\ x, & a \le x \le b \\ 0, & x > b \end{cases}$$

Ans. $\sqrt{\frac{2}{\pi}} \left\{ \frac{1}{s} (-b \cos bs + a \cos as) + \frac{1}{s^2} (\sin bs - \sin as) \right\}$

12. Find $f(x)$, if

$$\int_0^\infty f(x)\cos sx\,dx = \begin{cases} 1-x, & 0 \le s \le 1 \\ 0, & s > 1 \end{cases}$$

Hence prove $\int_0^\infty \frac{\sin^2 t}{t^2}\,dt = \pi/2$

Ans. $f(x) = \frac{4\sin x}{\pi x^2}$

13. Using Fourier integrals, prove

$$\int_0^\infty \frac{\sin \pi\lambda \sin \lambda x}{1-\lambda^2} = \begin{cases} \frac{\pi}{2}\sin x, & 0 \le x \le \pi \\ 0, & x > \pi \end{cases}$$

14. Using Fourier integrals, show that

(i) $\int_0^\infty \frac{\lambda \sin \lambda x}{a^2+\lambda^2}\,d\lambda = \frac{\pi}{2}e^{-ax}, x > 0, a > 0$

(ii) $\int_0^\infty \frac{\cos \lambda x}{1+\lambda^2} = \frac{\pi}{2}e^{-x}, x \ge 0$

(Kerala 90, Mysore 94S, Calicut 89, 94)

(ii) $\int_0^\infty \frac{\cos \lambda x}{1+\lambda^2} = \frac{\pi}{2}e^{-x}, x \ge 0$

(Kerala 90, Mysore 94S, Calicut 89, 94)

15. Solve the integral equation

$$\int_0^\infty f(x)\cos \lambda x\,dx = e^{-\lambda}.$$

(Madras 94S)

Ans. $f(x) = \frac{2}{\pi(1+x^2)}$

2.27 PROPERTIES OF FOURIER TRANSFORMS

(I). Linearity of Transform

If $f(x)$ and $g(x)$ be two functions with Fourier transforms $\bar{f}(s), \bar{g}(s)$, the with any constants C_1 and C_2,

$$F\{C_1 f(x) + C_2 g(x)\} = C_1 F\{f(x)\} + C_2 F\{f(x)\} = C_1 \bar{f}(s) + C_2 \bar{g}(s)$$

The proofs of all theorems below follows by writing the transform integral so they are left to the reader to verify.

(II). Change of Scale Property

$$\bar{F}[f(as); s] = \frac{1}{a}\bar{F}\left(\frac{s}{a}\right)$$

(III). Shifting Property

$$\overline{F}\{f(x-a); s\} = e^{ias} F(f(x); s]$$
$$= e^{ias} \overline{f}(s).$$
$$\overline{F}[e^{iax} f(x); s] = \overline{F}[f(x); (s+a)]$$

(IV). Convolution Theorem

Convolution $f * g$ of two functions $f(x)$ and $g(x)$ defined over $(-\infty, \infty)$ is defined, as usual, as

$$f * g = \int_{-\infty}^{\infty} f(u)\, g(x-u)\, du = h(x).$$

The Fourier transform of the convolution of $f(x)$ and $g(x)$ is the product of their Fourier transforms, i.e.,

$$F\{f(x) \times g(x)\} = F\{f(x)\} \cdot F\{g(x)\}$$

PROOF. L.H.S. $= F\left\{\int_{-\infty}^{\infty} f(u)\, g(x-u)\, du\right\}$

$$= \int_{-\infty}^{\infty}\int_{-\infty}^{\infty} g(u)\, g(x-u)\, e^{ixs}\, du\, dx \text{ on changing the order}$$

$$= \int_{-\infty}^{\infty} f(u)\left\{\int_{-\infty}^{\infty} g(x-u)\, e^{isx}\, dx\right\} du$$

Let $x - u = t$

$$= \int_{-\infty}^{\infty} f(u)\left\{\int_{-\infty}^{\infty} g(t)\, e^{is(u+t)}\, dt\right\} du$$

$$= \int_{-\infty}^{\infty} f(u)\, e^{isu}\, du \cdot \int_{-\infty}^{\infty} g(t)\, e^{ist}\, dt = \overline{f}(s)\, \overline{g}(s)$$

$$= F\{f(x)\}\, F\{g(x)\}$$

2.28 PARSEVAL'S IDENTITY FOR FOURIER TRANSFORMS

Let $F\{F(x)\} = F(s)$, $F\{g(x)\} = G(s)$ be Fourier transforms of $f(x)$ and $g(x)$ respectively, then

(i) $\dfrac{1}{2\pi}\displaystyle\int_{-\infty}^{\infty} F(s)\,\overline{G}(s)\, ds = \int_{-\infty}^{\infty} f(x)\,\overline{g}(x)\, dx$

where bar here **implies the complex conjugate.**

PROOF. As $\quad g(x) = \dfrac{1}{2\pi}\displaystyle\int_{-\infty}^{\infty} G(s)\, e^{-isx}\, ds$

$$\bar{g}(x) = \frac{1}{2\pi}\int_{-\infty}^{\infty} \overline{G}(s)\, i^{isx}\, ds$$

So
$$\text{R.H.S.} = \frac{1}{2\pi}\int_{-\infty}^{\infty} f(x) \int_{-\infty}^{\infty} \overline{G}(s)\, e^{isx}\, ds\, dx$$

$$= \frac{1}{2\pi}\int_{-\infty}^{\infty} \overline{G}(s) \left\{\int_{-\infty}^{\infty} f(x)\, e^{isx}\, dx\right\} dx$$

$$= \frac{1}{2\pi}\int_{-\infty}^{\infty} \overline{G}(s)\, F(s)\, ds = \text{L.H.S.}$$

Taking $f(x) = g(x)$, we have

(ii) $$\frac{1}{2\pi}\int_{-\infty}^{\infty} |F(s)|^2\, ds = \int_{-\infty}^{\infty} |f(x)|^2\, dx.$$

Parseval's identities for Fourier Cosine and sine transforms are

$$\frac{2}{\pi}\int_0^{\infty} F_C(s)\, G_C(s)\, ds = \int_0^{\infty} f(x)\, g(x)\, dx$$

and
$$\frac{2}{\pi}\int_0^{\infty} F_s(s)\, G_s(s)\, ds = \int_0^{\infty} f(x)\, g(x)\, dx.$$

Example 2.40. Using Parseval's identities, prove that

(i) $$\int_0^{\infty} \frac{dt}{(a^2+t^2)(b^2+t^2)} = \frac{\pi}{2ab(a+b)}$$ *(Madras 91)*

(ii) $$\int_0^{\infty} \frac{\sin at}{t(a^2+t^2)}\, dt = \frac{\pi}{2}\left(\frac{1-e^{-a^3}}{a^2}\right)$$

Solution : Let $f(x) = e^{-\alpha x}$ So $\overline{F}_C(s) = \int_0^{\infty} e^{-\alpha x} \cos sx\, dx$

$$= \left[e^{-\alpha x}\frac{\{-\alpha\cos sx + s\sin sx\}}{\alpha^2+s^2}\right]_0^{\infty} = \frac{\alpha}{\alpha^2+s^2} \quad \text{...(1)}$$

Similarly for $g(x) = e^{-\beta x}$, $\overline{G}_C(s) = \dfrac{\beta}{\beta^2+s^2}$ ...(2)

So
$$\frac{2}{\pi}\int_0^{\infty} F_C(s)\, G_C(s) = \frac{2}{\pi}\alpha\beta\int_0^{\infty} \frac{1\, ds}{(\alpha^2+s^2)(\beta^2+s^{2})}$$

$$\text{By Parseval's identity} = \int_0^\infty e^{-\alpha x} e^{-\beta x}\, dx = \frac{1}{\alpha+\beta}$$

Hence $\displaystyle\int_0^\infty \frac{ds}{(\alpha^2+s^2)(\beta^2+s^2)} = \frac{\pi}{2\alpha\beta}\,\frac{1}{(\alpha+\beta)}$. (Proved)

(ii) Let $f(x) = e^{-\alpha x}$ so $\bar{F}_C(s) = \dfrac{\alpha}{\alpha^2+s^2}$

$$g(x) = \begin{cases} 1, & 0 < x < \alpha \\ 0, & x > \alpha \end{cases}$$

$$G_C(s) = \int_0^\alpha 1 \cos sx\, dx + 0 = \frac{\sin s\alpha}{s}$$

Hence $\displaystyle\frac{2}{\pi}\int_0^\infty F(s)\, G(s)\, ds = \frac{2\alpha}{\pi}\int_0^\infty \frac{\sin s\alpha}{s(s^2+\alpha^2)}\, ds = \int_0^\infty f(x)\, g(x)\, dx$

$$= \int_0^\alpha e^{-\alpha x}\cdot 1\, dx = \frac{[e^{-\alpha x}]_0^\alpha}{-\alpha} = \frac{1-e^{-\alpha^3}}{\alpha}$$

Hence $\displaystyle\frac{2\alpha}{\pi}\int_0^\infty \frac{\sin s\alpha}{s(s^2+\alpha^2)}\, ds = \frac{1-e^{-\alpha^2}}{\alpha}$

So $\displaystyle\int_0^\infty \frac{\sin \alpha t}{t(\alpha^2+t^2)} = \frac{\pi}{2}\left(\frac{1-e^{-\alpha^2}}{\alpha^2}\right)$

Example 2.41. Using Parseval's identity, show that

(i) $\displaystyle\int_0^\infty \frac{dx}{(x^2+1)^2} = \frac{\pi}{4}$ **and**

(ii) $\displaystyle\int_0^\infty \frac{x^2}{(x^2+1)^2}\, dx = \frac{\pi}{4}.$

Solution : (i) Taking $f(x) = e^{-x}$,

$$F_C\{f(x)\} = \int_0^\infty e^{-x} \cos sx\, dx$$

$$= \left[e^{-x}\,\frac{(-\cos sx + s \sin sx)}{1+s^2}\right]_0^\infty = \frac{1}{1+s^2}$$

So $\displaystyle\frac{2}{\pi}\int_0^\infty \{F(s)\}^2 = \frac{2}{\pi}\int_0^\infty \frac{1}{(1+s^2)^2}\, dx$

$$= \int_0^{\infty} \{f(x)\}^2 \, dx$$

$$= \int_0^{\infty} e^{-x} e^{-x} \, dx = \frac{[e^{-2x}]_0^{\infty}}{-2} = \frac{1}{2}$$

Hence $\displaystyle\int_0^{\infty} \frac{1}{(1+s^2)^2} \, dx = \frac{\pi}{4}$, so proved

(ii) Taking Fourier sine transform of $f(x) = e^{-x}$

$$F_s \{f(x)\} = \int_0^{\infty} e^{-x} \sin sx \, dx$$

$$= \left[e^{-x} \frac{(-\sin sx - s\cos sx)}{1+s^2} \right]_0^{\infty} = \frac{s}{1+s^2}$$

Hence $\displaystyle\frac{2}{\pi} \int_0^{\infty} \{F f(x)\}^2 \, dx = \frac{2}{\pi} \int_0^{\infty} \frac{x^2}{(1+x^2)^2} \, dx$

$$= \int_0^{\infty} \{f(x)\}^2 = \frac{1}{2} \text{ as above.}$$

Hence $\displaystyle\int_0^{\infty} \frac{x^2}{(1+x^2)^2} \, dx = \frac{\pi}{4}$

PROBLEM SET 2.10

1. Using Parseval's identity prove $\displaystyle\int_0^{\infty} \left(\frac{1-\cos x}{x} \right)^2 = \frac{\pi}{2}$

2. Using Parsevel's identity prove $\displaystyle\int_0^{\infty} \frac{\sin^4 x}{x^2} \, dx = \frac{\pi}{2}.$

3. Verify Convolution theorem for $f(x) = g(x) = e^{-x^2}$. *(V.T.U. 2000S)*

4. If $f(x) = \begin{cases} 1, & |x| < a \\ 0, & |x| > a \end{cases}$ show that $F_C(s) = \dfrac{2 \sin 98}{s}$ $(s \neq 0)$ and hence prove $\displaystyle\int_0^{\infty} \frac{\sin^2 ax}{x^2} = \frac{\pi a}{2}$

(Bangalore 93)

2.29 APPLICATION OF FOURIER TRANSFORMS IN THE SOLUTION OF BOUNDARY VALUE PROBLEMS OF PARTIAL DIFFERENTIAL EQUATIONS

If $u(x, t) = f(x, t)$ be a function of two independent variables x and t, on taking Fourier transforms w.r.t. x, we get the following $\overline{F}(s, t) = \overline{F}(f(x, t); x \to s)$

$$\overline{F}_C(s, t) = \overline{F}_C(f(x, t); x \to s)$$

$$\overline{F}_s(s, t) = \overline{F}_s(f(x, t); x \to s)$$

$$\overline{F}\left[\frac{\partial f}{\partial x}; x \to s\right] = -is\,[\overline{F}(x, t); x \to s]$$

$$\overline{F}\left[\frac{\partial^2 f}{\partial x^2}; x \to s\right] = -s^2\,[\overline{F}(x, t); x \to s] = -s^2\,\overline{F}(s, t)$$

For Cosine Transform

$$\overline{F}_C\left[\frac{\partial f}{\partial x}\right] = -f(0, t) + s\,\overline{F}_s$$

$$\overline{F}_C\left[\frac{\partial^2 f}{\partial x^2}\right] = -f_x(0, t) - s^2\,\overline{F}_C$$

For

$$\overline{F}_s\left[\frac{\partial f}{\partial x}\right] = -s\,\overline{F}_C$$

$$\overline{F}_s\left[\frac{\partial^2 f}{\partial x^2}\right] = sf(0, t) - s^2\,\overline{F}_C$$

Example 2.42. Determine the temperature distribution in the semi-infinite medium $x > 0$, when $u(0, t) = 0$ and $u(x, 0) = f(x)$. u is bounded for $x \geq 0, t \geq 0$.

Solution : The heat flow is governed by

$$\frac{\partial u}{\partial t} = C^2\,\frac{\partial^2 u}{\partial x^2}\ (x > 0, t > 0).$$

Taking Fourier sine transform

$$\frac{d\,\overline{u}_s}{dt} = C^2\,\{-s^2\,\overline{u}_s - s\,u(0, t)\}$$

So
$$\left(\frac{d}{dt} + c^2 s^2\right)\overline{u}_s = 0$$

So
$$\overline{u}_s = \overline{f}(s)\,e^{-c^2 s^2 t}$$

So
$$u(x, t) = \frac{2}{\pi}\int_0^\infty \overline{f}(s)\sin sx\,e^{-c^2 s^2 t}\,ds.$$

Example 2.43. **Solve** $\frac{\partial u}{\partial t} = c^2 \frac{\partial^2 u}{\partial x^2}$, **given** $\frac{\partial u(0,t)}{\partial x} = 0$, $u(x,0) = \begin{cases} x, & 0 < x < 1 \\ 0, & x > 1 \end{cases}$ $u(x,t)$ **is bounded for** $x > 0, t > 0$.

Solution : As $\frac{\partial u}{\partial x}(0, t)$ is given, so we take cosine transform.Taking Fourier cosine transform of the given equation

$$\frac{d}{dt}\bar{u} = c^2 \{-s^2 \bar{u} - u_x(0,t)\}, \text{ as } u_x(0,t) = 0$$

So $$\frac{\partial \bar{u}}{dt} + c^2 s^2 \bar{u} = 0$$

Sso $$\bar{u} = \bar{f}(s)\, e^{-c^2 s^2 t}$$

Hence $$u = \frac{2}{\pi}\int_0^\infty \bar{f}(s)\, e^{-c^2 s^2 t} \cos sx\, ds$$

$$\bar{f}(s) = \int_0^1 x \cos sx\, dx = \left[\frac{x \sin sx}{s} + \frac{\cos sx}{s^2}\right]_0^1 = \frac{\sin s}{s} + \frac{\cos s - 1}{s^2}$$

Hence $$u = \frac{2}{\pi}\int_0^\infty \left\{\frac{\sin s}{s} - \frac{1 - \cos s}{s^2}\right\} e^{-c^2 s^2 t} \cos sx\, dx.$$

Example 2.44. **Solve** $\frac{\partial u}{\partial t} = 2\frac{\partial^2 u}{\partial x^2}$, **given** $u(0,t) = 0$, $u(x,0) = e^{-t}$ $(x > 0)$ $u(x,t)$ **is bounded when** $x > 0, t > 0$.

Solution : Since $u(0, t)$ is given, we take Fourier sine transform of the given equation and have

$$\frac{d(\bar{u}(s))}{dt} = 2\int_0^\infty \frac{\partial^2 u}{dx^2} \sin sx\, dx$$

$$= \left[\sin sx \frac{\partial u}{\partial x}\right]_{x=0}^\infty - 2s\int \frac{\partial u}{\partial x}\cos sx\, dx$$

$$= \left(\text{assuming } \frac{\partial u}{\partial x} \to 0 \text{ as } x \to \infty\right) - 2s\{[u \cos sx]_0^\infty - s^2 \bar{u}\}$$

$$= 2[+s\, u(0,t) - s^2 \bar{u}] \text{ so } \frac{d\bar{u}}{dt} + 2s^2 \bar{u} = 0$$

So $$\bar{u}(s,t) = c\, e^{-2s^2 t}$$

Given $$u(x,0) = e^{-x}$$

$$\bar{u}(s,0) = \int_0^\infty e^{-x} \sin sx\, dx \left[e^{-x}\frac{\{-\sin sx - s\cos sx\}}{1+s^2}\right]_{x=0}^\infty = \frac{1}{1+s^2}$$

Hence $$\bar{u}(s,t) = \frac{s}{1+s^2} e^{-2s^2 t}$$

So $\quad u(x, t) = \frac{2}{\pi} \int_0^\infty \frac{x}{+ x^2} e^{-2s^{2t}} \sin sx \, dx.$

Example 2.45. Temperature u in a semi infinite rod of determined by $\frac{\partial u}{\partial t} = c^2 \frac{\partial^2 u}{\partial x^2}$, for $0 \le x < \infty$, with conditions

(i) $u = 0$, at $t = 0, x > 0$ so $\frac{\partial u}{\partial x}$ also $= 0$ when $x \to \infty$

(ii) $\frac{\partial u}{\partial x} = -\mu$ at $x = 0$,

(iii) $\frac{\partial u}{\partial x} \to 0$ as $x \to \infty$. Find $u(x, t)$.

Solution : As $\frac{\partial u}{\partial x}$ is given so we apply cosine transform to the given equation.

$$\int_0^\infty \frac{\partial u}{\partial t} \cos xs \, dx = c^2 \int_0^\infty \frac{\partial^2 u}{\partial x^2} \cos sx \, dx$$

$$\frac{\partial \bar{u}}{dt} = c^2 \left\{ \frac{\partial u}{\partial x} \cos sx - su \sin sx \right\}_{x=0}^{\infty} - s^2 c^2 \bar{u}$$

$$= \mu c^2 - c^2 s^2 \bar{u}$$

or $\quad \frac{\partial \bar{u}}{dt} + c^2 s^2 \bar{u} = \mu c^2$. It is a linear differential equation

$$\text{C.F.} = e^{-\int c^2 s^2 dt}$$

$$\text{P.I.} = \mu c^2 ovr0 + c^2 s^2 = \frac{\mu}{s^2}$$

So $\quad \bar{u} = c_1 e^{-c^2 s^2 t} + \frac{\mu}{s^2}$ at $t = 0, u = 0$, so $\bar{u} = 0$

So $\quad c_1 = -\frac{\mu}{s^2}$

Hence $\quad \bar{u} = \frac{\mu}{s^2}(1 - e^{-c^2 s^2 t})$

So $\quad u(x, t) = \frac{2\mu}{\pi} \int_0^\infty \frac{1 - e^{-c^2 s^2 t}}{s^2} \cos sx \, ds.$

Example 2.46. Use the method of Fourier transform to determine the displacement $u(x, t)$, of an infinite string, given that the string is initially at rest and the initial displacement is $f(x)$, $-\infty < x < \infty$. Show that the solution can be part in the form $u(x, t) = \frac{f(x + ct) + f(x - ct)}{2}$.

Solution : Taking Fourier transform w.r.t. x_1 of the equation

$$\frac{\partial^2 y}{\partial t^2} = c^2 \frac{\partial^2 y}{\partial x^2}, \text{ with conditions} \quad ...(1)$$

$$\left(\frac{\partial y}{\partial t}\right)_{t=0} = 0$$

and $y(x, 0) = f(x), -\infty < x < \infty, t > 0$

$$\frac{d^2 \bar{y}}{dt^2} = c^2 \int_{-\infty}^{\infty} \frac{\partial^2 u}{\partial x^2} e^{isx} dx$$

So
$$\frac{\partial^2 \bar{u}}{dt^2} = c^2 \left[\frac{\partial y}{\partial x} e^{isx} - is\, ye^{isx}\right]_{-\infty}^{\infty} + i^2 s^2 c^2 \bar{y}$$

as y and $\frac{\partial y}{\partial x}$ both $\to 0$ as $x \to \pm\infty$. So

We have
$$\frac{d^2 \bar{y}}{dt^2} + c^2 s^2 \bar{y} = 0$$

or
$$\bar{y} = c_1 \cos cst + c_2 \sin cst. \quad ...(2)$$

String is initially as rest

$\frac{\partial y}{\partial t}(x, 0) = 0$, taking its transform

$$\frac{\partial \bar{y}(s, 0)}{\partial t} \text{ also } = 0 \quad ...(3)$$

$y = f(x, 0)$ so
$$\bar{y}(s, 0) = \bar{f}(s) \quad ...(4)$$

From (2) $\bar{f} = c_1 + 0$

and
$$0 = \left(\frac{\partial \bar{y}}{\partial t}\right)_{t=0} = 0 + c_2 cs \text{ so } c_2 = 0$$

Hence
$$\bar{y} = \bar{f}(s, 0) \cos cst$$

So
$$y = \frac{1}{2\pi} \int_{-\infty}^{\infty} \bar{f}(s) \cos cst\, e^{isx} ds$$

$$= \frac{1}{2\pi} \int_{-\infty}^{\infty} \bar{f}(s) e^{isx} \frac{(e^{icst} + e^{-icst})}{2} ds$$

$$= \frac{1}{4\pi} \int_{-\infty}^{\infty} \bar{f}(s) \{e^{i(x+ct)s} + e^{i(x-ct)s}\} ds.$$

$$= \frac{1}{2} \{f(x - ct) + f(x + ct)\}$$

PROBLEM SET 2.11

1. Solve $\frac{\partial^2 u}{\partial t} = 2\frac{\partial^2 u}{\partial x^2}$, if $u(0, t) = 0$, $u(x, 0) = e^{-x}$, $x > 0$ $u(x, t)$ is bounded.

Ans. $u(x, t) = -\frac{2}{\pi}\int_0^\infty \frac{s\, e^{-2s^2 t} \sin sx}{1+s^2} \cdot ds$

2. Solve $\frac{\partial u}{\partial t} = k\frac{\partial^2 u}{\partial x^2}$, given $u = u_0$ at $x = 0, t > 0$, $u = 0$ at $t = 0$, $x > 0$, $u = 0$ as $x \to \infty$, $\frac{\partial u}{\partial x} \to 0$ as $x \to \infty$

Ans. $u = u_0\, [/1 - \frac{2}{\pi}\int_0^\infty \frac{e^{-ks^2 t}}{s} \sin sx\, dx$

3. An infinite string is initially at rest and that the initial displacement is $f(x)$, $(-\infty < x < \infty)$. Determine thd displacement $y(x, t)$ of the string.

Ans. $y(x, t) = \frac{1}{2}\, [f(x - ct) + f(x + ct)]$.

4. An infinitely long string having one end at $x = 0$, is initially at rest along the x-axis. The end $x = 0$ is given a transverse displacement $f(t)$, $t > 0$. Find the displacement of any point of the string at any time. ***(Delhi 91, Gorakhpur 91)***

Ans. $y(x, t) = f\left(t - \frac{x}{c}\right)$.

5. Solve $\frac{\partial V}{\partial t} = \frac{\partial^2 V}{\partial x^2}$, $0 \le x \le \pi$, $t \ge 0$, where $V(0, t) = 0 = V(\pi, t)$ and $V(x, 0) = V_0$

Ans. $V(x, t) = \frac{V_0}{\pi}\Sigma \frac{(1 - \cos n\pi)}{n} e^{-n^2 t \sin n x_0}$

3

Laplace Transformation

3.1 INTRODUCTION

Oliver Heaviside (1850-1925), developed a powerful method, known as **operational calculus** or **transform methods** for the solution of boundary value problems of differential equations. The transform methods are used in mostly all branches of engineering. The **French mathematician J. B. J. Fourier** (1768-1830) showed that any periodic function $f(x)$ can be represented in its period, as a series of sine and cosines

$$f(x) = a_0 + \sum_{1}^{\infty} \cos\left(\frac{2\pi}{T_0} nx\right) + \sum_{1}^{\infty} \sin\left(\frac{2\pi}{T_0} nx\right)$$

of multiples of $\frac{2\pi}{T_0} x$ where T_0 is the **period** and $\omega_0 = \frac{2\pi}{T_0}$ is the **fundamental frequency**. In the case of a non-periodic function, the function is regarded to be periodic over a period T, which tends to infinity. In that case the frequencies of successive terms $\omega_0, 2\omega_0 \ldots$ all $\to 0$ and the Fourier series tends to become continuous which is, then represented by an integral, known as **Fourier integral**. The Fourier transform and its inverse are given by

$$\textbf{Fourier transform of } f(t) \equiv F(\omega) = \int_{-\infty}^{\infty} f(t)\, e^{-i\omega t}\, dt$$

Inverse Fourier transform of $F(w)$ gives $f(t) = \frac{1}{2\pi} \int_{-\infty}^{\infty} F(\omega)\, e^{i\omega t}\, d\omega$, $e^{-i\omega t}$ are $e^{i\omega t}$ are the kernels of the transform and its inverse transform. We first take up the Laplace trasnform.

3.2 LAPLACE TRANSFORM

The two sided **Laplace transform** of function $f(t)$ is defined by

$$F(s) = \int_{-\infty}^{\infty} f(t)\, e^{-st}\, dt \qquad ...(1)$$

The Laplace's transform of $f(t)$ is denoted by $\boldsymbol{F(s)}$ or $\boldsymbol{L\{f(t)\}}$ or simply by $\bar{f}(\boldsymbol{s})$.

3.3 INVERSE LAPLACE TRANSFORM

If in the above definition of Laplace transform, **s be taken to be complex**, given by $s = \sigma + i\omega$, where $\sigma > 0$, for convergence, then

$$F(s) = \int_{-\infty}^{\infty} (f(t)\, e^{-\sigma t})\, e^{-i\omega t}\, dt \qquad ...(1)$$

But it is the Fourier transform of the function $f(t)\, e^{-\sigma t}$, whose inversion is given by

$$f(t)\, e^{-\sigma t} = \frac{1}{2\pi} \int_{-\infty}^{\infty} F(s)\, e^{i\omega t}\, d\omega.$$

If we let $\sigma + i\omega = s$ so that $id\omega = ds$, we have

$$f(t)\, e^{-\sigma t} = \frac{1}{2\pi i} \int_{\sigma - i\infty}^{\sigma + i\infty} F(s)\, e^{(s-\sigma)t}\, ds$$

$$= e^{-\sigma t} \frac{1}{2\pi i} \int_{\sigma - i\infty}^{\sigma + i\infty} F(s)\, e^{st}\, ds$$

Hence $$\boldsymbol{L^{-1}(F(s)) = F(t) = \frac{1}{2\pi i} \int_{\sigma - i\infty}^{\sigma + i\infty} F(s)\, e^{st}\, ds} \quad \sigma > 0$$

defines the **inverse Laplace transform** of the Laplace transform $L\{f(t)\} = F(s)$. Since it involves fair knowledge of complex integration, we will consider only such problems where inverse Laplace transform **is found only on the basis of knowledge of Laplace transform of functions.** Here we consider only the **one sided Laplace transform**, defining it as

$$\boldsymbol{L\, f(t) = \bar{f}(s)} = \int_0^{\infty} e^{-st} f(t)\, dt,\ s > 0.$$

$\boldsymbol{e^{-st}}$ is called the **kernel** of the Laplace transform. For every transform the region in which the integral exists, *i.e.*, in which it is finite called the region of its convergence should always be found out. The above integral is an improper (because of one of the infinite limits). This integral exists in its region of convergence when the function is either continuous or if not so, it has only a finite number of finite discontinuities, which means that the function to piece-wise or **sectionally continuous** in $(0, \infty)$.

Conditions for a transform to exist are :

(i) Function be sectionally continuous,

(ii) The integral be convergent.

3.4 SECTIONALLY CONTINUOUS FUNCTION

A function $f(x)$ defined on $[a, b]$ is said to be sectionally continuous on $[a, b]$ when either $f(x)$ is continuous in $[a, b]$ or if not so then it has only a finite number of finite discontinuities in each of the sub intervals in which $f(x)$ is defined. Graph of a piece-wise continuous function is as shown below. It should also have a finite number of maximas and minimas.

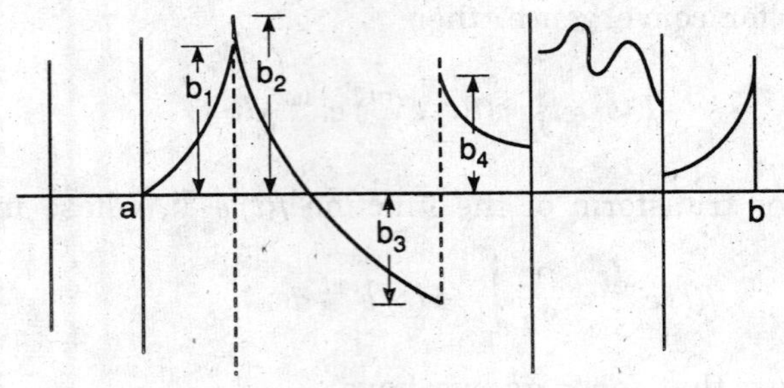

Fig. 3.1

(ii) Another condition for the transform to exist is that the parameter s should be such that the value of the integral remains be finite.

Exponential Order

A function $f(x)$ is said to be of **exponential order** a if $\lim_{x \to \infty} e^{-ax} f(x)$ = a finite quantity.

The Laplace transform $L\{f(x)\}$ is convergent when for $s > 0$, where $f(x)$ is of finite exponential order.

Existence Conditions

(i) The integral $\int_0^\infty e^{-st} f(t)\, dt$ must exists, Let $\int_0^a e^{-st} f(t)\, dt = F_a(s)$.

If $\lim_{s \to \infty} F_a(s)$ exists then $F(s)$ exists and the limiting value is the Laplace transform of $f(t)$.

(ii) If $f(x)$ be of exponential order a then integral exists for all $s > a$.

Finding Laplace Transforms of some functions

(i) $$L(1) = \int_0^\infty e^{-st} \cdot 1\, dt = \frac{[e^{-st}]_{t=0}^{\infty}}{-s} = \frac{1}{s} \quad ...(1)$$

(ii) $$L(e^{at}) = \int_0^\infty e^{-st} e^{at}\, dt = \frac{[e^{-(s-a)t}]_0^\infty}{-(s-a)} = \frac{1}{s-a} \quad ...(2)$$

when $s > a$.

(iii) $L(e^{iat})$ as above $= \dfrac{1}{s-(ia)} = \dfrac{s+ia}{s^2+a^2}$

Separating into real and imaginary parts

(iv) $$L(\cos at + i \sin at) = \frac{s}{s^2+a^2} + i\frac{a}{s^2+a^2}$$

So $$L(\cos at) = \frac{s}{s^2+a^2} \qquad ...(3)$$

(v) $$L(\sin at) = \frac{a}{s^2+a^2} \qquad ...(4)$$

Replacing a by ia and using the results $\sin(iat) = i \sinh at$ and $\cos(iat) = \cosh at$ or finding directly the Laplace transforms of e^{at} and e^{-at} separately

(vi) $$L(\sinh at) = L\left\{\left(\frac{e^{at}-e^{-at}}{2}\right)\right\} = \frac{a}{s^2-a^2}, \qquad ...(5)$$

(vii) $$L(\cosh at) = L\left\{\left(\frac{e^{at}+s^{-at}}{2}\right)\right\} = \frac{s}{s^2-a^2}, \qquad ...(6)$$

(viii) $$L(t^n) = \int_0^\infty t^{(n+1)-1} e^{-st}\,dt = \frac{\Gamma n+1}{s^{n+1}} \text{ (by definition of Gamma integral)}$$

$$= \frac{n!}{s^{n+1}}, \text{ if } n \text{ be zero or a positive integer,}$$

Example 3.1. **Find the Laplace transform of**

(i) sin t cos t **(ii) sin^3 2t** ***(Bhopal 91)***

(iii) cosh^3 2t ***(Bhopal 91, Andhra 86S)***

Solution : (i) $L(\sin t \cos t) = \dfrac{1}{2} L(\sin 2t) = \dfrac{1}{2}\dfrac{2}{s^2+2^2} = \dfrac{1}{s^2+4}$

(ii) $$L(\sin^3 2t) = L\left(\frac{3\sin 2t - \sin 6t}{4}\right) = \frac{3}{4}\frac{2}{s^2+4} - \frac{6}{4(s^2+36)}$$

$$= \frac{3}{2}\frac{(32)}{(s^2+4)(s^2+36)}$$

(iii) $$L(\cosh^3 2t) = L\left\{\frac{e^{2t}+e^{-2t}}{2}\right\}^3$$

$$= \frac{1}{8} L\{e^{6t} + e^{-6t} + 3(e^{2t}+e^{-2t})\}$$

$$= \frac{1}{8}\left[\left(\frac{1}{s-6}+\frac{1}{s+6}\right) + 3\left(\frac{1}{s-2}+\frac{1}{s+2}\right)\right]$$

$$= \frac{1}{4}\left\{\frac{s}{s^2-36} + \frac{3s}{s^2-4}\right\}$$

$$= \frac{s(s^2-28)}{(s^2-4)(s^2-36)}$$

Example 3.2. **If** $f(t) = \begin{cases} t, & 0 < t < 4, \\ 5, & t > 4 \end{cases}$

Solution : $$Lf(t) = \int_0^4 t\, e^{-st}\, dt + 0 = \left[\left(-\frac{1}{s}t + \frac{1}{s^2}\right) e^{-st}\right]_0^4$$

$$= \frac{4e^{-4s} - 0}{-s} - \frac{e^{-4s} - 1}{s^2} + \frac{5(0 - e)^{-4s}}{-s} = \frac{e^{-4s}}{s} + \frac{1}{s^2}(1 - e^{-4s})$$

3.5 PROPERTIES OF LAPLACE TRANSFORM

(I) Linearity Property

An operator L is linear when it satisfies

$$\boldsymbol{L\{af(t) + b\,g(t)\} = a\,L\{f(t)\} + bL\{g(t)\}}$$

The Laplace transform is a linear operation, as

$$\boldsymbol{L\{af(t) + b\,g(t)\}} = \int_0^\infty e^{-st}\{af(t) + bg(t)\}\,dt$$

$$= a\int_0^\infty e^{-st} f(t)\,dt + b\int_0^\infty e^{-st} g(t)\,dt = \boldsymbol{aL\{f(t)\} + bL\{g(t)\}}$$

(II) First Shifting Property

If $L\{f(t)\} = \bar{f}(s)$, then

$$\boldsymbol{L\{e^{at} f(t)\} = \bar{f}(s - a)}, \text{ provided } \boldsymbol{s - a > 0}$$

Proof. $$L\{e^{at} f(t)\} = \int_0^\infty e^{-st} e^{at} f(t)\,dt = \int_0^\infty e^{-(s-a)t} f(t)\,dt$$

Replacing the parameter s by $(s - a) = \bar{f}(s - a)$, where $s - a > 0$.

So all the standard results are revised by this property.

Example 3.3. **Find the Laplace transform of the following :**

(i) $\boldsymbol{e^{-at} \sinh bt}$

(ii) $\boldsymbol{e^{-2t} \sin 4t}$ *(Bhopal 91)*

(iii) $\boldsymbol{e^{-3t} t^3}$ *(Kuvempu 96)*

(iv) cosh $\boldsymbol{at}$ **sin** $\boldsymbol{at}$ *(Kerala 95)*

Solution. (i) $L(\sinh bt) = \dfrac{b}{s^2 - b^2}$ so $L(e^{-at} \sinh bt) = \dfrac{b}{(s + a)^2 - b^2}$

(ii) $L(\sinh 4t) = \dfrac{4}{s^2 + 4^2}$ so $L(e^{-2t} \sin 4t) = \dfrac{4}{(s + 2)^2 + 4^2}$

(iii) $L(t^3) = L(t^{4-1}) = \dfrac{!4}{s^4}$ so $L(e^{-3t} t^3) = \dfrac{3!}{(s + 3)^4}$

(iv) $\cosh at \sin at = \dfrac{e^{at} \sin at}{2} + \dfrac{e^{-at} \sin at}{2}$

So $L(\cosh at \sin at) = \dfrac{1}{2} \dfrac{a}{(s-a)^2 + a^2} + \dfrac{1}{2} \dfrac{a}{(s+a)^2 + a^2}$

$$= \frac{a}{2} \frac{2(s^2 + 2a^2)}{(s^2 + 2a^2)^3 - 4a^2 s^2} = \frac{a(s^2 + 2a^2)}{s^4 + 4a^4}$$

Example 3.4. **Find the Laplace transform of the following :**

(i) $f_1(t) = e^{-3t}$ (2 cos 5t – 3 sin 5t) *(J.N.U. 99)*

(ii) $f_2(t) = e^{-t} \sin^2 t$ *(Bangalore 90)*

Solution. (i) $L\{2 \cos 5t - 3 \sin st\} = 2L\{\cos 5t\} - 3L\{\sin st\} = 2 \cdot \dfrac{s}{s^2 + 25} - 3 \cdot \dfrac{5}{s^2 + 25}$

$$= \frac{2s - 15}{s^2 + 25}$$

$\therefore$ $L\{e^{-3t}(2 \cos 5t - 3 \sin 5t)\} = \dfrac{2(s+3) - 15}{(s+3)^2 + 25} = \dfrac{2s - 9}{s^2 + 6s + 34}$

(ii) $l\{\sin^2 t\} = L\left\{\dfrac{1 - \cos 2t}{2}\right\} = \dfrac{1}{2}[L\{1\} - L\{\cos 2t\}]$

$$= \frac{1}{2}\left[\frac{1}{s} - \frac{s}{s^2 + 4}\right] = \frac{1}{2}\left[\frac{s^2 + 4 - s^2}{s(s^2 + 4)}\right] = \frac{1}{2}\left[\frac{4}{s(s^2 + 4)}\right]$$

$$= \frac{2}{s(s^2 + 4)}$$

$\therefore$ $L\{e^{-t} \sin^2 t\} = \dfrac{2}{(s+1)[(s+1)^2 + 4]} = \dfrac{2}{(s+1)(s^2 + 2s + 5)}$

(III) Second Shifting Theorem

If $\boldsymbol{L\{f(t)\} = \bar{f}(s)}$ and $g(t)$ be a function such that

$$g(t) = \begin{cases} 0, & \text{for } t < 0 \\ f(t-a), & t \geq a \end{cases} \quad \text{then} \quad \boldsymbol{L\{g(t)\} = e^{-as} \bar{f}(s)}$$

$$L\{g(t)\} = 0 + \int_a^\infty f(t-a)\, e^{-st}\, dt \text{ Let } t - a = z$$

$$= \int_0^\infty f(z) = e^{-s(z+a)}\, dz = e^{-as} \int_0^\infty f(z)\, e^{-sz}\, dz = e^{-as} \bar{f}(s)$$

Example 3.5. **If the unit step function $U(t-a)$ be defined as, find its Laplace transform.**

$$\boldsymbol{u(t-a) = \begin{cases} 0, & t < a \\ 1, & t > a \end{cases}}$$

Solution : $\boldsymbol{L\{U(t-a)\}} = \displaystyle\int_0^a 0\, dt + \int_a^\infty 1\, e^{-st}\, dt = \dfrac{[e^{-st}]_a^\infty}{-s} = \dfrac{0 - e^{-as}}{-s} = \dfrac{e^{-as}}{s}.$

Example 3.6. **If** $f(t) = \frac{1}{\tau} t$, **for** $t < \tau$

$= \frac{1}{\tau}$, **for** $t > \tau$.

Show $L\{f(t)\} = \frac{1 - e^{-st}}{s^2 \tau}$.

Solution :

$$L\{f(t)\} = \frac{1}{\tau} \int_0^{\tau} e^{-st} \frac{1}{\tau} dt + \int_{\tau}^{\infty} \frac{1}{\tau} e^{-st} dt$$

$$= \frac{1}{\tau} \left\{ \frac{t\, e^{-st}}{-s} - \frac{e^{-st}}{s^2} \right\}_0^{\tau} + \frac{\{e^{-st}\}_{\tau}^{\infty}}{-s\tau}$$

$$= \frac{1}{s\tau} e^{-s\tau} - \frac{1}{s^2 \tau} (e^{-s\tau} - 1) + \frac{0 - e^{-s\tau}}{-s\tau}$$

$$= e^{-s\tau} \left\{ \frac{1}{s\tau} - \frac{1}{s^2\tau} + \frac{1}{s\tau} \right\} + \frac{1}{s^2\tau} = \frac{1 - e^{-s\tau}}{s^2\tau}$$

3.6 LAPLACE TRANSFORM OF A PERIODIC FUNCTION

A function $f(t)$ is said to be a **periodic function** with period T if $f(t + nt) = f(t)$, where n is any integer.

Example 3.7. **If $f(t)$ be a periodic function with period a, prove**

$$L\{f(t)\} = \frac{1}{1 - e^{-as}} \int_0^a e^{-st} f(t)\, dt.$$

Solution :

$$L\, f(t) = \int_0^a e^{-st} f(t)\, dt + \int_a^{2a} e^{-st} f(t)\, dt + \int_{2a}^{3a} e^{-st} f(t)\, dt + \ldots$$

$$= \sum_{r=1}^{\infty} \int_{(r-1)a}^{ra} e^{-st} f(t)\, dt$$

Let $(r - 1)\, a + t = z$

So $dt = dz$

$$= \sum_{r=1}^{\infty} \int_0^a f\{z + (r-1)a\}\, e^{-s\{z + (r-1)a\}}\, dz$$

As $f\{(r - 1)\, a + z\} = f(z)$, because a is the period of $f(t)$.

$$= \sum_{r=1}^{\infty} e^{-s(r-1)a} \int_0^a f(z)\, e^{-sz}\, dz$$

$$= \{1 + e^{-sa} + e^{-2sa} + \ldots\}.\, I.$$

Hence $$L\,f(t) = \frac{1}{1-e^{-as}}\,I$$ Hence Proved.

It is an **Infinite G.P.**

Example 3.8. **Find the Laplace transform of**

(i) $f(t) = \cos t,\ 0 < t < 2\pi,$

$= 0, \qquad t > 2\pi$

(ii) $f_\varepsilon(t) = \frac{1}{\varepsilon}, \quad t < \varepsilon$

$= 0, \quad t > t$

Show $\lim L\{f_\varepsilon(t)\}$

$\varepsilon \to 0 = 1$

Solution : (i) $$L\{f(t)\} = \int_0^{2\pi} e^{-st}\cos t\,dt + 0 = \left[\frac{e^{-st}\{-s\cos t + \sin t\}}{1+s^2}\right]_{2\pi} = \frac{s(1-e^{-2\pi s})}{1+s^2}$$

(ii) $$L\{f_\varepsilon(t)\} = \frac{1}{\varepsilon}\int_0^{\varepsilon} e^{-st}\,dt + 0 = \frac{[e^{-st}]_0^{\varepsilon}}{-st} = \frac{1-e^{-st}}{\varepsilon s}$$

$$\lim_{\varepsilon \to 0} \frac{1-e^{-st}}{\varepsilon s} = \frac{1-\left(1 - s\varepsilon + \frac{s^2\varepsilon^2}{!2} + \ldots\right)}{st} = 1.$$

(IV) Change of Scale Property

If $L\{f(t)\} = \bar{f}(s)$, then $L\,f(at) = \frac{1}{a}\bar{f}\left(\frac{s}{a}\right)$

Proof. $$L\{f(at)\} = \int_0^{\infty} f(at)\,e^{-st}\,dt$$ Let $at = z$

$$= \int_0^{\infty} F(z)\,e^{-\left(\frac{s}{a}\right)z}\,\frac{dz}{a} = \frac{1}{a}\bar{f}\left(\frac{s}{a}\right)$$

Example 3.9. **Find the Laplace transform of**

$f(t) = |t-1| + |t+1|,\ t \geq 0$ *(A.M.I.E. 1997W)*

Solution : $|t-1| = 1-t$ and $|t+1| = t+1$. For $t > 1$.

For $0 < t < 1$, $|t+1| = t+1$. Dividing the integral in two integrals one from 0 to 1 and other from 1 to ∞.

$$\text{So } L\,f(t) = \int_0^1 \{(1-t)+(1+t)\}\,e^{-st}\,dt + \int_1^{\infty} \{(t-1)+(t+1)\}\,e^{-st}\,dt$$

$$= 2\,\frac{[e^{-st}]_0^1}{-s} + 2\left\{\frac{t\,e^{-st}}{-s} - \frac{e^{-st}}{s^2}\right\}_1^{\infty}$$

$$= 2\frac{1-e^{-s}}{s} + 2\left\{\frac{0+e^{-s}}{s} + \frac{e^{-s}}{s^2}\right\} = 2\left\{\frac{s+e^{-s}}{s^2}\right\}$$

Example 3.10. Find the Laplace transform of $f(t) = (e^{-4t}\sin 3t)\, t$.

Solution : $f(t) =$ Imaginary part of $e^{(-4+3i)t} \cdot t$

$$L\,(-4+3i)t \cdot t = \frac{2!}{(s+4-3i)^2} \times \frac{(s+4+3i)^2}{(s+4+3i)^2}$$

$$= \frac{\{s+4+3i\}^2}{\{(s+4)^2+9\}^2} = \frac{(s+4)^2-9}{\{(s+4)^2+9\}^2} + \frac{6(s+4)}{\{(s+4)^2+9\}^2}$$

So $\qquad L\,\{f(t)\} =$ Imaginary part of above

$$= \frac{6(s+4)}{\{(s+4)^2+9\}^2} = \frac{6(s+4)}{(s^2+8s+25)^2}$$

Example 3.11. Find the Laplace transform of

(i) $(\sin at - at\cos at)$,

(ii) $\dfrac{e^{-t}\sin t}{t}$ *(AUUP 2008)*

(iii) $\dfrac{1-\cos t}{t^2}$ *(AUUP 2008)*

Solution : (i) $L\,(\sin at) = \dfrac{a}{s^2+a^2}$

$$L\, at\cos at = \text{Real part of } L\,(at\, e^{iat})$$

$$= R\frac{a}{(s-ia)^2} = R\frac{a(s+ia)^2}{(s^2+a^2)^2} = \frac{a(s^2-a^2)}{(s^2+a^2)^2}$$

So $$L(\sin at - at\cos at) = \frac{a\,\{(s^2+a^2)-(s^2-a^2)\}}{(s^2+a^2)^2} = \frac{2a^3}{(s^2+a^2)^2}$$

(ii) $L\,\{e^{-t}\sin t\} = \dfrac{1}{(s+1)^2+1}$

$$\Rightarrow \qquad L\left\{\frac{e^{-t}\sin t}{t}\right\} = \int_s^\infty \frac{1}{(s+1)^2+1}\,ds$$

$$= [\tan^{-1}(s+1)]_s^\infty$$

$$= \frac{\pi}{2} - \tan^{-1}(s+1) = \cot^{-1}(s+1)$$

(iii) $L\{1-\cos t\} = \dfrac{1}{s} - \dfrac{s}{s^2+1}\,ds$

$$L\left\{\frac{1-\cos t}{t}\right\} = \int_s^\infty \left(\frac{1}{s} - \frac{s}{s^2+1}\right)ds$$

$$= \left[\log s - \frac{1}{2} \log (s^2 + 1) \right]_s$$

$$= -\frac{1}{2} \log \left(\frac{s^2}{s^2 + 1} \right) = \frac{1}{2} \log \left(\frac{s^2 + 1}{s^2} \right)$$

Now, $$L \left\{ \frac{1 - \cos t}{t^2} \right\} = \int_s^\infty \frac{1}{2} \log \left(\frac{s^2 + 1}{s^2} \right) ds = \frac{1}{2} \int_s^\infty [\log (s^2 + 1) - 2 \log s] ds$$

$$= \frac{1}{2} \left[\{\log (s^2 + 1) - 2 \log s\} s - \int \left(\frac{2s}{s^2 + 1} - \frac{2}{s} \right) \cdot s ds \right]_s^{ds}$$

$$= \left[\frac{s}{s} \log \left(\frac{s^2 + 1}{s^2} \right) \right]_s^{ds} + \int_s^\infty \frac{ds}{s^2 + 1}$$

$$= -\frac{s}{2} \log \left(1 + \frac{1}{s^2} \right) + \frac{\pi}{2} - \tan^{-1} s$$

$$\Rightarrow \quad L \left\{ \frac{1 + \cos t}{t^2} \right\} = \cot^{-1} s - \frac{s}{2} \log \left(1 + \frac{1}{s^2} \right)$$

3.7 UNIT STEP FUNCTION

The function $U(t)$ defined as $U(t) = 1, \quad t \geq 0$

$= 0 \quad t < 0$ is called the **unit step function.**

Example 12. **Find the Laplace transform of**

(i) $f_1(b)\ t^2\ U(t - 3)$,

(ii) $f_2(t) = e^{t - a}\ u(t - a)$,

(iii) $f_3(t) = (t - 1)^2\ u(t - 1)$

Solution : $$L f_1(t) = \int_0^3 0 + \int_3^\infty t^2 e^{-st} t$$

Let $t = 3 + z$

$$= \int_0^\infty (3 + z)^2 e^{-s(3 + z)} = e^{-3s} \{L(9 + 6z + z^2)\}$$

$$= e^{-3s} \left\{ \frac{9}{s} + \frac{6}{s^2} + \frac{2}{s^3} \right\} = \frac{1}{s^3} (2 + 6s + 9s^2) e^{-3s}$$

(ii) $$L \{e^{t - a} U(t - a)\} = \int_a^\infty e^{t - a} e^{-st} dt.$$

Let $$t - a = z = e^{-as} \int_0^\infty e^z e^{-sz} = \frac{e^{-as}}{s - 1}$$

(iii) $L(t-1)^2\, U(t-1) = \int_1^{\infty} (t-1)^2 e^{-st}\, dt$

Let $(t-1) = z$, $I = \int_0^{\infty} e^{-s} z^2 e^{-sz}\, dz = e^{-s} \frac{!3}{s^3} = \frac{2e^{-s}}{s^3}$

PROBLEM SET 3.1

1. Find the Laplace transform of the following functions :

(i) $\sin^2 3t$ *(Warangal 95)*

(ii) $\sin 2t \cos 3t$,

(iii) $e^{-t} \sin^2 t$ *(Bangalore 90)*

(iv) $e^{-2t} \sin 4t$ *(Bhopal 91)*

(v) $\frac{e^{at} - 1}{a}$

Ans. (i) $\frac{36}{s(s^2+36)}$, (ii) $\frac{2s^2-10}{(s^2+25)(s^2+1)}$, (iii) $\frac{2}{(s+1)(s^2+2s+5)}$, (iv) $\frac{4}{(s+2)^2+16}$,

(v) $\frac{1}{s(s-a)}$

2. Find the Laplace transform of—

(i) $(1 - te^{-t})^3$

(ii) $f(t) \begin{cases} 0, & 0 \le t \le 1 \\ (t-1)^2, & t > 1 \end{cases}$

Ans. (i) $\frac{1}{s} + \frac{3}{(s+1)^2} + \frac{6}{(s+2)^3} + \frac{6}{(s+2)^4}$, (ii) $\frac{2e^{-s}}{s^3}$

3. Find the Laplace transform of

(i) $\cosh at - \cos at$

(ii) $H(t) = \begin{cases} t+1, & 0 \le t \le 2 \\ 3, & t > 2 \end{cases}$

Ans. (I) $\frac{2a^2 s}{s^4 - a^4}$ (ii) $\frac{1 + s - e^{-2s}}{s^2}$

4. Find the Laplace transform of

(i) $e^{2t} + 4t^3 - 2\sin 3t + 3\cos 3t$,

(ii) $\cos(at+b)$

(iii) $(\sin t - \cos t)^2$

Ans. (i) $\frac{1}{s-2} + \frac{24}{s^4} + \frac{3(s-2)}{s^4+9}$, (ii) $\frac{s\cos b - a\sin b}{s^2+a^2}$, (iii) $\frac{s^2-2s+4}{s(s^2+4)}$

Find the Laplace transform of the following functions :

5. $(t - \sinh 2t)$

Ans. $\dfrac{4+s^2}{s^2(4-s^2)}$

6. $\sin at \sin bt$

Ans. $\dfrac{2abs}{\{s^2+(a+b)^2\}\{s^2+(a-b)^2\}}$

7. $\sinh 2t \cos^2 t$ *(Madras 2000)*

Ans. $\dfrac{3}{2}\left[\dfrac{1}{s^2-9}+\dfrac{s^2-13}{s^4-10s^2+169}\right]$

8. $f(t) = e^t,\ 0 < t < 1$
$= 0,\ t > 1$ *(Madras 2000S, Coimbatore 1999)*

Ans. $\dfrac{e^{1-s}-1}{1-s}$

9. $f(t) = \begin{cases} \cos(t - 2\pi/3) & t > 2\pi/3 \\ 0 & t < 2\pi/3 \end{cases}$ *(Andhra 99)*

Ans. $\dfrac{s}{s^2+1} e^{-\frac{2\pi s}{3}}$

10. $f(t) = \begin{cases} \sin t, & 0 < t < \pi \\ 0, & t > \pi \end{cases}$

Ans. $\dfrac{1+e^{-\pi s}}{1+s^2}$

11. $f(t) = \begin{cases} t^2, & 0 < t < 2 \\ t-1, & 2 < t < 3 \\ 7, & t > 3 \end{cases}$ *(S. Patel 96S)*

Ans. $\dfrac{2}{s^3} + \dfrac{e^{-2s}(2+3s+3s^2)}{s^3} + \dfrac{e^{-3s}(5s-1)}{s^2}$

12. $f(t) = \begin{cases} \sin t, & 0 < t < \pi \\ \theta, & t > \pi \end{cases}$

Ans. $\dfrac{1+e^{-\pi s}}{1+s^2}$

(V) Laplace Transform of Derivatives

(i) If $L\{f(t)\} = \bar{f}(s)$, then $\boldsymbol{L\{f'(t)\} = s\bar{f}(s) - f(0)}$.

$$I = L\,|f'(t)| = \int_0^\infty \underset{I}{f'(t)}\, e^{-st}\, dt.$$ Integrating, by parts

$$I = [f(t)\, e^{-st}]_0^\infty - (-s)\int_0^\infty f(t)\, e^{-st}\, dt = -f(0) + s\bar{f}(s)$$

(ii) $L\{f^n(t)\} = \int_0^\infty \underset{I}{e^{-st}} \underset{II}{f^n(t)}\, dt\, dt$, Integrating by parts

$$I_n = [e^{-st} f^{n-1}(t)]_0^\infty + s \int_0^\infty e^{-st} f^{n-1}(t)\, dt$$

$$= 0 - f^{n-1}(0) + s\, I_{n-1}$$

$$sI_{n-1} = s\,(-f^{n-2}(0) + s\, I_{n-2})$$

.....

$$s^{n-1} I_1 = s^{n-1}(-f(0) + sI_0)$$

Hence, in general

$$\boldsymbol{I_n = s^n \bar{f}(s) - s^{n-1} f(0) - s^{n-1} f'(0) \ldots - s' s^{n-2}(0) - f^{n-1}(0).}$$

Assuming $\lim\limits_{t \to \infty} e^{-st} f^{n-1}(t) = 0$ for $n = 1, 2, 3, \ldots, n$.

This theorem is used in solving differential equations, using Laplace transform.

Example 3.13. **If** $\boldsymbol{L\{t \sin at\} = \dfrac{2as}{(s^2 + a^2)^2}}$, **evaluate :**

(i) $\boldsymbol{L\{at \cos at + \sin at\}}$

(ii) $\boldsymbol{L\{2 \cos at - at \sin at\}}$

Solution : Let $F(t) = t \sin at$

$\Rightarrow \quad F'(t) = at \cos at + \sin at$

and $\quad F''(t) = 2a \cos at - a^2 t \sin at$

Also $\quad F(0) = 0 = F(0)', F''(0) = 2a$

It is given that

$$f(s) = \frac{2as}{(s^2 + a^2)^2}$$

(i)
$$L\{at \cos at + \sin at\} = s \cdot \frac{2as}{(s^2 + a^2)^2} - 0$$

$$= \frac{2as^2}{(s^2 + a^2)^2}$$

(ii)
$$L\{F''(t)\} = s^2 f(s) - sF(0) - F'(0)$$

$$= s^2 \frac{2as}{(s^2 + a^2)^2} - s \,.\, 0 - 0$$

$$= \frac{2as^3}{(s^2 + a^2)^2}$$

$\therefore$
$$L\{2 \cos at - at \sin at\} = \frac{2s^3}{(s^2 + a^2)^2}$$

3.8 LAPLACE TRANSFORM OF $\{t^n f(t)\}$, n BEING A POSITIVE INTEGER

Property VI

If $L\{f(t)\} = \bar{f}(s)$, then

$$L\{t^n f(t)\} = (-1)^n \frac{d^n}{ds^n} \{\bar{f}(s)\}.$$

Proof. When the series or integral is uniformly convergent, it can be differentiated under the integral sign. So when the Laplace transform exists, differentiating

$$\bar{f}(s) = \int_0^\infty e^{-st} f(t)\, dt \qquad ...(1)$$

partially w.r.t. both the sides

$$\frac{d\bar{f}(s)}{ds} = \int_0^\infty \frac{\partial}{\partial s}(e^{-st}) f(t)\, dt = -\int_0^\infty t\, e^{-st} f(t)\, dt.$$

Differentiating successively n times, we get

$$\frac{d^n \bar{f}(s)}{ds^n} = (-1)^n \int_0^\infty t^n e^{-st} f(t)\, dt.$$

or

$$\int_0^\infty t^n e^{-st} f(t)\, dt = (-1)^n \frac{d^n \bar{f}(s)}{ds^n}.$$

It can also be proved by Mathematical Induction.

Example 3.14. **Find the Laplace transform of**

(i) $t\, e^{-2t} \sin 2t$ *(Madras 96S)*

(ii) $t^2 e^{-3t} \sin 2t$ *(Madras 2000S)*

(iii) $t^3 e^{-3t}$. *(Kuvempu 96)*

Solution : (i) $L(\sin 2t) = \dfrac{2}{s^2 + 4}$

So $L(t \sin 2t) = \dfrac{(-1)2\,(-2s)}{(s^2 + 4)^2}$

Hence $L\{e^{-2t}(t \sin 2t)\} = \dfrac{4(s+2)}{\{(s+2)^2 + 4\}^2}$

(ii) $L(e^{-3t} \sin 2t) = \dfrac{2}{(s+3)^2 + 2^2}$

So $$L(t^2 e^{-3t} \sin 2t) = (-1)^2\, 2 \frac{d^2}{d^2} (s^2 + 6s + 13)^{-1}$$

$$= \frac{d}{ds} \{-2\,(2s+6)\,(s^2 + 6s + 13)^{-2}\}$$

$$= -4(s^2 + 6s + 13)^{-2} + 16(s+3)^2 (s^2 + 6s + 13)^{-3}$$

$$= \frac{4(3s^2 + 18s + 23)}{(s^2 + 6s + 13)^3}$$

(iii) $L(t^3 e^{-3t}) = (-1)^3 \frac{d^3}{ds^3} (s + 3)^{-1} = 6(s + 3)^{-4}$

Property VII. Laplace Transform of $\left\{\frac{1}{t} f(t)\right\}$

If $L\{f(t)\} = \bar{f}(s)$, then

$$L\left\{\frac{1}{t} f\right\} = \int_s^{\infty} \bar{f}(s)\, ds,$$

provided the integral exists.

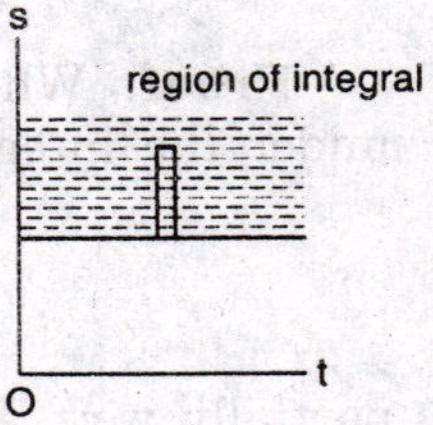

s

region of integral

s

O t

Fig. 3.2

Proof. $\bar{f}(s) = \int_0^{\infty} e^{-st} f(t)\, dt$ ...(1)

Integrating both sides w.r.t. from s to ∞

$$\int_s^{\infty} \bar{f}(s)\, ds = \int_s^{\infty} \left\{\int_0^{\infty} e^{-st} f(t)\, dt\right\} ds.$$

$$= \int_{t=0}^{\infty} \int_s^{\infty} \{e^{-st} f(t)\, ds\}\, dt$$

$$= \int_0^{\infty} f(t) \left[\frac{e^{-st}}{-t}\right]_s^{\infty} dt = \int_0^{\infty} \frac{1}{t} f(t)\, e^{-st}\, dt = L\left\{\frac{1}{t} f(t)\right\}$$

Example 3.15. Find the Laplace transform of

(i) $\frac{1}{t}(1 - e^t)$

(ii) $\frac{1}{t}(\cos at - \cos bt)$

(Madras 2000PT; Mangalore 99)

Solution. $L(1 - e^t) = \left\{\frac{1}{s} - \frac{1}{s-1}\right\}$

So $L\frac{1}{t}(1 - e^t) = \int_s^{\infty} \left\{\frac{1}{s} - \frac{1}{s-1}\right\} ds = \left[\log \frac{s}{s-1}\right]_s^{\infty}$

$$= \log \frac{s-1}{s} \quad \left[\text{as } \lim_{s\to\infty} \frac{s}{s-1} = \lim_{s\to\infty} \frac{1}{1 - \frac{1}{s}} = 1 \text{ and } \log 1 = 0\right]$$

(ii) $L(\cos at - \cos bt) = \left\{\frac{s}{s^2 + a^2} - \frac{s}{s^2 + b^2}\right\}$

So $L\,\frac{\cos at - \cos bt}{t} = \int_s^{\infty} \left\{\frac{s}{s^2 + a^2} - \frac{s}{s^2 + b^2}\right\} ds$

$$= \left[\frac{1}{2}\log\frac{s^2+a^2}{s^2+b^2}\right]_s^\infty = 0 - \frac{1}{2}\log\frac{s^2+a^2}{s^2+b^2} = \frac{1}{2}\log\left(\frac{s^2+b^2}{s^2+a^2}\right)$$

Example 3.16. **Evaluate** $\int_0^t \frac{e^t \sin t}{t}\, dt.$

Solution. (i) $L(\sin mt) = \frac{m}{s^2+m^2}$

So $$L\left(\frac{\sin mt}{t}\right) = m\int_0^\infty \frac{1}{s^2+m^2}\, ds = \frac{m}{m}\left[\tan^{-1}\frac{s}{m}\right]_s^\infty$$

$$= \frac{\pi}{2} - \tan^{-1}\frac{s}{m} = \cot^{-1}\left(\frac{s}{m}\right)$$

Hence $$\int_0^\infty e^{-st}\frac{\sin mt}{t}\, dt = \frac{\pi}{2} - \tan^{-1}\frac{s}{m}$$

Taking limit of both sides as $s \to 0$

$$\lim_{s\to 0}\int_0^\infty e^{-st}\frac{\sin mt}{t}\, dt = \int_0^\infty \frac{\sin mt}{t}\, dt = \frac{\pi}{2} - \lim \tan^{-1}\left(\frac{s}{m}\right)$$

$$= \pi/2, \text{ if } m > 0$$

$$= -\pi/2, \text{ if } m < 0 \quad \left[\textbf{Note: } \text{when } m < 0 \lim_{s\to 0} \tan^{-1}\frac{s}{m} = \pi\right]$$

(ii) $L(e^t \sin t) = \frac{1}{(s-1)^2+1}$

So $$L\left\{\frac{1}{t}(e^t \sin t)\right\} = \int_0^\infty \frac{1}{(s-1)^2+1}\, ds = \frac{1}{1}\left[\tan^{-1}\frac{s-1}{1}\right]_s^\infty$$

$$= \frac{\pi}{2} - \tan^{-1}(s-1)\cot^{-1}(s-1)$$

Property VIII. Laplace transform of integrals

Laplace transform of $\int_0^t f(u)\, du.$

If $L\{f(t)\} = \bar{f}(s)$

then $$L\left\{\int_0^t f(u)\, du\right\} = \frac{1}{s}\bar{f}(s)$$

Let $\phi(t) = \int_0^t f(u)\, du,$

So $\phi'(t) = f(t)$ and $\phi(0) = 0$

Now $$L\{\phi'(t)\} = s\phi(t) - \phi(0) = s\phi(t) - 0$$

Hence $$\phi(t) = \frac{1}{s} L\{\phi'(t)\}$$

Example 3.17. **Evaluate** $L \int_0^t \frac{e^t \sin t}{t} dt.$

Solution : $$L(e^t \sin t) = \frac{1}{(s-1)^2 + 1}$$

So $$L\left(\frac{1}{t} e^t \sin t\right) = \int_s^\infty \frac{1}{(s-1)^2 + 1} ds$$

$$= \left[\tan^{-1} \frac{(s-1)}{1}\right]_s^\infty$$

$$= \frac{\pi}{2} - \tan^{-1}(s-1) = \cot^{-1}(s-1)$$

So $$L \int_0^t \frac{1}{t} e^t \sin t \, dt = \frac{1}{s} \cot^{-1}(s-1)$$

PROBLEM SET 3.2

Find the Laplace transform of the following functions :

1. $t^2 e^{-2t} \sin t$

Ans. $\dfrac{2(3s^2 + 12s + 11)}{(s^2 + 4s + 5)^3}$

2. $t \cos at$ ***(Assam 99 Andhra 99)***

Ans. $\dfrac{s^2 - a^2}{(s^2 + a^2)^2}$

3. $t^2 \sin at$

Ans. $\dfrac{2a(3s^2 - a^2)}{(s^2 + a^2)^3}$

4. $t e^{-t} \sin 3t$

Ans. $\dfrac{6(s + 1)}{(s^2 + 2s + 10)^2}$

5. If $L\{f(t)\} = \bar{f}(s)$ Prove :

(i) $L\{tf(t)\} = -\dfrac{d}{ds}\{\bar{f}(s)\}$

(ii) $L\left\{\frac{1}{t} f(t)\right\} = \int_s^\infty \bar{f}(s)\, ds.$

6. Find the Laplace transform of

(i) $\frac{\sin 2t}{t}$ *(Madras 93)*

Ans. (i) $\cos^{-1} \frac{s}{2}$

(ii) $\frac{1-e^t}{t}$ *(Karnataka 93, Rewa 90)*

Ans. $\log \frac{s-1}{s}$

7. Find the Laplace transform of

(i) $\frac{\cos 2t - \cos 3t}{t}$ *(Madurai 88)*

Ans. (i) $\frac{1}{2} \log \frac{s^2+9}{s^2+4}$

(ii) $\frac{\sin^2 t}{t}$

Ans. $\frac{1}{4} \log \frac{s^2+4}{s^2}$

8. Find the Laplace transform of

(i) $\frac{\sinh t}{t}$,

Ans. $\frac{1}{2} \log \frac{s-1}{s+1}$

(ii) $\frac{e^{-3t} - e^{-6t}}{t}$ *(Kerala 97S)*

Ans. $\log\left(\frac{s+6}{s+3}\right)$

9. If $L\left\{\frac{1-\cos at}{a^2}\right\} = \frac{1}{s(s^2+a^2)}$. Show that $L\left\{\frac{t(1-\cos at)}{a^2}\right\} = \frac{3s^2+a^2}{s^2(s^2+a^2)^2}$

10. If $L\left\{\frac{\sin at}{t}\right\} = \tan^{-1}\left(\frac{1}{s}\right)$. Show $L\left\{\frac{\sin at}{t}\right\} = \tan^{-1} \frac{a}{s}$

11. Prove that (i) $\int_0^\infty \frac{e^{-t} - e^{-3t}}{t} = \log_e 3$, (ii) $\int_0^\infty \frac{e^{-t} \sin^2 t}{t}\, dt = \frac{1}{4} \log 5$

12. Evaluate (i) $L\left\{\int_0^t \frac{\sin t}{t}\, dt\right\}$, *(Delhi 97)*

(ii) $\int_0^t e^{-t} \cos t \, dt$

Ans. (i) $\frac{1}{s} \cot^{-1}(s)$, (ii) $\frac{1}{s} \cdot \frac{s+1}{s^2 + 2s + 2}$

13. Find the Laplace transform of

(i) $\frac{1 - \cos 2t}{t}$ *(Mysore 97)*

Ans. $\frac{1}{2} \log \frac{s^2 + 4}{s^2}$

(ii) $\frac{e^{at} - \cos bt}{t}$ *(Madras 99)*

Ans. $\log \frac{s^2 - b^2}{s - a}$

14. Find the Laplace transform of

(i) $\frac{1 - \cos t}{t^2}$

Ans. $\cot^{-1} s - \frac{s}{2} \log (1 + s^{-2})$

(ii) $t\, e^{-t} \cosh t$ *(Assam 99)*

Ans. $\frac{s^2 + 2s + 2}{(s^2 + 2s)^2}$

15. Find the Laplace transform of

(i) $t^2 \cos at$

Ans. (i) $\frac{2s^2 - 6a^2 s}{(s^2 + a^2)^3}$

(ii) $t \sinh at$

Ans. $\frac{2as}{(s^2 - a^2)^2}$

16. Given $L\left\{2\sqrt{\frac{t}{\pi}}\right\} = s^{-3/2}$, show $L\left(\frac{1}{\sqrt{\pi t}}\right) = s^{-\frac{1}{2}}$ *(Gulbarga 99s)*

3.9 INVERSE LAPLACE TRANSFORM

Using the results of Laplace transform of a function $f(t)$ $L\{f(t)\} = \bar{f}(s)$, we define the inverse transform denoted as $L^{-1}\{\bar{f}(s)\} = f(t)$ and have the following results :

(i) As $L(1) \frac{1}{s}$, so $L^{-1}\left(\frac{1}{s}\right) = 1$. Similarly

(ii) $L^{-1} \frac{1}{s - a} = e^{at}$

(iii) $L^{-1}\left(\frac{1}{s^n}\right) = \frac{t^{n-1}}{\lfloor n} = \frac{t^{n-1}}{n! - 1}$ if n be a positive integer as $n = \lceil n = \lfloor n-1$.

(iv) $L^{-1}\left(\frac{1}{s^2 + a^2}\right) = \frac{1}{a} \sin at$

(v) $L^{-1}\left(\frac{s}{s^2 + a^2}\right) = \cos at$

(vi) $L^{-1} \frac{1}{s^2 - a^2} = \frac{1}{a} \sinh at$

(vii) $L^{-1} \frac{s}{s^2 - a^2} = \cosh at$

(viii) $L^{-1} \frac{1}{(s-a)^2 + a^2} = \frac{1}{a} e^{at} \sin at$

(ix) $L^{-1} \frac{s-a}{(s-a)^2 + a^2} = e^{at} \cos at.$

(x) $L^{-1} \frac{s}{(s + a^2)^2} = \frac{1}{2a} (t \sin at)$

(xi) $L^{-1} \frac{1}{(s^2 + a^2)^2} = \frac{\sin at - at \cos at}{2a^3}$

(xii) $L^{-1} \frac{1}{(s-a)^n} = e^{at} \frac{t^{n-1}}{\lfloor n} = \frac{e^{at}\, t^{n-1}}{!\, n-1}$ if n be a positive integer.

To find the inverse Laplace transform of a compound fraction as $\frac{1}{(s-1)(s-2)}$, it should first be broken into partial fractions and after that, some of the above formulae which applicable should be applied on each fraction.

Property I. Linearty Property :

If a_1 and b_1 are constants and

$$L\{f_1(t)\} = \bar{f}_1(s) \text{ and } L\{f_2(t) = \bar{f}_2(s), \text{ than}$$

$$L^{-1}\{a_1\bar{f}_1(s) + a_2\bar{f}_2(s)\} = a_1L^{-1}\{\bar{f}_1(s)\} + a_2L^{-1}\{\bar{f}_2(s)\}$$

Example 3.18. Find the inverse Laplace transform of $\frac{1}{s+2} + \frac{3s}{s^2+4}$

Solution : $L^{-1}\left\{\frac{1}{s+2}\right\} = e^{-2t}$ and $L^{-1}\left\{\frac{s}{s^2+4}\right\} = \cos 2t$

$$\therefore \quad L^{-1}\left\{\frac{1}{s+2} + \frac{3s}{s^2+4}\right\} = L^{-1}\left\{\frac{1}{s+2}\right\} + 3L^{-1}\left\{\frac{s}{s^2+4}\right\}$$

$$= e^{-2t} + 3\cos 2t$$

Property II. First Shifting Property :

If $L^{-1}\{\bar{f}(s)\} = \bar{f}(t)$, then $L^{-1}\{\bar{f}(s-a)\} = e^{at} F(t)$.

Example 3.19. Find the inverse Laplace transform of $\dfrac{s+1}{s^2+2s+1}$

Solution :

$$\bar{f}(s) = \frac{s+1}{s^2+2s+4} = \frac{s+1}{(s+1)^2+3}$$

$$\because \quad L^{-1}\left\{\frac{s}{s^2+3}\right\} = \cos\sqrt{3}t$$

$$\therefore \quad L^{-1}\left\{\frac{s+1}{s^2+2s+4}\right\} = e^{-t}\cos\sqrt{3}t$$

Property III. Second Shifting Property :

If $L^{-1}\{f(s)\} = f(t)$, then $L^{-1}\{e^{-as}f(s)\} = g(t)$, where $g(t) = \begin{cases} f(t-a), & t > a \\ 0, & t < a \end{cases}$.

Example 3.20. Find inverse Laplace transform of $\left(\dfrac{e^{-s}-e^{-3s}}{s^2}\right)$

Solution :

$$\because \quad L^{-1}\left\{\frac{1}{s^2}\right\} = t = f(t) \text{ (say)}$$

$$\therefore \quad L^{-1}\left\{\frac{e^{-s}}{s^2}\right\} = L^{-1}\left\{e^{-s}\cdot\frac{1}{s^2}\right\} = \begin{cases} t-1, & t > 1 \\ 0, & t < 1 \end{cases} \quad \text{(By second shifting property)}$$

$$= (t-1)\,u(t-1)$$

and $$L^{-1}\left\{\frac{e^{-3s}}{s^2}\right\} = L^{-1}\left\{e^{-3s}\cdot\frac{1}{s^2}\right\} = \begin{cases} t-3, & t > 3 \\ 0, & t < 3 \end{cases} = (t-3)\,u(t-3)$$

$$\therefore \quad L^{-1}\left\{\frac{e^{-s}-e^{-3s}}{s^2}\right\} = (t-1)\,u(t-1) - (t-3)\,4(t-3)$$

Property IV.

If $L^{-1}\{\bar{f}(s)\} = f(t)$, then $L^{-1}\{\bar{f}(as)\} = \dfrac{1}{a} f\left(\dfrac{t}{a}\right)$

Example 3.21. $L^{-1}\left\{\dfrac{e^{-1/s}}{\sqrt{s}}\right\} = \dfrac{\cos 2\sqrt{t}}{\sqrt{\pi t}}$, find $L^{-1}\left\{\dfrac{e^{-a/s}}{\sqrt{s}}\right\}$ *(AUUP 2008)*

Solution : It is given that $L^{-1}\left\{\dfrac{e^{-1/s}}{\sqrt{s}}\right\} = \dfrac{\cos 2\sqrt{t}}{\sqrt{\pi t}} = f(t)$ (say)

Then $$\frac{e^{-a/s}}{\sqrt{s}} = \frac{1}{\sqrt{a}}\left[\frac{e^{-a/s}}{\sqrt{s/a}}\right]$$

$$\therefore \quad L^{-1}\left\{\frac{e^{-a/s}}{\sqrt{s}}\right\} = \frac{1}{\sqrt{a}} L^{-1}\left[\frac{e^{-a/s}}{\sqrt{s/a}}\right]$$

$$= \frac{1}{\sqrt{a}}\, a \cdot \frac{\cos 2\sqrt{at}}{\sqrt{\pi a t}} = \frac{\cos 2\sqrt{at}}{\sqrt{\pi t}}$$

Property V : Inverse Laplace Transform of Derivatives :

If $L^{-1}\{\bar{f}(s)\} = f(t)$, then $L^{-1}\{\bar{f}^{(n)}(s)\} = L^{-1}\left\{\frac{d^n}{ds^n}\bar{f}(s)\right\} = (-1)^n t^n f(t)$

Example 3.22. Find the inverse laplace transform of $\tan^{-1}\left(\frac{1}{s}\right)$

Solution :

$$L^{-1}\left\{\tan^{-1}\frac{1}{s}\right\} = -\frac{1}{t} L^{-1}\left\{\frac{d}{ds}\tan^{-1}\frac{1}{s}\right\}$$

$$= -\frac{1}{t} L^{-1}\left\{\frac{1}{1+\frac{1}{s^2}}\left(-\frac{1}{s^2}\right)\right\} = \frac{1}{t} L^{-1}\left\{\frac{1}{1+s^2}\right\}$$

$$= \frac{\sin t}{t}$$

Example 3.23. Find the inverse Laplace tranform of $\log\left(\frac{s+a}{s+b}\right)$.

Solution :

$$L^{-1}\left\{\log\left(\frac{s+a}{s+b}\right)\right\} = -\frac{1}{t} L^{-1}\left\{\frac{d}{ds}\log\frac{(s+a)}{(s+b)}\right\}$$

$$= -\frac{1}{t} L^{-1}\left\{\frac{d}{ds}(\log(s+a) - \log(s+b))\right\}$$

$$= -\frac{1}{t} L^{-1}\left\{\frac{1}{s+a} - \frac{1}{s+b}\right\} = -\frac{1}{t}\left[L^{-1}\left\{\frac{1}{s+a}\right\} - L^{-1}\left\{\frac{1}{s+b}\right\}\right]$$

$$= -\frac{1}{t}[e^{-at} - e^{-bt}] = \frac{e^{-bt} - e^{-at}}{t}$$

Property VI : Multiplication by *s*

If $L^{-1}\{\bar{f}(s)\} = f(t)$, and $f(0) = 0$, then $L^{-1}\{s\bar{f}(s)\} = f'(t)$.

Example 3.24. Using property VI. Find inverse Laplace transform of $\frac{s}{s^2+4}$.

Solution :

$$\because \quad L^{-1}\left\{\frac{1}{s^2+4}\right\} = \frac{1}{2}\sin 2t$$

$$\therefore \quad L^{-1}\left\{s \cdot \frac{1}{s^2+4}\right\} = \frac{d}{dt}\left[\frac{1}{2}\sin 2t\right]$$

$$= \frac{1}{2}\, 2\cos 2t = \cos 2t$$

Property VII : Division by *s*

If $L^{-1}\{\bar{f}(s)\} = f(t)$, then $L^{-1}\left\{\frac{\bar{f}(s)}{s}\right\} = \int_0^t f(u)du$

and $L^{-1}\left\{\frac{\bar{f}(s)}{s^n}\right\} = \int_0^t \int_0^t \dots \int_0^t f(u)du$

Example 3.25. Find the inverse Laplace transform of $\frac{1}{s(s^2+4)}$.

Solution : $\because \quad L^{-1}\left\{\frac{1}{s^2+4}\right\} = \frac{1}{2}\sin 2t$

$$\therefore \quad L^{-1}\left\{\frac{1}{s(s^2+4)}\right\} = \int_0^t \frac{1}{2}\sin 2u\, du$$

$$= \frac{-1}{2}\left[\frac{\cos 2u}{2}\right]_0^t$$

$$= \frac{-1}{4}[\cos 2t - \cos 0] = \frac{1}{4}[1 - \cos 2t]$$

Property VIII : Heaviside's Expansion Formula for Inverse Laplace Transform :

Let $\bar{f}(s)$ and $\bar{g}(s)$ be two polynomial function of s, such that degree of $\bar{g}(s)$ is greater than that of $\bar{f}(s)$ and if $\bar{g}(s)$ have distinct roots, (*i.e.*, $\bar{g}(s) = (s-\alpha_1)(s-\alpha_2)\dots(s-\alpha_n)$, where $\alpha_1, \alpha_2, \dots, \alpha_n$ are distinct roots of $\bar{g}(s)$. Then

$$L^{-1}\left\{\frac{\bar{f}(s)}{\bar{g}(s)}\right\} = \sum_{r=1}^{n} \frac{\bar{f}(\alpha_\gamma)}{\bar{g}'(\alpha_\gamma)} e^{\alpha_\gamma t}$$

Example 3.26. Apply Heaviside's Expansion formula, to find the inverse Laplace transform of $\left(\frac{2s^2+5s-4}{s^3+s^2-2s}\right)$.

Solution : Here we get $\bar{f}(s) = 2s^2 + 5s - 4$ and $\bar{g}(s) = s^3 + s^2 - 2s$ obviously $\alpha_1 = 0$, $\alpha_2 = 1$ $\alpha_3 = 2$ are distinct roots of $\bar{g}(s)$ and $g'(s) = 3s^2 + 2s - 2$.

$$\therefore \quad L^{-1}\left\{\frac{2s^2+5s-4}{s^3+s^2-2s}\right\} = \frac{\bar{f}(0)}{\bar{g}'(0)}e^{0.t} + \frac{\bar{f}(1)}{\bar{g}'(1)}e^{1.t} + \frac{\bar{f}(-2)}{\bar{g}'(-2)}e^{-2t}$$

$$= \frac{-4}{-2}\cdot 1 + \frac{(3)}{(3)}e^t + \left(\frac{-6}{6}\right)e^{-2t}$$

$$= 2 + e^t - e^{-2t}$$

Example 3.27. **Find the inverse Laplace transform of the following :**

(i) $L^{-1}\left\{\dfrac{s}{(s^2+a^2)^2}\right\}$,

(ii) $L^{-1}\left\{\dfrac{s^2-a^2}{(s^2+a^2)^2}\right\}$

Solution : We know

(ii) $L(\sin at) = \dfrac{a}{s^2+a^2}$

differentiating both sides w.r.t. a

$$L(t\cos at) = \frac{1\cdot(s^2+a^2)-2a^2}{(s^2+a^2)^2} = \frac{s^2-a^2}{(s^2+a^2)^2}$$

Hence $$L^{-1}\left(\frac{s^2-a^2}{(s^2+a^2)^2}\right) = t\cos at.$$

(i) $$L(\cos at) = \left\{\frac{s}{s^2+a^2}\right\}$$

differentiating both sides w.r.t. a

$$L(-t\sin at) = \frac{-2as}{(s^2+a^2)^2}$$

Hence $$L\left(\frac{t\sin at}{2a}\right) = \frac{s}{(s^2+a^2)^2}$$

So $$L^{-1}\frac{s}{(s^2+a^2)^2} = \frac{t\sin at}{2a}.$$

Second Method

$$L(e^{iat}\,t) = \frac{1}{(s-ia)^2} = \frac{(s+ia)^2}{(s^2+a^2)^2}$$

So $$L\{t(\cos at + i\sin at)\} = \frac{s^2-a^2}{(s^2+a^2)^2} + 2i\,\frac{as}{(s^2+a^2)^2}$$

Equation real and imaginary parts

$$L(t\cos at) = \frac{s^2-a^2}{(s^2+a^2)^2}$$

So $$L^{-1}\left\{\frac{s^2-a^2}{(s^2+a^2)^2}\right\} = t\cos at$$

and $$L^{-1}\frac{s}{(s^2+a^2)^2} = \frac{1}{2a}(t\sin at)$$

Example 3.28. **Find the inverse Laplace transform of**

(i) $\dfrac{5s+3}{(s-1)(s^2+2s+5)}$ *(Bangalore 90)*

(ii) $\dfrac{s}{s^4 + 4a^4}$ *(Delhi 94, Kerala 95)*

Solution. Let $\dfrac{5s+3}{(s-1)(s^2+2s+5)} \approx \dfrac{A}{s-1} + \dfrac{Bs+C}{s^2+2s+5}$

then $$A = \lim_{s \to 1} (s-1) f(s) = \frac{5 \times 1 + 3}{1+2+5} = 1$$

$$Bs + C = \lim_{s^2+2s+5 \to 0} (s^2+2s+5) f(s) = \lim \frac{5s+3}{s-1}$$

or $$(Bs+C)(s-1) = 5s+3$$

or $$Bs^2 + (C-B)s - C = 5s+3$$

As $$s^2 + 2s + 5 \to 0$$

So $$s^2 \to -(2s+5)$$

$$-B(2s+5) + (C-B)s - C$$

Comparing coefficients of s and constant term

$C - 3B = 5, \; -5B - C = 3$

So $B = -1, \; C = 2$

So $$L^{-1}\bar{f}(s) = L^{-1}\left\{\frac{1}{s-1} + \frac{(-1)(s+1)}{(s+1)^2+2^2} + \frac{2+1}{(s+1)^2+2^2}\right\}$$

$$= e^t - e^{-t}\cos 2t + \frac{3}{2}e^{-t}\sin 2t.$$

Example 3.29. Find the inverse Laplace transform of the following :

(i) $\log \dfrac{s+1}{s-1}$

(ii) $\dfrac{1-s}{s(s+1)}$

Solution : We know $$L\{t\,f(t)\} = -\frac{d\bar{f}(s)}{ds}$$

where $$\bar{f}(s) = L\,f(t)$$

$$= -\frac{d}{ds}\{\log(s+1) - \log(s-1)\}$$

$$= -\frac{1}{s+1} + \frac{1}{s-1}$$

Hence $$t\,f(t) = -L^{-1}\frac{1}{s+1} + L^{-1}\frac{1}{s-1} = -e^{-t} + e^t$$

Hence $$f(t) = \frac{2\sinh t}{t}$$

(ii) $$\frac{s^2+1}{s(s+1)} = \frac{1-s}{s(s+1)} = \frac{1}{s}\frac{-2}{s+1} = \bar{f}(s)$$

$$L\{t\,f(t)\} = -\frac{d\bar{f}(s)}{ds} = \frac{1}{s^2} - \frac{2}{(s+1)^3}$$

So $$t\,f(t) = L^{-1}\left(\frac{1}{s^2}\right) - 2\,L^{-1}\frac{1}{(s+1)^3}$$

$$= \frac{t^2}{!2} - \frac{2e^{-t}\,t^2}{!2}$$

Hence $f(t) = t - 2e^{-t}\,t = \boldsymbol{t\,(1 - 2e^{-t})}$

Example 3.30. Find the inverse Laplace transforms of the following :

(i) $\log \dfrac{s^2+1}{s(s+1)}$

(ii) $\cot^{-1}\dfrac{s}{2}$

(iii) $\tan^{-1}\dfrac{2}{s^2}$.

Solution. (i) $L\,\{t\,f(t)\} = -\dfrac{d}{ds}\,\{\log(s^2+1) - \log s - \log(s+1)\}$

$$= -2\,\frac{s}{s^2+1} + \frac{1}{s} + \frac{1}{s+1}$$

Hence $$t\,f(t) = L^{-1}\left(-2\,\frac{s}{s^2+1} + \frac{1}{s} + \frac{1}{s+1}\right)$$

$$= \boldsymbol{-2\cos t + 1 + e^{-t}}$$

(ii) $$L\,\{t\,f(t)\} = -\frac{d}{ds}\cot^{-1}\left(\frac{s}{2}\right) = \frac{1}{1+\frac{s^2}{4}} \times \frac{1}{2} = \frac{2}{s^2+4}$$

Hence $$t\,f(t) = L^{-1}\left(\frac{2}{s^2+4}\right) = \sin 2t.$$

So $$f(t) = \frac{1}{t}\sin 2t.$$

(iii) $$L\,\{t\,f(t)\} = -\frac{d}{ds}\tan^{-1}\left(\frac{2}{s^2}\right) = -\frac{d}{ds}\cot^{-1}\left(\frac{s^2}{2}\right) = \frac{s}{1+\frac{s^4}{4}}$$

$$= \frac{4s}{(s^2+2)^2 - (2s)^2}$$

$$= \left\{\frac{1}{s^2-2s+2} - \frac{1}{s^2+2s+2}\right\}$$

$$= \boldsymbol{\frac{1}{(s-1)^2+1} - \frac{1}{(s+1)^2+1}}$$

Hence $$t\,f(t) = L^{-1}\frac{1}{(s-1)^2+1} - L^{-1}\frac{1}{(s+1)^2+1}$$

$$= e^{t}\sin t - e^{-t}\sin t = 2\sin t\sinh t$$

So $$f(t) = \boldsymbol{\frac{2}{t}\sin t\sinh t.}$$

PROBLEM SET 3.3

Find the inverse Laplace transform of the following :

1. $\dfrac{s^2 - 3s + 4}{s^3}$

Ans. $1 - 3t + 2t^2$

2. $\dfrac{3(s^2 - 2)^2}{2s^5}$

Ans. $\dfrac{3}{2} - 3t^2 + \dfrac{t^4}{4}$

3. $\dfrac{3s + 4}{4s^2 + 12s + 9}$

Ans. $\dfrac{1}{8}(6 - t)\, e^{-\frac{3}{2}t}$

4. $\dfrac{3s^2}{s^3 - a^3}$

Ans. $e^{at} + 2\, e^{\frac{-at}{2}} \cos\left(\dfrac{a}{2}\sqrt{3}\, t\right)$

5. $\dfrac{s}{(s + 1)^2 (s^2 + 1)}$

Ans. $\dfrac{1}{2}(\sin t - t\, e^{-t})$

6. $\dfrac{1}{s^3 - a^3}$ *(Gulbarga 96)*

Ans. $\dfrac{1}{3a^2}\left[e^{at} - e^{\frac{-at}{2}} \cos a \dfrac{\sqrt{3}}{2} t - \sqrt{3}\, e^{-at/2} \sin a \dfrac{\sqrt{3}}{2} t\right]$

7. $\dfrac{1}{s^4 - 4}$

Ans. $\dfrac{1}{2a^3}\{\sinh at - \sin at\}$

8. $\dfrac{2s^2 - 6s + 5}{s^3 - 6s^2 + 11s - 6}$

Ans. $\dfrac{1}{2} e^{t} - e^{2t} + \dfrac{5}{2} e^{3t}$

9. $\dfrac{s^2 + s - 2}{s(s + 3)(s - 3)}$ *(Assam 99)*

Ans. $\dfrac{1}{3} + \dfrac{4}{15} e^{-3t} + \dfrac{2}{5} e^{2t}$

10. $\dfrac{1+2s}{(s+2)^2 (s-1)^2}$ *(Madurai 91)*

Ans. $\dfrac{t}{3}(e^t - e^{-2t})$

11. $\dfrac{s^3}{s^4 - a^4}$ *(Bhopal 91)*

Ans. $\dfrac{1}{2}(\sin t - t\, e^{-t})$

12. $\dfrac{s}{(s-3)(s^2+4)}$

Ans. $\dfrac{1}{13}(3\,e^{3t} - 3\cos 2t + 2\sin 2t)$

13. $\dfrac{s^2+6}{(s^2+1)(s^2+4)}$ *(Andhra Mech 90)*

Ans. $\dfrac{1}{3}(5\sin t - \sin 2t)$

14. $\dfrac{2s-3}{s^2+4s+13}$ *(Bangalore 91)*

Ans. $\dfrac{1}{3}e^{-2t}(6\cos 3t - 7\sin 3t)$

15. $\dfrac{s+3}{(s^2-5s+13)^2}$ *(Calicut 94)*

Ans. $3e^{-3t}(t\sin t)$

16. $\dfrac{s^2+s}{(s^2+1)(s^2+2s+2)}$

Ans. $\dfrac{1}{5}(1+e^{-t})\sin t + \dfrac{3}{5}(1-e^{-t})\cos t$

17. $\dfrac{s}{s^4+s^2+1}$

Ans. $\dfrac{2}{\sqrt{3}}\sinh\dfrac{t}{2}\sin\dfrac{\sqrt{3}\,t}{2}$

18. $\dfrac{a(s^2-2a^2)}{s^4+4a^4}$ *(Bhopal 91)*

Ans. $\cos at \sinh at$

19. $\dfrac{1}{(s^2+a^2)^2}$ *(Mysore 95)*

Ans. $\dfrac{1}{2a^3}(\sin at - at\cos at)$

20. If $u(t-a) = 0, \quad t < a$
$\qquad\qquad = 1, \quad t \geq a$

Show $L\, U(t-a) = \frac{1}{s} e^{-as}$.

21. $\frac{s}{s^2 - a^2} e^{-as}$

Ans. $\cosh \omega(t-a)\, U(t-a)$

22. $\frac{e^{-3s}}{s-3}$

Ans. $e^{3(t-2)}\, u(t-2)$

23. $\frac{e^{-as}}{s^2}\; a > 0$

Ans. $(t-a)\, U\,(t-a)$

3.10 INITIAL AND FINAL VALUE THEOREMS

(i) $$\lim_{s \to \infty} s\,\bar{f}(s) = \lim_{t \to 0} f(t) \qquad \ldots(1)$$

(ii) $$\lim_{s \to 0} s\,\bar{f}(s) = \lim_{t \to \infty} f(t) \qquad \ldots(2)$$

Solution. (i) $$\int_0^\infty e^{-st} f'(t)\, dt = s\,\bar{f}(s) - f(0) \qquad \ldots(3)$$

Taking limit in (3) as $s \to \infty$

$$0 = \lim_{s \to \infty} s\,\bar{f}(s) - \lim_{t \to 0} f(t)$$

Hence the initial value theorem is

$$\lim_{s \to \infty} s\,\bar{f}(s) = \lim_{t \to 0} f(t) \quad \text{proved.} \qquad \ldots(4)$$

(ii) Taking limit in (3) as $s \to 0$

$$\int_0^\infty \lim_{s \to 0} e^{-st} f'(t)\, dt = \lim_{s \to 0} \{s\,\bar{f}(s)\} - f(0)$$

or $$[f(t)]_0^\infty = \lim_{t \to \infty} f(t) - f(0) = \lim_{s \to 0} s\,\bar{f}(s) - f(0)$$

Hence the final value theorem is

$$\lim_{s \to 0} s\,\bar{f}(s) = \lim_{t \to \infty} f(t) \quad \text{proved.} \qquad \ldots(5)$$

3.11 CONVOLUTION THEOREM (OR FALTING THEOREM)

(AUUP 2008)

Let $\bar{f}(s)$ and $\bar{g}(s)$ be Laplace transforms of $f(t)$ and $g(t)$ respectively then by convolution of f and g, denoted by $f * g$, is meant. The theorem states, "Inverse Laplace transform of the product $\bar{f}(s)\,\bar{g}(s)$ is given by

$$f * g = L^{-1}\{\bar{f}(s)\,\bar{g}(s)\} = \int_0^t f(u)\,g(t-u)\,du.$$

f convolution g is denoted by $f * g$.

So $$\boldsymbol{f * g = L^{-1}\{\bar{f}(s)\,\bar{g}(s)\} = \int_0^t f(u)\,g(t-u)\,du.}$$

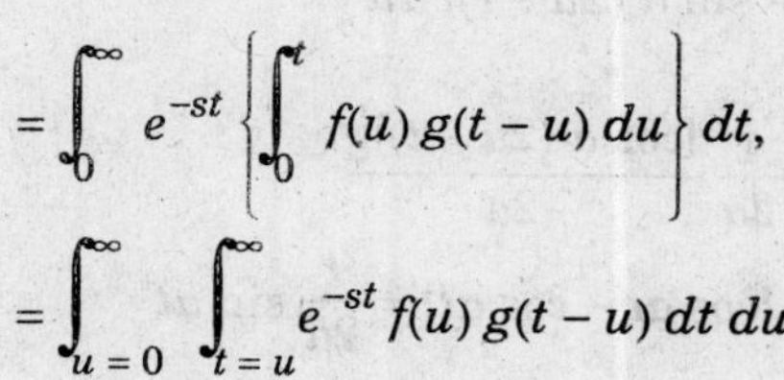

Fig. 3.3

Proof : Laplace transform of $\int_0^t f(u)\,g(t-u)\,du$

$$= \int_0^\infty e^{-st}\left\{\int_0^t f(u)\,g(t-u)\,du\right\}dt, \quad \text{on changing order of integration}$$

$$= \int_{u=0}^\infty \int_{t=u}^\infty e^{-st} f(u)\,g(t-u)\,dt\,du$$

Let $t - u = z$

$$= \int_0^\infty \int_0^\infty e^{-s(u+z)} f(u)\,g(z)\,dz\,du$$

As the limits arre independent,

So $$L\int_0^t f(u)\,g(t-u)\,du = \int_0^\infty e^{-su} f(u)\,du \int_0^\infty e^{-sz} g(z)\,dz = \bar{f}(s)\,\bar{g}(s).$$

Hence $= f * g$

or $$= L^{-1}\{\bar{f}(s)\,\bar{g}(s)\} = \int_0^t f(u)\,g(t-u)\,du.$$

Example 3.29. Apply convolution theorem to evaluate

(i) $$L^{-1}\left\{\frac{s^2}{(s^2+a^2)\,(s^2+b^2)}\right\}$$

(Delhi 94, Bhopal 91, Punjab 87b, AUUP 2007)

(ii) $$L^{-1}\left\{\frac{s}{(s^2+a^2)^2}\right\}$$

Solution : $$L^{-1}\left\{\frac{s}{s^2+a^2}\,\frac{s}{s^2+b^2}\right\} = \int_0^t \cos au \cos b\,(t-u)\,du$$

$$\frac{1}{2}\int_0^t [\cos\{(a-b)u+bt\}+\cos\{(a+b)u-bt\}]\,du$$

$$=\frac{1}{2}\left[\frac{\sin\{(a-b)\,u+bt\}}{a-b}+\frac{\sin\{(a+b)u-bt\}}{a+b}\right]_{u=0}^{t}$$

$$=\frac{1}{2}\left[\frac{\sin at-\sin bt}{a-b}+\frac{\sin st+\sin bt}{a+b}\right]$$

$$\frac{1}{(a^2+b^2)}\{a\sin at-b\sin bt\}.$$

(ii) $$L^{-1}\left\{\frac{s}{(s^2+a^2)}\frac{1}{s^2+a^2}\right\}=\frac{1}{2}\int_0^t \cos au\sin a(t-u)\,du$$

$$=\frac{1}{2a}\int_0^t \{\sin at-\sin a\,(2u-t)\}\,du$$

$$=\frac{\sin at}{2a}\cdot[u]_0^t-\frac{1}{2a}\,\frac{[\cos a\,(2u-t)]_0^t}{-2a}$$

$$=\frac{t\sin at}{2a}+\frac{1}{4a^2}\{\cos at-\cos at\}=\frac{t}{2a}\sin at$$

Example 3.30. Use convolution theorem to evaluate :

(i) $L^{-1}\left[\dfrac{1}{s^2\,(s+1)^2}\right]$

(ii) $L^{-1}\dfrac{1}{(s^2+1)^3}$

(iii) $L^{-1}\left[\dfrac{s^2}{s^4-a^4}\right]$.

Solution : (i) We know

$$L(t)=\frac{1}{s^2},\ L\,(e^{-t}\,t)=\frac{1}{(s+1)^2}$$

$$L^{-1}\,(f*g)=\int_0^t \underset{II}{e^{-u}}\ \underset{I}{u(t-u)}\,du$$

$$=[e^{-4}\,\{-4t+u^2-t+2u+2\}]_{u=0}^{t}$$

$$=e^{-t}\,(2t+2)+t-2$$

(ii) We know $L^{-1}\left(\dfrac{1}{1+s^2}\right)=\sin t$ ...(1)

So $$L^{-1}\left(\frac{1}{1+s^2}\,\frac{1}{1+s^2}\right)=\int_0^t \sin u\sin(t-u)\,du$$

$$= \frac{1}{2}\int_0^t \{\cos(-t+2u) - \cos t\}\, du$$

$$= \frac{1}{2}\left[\frac{\sin(2u-t)}{2} - 4\cos t\right]_{=0}^{t}$$

$$= \frac{1}{2}\left[\frac{\sin t - \sin(0-t)}{2} - t\cos t\right] = \frac{1}{2}(\sin t - t\cos t) \quad \text{...(2)}$$

Hence $L^{-1}\dfrac{1}{(1+s^2)^2(1+s^2)}$

$$= \int_0^t \frac{1}{2}\{\sin u - u\cos u\}\sin(t-u)\, du$$

$$= \frac{1}{4}\int_0^t \{\cos(2u-t) - \cos t - u\sin t - u\sin(t-2u)\}\, du$$

$$= \frac{1}{4}\left[\frac{\sin(2u-t)}{2} - 4\cos t\right]_{u=0}^{t} - \int_0^t \frac{u}{4}\sin t\, du - \frac{1}{4}\int_0^t u\sin(t-2u)\, du$$

$$= \frac{1}{4}\left[\frac{\sin t - \sin(-t)}{2} - t\cos t\right] - \frac{\sin t}{4}\frac{t^2}{2} - \frac{1}{4}\left[\frac{u\cos(t-2u)}{2} - \frac{1}{2}\int_0^t \cos(t-2u)\, du\right.$$

$$= \frac{1}{4}(\sin t - t\cos t) - \frac{t^2\sin t}{8} - \frac{1}{8}\left[u\cos(t-2u) + \frac{\sin(t-2u)}{2}\right]_{u=0}^{t}$$

$$= \frac{1}{4}(\sin t - t\cos t) - \frac{t^2\sin t}{8} - \frac{1}{8}\left[t\cos t + \frac{(\sin -t) - \sin t}{2}\right]$$

$$= \left(\frac{1}{4} + \frac{1}{8}\right)(\sin t - t\cos t) - \frac{t^2\sin t}{8}$$

$$= \frac{1}{8}\{(3-t^2)\sin t - 3t\cos t\}$$

(iii) $L^{-1}\left\{\dfrac{s}{s^2-a^2}\,\dfrac{s}{s^2+a^2}\right\}$.

As $\cosh au = \cos aui$,

$$= \int_0^t \cos(aui)\cos a(t-u)\, du$$

$$= \frac{1}{2}\int_0^t [\cos\{at + au(i-1)\} + \cos\{ua(i+1) - at\}]\, du$$

$$= \frac{1}{2}\left[\frac{\sin\{at + a(i-1)u\}}{a(i-1)} + \frac{\sin\{a(i+1)u - at\}}{a(i+1)}\right]_{=0}^{t}$$

$$= \frac{1}{2}\left[\frac{\sin ait - \sin at}{a(i-1)} + \frac{\sin ait - \sin(-at)}{a(i+1)}\right]$$

$$\frac{1}{2a}\sinh at\left\{\frac{i}{i-1} + \frac{i}{i+1}\right\} + \frac{\sin at}{2a}\left\{\frac{1}{i+1} - \frac{1}{i-1}\right\}$$

$$\frac{1}{2}a\left(\frac{2i^2}{-2}\right)\sinh at + \left(\frac{-2}{-2}\right)\frac{\sin at}{2a} = \frac{\sinh at + \sin at}{2a}$$

PROBLEM SET 3.4

Find the inverse Laplace transform of

1. $\frac{1}{s^2(s^2+a^2)}$ *(JNTU 95S)*

Ans. $\frac{1}{a^2}\left(t - \frac{\sin at}{a}\right)$

2. $\frac{2as}{(s^2+a^2)^2}$ *(Delhi 97)*

Ans. $t \sin at$.

3. $\log \frac{(s+1)}{(s+2)(s+3)}$ *(Combatore)*

Ans. $e^{-t} - e^{-2t} - e^{-3t}$

4. $\log \frac{s^2+1}{(s-1)^2}$. *(Madras 2000S)*

Ans. $\frac{2}{t}(e^t - \cos t)$

5. $\cot^{-1}(s+1)$ *(AMIE 97W)*

Ans. $\frac{e^{-t}\sin t}{t}$

Use convolution theorem, evaluate

6. $L^{-1}\frac{1}{(s+a)(s+b)}$ *(Madras 99)*

Ans. $\frac{e^{-bt} - e^{-at}}{a-b}$

7. $L^{-1}\frac{1}{(s^2+a^2)^2}$ *(Madras 97S)*

Ans. $\frac{\sin at - at\cos at}{2a^3}$

8. $\dfrac{1}{s^2 (s+1)^2}$ ***(Mysore 97)***

Ans. $t(e^{-t} + 1) + 2(e^{-t} - 1)$

9. $L^{-1} \dfrac{s}{(s^2+1)(s^2+4)}$ ***(Madras 2000S)***

Ans. $\dfrac{\cos t - \cos 2t}{3}$

10. Show that

(i) $L^{-1}\left\{\dfrac{1}{s} \sin \dfrac{1}{s}\right\} = t - \dfrac{t^3}{(!\,3)^2} + \dfrac{t^5}{(!\,5)^2} \dots$ ***(Mysore 99, Marathwada 99)***

Hint expand $\sin \dfrac{1}{s}$ and find L^{-1} term by term.

(ii) $L^{-1}\left(\dfrac{1}{s} \cos \dfrac{1}{s}\right) = 1 - \dfrac{t^2}{(!\,2)^2} + \dfrac{t^4}{(!\,4)^2} + \dots$

3.12 SOLUTION OF ORDINARY DIFFERENTIAL EQUATIONS, USING LAPLACE TRANSFORM

Basic formulae used here are :

(i) In general $\qquad L\left\{\dfrac{d^n f(t)}{dt^n}\right\} = s^n \bar{f}(s) - s^{n-1} f(0) \dots - s f^{n-2}(0) - f^{n-1}(0).$

In particular for $n = 1$, $\qquad L\left\{\dfrac{d f(t)}{dt}\right\} = s \bar{f}(s) - f(0)$

for $n = 2$, $\qquad L\{f''(t)\} = s^2 \bar{f}(s) - s f(0) - f'(0)$

(ii) $\qquad L\{t^n f(t)\} = (-1)^n \dfrac{d^n}{ds^n} \{\bar{f}(s)\}$

Subject to the condition that

$$e^{-st} f(t) = 0 \quad \text{as} \quad t \to \infty$$

By the use of Laplace transform, the differential equations of order one get reduced to simple algebraic equations. Then using the given initial values of $f(0)\, f'(0)$ etc. and breaking the expression for $\bar{f}(s)$ into partial fractions and then taking the inverse transform of each term, we have the solution of the equation.

Example 3.31. Solve by Laplace transform, the equations

(i) $\dfrac{dx}{dt} - 2x = 3e^t$, **given** $x(0) = 1$

(ii) $\dfrac{d^2x}{dt^2} - 3\dfrac{dx}{dt} + 2x = e^{-t}$, **given** $x(0) = x'(0) = 1.$

Solution : (i) Taking Laplace's transform, we get

$$s\,\bar{x}(s) - x(0) - 2\bar{x}(s) = \frac{3}{s-1}$$

or $$\bar{x}(s-2) = 1 + \frac{3}{s-1} = \frac{s+2}{s-1}$$

So $$\bar{x} = \frac{s+2}{(s-1)(s-2)},$$ on breaking into partial fractions

$$= \frac{-3}{s-1} + \frac{4}{s-2}$$

So $$x(t) = L^{-1}\left(\frac{-3}{s-1} + \frac{4}{s-2}\right) = -3\,e^{t} + 4\,e^{2t}$$

(ii) Taking L-ttransform of both sides, we have

$$s^2\,\bar{x}(s) - s\,x(0) - x'(0) - 3s\,\bar{x}(s) + 3x(0) + 2\,\bar{x}(s) = \frac{1}{s+1}$$

or $$(s^2 - 3s + 2)\,\bar{x} = s + 1 - 3 + \frac{1}{s+1} = \frac{s^2 - s - 1}{(s+1)}$$

So $$\bar{x} = \frac{s^2 - s - 1}{(s+1)(s-1)(s-2)},$$ on breaking into partial fractions

$$= \frac{1}{6(s+1)} + \frac{1}{2(s-1)} + \frac{1}{3(s-2)}$$

Hence $$x(t) = L^{-1}\left\{\frac{1}{6(s+1)} + \frac{1}{2(s-1)} + \frac{1}{3(s-2)}\right\}$$

$$= \left\{\frac{1}{6}e^{-t} + \frac{1}{2}e^{t} + \frac{1}{3}e^{2t}\right\}$$

Example 3.32. Solve by use of Laplace transform, the equation

$$\frac{d^2y}{dx^2} + 4y = 2\sin x + 3\cos x, \text{ given } y(0) = y'(0) = 2$$

(Raj 2001)

Solution. Taking L-transform of the equation,

$$s^2\,\bar{y} - s\,y(0) - y'(0) + 4\bar{y} = \frac{2}{s^2+1} + \frac{3s}{s^2+1}$$

or $$(s^2+4)\,\bar{y} = 2s + 2 + \frac{2+3s}{s^2+1} = \frac{2s^3 + 2s^2 + 5s + 4}{s^2+1}$$

or $$\bar{y} = \frac{2s^3 + 2s^2 + 5s + 4}{(s^2+1)(s^2+4)} = \frac{As+B}{s^2+1} + \frac{Cs+D}{s^2+4}$$

So $$2s^3 + 2s^2 + 5s + 4 = (As+B)(s^2+4) + (s^2+1)(Cs+D)$$

$$= (A+C)\,s^3 + (B+D)\,s^2 + (4A+C)\,s + (4B+D)$$

Comparing coefficients

$$A + C = 2$$

$$4A + C = 5 \text{ so } A = C = 1$$

$$B + D = 2$$

$$4B + D = 4$$

So $B = \frac{2}{3}, D = \frac{4}{3}$

Hence $$y(t) = L^{-1}\left\{\frac{s}{s^2+1} + \frac{2}{3}\frac{1}{s^2+1} + \frac{s}{s^2+4} + \frac{4}{3}\frac{1}{s^2+4}\right\}$$

$$= \left\{\cos t + \frac{2}{3}\sin t + \cos 2t + \frac{2}{3}\sin 2t\right\} \textbf{ Ans.}$$

Example 3.33. Solve the simultaneous equations

$$(D + 2)\, x + 3y = 0 \qquad ...(1)$$

$$3x + (D + 2)\, y = 2e^t \qquad ...(2)$$

given at $t = 0$, $x = 0$, $y = 0$

Solution. Taking L-transform of the equations, we have from (1)

$$s\,\bar{x}\,(s) + 2\,\bar{x}\,(s) - x(0) + 3\,\bar{y} = 0$$

or $$(s + 2)\,\bar{x} + 3\,\bar{y} = 0 \qquad ...(3)$$

and from (2)

$$3\,\bar{x} + (s + 2)\,\bar{y} + y(0) = \frac{2}{s-1}$$

or $$3\,\bar{x} + (s + 2)\,\bar{y} - \frac{2}{s-1} = 0 \qquad ...(4)$$

from (3) and (4)

$$\frac{\bar{x}}{-6-0} = \frac{\bar{y}}{2(s+2)} = \frac{1}{(s-1)\,\{(s+2)^2 - 9\}}$$

So $$\bar{x} = \frac{-6}{(s-1)^2\,(s+5)}$$

and $$\bar{y} = \frac{2(s+2)}{(s-1)\,(s-1)\,(s+5)}$$

$$= \left\{\frac{A}{s-1} + \frac{C}{s+5} + \frac{B}{(s-1)^2}\right\}$$

So $\quad -6 = A(s-1)\,(s+5) + B(s+5) + C(s-1)^2$

Putting $s = 1$; $-6 = B(6)$ or $B = 1$

Putting $s = -5$; $-6 = 0 + 0 + 36C$ so $C = \frac{-6}{36} = -\frac{1}{6}$

Putting $s = 0$; $-6 = -5A + 5B + C$

So $\quad 5A = -5 - \frac{1}{6} + 6 = \frac{5}{6}$ or $A = \frac{1}{6}$

Hence $$x(t) = L^{-1}\left\{\frac{1}{6(s-1)} - \frac{1}{(s-1)^2} - \frac{1}{6(s+5)}\right\}$$

$$= \frac{1}{6}e^t + t\,e^t - \frac{1}{6}e^{-5t}$$

$$y = -\frac{1}{3}\left(\frac{dx}{dt} + 2x\right)$$

$$= \frac{-1}{3}\left\{\left(\frac{1}{6}+2\right)e^t + (t+1+2t)\,e^t + \left(\frac{5}{6}-\frac{1}{12}\right)e^{-5t}\right\}$$

$$= -\frac{19}{18}e^t - t\,e^t + \frac{1}{18}e^{-5t}$$

Example 3.34. Solve by Laplace transform

$$(D^2 + m^2)\,y(t) = a\cos nt, \text{ given } y(0) = y'(0) = 0$$ ***(Raj 2003, MREC 2001)***

Solution. Taking L-transform of the equation

$$(s^2 + m^2)\,\bar{y} - s\,y(0) - y'(0) = a\,\frac{s}{s^2+n^2}$$

So $$\bar{y} = a\,\frac{s}{(s^2+m^2)(s^2+n^2)} = \frac{a}{m^2-n^2}\left\{\frac{s}{s^2+n^2} - \frac{s}{s^2+m^2}\right\}$$

Hence $$y(t) = L^{-1}(\bar{y}) = \frac{a}{m^2-n^2}\{\cos nt - \cos mt\}$$

Example 3.35. Solve $(D^2 + n^2)\,x = a\sin(nt+\alpha)$ given at $t = 0$, $x = x' = 0$.

Solution : Taking the Laplace transform of the equation

$$\{s^2\bar{x} - s\,x(0) - x'(0)\} + n^2\bar{x} = aL\{\sin nt\cos\alpha + \cos nt\sin\alpha\}$$

$$= a\left\{\frac{n\cos\alpha + s\sin\alpha}{s^2+n^2}\right.$$

So $$\bar{x} = ax\cos\alpha\left\{\frac{1}{(s^2+n^2)^2}\right\} + a\sin\alpha\,\frac{s}{(s^2+n^2)^2}.$$

So $$x(t) = \frac{an\cos\alpha}{n^2}L^{-1}\left\{\frac{n}{s^2+n^2}\,\frac{n}{s^2+n^2}\right\} + a\sin\alpha\,L^{-1}\left\{\frac{1}{s^2+n^2}\,\frac{s}{s^2+n^2}\right\}$$

$$= \frac{a\cos\alpha}{n}\int_0^t \sin nu\,\sin n(t-u)\,du + \frac{a\sin\alpha}{n}\int_0^t \sin nu\,\cos n(t-u)\,du$$

$$= \frac{a}{2n^2}[\sin nt\cos\alpha - nt\cos(nt+\alpha)]$$

3.13 APPLICATION OF LAPLACE TRANSFORM TO ELECTRICAL CIRCUITS

The current in a circuit containing resistance R, and inductance L and a capacitance C with e.m.f. source E is governed by

$$L\frac{di}{dt} + Ri + \frac{1}{C}Q = \dot{E} \qquad \text{...(1)}$$

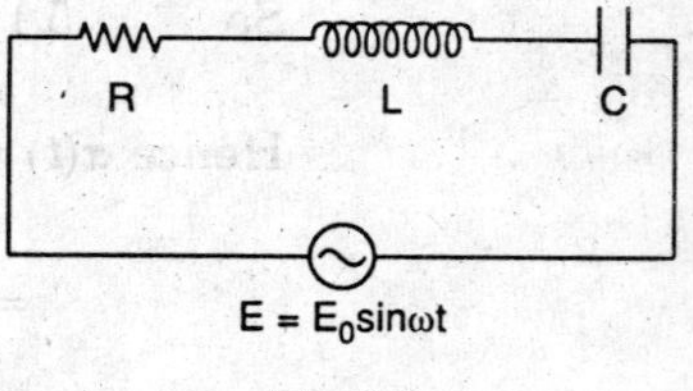

Fig. 3.4

where $i = \dfrac{dQ}{dt}$

or $$L\frac{d^2Q}{dt^2} + R\frac{dQ}{dt} + \frac{1}{C}Q = E \qquad \text{...(2)}$$

Where the source of e.m.f. may be a constant source $E = E_0$ or a sinusoidal alternating source where $E = S_0 \sin \omega t$ or an exponentially decaying source where $E = E_0 e^{-\alpha t}$.

Example 3.36. An inductor of 2 henrys, a resistor of 16 ohms and a capacitor of ·02 farads are connected is given with an e.m.f. $E = E_0$ volts.

If at $t = 0$, q the charge in the capacitor is zero and the current in the circuit is also zero, Find the charge and current in the circle for $t > 0$, if $E_0 = 300$ volts.

Solution. The equation governing the charge is

$$L \frac{d^2Q}{dt^2} + R \frac{dQ}{dt} + \frac{1}{C} Q = E_0$$

Where $L = 2$, $R = 16$, $C = ·02$, $E_0 = 300$

So $$\frac{d^2Q}{dt^2} + 8 \frac{dQ}{dt} + 25Q = 150 \quad ...(1)$$

With $Q(0) = 0$, $i(\theta) = Q'(0) = 0$.

Taking L transform of (1), we have

$$(s^2 + 8s + 25)\,\overline{Q} - sQ(0) - Q'(0) - 8Q(0) = \frac{150}{s}$$

as $Q(0) = Q'(0) = 0$

So $$\overline{Q} = 150 \frac{1}{s(s^2 + 4s + 25)}$$

On breaking into partial fractions

$$\overline{Q} = \frac{150}{25} \left\{ \frac{1}{s} - \frac{s+4}{(s+4)^2 + 3^2} \right\}$$

So $$Q = 6\left[1 - e^{-4t} (\cos 3t + 4/3 \sin 3t)\right]$$

and current $i = \dfrac{dQ}{dt} = 50\, e^{-4t} \sin 3t$.

PROBLEM SET 3.5

Solve the following differential equations, using Laplace transform :

$$\left[\textbf{Notations: } \frac{dx}{dt} = x' \textbf{ etc.}\right]$$

$\dfrac{dy}{dx} = y'$, **differentiation with respect to independent variable.**

1. $\dfrac{d^2x}{dt^2} - 2\dfrac{dx}{dt} + x = e^t$, given at $t = 0$, $x = 2$, $\dfrac{dx}{dt} = -1$.

   Ans. $x = 2e^t - 3t\,e^t + \frac{1}{2} t^2 e^t$.

2. $y'' + 3y' - 4y = x$, given $y(0) = 0$, $y'(0) = 1$

Ans. $y(x) = \left\{-\frac{3}{16} - \frac{x}{4} + \frac{2}{5}e^x - \frac{17}{80}e^{-4x}\right\}$

3. $(D^2 + 1)y = t$, given $y(0) = 1$, $y'(0) = 2$ *(Raj, 2001, 2002)*

Ans. $y(t) = t + \cos t + \sin t$

4. Solve the simultaneous equations

$$\frac{dx}{dt} - y = e^t, \; \frac{dy}{dt} + x = \sin t,$$

given $x(0) = 1$, $y(0) = 0$

Ans. $x = \frac{1}{2}[e^t + \cos t + 2\sin t - t\cos t]$; $y = \frac{1}{2}[-e^t + \cos t - \sin t + t\,e^t]$.

5. Solve $\frac{d^2x}{dt^2} + 9x = \cos 2t$, if $x(0) = 1$,

$x(\pi/2) = -1$ *(Kanpur 95, Calicut 94)*

Ans. $x = \frac{1}{5}\{\cos 2t + 4\sin 3t + 4\cos 3t\}$

6. $y'' + y = t$, given $y(0) = 1$, $y'(0) = -2$ *(Assam 99)*

Ans. $y = t - 3\sin t + \cos t$.

7. $y'' + 2y' - 3y = \sin t$, given $y(0) = y'(0) = 0$ *(Madras 90S)*

Ans. $y = \frac{1}{8}e^t - \frac{1}{40}e^{-3t} - \frac{1}{10}(2\sin t + \cos t)$.

8. $y'' - 3y' + 2y = 4t + e^{3t}$, given $y(0) = 1$, $y'(0) = -1$ *(Andhra 2000, Mangalore 99)*

Ans. $y = 2t + 3 + \frac{1}{2}(e^{3t} - e^t) - 2e^{2t}$

9. $y''' + 2y'' - y' - 2y = 0$ given at $t = 0$, $y = 1$, $y' = 2$, $y'' = 2$

Ans. $y = \frac{1}{3}(5e^t + e^{-2t}) - e^{-t}$.

10. $y'' + 2y' + 5y = e^t \sin t$, given at $t = 0$, $y = 0$, $y' = 1$ *(Assam 99, Delhi 97, Mangalore 97)*

Ans. $y = \frac{11}{3}e^{-t}\{\sin t + \sin 2t\}$.

11. A resistor of R ohms is connected is series with a capacitor of capacity C farads in a circuit having a source of E volts e.m.f. At $t = 0$, charge on the capacitor in zero find the charge and the current at $t > 0$, when
(i) $E = E_0$, a constant, (ii) $E = E_0 e^{-\alpha t}$.

Ans. (i) $Q = E_0 C[1 - e^{-t/RC}]$, $I = \frac{E_0}{R}e^{-\frac{1}{RC}t}$.

(ii) $Q(t) = \frac{E_0 C}{1 - \alpha RC}\left(e^{-\alpha t} - e^{-\frac{1}{RC}t}\right)$;

$$I = \frac{dQ}{dt} = \frac{E_0 C}{1 - \alpha RC}\left\{\frac{1}{RC}e^{-\frac{1}{RC}t} - \alpha e^{-\alpha t}\right\}.$$

12. A resistance R in series with inductance L is connected with a source of emf E volt where $E = E(t)$. If the current is given by $L\frac{di}{dt} + Ri = E(t)$. Find current at any time t, if the swtich is connected at $t = 0$ and disconnected at $t = t_1$.

Hint : $E(t) = \begin{cases} E_0, & 0 < t < t_1 \\ 0, & t > t_1 \end{cases}$

$$i = \frac{E_0}{R}\left\{1 - e^{-\frac{R}{L}t}\right\} - \frac{E_0}{R}\left\{1 - e^{-\frac{R}{l}(t-t_1)}\right\} U(t - t_1)$$

where $U(t - t_1)$ is the unit step function $U(t - t_1) = \begin{cases} 0, & t < t_1 \\ 1, & t > t_1 \end{cases}$ and $L\{U(t - t_1) f(t)\} = e^{-t_1 s}\bar{f}(s)$.

So $$i = \frac{E_0}{R}\left[1 - e^{-\frac{R}{L}t}\right], \; 0 < t < t_1$$

$$= \frac{E_0}{R}\left[e^{-\frac{R}{L}(t-t_1)} - e^{-\frac{R}{L}t}\right], \; t > t_1$$

13. Solve $(D^2 + m^2)\, x = a \cos nt,\; t > 0$ given at $t = 0$, $x = x_0$, $x' = x_1$ and $m \neq n$

Ans. $x = \frac{x_1}{m}\sin mt + \left(x_0 - \frac{a}{m^2 - n^2}\right)\cos mt + \frac{a}{m^2 - n^2}\cos nt.$

14. Solve $(D^2 + 1)\, y = t \cos 2t,\; t > 0$ given $y(0) = y'(0) = 0$ ***(MREC 2001, Raj 2002)***

Ans. $y = -\frac{5}{a}\sin t + \frac{4}{a}\sin 2t - \frac{1}{3}t\cos 2t.$

15. $(D^4 - 1)y = 1$, given $y(0) = y'(0) = y''(0) = y'''(0) = 0$

Ans. $y = -1 + \frac{1}{2}\cosh t + \frac{1}{2}\cos t.$

16. $(D^2 + 1)\, y = \sin t \sin 2t$, given for $t = 0, y = y' = 0$

Ans. $y = \frac{15}{16}\cos t + \frac{1}{4}t\sin t + \frac{1}{16}\cos 3t$

17. Solve $(D^2 + n^2)y = a \sin(nt + \alpha)$, given $y(0) = y'(0) = 0$

Ans. $y = \frac{a}{2n^2}[\sin nt \cos\alpha - nt\cos(nt + \alpha)]$

18. Solve $(D^2 - 1)y = a \cosh t$, given $y(0) = y'(0) = 0$

Ans. $y = \frac{at}{2}\sinh t.$

Solve the simultaneous differential equations

19. $(D - 2)x + 3y = 0;\; 2x + (D - 1)y = 0$, given $x(0) = 8$, $y(0) = 3$

Ans. $x = 5e^{-t} + 3e^{4t};\; y = 5e^{-t} - 2e^{4t}.$

20. $(D + 1) + (D + 1)y = 1$, given $x(0) = 0$, $y(0) = 1$; $(D - 1)\, y - 2x = 0$

Ans. $x = e^{-t} - 1;\; y = 2 - e^{-t}$

21. $(D^2 - 3)x - 4y = 0$, $(D^2 + 1)y + x = 0$, given at $t = 0$, $x = y = y' = 0$

Ans. $x = 2t\cosh t$, $y = [\sinh t - t\cosh t]$ and $x' = 2$.

22. A voltage $E\,e^{-\alpha t}$ is applied at $t = 0$, in a circuit containing inductance L and resistor R. Show that the current at time t is given by $i = \dfrac{E}{R - \alpha L}\left\{e^{-\alpha t} - e^{-\frac{R}{L}t}\right\}$

23. An inductor of 3 henry is in series with a resistor of 30 ohms and an e.m.f. $E = 150 \sin 2t$ volts. Assuming that at $t = 0$, the current is zero, find the current for $t > 0$.

Ans. $I = (\sin 20t - 2\cos 20t + 2e^{-10t})$

24. An inductor of 3 henries is in series with a resistor of 30 ohms an e.m.f. of 150 volts. Assuming the current to be zero at $t = 0$, find the current at any time $t > 0$.

Ans. $I = 5\,(1 - e^{-10t})$.

3.14 LAPLACE TRANSFORMS OF SOME OTHER USEFUL FUNCTIONS

3.14.1 (Heaviside's) Unit Step Function

Definition

The unit step function $U(t - a)$ is defined as

$$U(t-a) = \begin{cases} 0, & t < a \\ 1, & t > a \end{cases}$$

Laplace transform of $U(t - a)$

$$= \int_0^\infty e^{-st}\,U(t-a)\,dt$$

Fig. 3.5

$$L\{U(t-a)\} = \int_a^\infty e^{-st}\,dt = \frac{[e^{-st}]_a^\infty}{-s} = \frac{0 - e^{-as}}{-s} = \frac{e^{-as}}{s}$$

If $a = 0$

$$U(t-a) = U(t-0) = U(t) = \begin{cases} 0, & t < 0 \\ 1, & t > 0 \end{cases}$$

and

$$L\{U(t)\} = \frac{e^{-0s}}{s} = \frac{1}{s}$$

Second Shifting Theorem

If $L\{f(t)\} = \bar{f}(t)$,

$$L\{f(t-a)\,U(t-a)\} = e^{-as}\,\bar{f}(s)$$

$$L\{f(t-a)\,U(t-a)\} = \int_a^\infty e^{-st}\,f(t-a)\cdot 1\,dt$$

Let $t - a = z$

$$= \int_0^\infty e^{-s(a+z)}\,f(z)\,dz = e^{-as}\,\bar{f}(s).$$

Example 3.37. Find Laplace transform of :

(i) $(t-1)^2\, U(t-1)$

(ii) $\sin t\, U(t-a)$

(iii) $e^{-3t}\, U(t-2)$

Solution. (i) $L\{(t-1)^2 U(t-1)\} = \int_1^\infty e^{-st}(t-1)^2 \cdot 1\, dt$ Let $t-1=2$

$$= \int_0^\infty e^{-s(1+z)} z^2\, dz = e^{-s}\frac{!3}{s^3} = \frac{2e^{-s}}{s^3}.$$

(ii) $L\{(\sin t)\, U(t-a)\} = \int_a^\infty e^{-st} \sin t \cdot 1\, dt$

Let $t-a=z$

$$= \int_0^\infty e^{-s(a+z)} \{\sin a \cos z + \cos a \sin z\}\, dz$$

$$= e^{-as}\left\{\frac{s \sin a + \cos a}{s^2+1}\right\}$$

Taking $a = \pi$ in particular,

So $L\{\sin t\, U(t-\pi)\} = \dfrac{e^{-\pi s}}{s^2+1}\{\cos \pi + s \sin \pi\} = \dfrac{-e^{-\pi s}}{s^2+1}$

(iii) $L\, e^{-3t}\, U(t-2) = \int_2^\infty e^{-st} e^{-3t}\, dt = e^{-2s}\int_0^\infty e^{-(s+3)z}\, dz$

$$= \frac{e^{-2(s+3)}}{s+3}$$

Example 3.38. Find the inverse Laplace transform of

(i) $\dfrac{se^{-s/2} + \pi e^{-s}}{s^2+\pi^2}$

(ii) $\dfrac{e^{-es}}{s^2(s+a)}\; C > 0$ *(VTU 2000)*

Solution. W know if $L\, f(t) = \bar{f}(s)$ $L\{f(t-a)\, U(t-a)\} = e^{-as}\bar{f}(s)$

So $L^{-1}\{e^{-as}\bar{f}(s)\} = f(t-a) \cdot U(t-a)$

(i) $L^{-1}\, e^{-s/2}\left\{\dfrac{s}{s^2+\pi^2}\right\} = \cos \pi\left(1-\dfrac{1}{2}\right) U\left(t-\dfrac{1}{2}\right)$

and $L^{-1}\dfrac{e^{-s}}{s^2+\pi^2} = \dfrac{1}{\pi}\sin \pi\,(t-1)\, U\,(t-1)$

$$= -\frac{\sin \pi t}{\pi}\, U(t-1)$$

Hence $L^{-1}\{\mathcal{F}(s)\} = \sin \pi t \, U\left(t - \frac{1}{2}\right) - \pi \frac{\sin \pi t}{\pi} U(t-1)$

(ii) $L^{-1} \frac{1}{s^2(s+a)} = L^{-1}\left\{\frac{A}{s} + \frac{B}{s^2} + \frac{C}{s+a}\right\}$

$$= L^{-1}\left\{\frac{-1/a^2}{s} + \frac{\frac{1}{a}}{s^2} + \frac{1/a^2}{s+a}\right\} = \left\{\frac{-1}{a^2} + \frac{t}{a} + \frac{e^{-ta}}{a^2}\right\}$$

Hence $L^{-1}\{\mathcal{F}(s)\, e^{-Cs}\} = U(t-c)\left[-\frac{1}{a^2} + \frac{t-C}{a} + \frac{1}{a^2} e^{(-t-C)\,a}\right]$

$$= \frac{1}{a^2}\left[a(t-c) - 1 + e^{-a(t-c)}\right] U(t-c)$$

Example 3.39. **Calculate the maximum deflection of beam of length l and having a uniformly distributed load of ω kg/m in $\left(\frac{l}{4} < x < \frac{3l}{4}\right)$ only in the central half position.**

Solution. Taking the origin at one end A and measuring y to be position down wards.

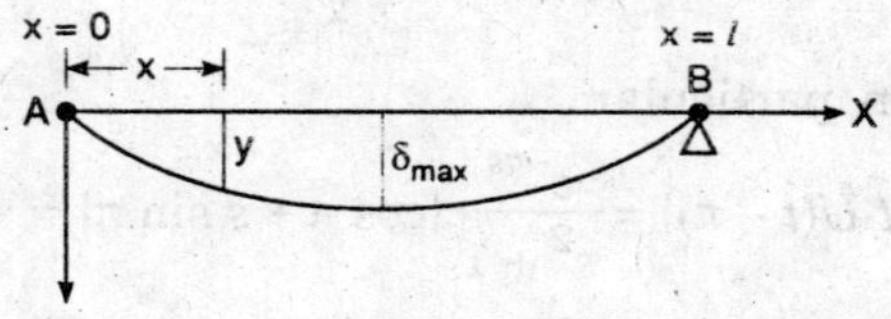

Fig. 3.6

So $\omega(x) = \omega\, U\left(x - \frac{1}{4}\right) - \omega\, U\left(x - \frac{3l}{4}\right)$

where V denotes the unit step function. The equation giving the deflection is

$$EI \frac{d^4y}{dx^4} = \omega(x)$$

$$= \omega\left\{U\left(x - \frac{l}{4}\right) - U\left(x - \frac{3l}{4}\right)\right\}$$

Taking L-transform of (1)

$$EI\,\{s^4 \bar{y} - s^3 Y(0) - s^2 y'(0) - s\, y{\rightarrow}(0) - y'''(0)\} = \left\{\frac{\omega\, e^{-\frac{1}{4}sl}}{s} - \frac{\omega\, e^{-\frac{3}{4}sl}}{s}\right\}$$

As $U(0) = U'(0) = 0$, taking $u{\rightarrow}(0) = c_1$, $U'''(0) = c_2$

$$EI\bar{Y} = \omega\left\{\frac{E^{-ls/4}}{s^5} - \frac{e^{\frac{-3ls}{4}}}{s^5}\right\} + \frac{c_1}{s^3} + \frac{c_2}{s^4} \quad ...(2)$$

Hence $EI\,(Y) = \frac{\omega}{24}\left[\left(x - \frac{l}{4}\right)^4 U\left(x - \frac{l}{4}\right) - \left(x - \frac{3l}{4}\right)^4 u\left(x - \frac{3l}{4}\right)\right] + \frac{c_1}{2}x^2 + \frac{1}{6}c_2 x^3$ ...(3)

For $x > \frac{3l}{4}\; EIY = \frac{\omega}{24}\left[\left(x - \frac{l}{4}\right)^4 - \left(x - \frac{3l}{4}\right)^4\right] = \frac{c_1 x^2}{2} + \frac{c_2 x^3}{6}$ ...(4)

Differentiating

$$EI\,\frac{dy}{dx} = \frac{\omega}{6}\left[\left(x - \frac{l}{4}\right)^3 - \left(x - \frac{3l}{4}\right)^3\right] + c_1 x + \frac{c_2 x^3}{2} \quad ...(5)$$

$\frac{dy}{dx} = 0$ at $x = l$, $y = 0$ at $x = 0$

So $0 = \frac{W}{24}\left[\left(\frac{3l}{4}\right)^4 - \left(\frac{l}{4}\right)^4\right] + c_1\frac{l^2}{2} + c_2\frac{l^3}{6}$

and $0 = \frac{W}{6}\left[\left(\frac{3l}{4}\right)^3 - \left(\frac{l}{4}\right)^3\right] c_1 l + c_2\frac{l^2}{2}.$

It gives $c_1 = \frac{11\omega l^2}{192}$, $\omega_2 = -\frac{\omega l}{4}.$

So for $\frac{l}{4} > x > \frac{3l}{4}$,

$$EIY = \frac{\omega}{24}\left(x + \frac{l}{4}\right)^4 + \frac{11\omega l^2}{384}x^2 - \frac{\omega l}{24}x^3.$$

Hence the maximum deflection

$$y\,(x = l/2) = \frac{13\omega l^4}{6144\,EI}$$

3.14.2. DIRAC-DELTA FUNCTION OR UNIT IMPULSE FUNCTION

$$\delta_\varepsilon(t) = \begin{cases} 0, & t < 0 \\ \frac{1}{\varepsilon}, & 0 < t < t \\ 0, & t > \varepsilon \end{cases}$$

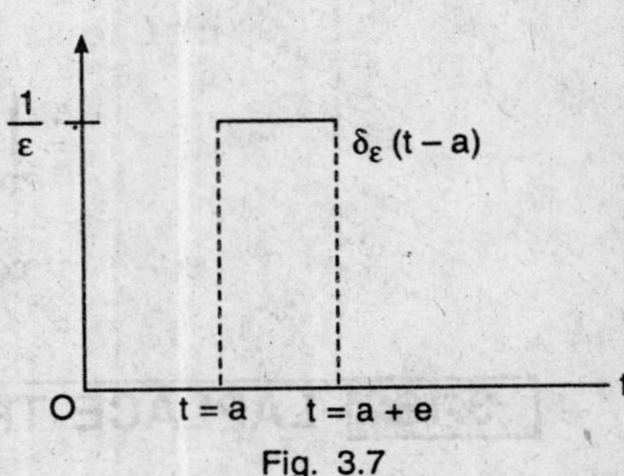

Fig. 3.7

Laplace transform $\delta_t(t) = \int_0^\infty e^{-st}\,\delta_t(t)\,dt = \int_0^\varepsilon \frac{e^{-st}}{\varepsilon}\,dt$

$$= \frac{1}{-s\varepsilon}\,[e^{-st}]_0^\varepsilon = \frac{e^{-st} - 1}{-s\varepsilon}$$

Expanding and taken limit as $\varepsilon \to 0$

$$\frac{1 - s\varepsilon + \frac{s^2\varepsilon^2}{!2} + \ldots - 1}{-s\varepsilon} = 1$$

3.15 LAPLACE TRANSFORM OF UNIT IMPULSE FUNCTION

(i) $L\{\delta(t)\} = \lim_{\varepsilon \to 0} \int_0^{\varepsilon} e^{-st} \frac{1}{\varepsilon} dt = \lim_{\varepsilon \to 0} \frac{[e^{-s\varepsilon}]_0^{\varepsilon}}{-s\varepsilon} = 1$

(ii) $L\{f(t)\, \delta(t-a)\} = \lim_{\varepsilon \to 0} \int_a^{a+\varepsilon} f(t) \frac{1}{\varepsilon} dt$

Let $t = a + y$

$y \to 0$

Expanding, $f(t) = \{f(a) + y f'(a)$ Apprx.

$$= \frac{1}{\varepsilon} \int_0^{\varepsilon} \{f(a) + yf'(a)\}\, dy = f(a) \text{ Apprx.}$$

(iii) $L\, \delta\,(t-a) = \frac{1}{\varepsilon} \int_a^{a+t} e^{-st}\, dt$

Let $t = a + z$

$$= \frac{1}{\varepsilon} e^{-as} \int_0^{\varepsilon} e^{-sz}\, dz = e^{-as}$$

Example 3.40. Find the Laplace transform of

(i) $t^3\, \delta(t-8)$

(ii) $\cos t \log t\, \delta(t-\pi)$

Solution : (i) $L\{t^3\delta(t-8) = \int_0^{\infty} e^{-st}\, t^3\delta(t-8)dt$

$= 8^3 e^{-8s}$ (As per definition)

$= 512e^{-8s}$

(ii) $L\{\cos t \log t\, \delta(t-\pi)\}$

$$= \int_0^{\infty} e^{-st} . \cos t \log t\, \delta(t-\pi)dt$$

$$= \cos \pi \log \pi\, e^{-\pi s} = -\log \pi\, e^{-\pi s}$$

3.16 LAPLACE TRANSFORM OF PERIODIC FUNCTION

If $f(t)$ be such that $f(t+T) = f(t)$, then $f(t)$ is called a periodic function with period T.

Prove that, if $f(t)$ is a periodic function with period T then

$$L\, f(t) = \frac{1}{1-e^{-st}} \int_0^{T} e^{-st} f(t)\, dt.$$

Proof. $$L\{f(t)\} = \int_0^T e^{-st} f(t)\,dt + \int_T^{2T} e^{-st} f(t)\,dt + \ldots = \sum_{r=1}^{\infty} \int_{(r-1)T}^{rT} f(t)\,e^{-st}\,dt$$

Let $t = (r-1)\,T + z$

$$= \sum_{r=1}^{\infty} \int_0^T f((r-1)\,T + z)\,e^{-s\{(r-1)T + z\}}\,dz$$

$$= \sum_{r=1}^{\infty} e^{-(r-1)Ts} \int_0^T f(z)\,e^{-sz}\,dz$$

$$= \{1 + \lambda + \lambda^2 + \ldots\}\,I \qquad \text{where } \lambda = e^{-Ts}$$

$$= \frac{1}{1-\lambda} I = \frac{1}{1-e^{-Ts}} \int_0^T e^{-st} f(t)\,dt.$$

Example 3.41. **Find the Laplace transform of** $f(t) = \begin{cases} \sin \omega t, & 0 < t < \dfrac{\pi}{\omega} \\ 0, & \dfrac{\pi}{\omega} < t < \dfrac{2\pi}{\omega} \end{cases}$

(Coimbatore 99, Madras 97, Kuvempu 96)

Solution : As the function is periodic with period $\dfrac{2\pi}{\omega}$

$$L\{f(t)\} = \frac{1}{1 - e^{-\frac{2\pi}{\omega}s}} \int_0^{\frac{2\pi}{\omega}} e^{-st} f(t) = dt$$

$$= \frac{1}{1 - e^{-\frac{2\pi}{\omega}s}} \left[\int_0^{\frac{\pi}{\omega}} e^{-st} \sin \omega t + 0\right] dt$$

$$= \frac{1}{1 - e^{-\frac{2\pi s}{\omega}}} = \frac{1}{s^2 + \omega^2} [e^{-st}\,(-s \sin \omega t - \omega \cos \omega t)]_0^{\pi/\omega}$$

$$= \frac{\omega}{(1 - e^{-\frac{2\pi s}{\omega}})\,(s^2 + \omega^2)}$$

Example 3.42. **Find the Laplace transform of** $f(t) = \begin{cases} \sin t, & 0 < b < \pi \\ 0, & \pi < t < 2\pi \end{cases}$**,** $f(t + 2\pi) = f(t)$**.**

Solution : $$L\{f(t)\} = \frac{1}{1 - e^{-2\pi s}} \int_0^{2\pi} f(t)\,e^{-st}\,dt$$

$$= \frac{1}{1 - e^{-2\pi s}} \left[\int_0^{\pi} \sin t\,e^{-st}\,dt + 0\right]$$

$$= \frac{1}{1-e^{-2\pi s}} \int_0^{\pi} e^{-st} \sin t dt = \frac{1}{1-e^{-2\pi s}} \left[\frac{e^{-st}(-s \sin t - \cos t)}{s^2+1} \right]_0^{\pi}$$

$$= \frac{1}{1-e^{-2\pi s}} \left[\frac{e^{-s\pi}(-s \,.\, \sin \pi - \cos \pi) - e^0(-s \,.\, \sin 0 - \cos 0)}{s^2+1} \right]$$

$$= \frac{1}{(1+s^2)(1+e^{-s\pi})}$$

PROBLEM SET 3.6

1. Express the following functions in terms of unit step function and find their Laplace transform.

(i) $f(t) = \begin{cases} 8 & t < 2 \\ 6 & t > 2 \end{cases}$

(ii) $f(t) = \begin{cases} t-1, & 1 < t < 2 \\ 3-t, & 2 < t < 3 \end{cases}$

(iii) $f(t) = \begin{cases} 1, & a < t < b \\ 0 & \text{otherwise} \end{cases}$

(iv) $f(t) = \begin{cases} 2t, & 0 \le t < 5 \\ 10, & t > 5 \end{cases}$

Ans. (i) $\frac{8}{s} - \frac{2e^{-2s}}{s}$, (ii) $\frac{e^{-s} - 2e^{-2s} + e^{-3s}}{s^2}$, (iii) $\frac{e^{-as} - e^{-bs}}{s}$, (iv) $\frac{2}{s^2}(1 - e^{-5s})$

2. Find the Laplace transform of

(i) $e^{t-2}\, U(t-2)$

(ii) $t^2\, U(t-3)$

(iii) $e^{2t}\, U(t-3)$

Ans. (i) $\frac{e^{-2s}}{s-1}$, (ii) $\frac{e^{-3s}(2+6s+9s^2)}{s^3}$, (iii) $\frac{e^{-3(s-2)}}{s-2}$

3. Find the Laplace transform of

(i) $\frac{\delta(t-\pi)}{t}$

(ii) $e^{-\pi t}\, \delta(t-a)$

Ans. (i) $\frac{e^{-s\pi}}{\pi}$, (ii) $e^{-a(\delta+\pi)}$

4. Find the Laplace transform of triangular wave of period 2π

$f(t) = t, \quad 0 < t < a$ ***(Madras 2000PT)***

$= 2a - t, \; a < t < 2a$ ***(Delhi 97, Mangalore 97)***

Ans. $\frac{1}{s^2} \tanh \frac{as}{2}$.

5. Find the Laplace transform of the square wave function of period a defined by

$$f(t) = 1, \quad 0 < t < \frac{a}{2}$$

$$= -1, \quad \frac{a}{2} < t < a$$

(JNTU 99, Madras 93, UPTU 2004)

Ans. $\frac{1}{s} \tanh \frac{as}{4}$.

6. Find the Laplace transform of saw lootted wave of period T, defined by $f(t) = \frac{1}{T}t$, $0 < t < T$.

Ans. $\frac{1}{s^2 T} - \frac{e^{-sT}}{s(1 - e^{-sT})}$.

7. Find the Laplace transform of full wave rectifier $f(t) = E \sin \omega t$, $0 < t < \pi/\omega$, having period $\frac{\pi}{\omega}$.

Ans. $\frac{E\omega}{s^2 + \omega^2} \coth \frac{\pi s}{2\omega}$.

8. Find the Laplace transform of

(i) $f(t) = \begin{cases} t, & 0 < t < 1 \\ 0, & 1 < t < 2 \end{cases}$, where $f(t + 2) = f(t)$

Ans. $\frac{1 - e^{-s}(s + 1)}{s^2(1 - e^{2s})}$

(ii) $f(t) = \begin{cases} 1, & 0 < t < 1 \\ -1, & 1 < t < 2 \end{cases}$, where $f(t + 2) = f(t)$

Ans. $\frac{1}{2} \tanh \frac{s}{2}$

4

Linear Programming

4.1 INTRODUCTION

In ordinary life, we take decisions merely by intuition and past experiences. But in complicated problems mere intuition cannot enable us to reach at the correct decision. So in the fields of management, engineering etc., where the problems have several aspects for consideration, the modeling technique and operations research methods are adopted for their solutions.

In such cases a **mathematical model of the problem** is prepared and an optimal solution is reached satisfying all the constraints in the problem. It is **known as mathematical programming.** After the World War II an independent subject known as **'Operations Research'** which embody the various programming methods and techniques of optimization, has come into existence. **Linear programming** is one such method applicable **where the objective function and the constraints** are both expressible **as linear functions of the decision variables.**

If the problem has n variables and m constraints expressed as a set of m linear simultaneous in-equations, (**in equalities**), then they bound a region of an n-dimensional hyperspace in side which they are true at every point. Every L.P. problem consists of seeking an optimal solution of a defined objective function in this **region known as the feasible region**. A theorem of linear programming establishes that the **optimal solution lies at one of the vertices of the hyper polyhedron** figure bounding the feasible region. So by calculating the value of the objective function at all these vertices, we find that vertex where the objection function **has the maximum** or minimum value as required.

4.2 LINEAR PROGRAMMING (L.P.)

Definition

Linear Programming is a method of finding an optimal solution of a problem defined as a linear function of its variables and subjected to constraints which are also linear.

The L.P. method is used in deciding diet composition, product mix and blending problems. Oil refineries, chemical industries, steel industries and food processing industry also use linear programming for the solution of their problems. The transportation and assignment problems are also L.P. problems.

4.3 LINEAR PROGRAMMING PROBLEM (L.P.P.)

A linear programming problem consists of three parts :

1. Objective Function

Hence the objective of the problem is expressible as a linear function of its variables and parameters. The problem consists in finding a solution which optimizes this function subject to the conditions of the problem.

2. Constraints

The constraints, imposed in the problem are also expressible as linear simultaneous equations or in-equations involving the variables. The region known as the feasible region has to be found where all the constraints are satisfied.

3. Non-negativity Restrictions

As the problem is not merely theoretical but represents some real situation, so the solution is meaningful from applications point of view only when the variables are non-negative. So the condition $x_i \geq 0$ is imposed for all variables x_i of the problem. These are called the non-negativity conditions.

4.4 FORMULATION OF THE PROBLEM

Using the given description of the problem which is to be solved by linear programming, the following steps are taken :

1. Identity the decision variables and denote them by x, y etc. or as $x_1, x_2 \ldots$ and so on.

2. Formulate the objective function. It involves the variables and given parameters of the problem. It is in the form of a linear algebraic expression.

3. Express the constraints as linear inequations (inequalities),

4. Impose the conditions $x_i \geq 0$ for all the variables x_i in the problem, for a feasible solution,

This is called the formulation of a L.P. problem and is illustrated by the following examples.

Example 4.1. **Old hens can be brought at Rs. 20.00 and young ones at Rs. 50.00. An old hen lays 3 and a young one 5 eggs a week. An egg is sold for Rs. 2.00. If the expenses incurred on their feeding be Rs. 7.00 per hen per week, find how many hens of each kind a person having Rs. 800.00 for investmemt should purchase so as to earn the maximum profit, if he has accommodation only for 20 hens in his house. Formulate it as a L.P. problem.**

Solution : Suppose the purchases x old and y young hens.

Then numberof laid down produced in a week $= 3x + 5y$.

Revenue from their sale $= 2(3x + 5y)$ Rs./week

Money spent on their feeding $= 7(x + y)$ Rs./week

Net income per week $= z = 2(3x + 5y) - 7x - 7y = (3y - 1x)$

Objective function

$$\text{Maximize } z = (3y - x)$$

Constraints

(i) amount spent on their purchase is to be less than Rs. 800/-

So $20x + 60y \le 800$.

(ii) total hens should not exceed 20.

So $x + y \le 20$

Non-Negativity conditions.

$$x \ge 0, y \ge 0$$

The negative values of the variables are only mathematical but impracticable. In the answer if the values of x and y come out in fractional form, they should be rounded to their positive integral parts before calculating z.

Example 4.2. **A firm manufacturing two types of electric items *A* and *B*, earns of profit of Rs. 2000/- and Rs. 3000/- on each items of type *A* and *B* respectively. Each unit of *A* requires 3 motors and 4 transforms, while that of *B* requires 2 motors and 4 transformers. The item *B* being of special variety is also fitted with a stabilizer. If the supply per month is limited to 210 motors, 300 transformersand 54 stabilizers, formulate it as a L.P problem for maximum profit.**

Solution : Let x_1, x_2 be the number of items of A and B produced by the firm every month. Then the profit earned $P = 2000x_1 + 3000x_2$.

P is to be maximized so objective function is Max. $z = 2000x_1 + 3000x_2$

Constraints

(i) for motors $3x_1 + 2x_2 \le 210$

(ii) for transformers $4x_1 + 4x_2 \le 300$

(iii) for stabilizers $x_2 \le 65$

Non-negativity restrictions : $x_1 \ge 0, x_2 \ge 0$.

Example 4.3. **A company makes two kinds of leather belts. Belt *A* is of superior quality. They give a profit of Rs. 8.00 and 6.00 per belt respectvely. Each belt of type *A* requires twice as much time as a belt of type *B* in its manufacture. The company could produce 1000 belts per day, if they all be of type *B*. The supply of leather is limited to that for 800 pieces of either type taken combined. Belt *A* requires a fancy bruckle whose supply is limited to 400 per day, while the supply of buckles used in *B* is limited to 700 per day. Formulate it as a L.P. problem for maximum profit.** *(Andhra 96)*

Solution : Let x_1 and x_2 be the number of units of A and B respectively produced by the company.

Then objective is Maximize $P = 8x_1 + 6x_2$

Constraints

For time $x_1(2t) + x_2t \le 1000t$

For leather $x_1 + x_2 \le 800$

For buckles $x_1 \le 400$

$x_2 \le 700$

Non-negativity restrictions : $x_1 \ge 0, x_2 \ge 0$.

Example 4.4. **A firm is engaged in breeding pigs. Apart from the farm products, each pig must be given 108 units, 36 units and 12 units of three foods X, Y, Z respectively everyday. Two types A and B of foods are available at the cost of Rs. 20 and Rs. 40 per unit respectively. The X, Y, Z contents in A and B are as shown below:**

	X	Y	Z	
A	36	03	20	Cost Rs. 20
B	06	12	10	Cost Rs. 40

Formulate it as a L.P. problem for minimum total expenditure. Let x_1 and x_2 units of A and B be purchased

Objective : Minimize $z = 20x_1 + 40x_2$

Constraitns for X $36x_1 + 6x_2 \ge 108$

for Y $3x_1 + 12x_2 \ge 36$

for Z $20x_1 + 10x_2 \ge 100$

Non-negativity conditions :

$x_1 \ge 0,\ x_2 \ge 0.$

Example 4.5. **A firm making castings, use electric furnace to melt iron with the following specifications :**

	Minimum	Maximum
Carbon	3.20%	3.40%
Silicon	2.25%	2.35%

Specification and costs of various raw materials used for this purpose are as given below :

Material	Carbon %	Silicon %	Cost (Rs.)	in tonnes
Steel Scrap	.4	.15	850/tonne	x_1
Cast iron Scrap	3.80	2.40	900/tonne	x_2
Remelt from boundary	3.50	2.30	500/tonne	x_3

If the total amount of iron metal required is 4 tonnes, find the weight of each raw material that must be used in the optimum mix and at least cost.

(JNTU 99S)

Solution : **Formulation of the Problems :**

Let the amounts of each raw material purchases in tonnes be x_1, x_2, x_3, then the objective is

$$\text{Minimize} \qquad z = 850x_1 + 900x_2 + 500x_3.$$

To meet the maximum and minimum requirement of carbon and silicon in the product, the restricts are

$$0.4x_1 + 3.8x_2 + 3.5x_3 \geq (3.2) \times 4$$

$$0.4x_1 + 3.8x_2 + 3.5x_3 \leq (3.40) \times 4$$

$$0.15x_1 + 2.40x_2 + 2.30x_3 \geq (2.25)4$$

$$0.15x_1 + 2.4x_2 + 2.3x_3 \leq (2.35)4$$

$$x_1 + x_2 + x_3 = 4$$

$x_1 \geq 0, x_2 \geq 0, x_3 \geq 0.$

To be solved by simplex method.

PROBLEM SET 4.1

Formulate the following problems as L.P. problems :

1. A firm manufactures 3 products A, B, C on which she earns a profit of Rs. 30/-, 20/-, 40/- per unit respectively. In production of these items machines M_1 and M_2 are employed. The processing times of the items on the machiens are are given below : Product

	A	B	C
Machine M_1 :	4	3	5 (in minute)
M_2 :	2	2	4

The machines M_1, M_2 have the available times of 2000, 2500 minutes respectively. The firm should purchase $100 \leq A \leq 150$, $200 \leq B$ $50 \leq C$. Formulate it as a L.P. Problem for maximum profit. ***(AUUP 2007, Kerala 96S, Madras 96)***

Max. $Z = 30x_1 + 20x_2 + 40x_3$.

Subject to $4x_1 + 3x_2 + 5x_3 \leq 2000$, $2x_1 + 2x_2 + 4x_3 \leq 2500$, $100 \leq x_1 \leq 150$, $200 \leq x_2$, $50 \leq x_3$.

2. A firm manufactures headache pills in two marks A and B. A contains 2 grains Asprin, 5 grains bicarbonate and 1 grain codeine while B has 1 grain asprin, 8 grains bicarbonate and 6 grains of codiene. It is found that the user should take 15 grains of aspirin, 74 grains bicarbonate and 24 grains of codiene each day for curing his disease. Formulate it as a L.P. problem to minimize the number of pills he should take daily for getting free from the disease.

3. A manufacturer produces two modes M_1 and M_2, each unit of M_1 requires 4 hours grinding and 2 hours polishing; whereas for M_2 the requirements are 2 hours grinding and 5 hours of polishing. The manufacturer has 2 grinders, 3 polishers. The grinder works for 40 hours and polisher for 60 hours in a week. The profit earned per unit

is Rs. 30/- and Rs. 40/- on M_1 and M_2 respectively. If all production be sold, formulate the above information as a L.P. problem for maximum profit per week.

4. A soft-drink producer has two bottling plants *A* and *B*. *A* is for use in 8 ounce and *B* for 16 ounce bottle packs. The timing of the plants which can also be used commonly with less speed, are as given below

Machine	8 ounce pack	16 ounce packs
A	100 per minute	40 per minute
B	60 per minute	75 per minute

If machiens can be run 8 hours per day on a five-day week. If the weekly production is to be limited to 3 lac ounces and the market demand be 25,000 for 8 ounce and 7,000 for 16 ounce packs. Formula the problem for maximum profit if the profit be Rs. 1.50 and Rs. 2.50 on the 8 ounce & 16 ounce packs respectively. ***(Kerala 91)***

Ans. Max $z = 1.5x_1 + 2.5x_2$ subject to $2x_1 + 5x_2 \leq 480{,}000$, $5x_1 + 4x_2 \leq 720{,}000$

$8x_1 + 16x_2 \leq 300{,}000$, $0 \leq x_1 \leq 25000$, $0 \leq x_2 \leq 7000$.

5. A firm produces an alloy with the following specifications :

(i) specific gravity $\leq .97$

(ii) chromium content > 15%;

(iii) melting temperature $\geq 494^\circ C$.

The alloys requires three raw materials *A, B, C* with the properties as follows :

	A	*B*	*C*
Sp. gravity:	0.94	1.00	1.05
Chronium content:	10%	15%	17%
Melting point:	470°C	500°C	520°C

Find the values of *A, B, C* to be used in production of 1 tonne alloy of desired properties under minimum production cost for the cost Rs. 105/tonne for *A*, Rs. 245/ tonne for *B* and Rs. 165/tonne for *C*. Formulate the above information as a L.P. problem.

6. A firm manufactures two items. it purchases raw castings which are then machined, bored and polished. Castings for items *A* and *B* cost Rs. 3.00 and Rs. 4 each which they are sold after finishing for Rs. 6.00 and Rs. 7.00 per piece respectively. Running costs of the three machines used one Rs. 20.00. Rs. 14.00 and Rs. 17.50 per hour respectively. Formulate it as a L.P. problem of the product manufacturing for maximum profit ? The capacities of the machines are :

	Part A	Part B
Machine	25 / h	40 / h
Boring	28 / h	35 / h
Polishing	25 / h	25 / h

Ans. Max $z = 1.2x_1 + 1.4x_2$;

Subject to $40x_1 + 25x_2 \leq 1000$, $35x_1 + 28x_2 \leq 980$, $25x_1 + 35x_2 \leq 875$, $x_1, x_2 \geq 0$.

7. A farmer has to plant trees of kinds A and B in a plot of 4400 m^2 in area. For a tree of type A 25 m^2 area of for B, 40 m^2 area is to be allotted. The water requirements of the types A and B are 30 units and 15 units respectively per tree. Only 3300 units of water is available. If the number of $A : B$ is not to remain less than 6/19 and not to exceed 17/8, Formulate it as a L.P. problem for maximum profit if the return from them is in the ratio 3 : 2 respectively. ***(Karnataka 94)***

Ans. 80 A and 60 B.

Max $P = 3x_1 + 2x_2$

$$25x_1 + 40x_2 \le 4400, \quad 30x_1 + 15x_2 \le 3300$$

$$\frac{x_1}{x_2} \ge \frac{6}{19}, \quad \frac{x_1}{x_2} \le \frac{17}{8}$$

$$19x_1 - 6x_2 \ge 0$$

$$-8x_1 + 17x_2 \ge 0$$

8. The manager of an oil refinery must decide on optimum mix of two possible blending processes of which the inputs and outputs per production seen are as follows :

Process (Units)	Input (Units)		Output	
	Grade A	Grade B	Gasoline X	Gasoline Y
1	5	3	5	8
2	4	5	4	4

The maximum amounts of A and B available are 200 of A and 150 units of B. Market requirements show that atleast 100 units of gasoline X and 80 units of Y must be produced. The profits per production seen for process 1 and 2 are Rs. 300/- and Rs. 400/- respectively. Formulate it as a L.P. problem and solve. ***(Gujrat 1998)***

Ans. 400/13 units under and 150/13 units

Under process z : Max. Profit 1,80,000/13.

4.5 GRAPHICAL METHOD OF SOLUTION FOR TWO DIMENSIONAL PROBLEMS

If a linear programming problem involves only two variables, it can be represented and solved graphically.

Steps of Graphical Solution

1. From the given description, the variables are decided and objective function and constraints are expressed as equations or inequalities as per given conditions. The non-negativity conditions are also written down.

2. Limiting lines corresponding to the in-equations of constraints are drawn. The proper side of the line on which the feasible region lies is indicated by arrows.

3. The lines may be drawn only in the first quadrant where $x \ge 0, y \ge 0$ are satisfied. The feasible region lies inside the a closed polygon when the religion it is bounded and all its vertices can be found. The optimal solution lies at some one of these vertices. So coordinates of the vertices are found by solving the equations of the limiting lines which intersect at them.

4. **The value of the objective function is found at each of these vertices.**

The vertex at which z is maximum or minimum, as the problem be, gives the solution according as it is a maximization or a minimization problem.

4.6 ISO-PROFIT or *Z*-LINE

If $z = c_1x + c_2y$ be the objective function. Draw the line $0 = c_1x + c_2y$, through origin. Then draw lines parallel to it. The line which is fartherest and passes through a vertex is the line for z_{max} and the co-ordinates (x, y) of the vertex gives the values of x and y for which z is maximum. Similarly if z_{min} is to be found, the line nearest to 0 and passing through a vertex is the requiré line with co-ordination of the vertex as required solution. These lines are called iso Z-lines.

Example 4.6. **Solve graphically the problem formulated in Example 2.**

Solution : The formulation of the problem is

Maximize $P = 2000x_1 + 3000x_2$

Subject to $3x_1 + 2x_2 \leq 210,$

$4x_1 + 4x_2 \leq 300,$

$1x_2 \leq 65;\ x_1 \geq 0,\ x_2 \geq 0.$ *(Raj 2003)*

The limiting lines $3x_1 + 2x_2 = 210$ ...(1)

$4x_1 + 4x_2 = 300$ ...(2)

$x_2 = 65$ ...(3)

are drawn graphically as shown here (Fig. 4.1).

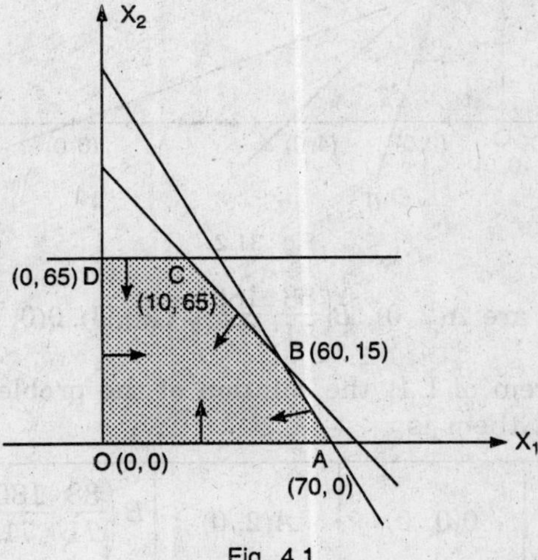

Fig. 4.1

The feasible region lies inside the polygon, with vertices 0(0, 0), A(70, 0), (0, 65), B(60, 15), C(10, 65) and D(0, 65). By theorem of L.P. the solution of the problem lies at one of these points.

The values of P at thus for vertices are as given below

Vertex	0(0, 0)	(70, 0)	C(10, 65)	D(0, 65)
$P = 2000x + 3000y$	0	140,000	215,000 Max	195,000

The maximum profit is = Rs. 215,000/- for producing 10 units of x_1 and 65 units of x_2

Example 4.7. **Solve graphically the problem**

Maximize $z = 5x + 7y$

subject to $x + y \le 4$

$3x + 8y \le 24$

$10x + 3y \le 20.$

Solution : The polygon $OABCO$ represents the feasible region in which all the inequalities are satisfied.

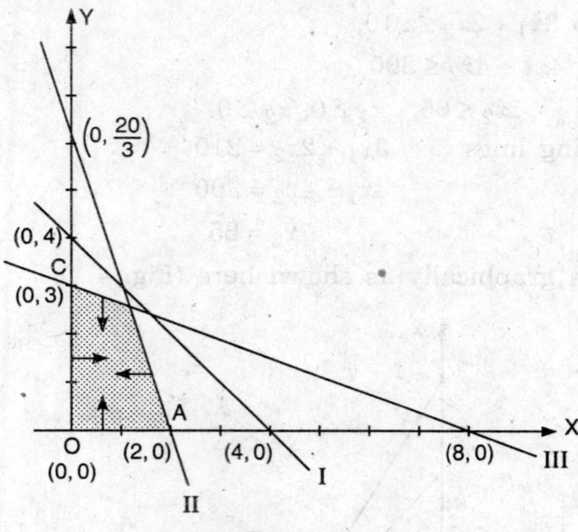

Fig. 31.2

The vertices are $A(2, 0)$, $B\left(\frac{88}{71}, \frac{180}{71}\right)$, $C(0, 3)$, $0(0, 0)$

By the theorem of L.P. the solution of the problem lies at one of them. The value of z at them is

Vertex	0(0, 0)	A(2, 0)	$B\left(\frac{88}{71}, \frac{180}{71}\right)$	Max.	< (0, 3)
$z = 5x + 7y$	0	10	$\frac{440 + 1260}{71} = \frac{1700}{71}$	= 23.94	21

Ans. z is max at $B(1.239, 2.535)$ with $z_{max} = 23.94$

Example 4.8. **Solve graphically the L.P. problem**
Maximize $z = 2x + y$,
subject to

$$x + 2y \leq 10 \quad ...(1)$$
$$x + y \leq 6 \quad ...(2)$$
$$x - y \leq 2 \quad ...(3)$$
$$x - 2y \leq 1 \quad ...(4)$$

$x \geq 0, y \geq 0.$

Solution : The limiting lines are drawn by joining the points where they meet the axes and are shown in the graph given below.

For making the proper side on which the feasible region, it easy for the lines (1), (2).

For $x - y \leq 2$

On the x-axis $y = 0$ we must have $x \leq 2$ So on x axis, its part on left of the point $x = 2$ would be on the feasible side. Similarly for $x - 2y \leq 1$. Then arrows should put which on part of the line which bounds the feasible area.

As is seen in the figure, the feasible region is bounded by lines having vertices $OABCDE$.

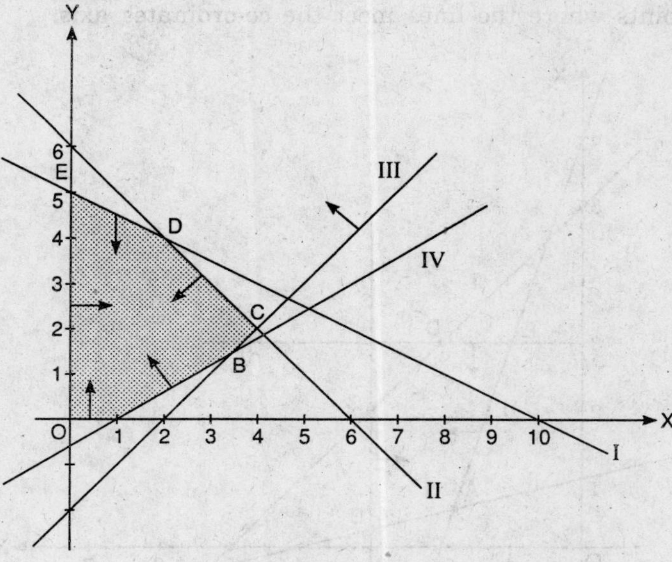

Fig. 4.3

The coordinates of these points on solving the lines which intersect at them are given as

$$0(0, 0);\ A(2, 0)\ B \begin{Bmatrix} x - y = 2 \\ x - 2y = 1 \end{Bmatrix} \Rightarrow (3, 1);$$

$$C \begin{Bmatrix} x + y = 6 \\ x - y = 2 \end{Bmatrix} \Rightarrow x, y) = (4, 2)$$

$$D\begin{cases} x + y = 6 \\ x + 2y = 10 \end{cases} \Rightarrow (2, 8).$$

The values of z at these points is given by

Vertex	0(0, 0)	A(2, 0)	B(2, 0)	C(4, 2)	D(2, 8)	E(0, 5)
$z = 2x + y$	0	4	6 + 1 = 7	8 + 2 = 10	4 + 8 = 12Max	0 + 5 = 5

By theorem of L.P., z is maximum at $x = 4, y = 2$, which is the solution with $z_{max} = 12$.

Example 4.9. **Solve the following L.P. problem graphically :**

Minimize $z = 3x_1 + 2x_2$

subject to $x_1 + x_2 \leq 5$ ...(1)

$3x_1 + x_2 \geq 6$ ...(2)

$x_1 + 4x_2 \geq 4$ ...(3)

$x_1 \leq 3$ ...(4)

$x_2 \leq 3$ ...(5)

$x_1 \geq 0, x_2 \geq 0.$

Solution : The limiting lines corresponding to the given inequalities are down by joining the points where the lines meet the co-ordinates axis.

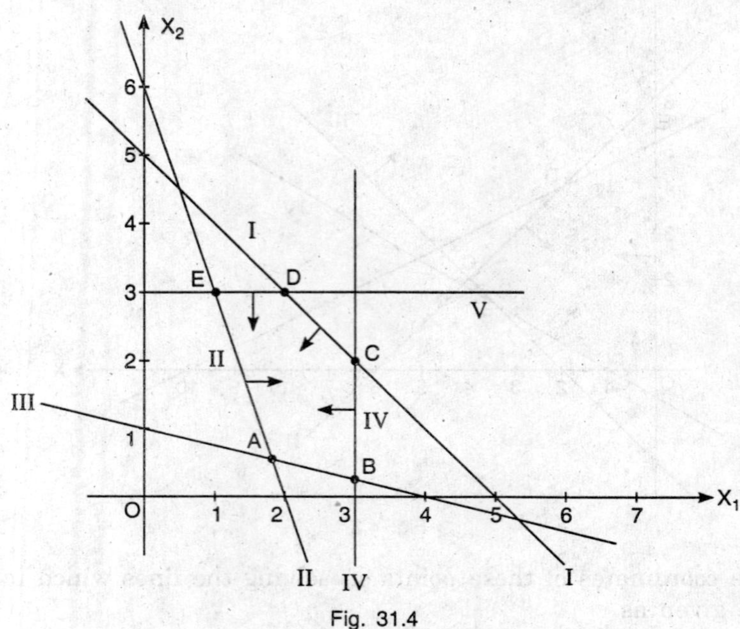

Fig. 31.4

Care should be taken in marketing the arrow on the line which indicate the side on which the feasible region lies. The inequality (2) is given in the form of greater than so arrow should be marked on its right. The feasible region is bounded by the lines with vertices A, B, C, D, E. Their co-ordinates are given by

$$A \left\{\begin{matrix} 3x_1 + x_2 = 6 \\ x_1 + 4x_2 = 4 \end{matrix}\right\} \Rightarrow \left(\frac{20}{11}, \frac{6}{11}\right)$$

$$B \left\{\begin{matrix} x_1 = 3 \\ x_1 + 4x_2 = 4 \end{matrix}\right\} \Rightarrow \left(3, \frac{1}{4}\right),$$

$$C \left\{\begin{matrix} x_1 + x_2 = 5 \\ x_1 = 3 \end{matrix}\right\} \Rightarrow (3,\ 2)$$

$$D = \left\{\begin{matrix} x_2 = 3 \\ x_1 + x_2 = 5 \end{matrix}\right\} \Rightarrow (2,\ 3),$$

$$E \left\{\begin{matrix} x_2 = 3 \\ 3x_1 + x_2 = 6 \end{matrix}\right\} \Rightarrow (1,\ 3)$$

By L.P. theorem, the solution lies at some one of these points,

Vertex	$A\left(\frac{20}{11}, \frac{6}{11}\right)$	$B\left(3, \frac{1}{4}\right)$	$C(3, 2)$	$D(2, 3)$	$E(1, 3)$
$z = 3x_1 + 2x_2$	$\frac{72}{11} = 6\frac{6}{11}$ Minimum	9.5	13 Max.	12	9

$$z_{\min} = 6\frac{6}{11} \text{ at } (x_1, y_1) = \left(\frac{20}{11}, \frac{6}{11}\right).$$

Example 4.10. Solve maximize $z = 3x_1 + 2x_2$

subject to $\quad x_2 - x_1 \le 0$

$\quad x_1 + x_2 \ge 3$

Solution : (i) $X_2 - X_1 = 0$, passes through (0, 0) and makes an angle of 45° with either axis.

On x_1 axis $x_2 = 0$ so $-x_1 \le 0$ or $x_1 \ge 0$.

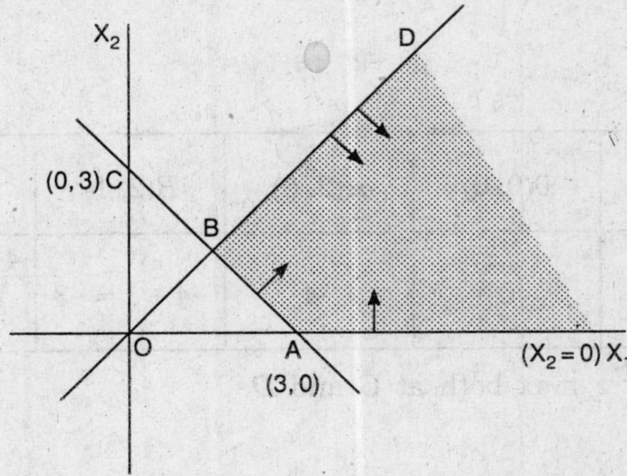

Fig. 4.5

So positive part of the x_1 axis lies in the feasible region.

$$x_1 - x_2 > 0$$

(ii) As $x_1 + x_2 \geq 3$, the part of the plane on right of the line ABC is in the feasible region. The feasible region as shown in the figure is unbounded going upto ∞ at $x_1 \to \infty$, x_2 having any value z also $\to \infty$. So the solution is unbounded. If the minimum of the function be required it will exist at A or B

Points	$A(3, 0)$	$B(3, 3)$
Min $z = 3x_1 + 2x_2$	$9 + 0$ min	$9 + 6$

z is minimum at $A(3, 0)$ with $z_{min} = 9$.

Example 4.11. **Solve graphically the L.P. problem**

Maximize $\quad z = y - 2x$

subject to $\quad x + y \leq 3 \quad$ ...(1)

$-2x + y \leq 1 \quad$ ...(2)

$x \leq 2 \quad$ ...(3)

$x \geq 0, y \geq 0$

Solution : Drawing the limiting lines and making the proper side of the line pointing inside the feasible region. The region is bounded by the polygon with vertices O, A, B, C, D, finding z at these vertices, we have

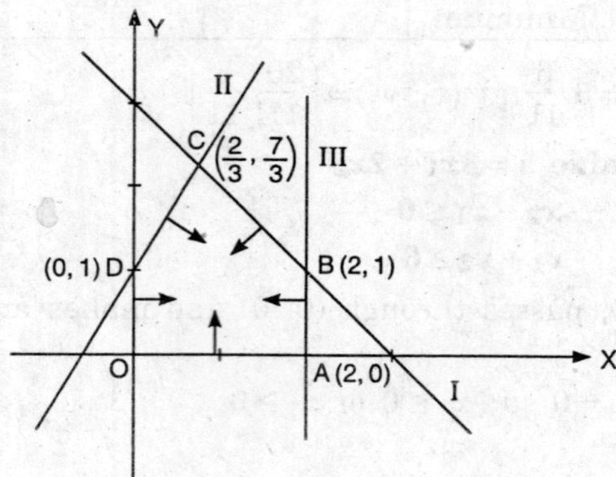

Fig. 4.6

Vertex	0(0, 0)	$A(2, 0)$	$B(2, 1)$	$C\left(\frac{2}{3}, \frac{7}{3}\right)$	$D(0, 1)$
$z = y - 2x$	0	-4	$-4 + 1 = -3$	$\frac{-4+7}{3}$ = 1Ma x	1 Max

We see that z max both at C and D.

If such be the case then z is max. = 1 at every point on the line segment BC. This is so because the line BC limiting line representing one of the constraints is parallel to the objective line $y - 2x = z$.

Example 4.12. **Maximize $z = x + y$**

subject to $2x - 3y \geq 4$

$y - 2x \geq 0$

Solution : $x > 0, y > 0$ implies that the feasible region is confined to the positive quadrant. For marking the proper side of $2x - 3y \geq 4$

Let us take $y = 0$ (x axis)

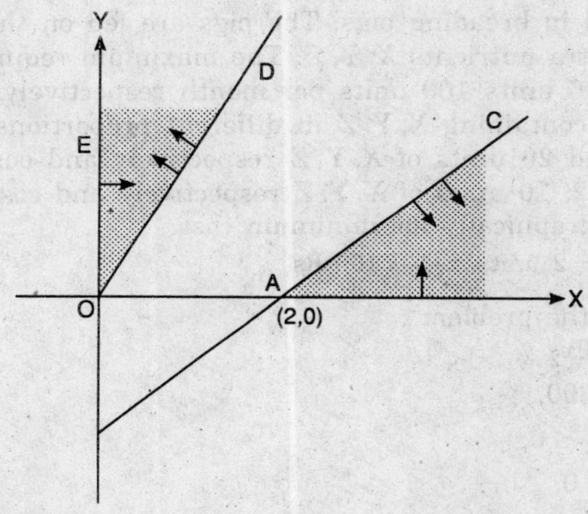

Fig. 4.7

We have $2x - 0 \geq 4$ so part of the x axis on which $x \geq 2$ will be in feasible region so one part of the feasible region lies in the angle $\angle CAB$. After drawing $y - 2x = 0$ which passes through (0, 0), if we take $x = 0$ (on y axis we get $y - 0 \geq 0$ so positive part of the y axis is in feasible region. So II part of the feasible region lies in $\angle EOD$. As these two regions **have nothing in common so the feasible region satisfying all the inequalities does not exist** or the constraints are in consistent. Hence the problem cannot be solved **or it has no solution.**

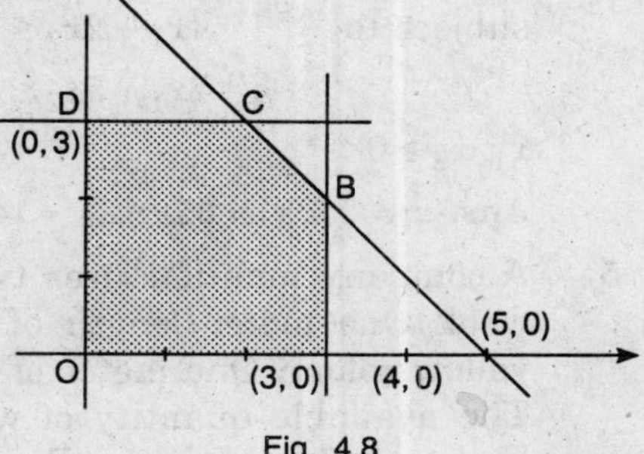

Fig. 4.8

Redundant constraint

If no part of the limiting line representing a constraint, forms a side of the polygon bounding the feasible region, then that constraint is useless or unnecessary or redundant. In the figure below. Among the constraints

$$x \leq 3, \quad y \leq 3$$

$$x + y \leq 5, \; x - y \leq 4$$

The constraint $x - y \leq 4$ is redundant.

PROBLEM SET 4.2

1. A company makes two kinds of leather belts. They give a profit of Rs. 4.00 and 3.00 per belt respectively. It requires twise as much time to manufacture a belt of type A than that of type B. If all belts be made of type B, than the company could makes 1000 pieces per day. The same leather is used in both types and a supply of it sufficient for 800 pieces is possible. Belt A is fitted with a fancy buckle and B with an ordinary one, whose respective supplies are limited to 400 and 700 per day. Solve the problem graphically for maximum profit. ***(Andhra 1996)***

   Ans. $x_1 = 200, x_2 = 600, z_{max} = 2600.$

2. A farm is engaged in breading pigs. The pigs are fed on the products grown on the form plus such extra nutrients X, Y, Z. The maximum requirements of each of them being 108 units, 36 units 100 units per month respectively. There are two varieties A and B of foods containing X, Y, Z in different proportions are available. One unit of A has 36, 3 and 20 units of X, Y, Z respectively and costs Rs. 20 per unit. One unit of B has 6, 12, 10 units of X, Y, Z respectively and costs Rs. 40 per unit. Solve the L.P. problem graphically for minimum cost.

   Ans. $A = 4$ units, $B = 2$ units, $z_{min} = 160$ Rs. ***(Raj 2003)***

3. Solve graphically the problem :

   Min $z = 3x_1 + 9x_2$

   s.t. $x_1 + x_2 \geq 800,$

   $2x_1 - 10x_2 \leq 0,$

   $3x_1 - x_1 \geq 0,$

   $x_1 \geq 0, x_2 \geq 0$

   Ans. $x_1 = 200,\ x_2 = 600,\ z_{min} = 6000.$

4. Solve graphically the problem :

   Maximize $z = 3x_1 + 4x_2$

   subject to $4x_1 + 2x_2 \leq 80,$

   $2x_1 + 5x_2 \leq 180,$

   $x_1, x_2 \geq 0$ ***(T.V.U. 2000S)***

   Ans. $x_1 = 2.5,\ x_1 = 35,\ z_{max.} = 147.5$

5. A company manufactures two types A and B of cloth, using three different coloured wool. One meter length of A requires 4 oz. of red wool, 5 oz. green, and 3 oz of yellow colour. One meter of B requires 5 oz, red, 2 oz. green and 8 oz. of yellow wool. The available quantity of wool is 1000 oz. red, 1000 oz. green and 1200 oz. yellow. If the profit earned be Rs. 5 per yard on type A and Rs. 3 per yd. on type B, find the quantities of each type to be produced to have the maximum profit by solving this L.P. problem graphically. ***(Madras 1992)***

   Ans. $x_1 = \dfrac{3000}{17}$ yds, $x_2 = \dfrac{1000}{17}$ yds. with $z_{max} = 1058.8.$

6. Solve graphically the L.P. problem
Maximize $z = 2x + 3y$
subject to $x + y \le 30$
$3 \le y \le 12$
$x - y \ge 0$
$x \le 20,\ x, y \ge 0$ *(Kerala 91)*

Ans. $x = 18, y = 12, z_{max} = 72$

7. Show that the following L.P. problem has multiple set of solutions. Also show that one of the constraints is rebundant.
Solve graphically, the L.P. problem
Maximize $z = 100x_1 + 40x_2$
subject to $10x_1 + 4x_2 \le 2000$
$3x_1 + 2x_2 \le 900$
$6x_1 + 12x_2 \le 3000,\ x_1, x_2 \ge 0$

Ans. z at any point on the part of the line $10x_1 + 4x_2 \le 3000$ has the max value 20,000. So $A(200, 0)$ and $B(125, 187.5)$ are two of its many solutions. The constraint $3x_1 + 2x_2 \le 900$, does not from any side of the polygon bounding the feasible region is therefore unnecessary (redundant).

8. Solve graphically the L.P. problem
Maximize $z = 3x + 5y$
subject to $x + 2y \le 200$
$x + y \le 150,$
$x \le 60,\ x \ge 0, y \ge 0$ *(Raj 2003)*

Ans. $x = 100,\ y = 50,\ z_{max} = 550$

Solve the L.P. problem Maximize $z = 2x_1 + 3x_2$
subject to $x_1 + x_2 \le 1$
$3x_1 + 4x_2 \le 4,\ x_1, x_2 \ge 0$

Ans. $x_1 = 0,\ x_2 = 1,\ z_{max} = 3$, constraint $3x_1 + 4x_2 \le 4$ is rebundant.

9. Solve graphically the L.P. problem
Minimize $z = 4x_1 + 2x_2$
subject to $x_1 + 2x_2 \ge 2$
$3x_1 + x_2 \ge 3$
$4x_1 + 3x_2 \ge 6,$
$x_1, x_2 \ge 0$ *(MNIT 2003)*

Ans. $x_1 = .6,\ x_2 = 1.2,\ z_{min} = 4.8$

10. Solve graphically the problem
Maximize $z = 4x_1 + 5x_2$
subject to $x_1 + x_2 \ge 1$
$-2x_1 + x_2 \le 1$
$4x_1 - 2x_2 \le 1,\ x_1, x_2 \ge 0$
The solution is unbounded

11. Maximize $z = 3x_1 + 4x_2$

subject to $x_1 - x_2 \le -1$

$-x_1 + x_2 \le 0$

$x_1, x_2 \ge 0$

The problem has no solution as the constraints are inconsistent.

12. Solve graphically the L.P. problem

$z = x_1 + x_2$

subject to $x_1 - x_2 \ge 0$

$3x_1 - x_2 \le -3,$

$x_1, x_2 \ge 0$

Ans. The feasible region does not lie in first quadrant so the problem has no solution.

13. Maximize $z = 3x_1 + 2x_2$

subject to $x_1 - x_2 \le 1$

$x_1 + x_2 \ge 3,$

$x_1, x_2 \ge 0$

Ans. The solution is unbounded

14. Maximize $z = 3x_1 - 2x_2$

subject to $x_1 + x_2 \le 1$

$2x_1 + 2x_2 \ge 4,$

$x_1 x_2 \ge 0$

Ans. No solution.

15. Solve graphically the problem

Max. $z = 5x_1 + 3x_2$

subjec to $3x_1 + 5x_2 \le 15;$

$5x_1 + 2x_2 \le 10,\ x\, x_2 > 0$

$x_1 = \dfrac{20}{19},\ x_2 = \dfrac{45}{19},\ z_{\max} = \dfrac{5}{19}.$ *(Madras 1993)*

16. Min $z = 20x_1 + 10x_2,$

subject to $x_1 + 2x_2 \le 40,$

$3x_1 + x_2 \ge 30,$

$4x_1 + 3x_2 \ge 60,\ \ x_1, x_2 \ge 0$ *(V.T.U. 2001)*

Ans. $x_1 = 6,\ x_2 = 12,\ z_{\min} = 240$

17. Solve graphically the problem

Maximize $z = 4x_1 + 3x_2$

subject to $x_1 + x_2 \le 50$

$x_1 + 2x_2 \le 80$

$2x_1 + x_2 \ge 20$

$x_1, x_2 \ge 0$ *(North Bengal 89)*

Ans. $x_1 = 50,\ x_2 = 0,\ z_{\max} = 200.$

4.7 GENERAL LINEAR PROGRAMMING PROBLEM

We have solved linear programming problems involing only two variables by the graphical method. Now we consider the **general problem, involving n variables $x_1, x_2 \ldots x_n$, with m constraints.** The problem can be represented as

Maximize/minimize $\quad z = c_1x_1 + c_2x_2 + \ldots + c_nx_n \quad$ ...(1)

Subject to the conditions :

$$\left.\begin{array}{l} a_{11}x_1 + a_{12}x_2 + \ldots + a_{1n}x_n \le b_1 \\ \ldots\ldots\ldots\ldots\ldots \\ \ldots\ldots\ldots\ldots\ldots \\ b_{m1}\,x_1 + a_{m2}\,x_2 + \ldots + a_{mn}\,x_n \le b_m \end{array}\right\} \quad \ldots(2)$$

with $\quad x_1\, x_2 \ldots x_n \ge 0 \quad$ ...(3)

4.8 DEFINITIONS

Solution to the L.P. problem

Any set of values $(x_1, x_2, \ldots x_n)$ which satisfy all the above constraints (2), will be called a solution.

4.9 FEASIBLE SOLUTION

The solution $(x_1, x_2, \ldots x_n)$ is meaningful where condition (3) are satisfied, *i.e.*, where all $x_i \ge 0$, $i = 1, 2 \ldots n$. Such a solution is called a **feasible solution.**

4.10 CHANGING THE INEQUALITIES INTO EQUATIONS

Mathematical manipulations are not possible unless the inequalities (2) are changed into equations. For this, we add variables $x_{n+1}, x_{n+2} \ldots x_{n+m}$ respectively in the m inequalities and have the m equations

$$\sum_{j=1}^{n} a_{ij}\,x_j + x_i = b_i, \qquad i = 1, 2 \ldots m.$$

4.10.1. Salck Variable

The **variables** x_i, so **added** to change the inequality of the form of less than (≤) into an equation are called **slack variables.** $b = (b_1, b_2, \ldots b_m)$ is called the **requirement** vector and $c = (c_1, c_2 \ldots c_n)$ as **cost vector.**

4.10.2. Surplus Variable

If any constraint be given in the form of (≥) as $\sum_{j=1}^{n} a_{ij}\,x_j \ge b_i$, then the variable x_i for changing it into an equation is subtracted instead of being added to keep it always to have positive value. In this case we have $\sum_{j=1}^{n} a_{ij}\,x_j - x_i = b_i$

The variable x_i which has thus to be subtracted, is called a **surplus varriable.**

Case I. Constraints are given in (≤) **less than form**

After adding the m surplus variables $x_{n+1} \dots x_{n+m}$

We have m equations $\sum_{j=1}^{n} a_{ij} x_j + x_{n+i} = b_i$ ...(1)

$i = 1, \dots m.$

They can be solved uniquely when they are reduced in ***m* equations** in ***m* unknowns** by assuming ***n*** of the $n + m$ variables to be each **equal to zero**. Such variables are called **non-basic** and those m variable whose values are found from the m equations as **basic variables.**

4.11 NON-BASIC VARIABLES

The n variables which are taken equal to be zero, **initially**, for having a solution of (1), are called the **non-basic variables**.

4.12 BASIC VARIABLES AND BASIS

The remaining m variables in (1) are called the **basic variables**. The matrix of the coefficient of these m variables has m rows and m columns. It is called the **basis matrix**. Denoting the columns of the basis matrix by $\alpha_1, \alpha_2 \dots \alpha_m$, these are called the basic vectors.

We have $\alpha_1 = \begin{pmatrix} 1 \\ 0 \\ \vdots \\ 0 \end{pmatrix}, \alpha_2 = \begin{pmatrix} 0 \\ 1 \\ 0 \\ \vdots \end{pmatrix}$ etc.

Thus $\alpha_1, \alpha_2, \dots$ **are unit vectors.**

4.13 BASIC SOLUTION

The solution of m equations in m **unknowns is called basic solution.**

If values of all the basic variables comes out to be non-negative (either positive or zero), the solution is caled a **basic feasible** solution.

4.14 NON-DEGENERATE SOLUTION

On solving the equations, if none of the basic variables has the value zero, in their solution, **the solution is called a non-degenerate basic solution.**

4.15 DEGENERATE BASIC SOLUTION

If values of one or more **basic variables comes out to be zero, the basic solution is called a degenerate basic solution.** Writing the m equations after relabeling them as

$$\alpha_1 x_1 + \alpha_2 x_2 \dots \alpha_n x_n = b$$

The solution will be degenerate when the vectors $\alpha_1, \alpha_2 \dots \alpha_n$ **are not linearly independent** *i.e.*, when some one of them is a linear combination of the remaining, otherwise it will be non-degenerate.

Example 4.13. Find the basic solutions of the equations

$$x_1 + 2x_2 + x_3 = 4, \quad 2x_1 + x_2 + 5x_3 = 5$$

Solution : (i) Let ($x_1 = 0$ be assumed to be non-basic) then $\begin{bmatrix} 2 & 1 \\ 1 & 5 \end{bmatrix}\begin{bmatrix} x_2 \\ x_3 \end{bmatrix} = \begin{bmatrix} 4 \\ 5 \end{bmatrix}$

Basic matrix is $B_X = \begin{bmatrix} 2 & 1 \\ 1 & 5 \end{bmatrix}$. $\begin{bmatrix} x_2 \\ x_3 \end{bmatrix} = B^{-1}\begin{bmatrix} 4 \\ 5 \end{bmatrix} = \begin{bmatrix} 5/3 \\ 2/3 \end{bmatrix}$, solution is feasible and non-degenerate.

(ii) Taking ($x_2 = 0$. as non-basic) then $B_X = \begin{bmatrix} 1 & 1 \\ 2 & 5 \end{bmatrix}$ Solution $\begin{bmatrix} X_1 \\ X_3 \end{bmatrix} = \begin{bmatrix} 5 \\ -1 \end{bmatrix}$

It is **not a feasible** solution as $x_3 = -1 < 0$.

(iii) Taking ($x_3 = 0$, as non-basic). Then $B_X = \begin{bmatrix} 1 & 2 \\ 2 & 1 \end{bmatrix}$, with $\begin{bmatrix} X_1 \\ X_2 \end{bmatrix} = \begin{bmatrix} 2 \\ 1 \end{bmatrix}$, feasible, non-degenerate solution.

Example 4.14. Find the basic solution of

$$x_1 + 2x_2 + 4x_3 = 4$$
$$2x_1 + x_2 + 5x_3 = 5$$

taking x_1 to be non-basic.

Soluiton : When $x_1 = 0$ is non basic, $B_X = \begin{bmatrix} 2 & 4 \\ 1 & 5 \end{bmatrix}$ and $\begin{bmatrix} x_2 \\ x_3 \end{bmatrix} = \begin{bmatrix} 0 \\ 1 \end{bmatrix}$.

The solution is degenerate as $x_2 = 0$, which is a basic variable.

Example 4.15. Change the following in equations with an initial basic feasible solution.

$$2x + 3y \le 10 \qquad \text{...(1)}$$
$$x + 5y \le -4 \qquad \text{...(2)}$$

Solution : The second equation on multiplying by (–1) changes to

$$-x - 5y \ge 4 \qquad \text{...(3)}$$

Now let $2x + 3y + x_1 + 0x_2 = 10$

$$-x - 5y + 0 + 1x_2 = 4$$

There are four variables and only two equations taking $x = 0, y = 0$ as **non-basic**

We have $1x_1 + 0x_2 = 10$

$$0x_1 + 1x_2 = 4$$

where from **$x_1 = 10, x_2 = 4$ is a basic feasible solution.**

Example 4.16. $x_1 = 2, x_2 = 3, x_3 = 1$, is a feasible solution of

$$2x_1 + 1x_2 + 4x_3 = 11, \quad 3x_1 + 1x_2 + 5x_3 = 14,$$

Find a basic feasible solution.

Solution : In a basic solution one variable must be zero. The three coeff. vectors $\alpha_1 = \begin{pmatrix} 2 \\ 3 \end{pmatrix}$, $\alpha_2 = \begin{pmatrix} 1 \\ 1 \end{pmatrix}$, $\alpha_3 = \begin{pmatrix} 4 \\ 5 \end{pmatrix}$ are three vectors in a two dimensional space. So these must be linearly dependent become in two dimensional space only two vectos and not make can be linearly independent. Let $\lambda_1 \alpha_1 + \lambda_2 \alpha_2 + \lambda_3 \alpha_3 = 0$,

So $\quad 2\lambda_1 + \lambda_2 + 4\lambda_3 = 0$

$\quad 3\lambda_1 + \lambda_2 + 5\lambda_3 = 0$

So $\quad \lambda_1 = k_1 \lambda_2 = 2k, \lambda_3 = -k$

Let $\quad \nu = \text{Max}\left\{\frac{k}{x_1}, \frac{2k}{x_2}, \frac{-k}{x_3}\right\} = \left\{\frac{1}{2}, \frac{2}{3}, \frac{-1}{1}\right\} = \frac{2}{3}$.

Taking $k = 1$,

So $\quad x' = \left(2 - \frac{\lambda_1}{\nu}, 3 - \frac{\lambda_2}{\nu}, 1 - \frac{\nu_3}{\nu}\right) = \left(2 - 1 \times \frac{3}{2}, 3 - 2 \times \frac{3}{2}, 1 + \frac{3}{2}\right)$

$= \left(\frac{1}{2}, 0, 5/2\right)$ is the required basic solution.

Example 4.17. Find all the basic solutions of $2x_1 + x_2 + 4x_3 = 11$, $3x_1 + x_2 + 5x_3 = 14$. *(V.T.U. 2000S)*

Investigate whether the basic solutions are non-degenerate or degenerate basic feasible solutions. Hence find the basic feasible solutions of the system. *(North Bengal 89)*

Solution : (i) Let $x_1 = 0$ be non-basic, then

$$x_2 = 4x_3 = 11$$

$$x_2 + 5x_3 = 14$$

Which gives the basic solution as $x_2 = 3$, $x_3 = -1$. It is not feasible as $x_3 < 0$.

(ii) Let $x_2 = 0$ be non-basic, then

$$2x_1 = 4x_3 = 11$$

$$3x_1 + 5x_3 = 14$$

which gives $x_1 = \frac{1}{2}$, $x_3 = \frac{10}{4}$ as basic solution which is feasible as

$x_1, x_3 > 0$ and non-degenerate as non of basic variables is zero.

(iii) Let $x_3 = 0$ be non-basic, then

$$2x_1 + x_2 = 11$$

$$3x_1 + x_2 = 14$$

which gives $x_1 = 3$, $x_2 = 5$ as a basic feasible non-degenerate solution.

The feasible non-degenerate solutions are

(i) $x_2 = 0$, $x_1 = \frac{1}{2}$, $x_3 = 5/2$;

(ii) $x_3 = 0$, $x_1 = 3\ x_2 = 5$

PROBLEM SET 4.3

1. Show that the vector (1, 0, 1, 6) is not a feasible solution to the system $x_1 = x_2 + x_3 = 2$, $2x_1 + 3x_2 + 4x_3 - x_4 = 0$.

2. Show that the vector (1, 1, 1) is a feasible solution to the system of equations

$$x_1 + x_2 + 2x_3 = 4$$
$$2x_1 - x_2 + x_3 = 2$$

Reduce it to a basic feasible solution

(i) $x_1 = 2, x_2 = 2, x_3 = 0,$

(ii) $x_1 = 0, x_2 = 0, x_3 = 2,$

(iii) $x_1 = 0, x_2 = 0, x_3 = 2.$

3. If $x_1 = 2, x_2 = 3, x_3 = 1$, be a feasible solution to

$$2x_1 + x_2 + 4x_3 = 11;$$
$$3x_1 + x_2 + 5x_3 = 14,$$

find a basic feasible solution.

Ans. $x_3 = 0, x_1 = 3, x_2 = 5$

4. Find an optimal solution to the L.P. problem by computing all basic solutions and then finding the one that maximizes the objective function

$$2x_1 + 3x_2 - x_3 + 4x_4 = 8;$$
$$x_1 - 2x_2 + 6x_3 - 7x_4 = -3;$$

$x_1, x_2, x_3, x_4 \geq 0$

Max. $z = 2x_1 + 3x_2 + 4x_3 + 7x_4$ ***(Kerala 95S, Calicut 92)***

Ans. Optimal basic feasible sol. is $x_1 = 0, x_2 = 0,\ x_3 = \frac{44}{17}, x_4 = \frac{45}{17}, z_{max} = 28.9.$

5. Show that the following system of equations $x_1 + 2x_2 + x_3 = 4$; $2x_1 + x_2 + 5x_3 - 5$, has two degenerate basic feasible and two non-degenerate non-feasible basic solutions. ***(North Bengal 88)***

6. Find all basic solutions of Maximize $z = x_1 + 3x_2 + 3x_3$ subject to $x_1 + 2x_2 + 3x_3 = 4$; $2x_1 + 3x_2 + 5x_3 = 7$, $x_1, x_2, x_3 > 0$.

which of then are degenerate and which are optimal feasible solutions ?

(i) basic $x_1 = 2, x_2 = 1, x_3 = 0$

(ii) $x_1 = x_3 = 1, x_2 = 0$

(iii) $x_2 = -1, x_3 = 2, x_1 = 0$

(a) first two are non degerate basic and feasible sols.

(b) first solution is optimal with $z_{max.} = 5$.

7. Obtain the basic solutions of the following system of linear equations $x_1 + 2x_2 + x_3 = 4$, $2x_1 + x_2 + 5x_3 = 5$.

Ans. (i) $x_1 = 2, x_3 = 1, x_3 = 0$ (non-basic);

(ii) $x_1 = 5, x_3 = -1,$

(iii) $x_2 = \frac{5}{3}, x_3 = \frac{2}{3}, x_1 = 0$. All these solutions $x_2 = 0$ are non-degenerate.

4.16 SOME IMPORTANT THEOREMS OF L.P.P.

Theorem 1. If a linear programming problem

Maximize $z = cX$, subject to $aX \le b, x \ge 0$ has at least one feasible solution then it also has a basic feasible solution.

Theorem 2. If one feasible solution of the L.P. problem

Max. $z = cX$, $AX \le b$, $X \ge 0$, be optimal then one basic feasible solution also exists which is optimal.

Theorem 3. If every set of m column vectors of the augmented matrix $[A, b]$ be linearly independent, the basic solutions of $AX = b$ will be non-degenerate.

Theorem 4. If $X_B = B^{-1} b$ be a non-degenerate basic feasible solution of $AX = b$ with $z = z'$ and if for some column α_i of matrix A, which is not in B, we have $z_i - c_i < 0$ with atleast one of the element y_{ji} of the column vector α_i to be positive then we can have a new basic feasible solution by introducing α_i in B and replacing some one of the column of B. The new solution $\hat{z}$ will make be greater then z'. The solution is optimal at the stage when all $z_i - c_i \ge 0$.

Theorem 5. (Unbounded Solution). If at some stage, some $z_i - c_i$ has most negative value but all elements of vector α_i be negative then the solution of the problem will be unbounded.

4.17 EVALUATION AND NET EVALUATION [Z_j AND ($z_j - c_j$)]

Let Maximize $z = cX$. with $aX = b, X \ge 0$ be a L.P. problem, Let X_B be a basis with c_B as the corresponding cost vector then

$z_j = \sum_{i=1}^{m} c_{Bi} y_{ij}$ is called the evaluation corresponding to α_j and $z_j - c_j$ is called the net **evaluation**. The solution is optimal at the stage when $z_j - c_j \ge 0$ for all j.

4.18 CANONICAL FORM OF L.P. PROBLEM

Before proceeding for solution of a L.P. problem by simplex method the following steps are to be taken:

1. **Objective function is to be made that of a maximizaton problem if it is not so.**

The **simplex method** is evolved only for the case when the objective function is to be maximized. So if in a problem we have Minimize $z = cX$ then on putting $-z = z'$, Min $(-z') = -$ Max z'

So it should be changed to Max $z' = -cX$, and than solved. The solution will also be solution of Min $z = cx$.

2. **All the constraints should be expressed in ($\le$) less than form.**

If we have a constraint $\sum_j -a_{ij}x_j \le -b_i$ we subtract variable s_i and have the equation $a_{ij} \cdot x_j - s_i = b_i$. But then the added vector $\begin{pmatrix} 0 \\ - \\ o \end{pmatrix}$ will not form a unit vector, required to include it in the initial basic matrix. So then an artificial variable will also have to be added.

3. **Variables should all be non-negative.**

If x_j be a variable for which $x_j \ge 0$ is not given i.e. if $x_j \le 0$ then

We let $x_j = x'_j - x''_j$ where x'_j, x''_j are both ≥ 0. The above conditions (2) and (3) are essential from the point of their importance while writing the dual.

4.19 STANDARDIZATION

In the case of constraints given in (≤) less than form a slack variable x_i is added to change them into an equation as

$$\sum_{j=1}^{n} a_{ij}x_j + x_i = b_i$$

If the problem be Min $z = CX$, the constraints are given in (≥) greater than or equal to form. Writing $z' = -z$, we have

$$CX = \text{Min } z = \text{Min } (-z') = -\text{ Max } z'$$

So that the problem becomes a maximization problem

$$\text{Max } z' = -CX$$

The constraints in a minimization problem are given in (≥) greater than form. They are changed into equations by subtracting surplus variables x_i are $\sum a_{ij}x_j - x_i = b_i$

Then an **artificial variable** x_{ia} is added so as to have the coefficients of basic variables to the unit vectors. We then have

$$\sum a_{ij}x_j - x_i + x_{ia} = b_i.$$

4.20 SIMPLEX METHOD

We first consider the simplex method for solving a standard L.P. problem not involving any artificial variable.

Maximize $Z = CX$,

Subject to $AX = b, X \ge 0$,

where A is a $m \times (n + m)$ matrix.

4.21 SIMPLEX ALGORITHM

1. Change the given problem into a maximization problem if it is not so.

2. Make all $b_i > 0$, so that the starting basic solution be a feasible solution (all $x_{n+1}, i = 1, 2 \ldots m > 0$) when the starting solution is a basic feasible solution then all subsequent solution will also be basic feasible, obtained by entering one new vector in the basis and departing are already existing into the basis.

3. The problem is brought to the standard form by adding the slack variables into the constraint inequalities.

4. As a starting basic solution, take all the main variables of the to be zero $(x_1 = x_2 = x_n = 0)$ problem then slack variables $x_i = b_i$ will form, the starting basic solution.

5. Write the simplex table as

			$C_B =$	C_1	C_2			y_{n+m}
C_B	X_B	X						
0	α_{n+1}	x_{n+1}	b_1	y_{11}				0
0	α_{n+2}	x_{n+2}	b_2	y_{21}				0 0
0	α_{n+m}	x_{n+m}	b_m	y_{m1}				1
				$z_1 - c_1$				$z_{n+m} - c_{n+m}$

Find
$$z_i = \sum_{i=1}^{m} C_{n+i}\,(y_{n+i,j}) \;\ldots\; j = 1, \ldots, n+m.$$

6. Find the most negative value of $(z_i - c_i)$. Suppose it corresponds to the rth column then the vector α_r will be **entering into the basis.**

7. Compute Min $\left\{\frac{b_i}{y_{ir}},\ y_{ir} > 0,\ i = 1, \ldots m\right\}$ Let the min be $\frac{b_k}{y_{kr}}$ then the kth vector α_k will be **departing from the basis.** The element $\boldsymbol{y_{kr}}$ is known as the pivot or **key element** for the percent change of basis vector. For changing the entering vector α_k as a unit vector, we do the following :

8. Divide the kth row by y_{ir} through out. Thus the element in the (r, k) place becomes unity.

9. In order to make all exception elements in the rth column to be zero, perform
$$\hat{y}_{ij} = y_{ij} - \frac{y_{kj}}{y_{kr}}\, y_{ir}$$
We already have $\hat{y}_{ir} = 1,\ i = 1, 2, \ldots m$ but $i \neq k$. For $i = k$.

10. With this new first table, start with the same procedure by calculating $z_i - c_i$. All subsequent steps are similar to what has been stated above. The solution will be optimal at the stage when all $z_i - c_i$ an positive for all i.

Example 4.18. Use simplex method to solve the L.P.P.

Maximize $\quad z = 4x_1 + 10x_2$

Subject to $\quad 2x_1 + x_2 \leq 50$

$$2x_1 + 5x_2 \leq 100 \quad x_1 \geq 0$$
$$2x_1 + 3x_2 \leq 90, \quad x_2 \geq 0.$$

Solution : Adding the stack variables x_3, x_4, x_5 in the given inequalities, we have Max

$$z = 4x_1 + 10x_2 + 0x_3 + 0x_4 + 0x_5$$

subject to,
$$\left.\begin{array}{r} 2x_1 + x_2 + 1x_3 + 0 + 0 = 50 \\ 2x_1 + 5x_2 + 0 + 1x_4 + 0 = 100 \\ 2x_1 + 3x_2 + 0 + 0 + 1x_5 = 90 \end{array}\right\} \rightarrow$$

Simplex Table 1

Cost of basic variable	Basis vector variable	$\vec{c}=$	4	10	0	0	0
C_B	$\alpha_B X_B$	$\vec{b}$	$\alpha_1 \downarrow$	$\alpha_2\downarrow$	$\alpha_3 \downarrow$	$\alpha_4 \downarrow$	$\alpha_5 \downarrow$
0	$\alpha_3\, x_3$	50	2	1	1	0	0
0	$\alpha_4\, x_4$	100	2	[5]	0	1	0
0	$\alpha_5\, x_5$	90	2	3	0	0	1
		$(z_i - c_i) =$	0-4	0-10 most negative	0	0	0

$\uparrow$ α_2 entering $\downarrow$ α_4 departing

$z_1 = 2 \times 0 + 2 \times 0 + 2 \times 0 = 0$ $c_1 = 4,$

$z_2 = 1 \times 0 + 5 \times 0 + 3 \times 0 = 0,$ $c_2 = 10,\ z_2 - i_2 = -10,\ c_3 = z_3 = 0.$

As $\dot{z}_2 - c_2 = -10$ is largest negative, so α_2 is the entering vector

Now $\quad \text{Min}\left\{\frac{b_1}{y_{12}}, \frac{b_2}{y_{22}}, \frac{b_3}{y_{32}}\right\} = \text{Min}\left\{\frac{50}{1}\ \frac{100}{5}\ \frac{90}{3}\right\} = 20$ for $r = 2$.

Second row basic vector, α_4 is departing, key element $= y_{22} = 5$

Performing $\quad R_2 \rightarrow \frac{R_2}{5},$

$$R_1 \rightarrow R_1 - y_{12} \times \frac{R_2}{5},$$

$$R_3 \rightarrow R_3 - y_{32} \times \frac{R_2}{5}$$

Simplex Table

			$c = 4$	10	0	0	0
Table II		$\vec{b}$	α_1	α_2	α_3	α_4	α_5
C_B	α_B	X_B					
0	α_3	x_3	$50 - 1 \times 20 = 30$	$2 - 1 \times \frac{2}{5} = 8/5$	$1 - 1 \times 1 = 0$	$1 - 1 \times 0 = 1$	$0 - \frac{1}{5} = \frac{-1}{5}$	$0 - 1 \times 0 = 0$
10	α_2	x_2	$\frac{100}{5} = 20$	$\frac{2}{5}$	$\frac{5}{5} = 1$	0	$\frac{1}{5}$	0 [(dividing whole row by key element)]
0	α_5	x_5	$90 - 3 \times 20 = 30$	$2 - 3 \times \frac{2}{5} = \frac{4}{5}$	$3 - 3 \times 1 = 0$	$0 - 3 \times 0 = 0$	$0 - \frac{3}{5} = -\frac{3}{5}$	$1 - 3 \times 0 = 1$
		$z_i - c_i$	$4 - 4 = 0$	$= 0$	$= 0$	$+2$	0

$$z_1 = \frac{8}{5} \times 0 + \frac{2}{5} \times 10 + \frac{4}{5} \times 0 = 4, \quad c_1 = 4; \quad z_1 - c_1 = 0$$

$$z_2 = 0 \times 0 + 1 \times 10 + 0 = 10, \quad c_2 = 10; \quad z_2 - c_2 = 0$$

As all $z_i - c_i \geq 0$. So the solution at this stage is optimal.

$$x_3 = 30, x_2 = 20, x_5 = 30;$$

$$z_{\max} = 0 + 10 \times 20 + 0 + 0 = \mathbf{200}$$

Note : For the non-basic variable $x_1, z_1 - c_1 = 0$ (non positive) so alternative basic solution is also possible.

By bringing α_1 in the basics Now α_3 will depart and the next table will give

$$x_1 = \frac{150}{8}, x_2 = \frac{25}{2}, x_5 = 15$$

$$z_{\max} = \frac{150}{8} \times 4$$

$$= \frac{25}{2} \times 10$$

$$= 75 + 125 = 200 \text{ (same) as above.}$$

Example 4.19. **Solve the L.P.P. by simplex method**

Maximize $z = 107x_1 + x_2 + 2x_3$

Subject to $\quad 14x_1 + x_2 - 6x_3 + 3x_4 = 7 \quad$ **...(1)**

$16x_1 + x_2 - 6x_3 + 0x_4 \leq 5 \quad$ **...(2)**

$3x_1 - x_2 - x_3 + 0x_4 \leq 0 \quad$ **...(3)**

Solution : As coefficients of x_4 in (2) and (3) are zero. $\alpha_4 = \begin{pmatrix}3\\0\\0\end{pmatrix} = 3\begin{pmatrix}1\\0\\0\end{pmatrix}$ so x_4 can be taken to be in the initial basis, after dividing (1) by 3. Adding slack variables x_6 and x_7 in (2) and (3) respectively we have

$$z = 107x_1 + 4x_2 + 2x_3 + 0x_4 + 0x_5 + 0x_6$$

and $$\frac{14}{3}x_1 + \frac{1}{3}x_2 - 2x_3 + 1x_4 + 0 + 0 = \frac{5}{3} \quad ...(4)$$

$$16x_1 + 1x_2 - 6x_3 + 0 + 1x_5 + 0 = 5 \quad ...(5)$$

$$3x_1 - x_2 - x_3 + 0 + 0 + 1x_6 = 0 \quad ...(6)$$

Simplex Table 1

			$c =$	107	1	2	0	0	0
$\overrightarrow{C_B}$	α_B	X_B	$\overrightarrow{b}$	α_1	α_2	α_3	α_4	α_5	α_6
0	α_4	x_4	7/3	$\frac{14}{3}$	1/3	–2	1	0	0
0	α_5	x_5	5	16	1	–6	0	1	0
0	α_6	x_6	0	$\boxed{3}$	–1	–1	0	0	1
			$z_i - c_i =$	– 107	0 – 1	0 – 2	0	0	0

↑ is most negative $z_i - c_i = z_1 - c_1$ for $i = 1$

so α_1 entering

$$[\mathbf{z_1} = 0 \times \frac{14}{3} + 0 \times 16 + 0 \times 3 = 0,\ c_1 = 107$$

So $\mathbf{z_1 - c_1 = -107}$

$$\mathbf{z_2} = 0 \times \frac{1}{3} + 1 \times 0 + (-1) \times 0,\ z_2 = c_2 = 0 - 2 = -2,$$

So $z_2 - c_2 = -1$ similarly $z_3 - c_3 = -2$, others = 0]

Most negative of all $z_i - c_i$ is $z_1 - c_1 = -107$. So α_1 **is the entering vector for the babis.** For choosing the departing vector from the basis, we find

$$\text{Min}\left\{\frac{b_i}{y_{i1}}, x_{i1} > 0; = \frac{5/3}{14/3}, \frac{5}{16}, \frac{0}{3} = 0\right\}.$$

So key element $= \frac{y}{31} = 3$ and α_6 is the departing vector

Table 2

			$c = 1$	107	2	6	0	0	0
			b	α_1	α_2	α_3	α_4	α_5	α_6
0	α_4	x_4	$\frac{7}{3}-\frac{14}{3}\times 0 = \frac{7}{3}$	$\frac{14}{3}-\frac{14}{3}\times 1 = 0$	$\frac{1}{3}-\frac{14}{3}(-\frac{1}{3}) = \frac{17}{9}$	$-2-\frac{14}{3}\left(-\frac{1}{3}\right) = -\frac{4}{9}$	$1-\frac{14}{3}\times 0 = 1$	$0-\frac{14}{3}\times 0 = 0$	$0-\frac{14}{3}\times\frac{1}{3} = -\frac{14}{9}$
0	α_5	x_5	$5-16\times 0 = 5$	$16-16\times 1 = 0$	$1-16\left(-\frac{1}{3}\right) = \frac{19}{3}$	$-6-16\left(\frac{-1}{3}\right) = -2/3$	$0-16\times 0 = 0$	$1-0\times 0 = 1$	$0-\frac{1}{3}\times 16 = -\frac{16}{3}$
107	α_1	x_1	$0 = 0$	$\frac{3}{3} = 1$	$-\frac{1}{3}$	$-\frac{1}{3}$	0	0	$\frac{1}{3}$
			$z_i - c_i =$	$107-107 = 0$	$-\frac{107}{3}-2$	$-\frac{107}{3}-6$	0	0	$\frac{107}{3}$

↑ α_3 entering

Most Negative

As $z_3 - c_3$ is most negative, α_3 is **the entering vector**. But **for selection of the departing vector**, we find all coefficients y_{i3} in 3rd column are negative ($y_{13} = -4/9, y_{23} = -2/3, y_{33} = -1/3$). So outgoing vector cannot be decided. When such is the case, the solution is unbounded. So the problem has an **unbounded solution.**

Example 4.20. **Solve the L.P. problem**

Maximize $z = 3x_1 + 5x_2 + 4x_3$

subject to $2x_1 + 3x_2 \le 8$ ...(1)

$2x_2 + 5x_3 \le 10$ ...(2)

$3x_1 + 2x_2 + 4x_3 \le 15$ ...(3)

$x_1, x_2, x_3 \ge 0$

by the simplex method. *(Raj 93, 96)*

Solution : Adding slack variables x_4, x_5, x_6 in (1), (2), (3) we have

$$\text{Max. } z = 3x_1 + 5x_2 + 4x_3 + 0x_4 + 0x_5 + 0x_6$$

subject to

$$2x_1 + 3x_2 + 0x_3 + 1x_4 + 0 + 0 = 8 \quad ...(1)$$

$$0x_1 + 2x_2 + 5x_3 + 0 + 1x_5 + 0 = 10 \quad ...(2)$$

$$3x_1 + 2x_2 + 4x_3 + 0 + 0 + 1x_6 = 15 \quad ...(3)$$

Simplex Table 1

			$\vec{c}=$	3	5	4	0	0	0
			$\vec{b}$	α_1	α_2	α_3	α_4	α_5	α_6
0	α_4	x_4	8	2	[3]	0	1	0	0
0	α_5	x_5	10	0	2	5	9	1	0
0	α_6	x_6	15	3	2	4	9	0	1
			$z_i - c_i$	0 − 3	0 − 5	0 − 4	0 − 0	0 − 0	0 − 0

↑ most negative α_2 entering ↓ α_4 departing vector

$$z_1 = 2 \times 2 + 0 \times 0 + 3 \times 0 \text{ etc.}$$

As the most negative value of $z_i - c_i = z_2 - c_2 = -5$ **so α_2 is the entering vector**. For deciding about the departing vector from the basis find out

$$\text{Min}\left\{\frac{\vec{b}}{y_{i2}}, y_{i2} \geq 0\right\}$$

$$= \text{Min}\left\{\frac{8}{3}\ \frac{10}{2}\ \frac{15}{2}\right\} = \frac{8}{3} \text{ for } r = 1$$

So key element $= y_{12} = 3$ and α_4 **will be the departing vector**. Performing

$$R_1 \to \frac{R_1}{3};\quad R_2 \to R_2 - y_{22}\, R_1/3;\quad R_3 \to R_3 - y_{32}\, \frac{R_1}{3}$$

Table 2

			$c =$	3	5	4	0	0	0
C_B	α_B	X_B	$\vec{b}$	α_1	α_2	α_3	α_4	α_5	α_6
			8/3	2/3	$\frac{3}{3} = 1$	0	1/3	0	0
5	α_2	x_2				0		0	0
0	α_5	x_5	$10 - 2 \times \frac{8}{3} = \frac{14}{3}$	$0 - 2 \times 2/3 = -4/3$	$2 - 2 \times 1 = 0$	5 − 0 [= 5]	0 − 2/3 = −2/3	1 − 0 = 1	0 − 0 = 0
0	α_6	x_6	15 − 2 × 8/3 = 29/3	$3 - 2 \times \frac{2}{3} = 5/3$	$2 - 2 \times 1 = 0$	4 − 0 = 4	0 − 2/3 = −2/3	0 = 0	1 = 1
			$z_i - c_i =$	$\frac{10}{3} + \frac{0}{-3} = 1/3$	$5 + 0 - 5 = 0$	0 − 4 = −4	5/3	0	0

↑ α_3 is entering ↓ α_4 is departing

As most negative value of $z_i - c_i = z_3 - c_3 = -4$. So α_3 is the entering vector.

$\downarrow \alpha_5$ departing

Now $\quad \text{Min}\left\{\frac{\vec{b}}{y_{i3}}, y_{03} > 0 = \frac{8/3}{0}\ \frac{\frac{14}{3}}{5}\ \frac{\frac{29}{3}}{4}\right\} = \frac{14}{15} = \frac{b_2}{y_{23}}$

So second row vector α_5 is departing, with key element

$$y_{23} = 5. \text{ Performing } R_2 \to \frac{1}{5} R_2$$

$$R_1 \to R_1 - y_{12}\frac{R_2}{5} = R_1 - 0$$

$$R_3 \to R_3 - y_{32}\left(\frac{R_2}{5}\right) = R_3 - \frac{4}{5}R_2$$

Simplex Table 3

			$\vec{b}$	3	3	4	0	0	0
C	B	X		α_1	α_2	α_3	α_4	α_5	α_6
5	α_2	x_2	$\frac{8}{3} - 0 = \frac{8}{3}$	$\frac{2}{3} - 0 = 2/3$	$1 - 0 = 1$	$0 - 0 = 0$	$\frac{1}{3} - 0 = \frac{1}{3}$	$0 - 0 = 0$	$0 - 0 = 0$
4	α_3	x_3	$\frac{14}{15}$	$\frac{-4}{15}$	0	1	$\frac{-2}{15}$	$\frac{1}{5}$	0
0	α_6	x_6	$\frac{29}{3} - \frac{56}{15} = \frac{89}{15}$	$\frac{5}{3} + \frac{16}{15} = \frac{41}{15}$	0	$4 - 4 = 0$	$\frac{-2}{3} + \frac{8}{15} = \frac{2}{15}$	$0 - \frac{4}{4} = -\frac{4}{5}$	$= 1$
			$z_i - c_i =$	$\frac{2}{3} \times 5 - \frac{4}{15} \times 4 + 0 - 3 = -11/15$	$5 \times 1 + 0 - 5 = 0$	$0 + 4 - 4 = 0$	$\frac{17}{15}$	$\frac{4}{5}$	0

$\uparrow \alpha_1$ is entering $\qquad\qquad \downarrow \alpha_6$ departing

Now $\quad \text{Min}\left\{\frac{b}{y_{i1}}, y_{i1} > 0 = \frac{8/3}{2/3}, \frac{14/14}{-\text{ive}}, \frac{89/15}{41/15}\right\} = \frac{89}{41}$

for $r = 3$ so $y_{31} = \frac{41}{15}$ is key element and α_6 is (third row) departing vector

departing performing $\quad R_3 \to \frac{R_3}{y_{31}} = \frac{15}{41} R_3 = R'_3$

Performing $\quad R_1 \to R_1 - \frac{2}{3} R'_3,$

$$R_2 \to R_2 + \frac{4}{15} R'_3.$$

Table 4

			$c =$	3	4	5	0	0	0
C_B	α_B	X_B	$\overrightarrow{b}$	α_1	α_2	α_3	α_4	α_5	α_6
5	α_2	x_2	$\frac{8}{3} - \frac{2}{3} \times \frac{89}{41} = \frac{50}{41}$	0	1	0	$\frac{15}{41}$	$= \frac{8}{41}$	$-\frac{10}{41}$
4	α_3	x_3	$\frac{14}{15} + \frac{4 \times 89}{15 \times 41} = \frac{62}{41}$	1	0	1	$-\frac{6}{41}$	$\frac{5}{41}$	$\frac{4}{41}$
3	α_1	x_1	$\frac{89}{15} \times \frac{15}{41} = \frac{89}{41}$	1	0	0	$\frac{2}{41}$	$-\frac{12}{41}$	$\frac{15}{41}$
			$z_i - c_i =$	$0 + 4 + 3 - 3 = 4$	$5 - 5 = 0$	$4 - 4 = 0$	$\frac{45}{41}$	$\frac{24}{41}$	$\frac{11}{41}$

As all $z_i - c_i \geq 0$, So the solution at **this stage is optimal.**

Solution is $\boldsymbol{x_1 = \frac{81}{41}, x_2 = \frac{50}{41}, x_3 = \frac{62}{41}, z_{max} = \frac{765}{41}}$

PROBLEM SET 4.4

Use simplex method to solve the following L.P. problems :

1. Maximize $z = 3x_1 + 2x_2$

subject to $x_1 + x_2 \leq 4;$

$x_1 - x_2 \leq 2;$

$x_1 \geq 0, x_2 \geq 0$ ***(Calicut 1990)***

Ans. $x_1 = 3,\ x_2 = 1,\ z_{max} = 11$

2. Maximize $z = 2x_1 + 3x_2,$

subject to $x_1 + x_2 \leq 4,$

$-x_1 + x_2 \leq 1,$

$x_1 + 2x_2 \leq 5,$

$x_1 \geq 0,\ x_2 \geq 0$ ***(Anantapur 90)***

Ans. $x_1 = 4,\ x_2 = 0,\ z_{max} = 8$ or $x_2 = 2,\ x_4 = 1,\ z_{max} = 8$

3. Maximize $z = x_1 - 3x_2 + 2x_3$

subject to $3x_1 - x_2 + 2x_3 \leq 7$

$-2x_1 + 4x_2 \leq 12$

$-4x_1 + 3x_2 + 8x_3 \leq 10,$

$x_1, x_2, x_3 \geq 0$ ***(Karnataka 92, Dibrugarh 95)***

Ans. $x_1 = 4,\ x_2 = 5,\ x_3 = 0,\ z_{max} = -11$

4. Solve $z = 4x_1 + 5x_2$

subject to $x_1 + x_2 \leq 3;\ 3x_1 + 4x_2 \leq 10;\ x_1, x_2 \geq 0$

Ans. $x_1 = 2,\ x_2 = 1,\ z_{max} = 13$

5. Maximize $z = x_1 + 2x_2 + x_3$
subject to $2x_1 + x_2 + x_3 \le 2,$
$2x_1 - x_2 + 5x_3 \le 6,$
$4x_1 + x_2 + x_3 \le 6,$
$x_1, x_2, x_3 > 0.$
Ans. $x_2 = 4,\ x_3 = 2,\ x_5 = 0,\ z_{max} = 10$

6. Maximize $z = x_1 + 3x_2$
subject to $x_1 + 2x_2 \le 10,\ 0 \le x_1 \le 5,\ 0 \le x_2 \le 4.$ ***(V.T.U. 2001)***
Ans. $x_1 = 0,\ x_2 = 20,\ z_{max} = 200$

7. Maximize $z = 10x_1 + x_2 + 2x_3$
subject to $x_1 + x_2 - 2x_3 \le 10$
$4x_1 + x_2 + x_3 \le 20,\ x_1, x_2, x_3 \ge 0$ ***(Kerala 90)***
$x_1 = 5,\ x_2 = x_3 = 0,\ z_{max} = 50$

8. Max $z + x_1 + 3x_2,$
subject to $x_1 + 2x_2 \le 10,\ 0 \le x_1 \le 5,\ 0 \le x_2 \le 4.$ ***(V.T.U. 2001)***
Ans. $x_1 = 2,\ x_2 = 4,\ z_{max} = 14$

9. Maximize $z = x_1 + x_2 + 3x_3$
subject to $3x_1 + 2x_2 + x_3 \le 3,$
$2x_1 + x_2 + 2x_3 \le 2,$
$x_1, x_2, x_3 \ge 0$ ***(Madras 92)***
Ans. $x_1 = x_2 = 0,\ x_3 = 1,\ z_{max} = 3$

10. Minimize $z = x_1 - 3x_2 + 2x_3$
subject to $2x_1 - x_2 + 2x_3 \le 7$
$-2x_1 + 4x_2 \le 12$
$-4x_1 + 3x_2 + 8x_3 \le 10,$
$x_1, x_2, x_3 \ge 0$ ***(JNTU 99S)***
Ans. $x_1 = 4,\ x_2 = 5,\ x_3 = 0,\ z_{min} = -11$

4.22 ARTIFICIAL VARIABLE TECHNIQUE

If some of the constraints in a L.P. problem be given in the form of an equation or as (greater than ($\ge$) $\Sigma\, a_{ij}\, x_j \ge b_i$, with $b_i > 0$, then either we do not require to add any variable or have to subtract one, which is called a slack variable. But then we do not have a unit matrix of the coefficients and can not have a starting **basic solution** which is essential **for solving by the simplex method.** So in all the constraints of the above form, a variable, called an **artificial variable** is added. But which **should not occur in the final solution in the final table**. So either the artificial variable should have been eliminated at some stage or if **it is present in the final basis, its value should be zero**. If it be present in the final solution (when all $z_i - c_i \ge 0$), with some **non-zero positive value**, it implies that the **problem does not have any solution**. As soon as an artificial variable goes out of the basis, the **corresponding column may be dropped from the simplex table.**

There are two methods of solution for problems involving the artificial variable they are :

(i) **The big-M method** and

(ii) **The Two-phase method.**

4.23 THE BIG-M METHOD

In this method a very large value $-M$ is assigned as cost with the artificial variable in the objective function. This helps in removing them one-one by from the basis and the simplex table. The value $-M$ is called penalty and the method is known as Charnes Penalty method. The procedure in the method of solution is almost the same and is illustrated by the exampels given below :

Example 4.21. Solve the L.P. Problem using the big-M method.

Max $z = -2x_1 - x_2$

subject to $3x_1 + x_2 = 3$ ...(1)

$x_1 + 2x_2 \le 4$

$4x_1 + 3x_2 \ge 6$ ...(2)

$x_1, x_2 \ge 0$

Solution : Introducing a slack variable x_3 in (3), a surplus variable $-x_4$ in (2) and artificial variables x_5, x_6 in (1) and (2) and also in the value of z with artificial variable x_5, x_6 having coefficients, $-M$ each where **M is supposed to be very large**, we thus have

$$\text{Max } z = -2x_1 - x_2 + 0x_3 + 0x_4 - Mx_5 - Mx_6$$

Subject to $3x_1 + 1x_2 + 0 + 1x_5 = 3$

$4x_1 + 3x_2 - x_4 + 0 + 1x_6 = 6$

$x_1 + 2x_2 + x_3 = 4,$ $x_1, x_2, \ge 0$

Simplex Table 1.

			$c =$	-2	-1	0	0	$-M$	$-M$
C_B	α_B	X_B	$\vec{b}$	α_1	α_2	α_3	α_4	α_5	α_6
$-M$	α_5	x_5	3	[3]	1	0	0	1	0
$-M$	α_6	x_6	6	4	3	0	-1	0	1
0	α_3	x_3	4	1	2	1	0	0	0
	$z_i - c_i$			$-2M - 4M + 2 = -7M + 2$	$-M - 3M + 1 = -4M + 1$	0	M	$-M + M = 0$	$-M + M = 0$

↑ α_1 entering ↓ α_5 departing

Value of $z_i - c_i$ is most negative for $i = 1$, so α_1 is the entering **vector in the basis.** For departing vector, find

$$\text{Min}\left\{\frac{\vec{b}}{y_{i1}}, y_{i1} \geq 0, = \frac{3}{3}\frac{6}{4}\frac{4}{1}\right\} = 1, \text{ for } \textbf{row 1}$$

So α_5 is the departing vector. Pivot value $= y_{11} = 3$

Performing $\quad R_1 \frac{R_1}{3}; \quad R_2\ R_2 - \left(\frac{4R_1}{3}\right); \quad R_3\ \frac{1R_1}{3}$

Table 2.

				-2	-1	0	0	$-M$	Dropping α_5
C_B	α_B	X_B	$\vec{b}$	α_1	α_2	α_3	α_4	α_6	from Table
-2	α_1	x_1	$1 = 1$	1	$\frac{1}{3}$	0	0	0	
$-M$	α_6	x_6	$6 - 4 \times 1 = 2$	$4 - 4 \times 1 = 0$	$3 - \frac{4}{3} = \frac{5}{3}$	$0 - 4 \times 0 = 0$	$-1 - 4 \times 0 = -1$	$1 - 0 = 1$	
0	α_3	x_3	$4 - 1 \times 1 = 3$	$1 - 1 \times 1 = 0$	$2 - \frac{1}{3} = +\frac{5}{3}$	$1 - 0 \times 0 = 1$	$0 - 0 \times 0 = 0$	$0 - 0 \times 0 = 0$	
			$z_i - c_i$	$-2 + 2$	$-\frac{5}{3}M - \frac{2}{3} + 1$	0	0	$-M + M = 0$	

↑ α_2 entering ↓ α_6 departing

As $z_i - c_i$ is most negative for $i = 2$, so α_2 **is the entering vector** in the basis.

$$\text{Min}\left\{\frac{\vec{b}}{y_{i2}}, y_{i2} \geq 0; \frac{1}{1/3}\ \frac{2}{5/3}\ \frac{3}{5/3}\right\} = \frac{6}{5} \text{ for } r = 2$$

So second row vector α_6 **is the departing vector with pivot value** $= \frac{5}{3}$

Performing

$$R_2 \to \frac{3}{5} R_2;$$

$$R_1 \to R_1 - \frac{1}{3} \cdot \frac{3}{5} R_2;$$

$$R_3 \to R_3 - \frac{5}{3} \cdot \frac{3}{5} R_2$$

and dropping α_6 from the simplex table, we have

Table 3.

			$c =$	-2	-1	0	0
C_B	B	X_B	b	α_1	α_2	α_3	α_4
-2	α_1	x_1	$1-\frac{1}{3}\left(\frac{6}{5}\right)=\frac{3}{5}$	1	$\frac{1}{3}-\frac{1}{3}\times 1=0$	0	$0-\left(\frac{1}{3}\right)\left(-\frac{3}{5}\right)=\frac{1}{5}$
-1	α_2	x_2	$2\times\frac{3}{5}=\frac{6}{5}$	0	$\frac{5}{3}\times\frac{3}{5}=1$	0	$-1\times\frac{3}{5}=-\frac{3}{5}$
0	α_3	x_3	$3-\frac{5}{3}\times\frac{6}{4}=1$	0	$\frac{5}{3}-\frac{5}{3}\times 1=0$	1	$0-\left(\frac{5}{3}\right)\left(-\frac{3}{5}\right)=1$
			$z_i-c_i=$	$-2-(-2)=0$	$-1-(-1)=0$	0	$-\frac{2}{5}+\frac{3}{5}-0=+\frac{1}{5}$

As all $z_i - c_i \geq 0$. The solution is optimal.

Ans. $x_1 = 3/5,\quad x_2 = \frac{6}{5},\quad (x_3 = 1$, not reqd.)

with $\quad z_{\max} = -\frac{6}{5} - \frac{6}{5} = -\frac{12}{5}.$

Example 4.22. Solve by big–M method, the following L.P. problem.

Maximize $\quad z = 3x_1 + 2x_2 + 3x_3$

Subject to $\quad 2x_1 + x_2 + x_3 \leq 2 \quad$ **...(1)**

$3x_1 + 4x_2 + 2x_3 \geq 8 \quad$ **...(2)**

$x_1, x_2, x_3 \geq 0$

Solution : Introducing slack variable x_4 in (1) and a surplus variable x_5 and **artificial variable** x_6 in (1) and (2) add x_6 also in z with coefficient $-M$, where M is assumed to be very large. Thus we have,

$$\text{Max } z = 3x_1 + 2x_2 + 3x_3 + 0x_4 + 0x_5 - Mx_6$$

Subject to $\quad 2x_1 + x_2 + x_3 + x_4 + 0 + 0 = 2 \quad$ ...(3)

$3x_1 + 4x_2 + 2x_3 + 0 - x_5 + x_6 = 8 \quad$ ...(4)

Simplex Table 1.

			$c =$	3	2	3	0	0	$-M$
C_B	α_B	X_B	$\vec{b}$	α_1	α_2	α_3	α_4	α_5	α_6
0	α_4	x_4	2	2	1	1	1	0	0
$-M$	α_6	x_6	8	3	4	2	0	-1	1
			$z_i - c_i =$	$0-3M-3$	$0-4M-2$	$0-2M$	0	M	$-M+M=0$

$\uparrow \alpha_2$ entering

The most negative value of $z_i - c_i$ is for $i = 2$. So α_2 is the entering vector.

$$\text{Min}\left\{\frac{\vec{b}}{y_{i2}}, y_{i2} > 0; \frac{2}{2}\frac{8}{4}\right\} = 2, 2,$$

So $r = 1$ or $r = 2$.

4.24 DEGENERACY

The case as above, where $\underset{i}{\text{Min}}\left\{\frac{x_{Bj}}{y_{jk}}, y_{jk} > 0\right\}$ is true for more than one value of r, There can be more than one vectors, which may be deleted from the basis at this stage. In such case we delete any one of them, if no further degeneracy arises, then the problem will be solved. In the above examples deleting α_4 from the basis and proceeding we get the solution as in the above case.

But if in the above example we delete α_6 instead of α_4, one of the basic variables becomes zero (which is the definition of degeneracy) and on applying the simplex method further, we find that the same sequence of simplex tables are repeated without improving the value of the objective function. **This is called cycling**. There exists procedures for preventing the cycling but those we will not consider here because of complicacy and being of beyond standard.

If some one of b_i be zero initially, the degeneracy (as the corresponding basic variable will be zero) then occurs at the very first iteration.

4.25 EXCEPTIONAL CASES

Case (i). Tie for Outgoing Vector

When there is a tie for the outgoing vector because of the same least value r corresponding to which there can be two vectors eligible for going out of the basis. If the min value is > 1 choose any one for outgoing and proceed. Such an arbitrary choice does not affect the optimal value. If min value is zero, the degeneracy has to be resolved.

Case (ii). Tie for Incoming Vector

When the most negative value of $z_i - c_i$ is equal for two values of i, any one of them may be taking in the basis and then be proceed. It will also not affect the final optimal solution.

As both the values are coming out equal. It would require the knowledge of revised simplex method (resolution of degeneracy) to find, which one of the two should be droppted. However in above Ex. 2, if on drop the vector α_4, we reach at a solution.

Key element then is $y_{12} = 1$

Performing $\quad R_1 \rightarrow \frac{R_1}{y_{12}} = \frac{R_1}{1} = R;$

$$R_2 \; R_2 - \frac{4R_1}{1}$$

				3	2	3	0	0	$-M$
C	B	X	$\overrightarrow{b}$	α_1	α_2	α_3	α_4	α_5	α_6
2	α_2	x_2	2	2	1	1	1	0	0
$-M$	α_6	x_6	$8-8=0$	$3-4\times 2$ $=-5$	$4-4\times 1$ $=0$	$2-4\times 1$ $=-2$	$0-4\times 1$ $=-4$	$-1-0$ $=-1$	$1-0$ $=1$
			$z_i - c_i =$	$2\times 4 - M(-5)$	$2-2$	$2+2M$	$4M+2$	M	0

We have all $z_i - c_i \geq 0$.

We have the artificial variable to be still in the basis but because its value is zero. So the solution is optimal with $x_1 = x_3 = 0$ and $x_2 = 2$.

Ans. $\boldsymbol{x_2 = 2,\ z_{max} = 3\times 0 + 2\times 2 + 3\times 0 = 0 = 4.}$

4.26 PROBLEM HAVING UNBOUNDED SOLUTION

Example 4.23. Solve the L.P. problem

Maximize $\boldsymbol{z = 3x_1 + 2x_2 + x_3,}$

subject to $\boldsymbol{-3x_1 + 2x_2 + 2x_3 = 8}$ **...(1)**

$\boldsymbol{-3x_1 + 4x_2 + x_3 = 7}$ **...(2)**

$\boldsymbol{x_1, x_2, x_3 \geq 0.}$

Solution : Adding artificial variables x_4 and x_5 in (2) and (3) and $-Mx_4$, $-Mx_5$ in z where M is very large, we have

$$\text{Max } z = 3x_1 + 2x_2 + 1x_3 - Mx_4 - Mx_5$$

$$-3x_1 + 2x_2 + 2x_3 + x_4 = 8$$

$$-3x_1 + 4x_2 + x_3 + x_5 = 7$$

			$c =$	3	2	1	$-M$	$-M$
C	α_B	X_B	$\overrightarrow{b}\ \alpha_i$	α_1	α_2	α_3	α_4	α_5
$-M$	α_4	x_4	8	-3	2	2	1	0
$-M$	α_5	x_5	7	-3	4	1	0	1
			$z_i - c_i =$	$+3M+3M-3$ $=6M-3$	$-2M-4M-2$ $=-6M-2$	$-2M-M+1$ $=-M+1$	$-M+M$ $=0$	$-M+M$ $=0$

↑ α_2 entering

As most negative value of $z_i - c_i$ is for $i = 2$, so α_2 is the entering vector.

$$\text{Min}\left\{\frac{\overrightarrow{b}}{y_{i2}} y_{i2} > 0; \frac{8}{2}, \frac{7}{4}\right\} = \frac{7}{4} \text{ for } r = 2$$

So secnd row **vector $\boldsymbol{\alpha_5}$ is departing** with key element $y = 22 = 4$

Also dropping the artificial vector α_5 from table

Performing $R_2 \to \frac{R_2}{y_{22}} = \frac{1}{4} R_2$

$$R_1 \to R_1 - y_{12}\left(\frac{R_2}{y_{22}}\right) = R_1 - \frac{1}{2} R_2$$

				3	2	1	$-M$
C_B	α_B	X_B	$\vec{b}$	α_1	α_2	α_3	α_4
$-M$	α_4	x_4	$8 - 2 \times \frac{7}{4} = \frac{9}{2}$	$-3 - 2\left(\frac{-3}{4}\right) = -\frac{3}{2}$	$2 - 2(1) = 0$	$2 - \frac{2}{4} = \frac{3}{2}$	$1 - 2 \times 0 = 1$
2	α_2	x_2	$\frac{7}{4}$	$\frac{-3}{4}$	1	$\frac{1}{4}$	0
			$z_i - c_i =$	$\frac{3M}{2} - 3 = \frac{-3}{2}$	2	$\frac{-3M}{2} + \frac{1}{2} = -1$	$-M + M$

↓ α_1 ↓ α_4 departing

$z_i - c_i = -\frac{3M}{2} - \frac{1}{2}$ is most negative for $i = 3$, so α_3 is the entering vector,

For finding the departing vector

$$\text{Min}\left\{\frac{\vec{b}}{y_{i3}}, y_{i3} > 0 = \frac{\frac{9}{2}}{3/2} \; \frac{\frac{7}{4}}{1/4}\right\} = \{3, 7\} = 3$$

for $r = 1$. So 1st row vector α_4 is departing. It is now dropped from the table, being an artificial vector.

Pivot element $= y_{13} = \mathbf{3/2}$

Performing $R_1 \to \frac{2R_1}{3}$, $R_2 \to R_2 - \frac{1}{4}\left(\frac{2R_1}{3}\right)$

We get

				3	2	1
C_B	α_B	X_B	$\vec{b}\,\alpha_i$	α_1	α_2	α_3
1	α_3	x_3	$3 = 3$	-1	0	1
2	α_2	x_2	$\frac{7}{4} - \frac{1}{4}(3) = 1$	$\frac{-3}{4} - \frac{1}{4}(-1) = \frac{-1}{2}$	$1 - \frac{1}{4}(0) = 1$	$1 - \frac{1}{4}(1) = 0$
			$z_i - c_i =$	$-1 - 1 - 3$	$-2 + 2$	$1 - 1$

↑ α_1 entering

As $z_i - c_i = -5$ (Most negative) for $i = 1$. So α_1 is the entering vector. For choosing the departing vector, we find

$$\text{Min}\left\{\frac{\vec{b}}{y_{i1}}, y_{i1} > 0 = \frac{3}{-\text{ive}}, \frac{1}{-\text{ive}}\right\}$$

As **departing vector does not exist. The solution is unbounded**. Let us check it from the equations.

The constraints are in the form of equations. Writing then as

$$2x_2 + 2x_3 - (8 + 3x_1) = 0$$
$$4x_2 + 1x_3 - (7 + 3x_1) = 0$$

We have solvign for x_2, x_3,

$$x_2 = 1 + \frac{3}{2}x_1, \quad x_3 = 3 + x_1$$

and
$$z = 3x_1 + \left(1 + \frac{3}{2}x_1\right) + 3 + x_1 = 4 + \frac{11}{4}x_1$$

when $x_1 \to \infty$, $z \to \infty$. So the solution is unbounded.

PROBLEM SET 4.5

Solve the following L.P. problems by he Big-*M* method :

1. Maximize $z = x_1 + 2x_2 + 3x_3 - x_4$

$$x_1 + 2x_2 + 3x_3 = 15$$
$$2x_1 + 2x_2 + 5x_3 = 20$$
$$x_1 + 2x_2 + x_3 + x_4 = 10,$$

$x_1, x_2, x_3, x_4, \geq 0$

Hint : As x_4 is present only in first and not in other two equations. So it may be taken in the
basis and only two artificial variables x_5, x_6 may be added in other two equations.

Ans. $x_1 = 5/2$, $x_2 = 5/2$, $x_3 = 5/2$, $x_4 = 0$, $z_M = 15$

2. Minimize $z = 2x_1 + 3x_2$
subject to $2x_1 + x_2 \geq 4$

$$x_1 + 7x_2 \geq 7,$$

$x_1, x_2 \geq 0$

Hint : First change $z' = -z = -2x_1 - 2x_2$. So Max $z' = -2x_1 - 2x_2$

Ans. $x_1 = \frac{21}{13}$, $x_2 = \frac{10}{13}$, $z_{\min} = -z = \frac{72}{13}$.

3. Maximize $z = 3x_1 + 2x_2$
subject to $2x_1 + x_2 \leq 2$

$$3x_1 + 4x_2 \geq 12,$$

$x_1, x_2 \geq 0$

Ans. No. solution as artificial vector with is non-zero value remains in basis when all $z_i - c_i \geq 0$.

4. Maximize $z = x_1 + 2x_2 + 3x_3 - x_4$
subject to $x_2 = 2x_2 + 3x_3 = 150$
$2x_1 + x_2 + 5x_3 = 200$
$x_1 = 2x_2 + x_3 + x_4 = 100,$
$x_1, x_2, x_3, x_4 \geq 0$
Ans. $x_1 = x_2 = x_3 = 25,\ z_{max} = 150$

5. Maximize $z = 2x_1 + x_2$
subject to $x_1 - x_2 \leq 10$
$2x_1 - x_2 \leq 40,\ x_1, x_2 \geq 0$
solution is unbounded.

6. Max $z = -5x_1 - 8x_2$
subject to $3x_1 + 2x_2 \geq 3$
$x_1 + 4x_2 \geq 4$
$x_1 + x_2 \leq 5,$
$x_1, x_2 \geq 0$
Ans. $x_1 = 0,\ x_2 = 5\ z_{min} = -40$

7. Maximize $z = 5x_1 + 3x_2$
subject to $x_1 + x_2 \leq 2$
$5x_1 + 2x_2 \leq 10,$
$3x_1 + 8x_2 \leq 12,$
$x_1, x_2 \geq 0.$
Ans. $x_1 = 2,\ x_2 = 0,\ z_{max} = 10$

8. Maximize $z = 3x_1 + 2x_2 + 3x_3$
subject to $2x_1 + x_2 + x_3 \leq 2$
$3x_1 + 4x_2 + 2x_3 \geq 8,$
$x_1, x_2, x_3 \geq 0$ ***(J.N.T.U. 99S)***
Ans. $x_1 = 0,\ x_2 = 2,\ x_3 = 0,\ z_{max} = 4$

9. Maximize $z = x_1 + 2x_2 + 3x_3 - x_4$
subject to $x_1 + 2x_2 + 3x_3 = 15$
$2x_1 + x_2 + 5x_3 = 20$
$x_1 + 2x_2 + x_3 + x_4 = 10,$
$x_1, x_2, x_3, x_4 \geq 0$ ***(Rourkela 88)***
Ans. $x_1 = x_2 = x_3 = \frac{5}{2},\ x_4 = 0,\ z_{max} = 15.$

4.27 TWO PHASE METHOD

This is another method (first was the Big-*M* method already considered) of solving L.P. problems in which artificial variables are introduced to change the constraints with a unit matrix of the coefficients.

The simplex method of solution of an L.P. problem requires an initial basic feasible solution to start with. In two-phase method, Phase-I is a technique to have such a basic solution of the problem, which may **not be optimal** but is **only a basic solution**. On which simplex method can be applied further in Phase-II.

For this, in phase I, we consider the maximization of a new objective function W, in which the **original variables are given cost zero** and **cost –1 is assigned to each of the artificial variables. Solving phase-I by simplex method, the following situations may arise :**

1. **No Solution** All $z_i - c_i \geq 0$ but an artificial variable is present in the basis with **some non-zero value**. In that case the problem has no solution.

2. **Redundant constraint** If the artificial variable (when all $z_i - c_i \geq 0$) is present in the basis but **its value is zero**. It only indicates that some of the constraints are unnecessary (redundant) and we should proceed **with this last simplex matrix for the solution of the original problem.**

3. **If no artificial variable is present, we have $W = 0$, then proceed for phase II as explained above.**

Example 4.24. Solve the following L.P. problem by two-phase method.

Minimize $z = x_1 + x_2$,

Subject to $2x_1 + x_2 \geq 4$,

$x_1 + 7x_2 \geq 7$,

$x_1, x_2 \geq 0$. *(Madras 98)*

Solution : Adding the surplus variables x_3, x_4, and artificial variables x_5, x_6, the problem becomes.

Minimize $z = x_1 + x_2$ Let $z' = -z$

or Maximize $z' = -x_1 - x_2$

Subject to

$$2x_1 + 1x_2 - x_3 + 0 + 1x_5 + 0 = 4 \quad ...(3)$$

$$1x_1 + 7x_2 + 0 - x_4 + 0 + x_6 = 7 \quad ...(4)$$

Phase I

Maximize $W = 0x_1 + 0x_2 + 0x_3 + 0x_4 - x_5 - x_6$

subject to constraints given in (3) and (4)

Table 1.

			$c =$	0	0	0	0	–1	–1
C_B	α_B	X_B	$\vec{b}$	α_1	α_2	α_3	α_4	α_5	α_6
–1	α_5	x_5	4	2	1	–1	0	1	0
–1	α_6	x_6	7	1	[7]	0	–1	0	1
			$z_i - c_i =$	$-2 - 1 = -3$	$-1 - 7 = -8$	1	1	$-1 + 1$	$-1 + 1$

↑ α_2 entering

The most negative $z_i - c_i = -8$ for $i = 2$. So α_2 **is the entering vector**. For choosing the departing vector we find

$$\text{Min}\left\{\frac{\vec{b}}{y_{i2}}, y_{i2} \geq 0; \frac{4}{1}\frac{7}{7}\right\} = 1 \text{ for } r = 2.$$

So α_6 is the departing variable, with pivot value $y_{22} = 7$

Performing $R_2 \to \frac{R_2}{y_{22}} = \frac{R_2}{7}$

$$R_1 \to R_1 - \frac{y_{12}}{y_{22}} R_2 = R_1 - \frac{1}{7} R_2$$

Phase I
Table II

			$c =$	0	0	0	0	-1
c_B	α_B	X_B	$\vec{b}$	α_1	α_2	α_3	α_4	α_5
-1	α_5	x_5	$4 - 1 = 3$	$2 - \frac{1}{7} = \boxed{\frac{13}{7}}$	$1 - 1 = 0$	$-1 - 0$	$0 + \frac{1}{7}$	$1 - 0$
0	α_2	x_2	$\frac{7}{7} = 1$	$\frac{1}{7}$	1	0	$\frac{-1}{7}$	0
			$z_i - c_i =$	$-\frac{13}{7}$	0	1	$-\frac{1}{7}$	$1 - 1$

↑ α_1 entering

$z_i - c_i$ is most negative $\left(= -\frac{13}{7}\right)$ for $i = 1$, so α_1 **is the entering vector**. For chosing the departing vector, we find

$$\text{Min}\left\{\frac{\vec{b}}{y_{i1}}, y_{i1} > 0;\right\} = \left\{\frac{3}{13/7}\ \frac{1}{1/7}\right\} = \left\{\frac{21}{13}, 7\right\} = \frac{21}{13} \text{ for } r = 1,$$

Ist row vector α_5 is departing. key element $= y_{11} = \frac{13}{7}$.

$$\text{Performing } R_1 \to \frac{7}{13} R_1,\ R_2 \to R_2 - \frac{1}{7} \times \frac{7}{13} R_1$$

Phase I
Table III

			$c =$	0	0	0	0
c_B	α_B	X_B	$\vec{b}$	α_1	α_2	α_3	α_4
0	α_1	x_1	$3 \times \frac{7}{13} = \frac{21}{13}$	1	0	$-\frac{7}{13}$	$\frac{1}{13}$
0	α_2	x_2	$1 - \frac{1}{7} \times \frac{21}{13} = \frac{10}{13}$	$\frac{1}{7} - \frac{1}{7} \times 1 = 0$	$1 - \frac{1}{7} \times 0 = 1$	$0 - \frac{1}{7}\left(\frac{-7}{13}\right) = \frac{1}{13}$	$-\frac{1}{7} - \frac{1}{7} \times \frac{1}{13} = -\frac{2}{13}$
			$(z_i - c_i)$	0	0	0	0

All $z_i - c_i \geq = 0$, so W is optimal $= 0$

The solution of **Phase I is**

$$x_1 = \frac{21}{13}, \; x_2 = \frac{10}{13} \text{ with basis } (\alpha_1, \alpha_2)$$

Considering the original problem with basis (α_1, α_2).

Phase II

			$c =$	-1	-1	0	0
c_B	α_B	x_B	$\vec{b}$	α_1	α_2	α_3	α_4
-1	α_1	x_1	$\frac{21}{13}$	1	0	$-\frac{7}{13}$	$\frac{1}{13}$
-1	α_2	x_2	$\frac{10}{13}$	0	1	$\frac{1}{13}$	$-\frac{2}{13}$
			$z_i - c_i =$	$-1+1 = 0$	$-1+1 = 0$	$\frac{7}{13} - \frac{1}{13} = \frac{6}{13}$	$\frac{1}{13} + \frac{2}{13} = \frac{3}{13}$

As all $z_i - c_i \geq 0$, The solution is optimal for the original problem also.

Ans. $x_1 = \frac{21}{13}, \; x_2 = \frac{10}{13}, \; x_{\min} = \frac{31}{13}$

Example 4.25. **Use two-phase method to solve the L.P. problem**

Minimize $\quad z = 7.5x_1 - 3x_2$

subject to $\quad 3x_1 - x_2 - x_3 \geq 3 \quad$ ...(1)

$\quad x_1 - x_2 + x_3 \geq 0 \quad$ ...(2)

$x_1, x_2, x_3 \geq 0$ *(Andhra 99)*

Solution : Adding surface variables x_4, x_5 and artificial variables x_6, x_7 in equations (2) and (3), we have

Maximize $\quad z' = -7.5x_1 + 3x_2$

where $z' = -z$

Subject to $\quad 3x_1 - x_2 - x_3 - x_4 = 0 + x_6 + 0 = 3$

$\quad x_1 - x_2 + x_3 + 0 - x_5 + 0 + x_7 = 2$

Phase I Let us

maximize $\quad W = 0x_1 + 0x_2 + 0x_3 + 0x_4 + 0x_5 - 1x_6 - 1x_7$

to obtain an initial basic solution for the original problem to be solved in Phase II.

Table 1.

			c	0	0	0	0	0	−1	−1
c_B	α_5	X_B	$\vec{b}$	α_1	α_2	α_3	α_4	α_5	α_6	α_7
−1	α_6	x_6	3	$\boxed{3}$	−1	−1	−1	0	1	0
−1	α_7	x_7	2	1	−1	1	0	−1	0	1
			$z_i - c_i =$	$-3-1$	$1+1$	$1-1$	1	1	0	0

↑ α_1 entering ↑ α_1 entering

$z_i - c_i$ is most negative $(= -4)$ for $i = 1$, so α_1 **is the entering vector.** For choosing the departing vector we find

$$\text{Min}\left\{\frac{\vec{b}}{y_{i1}}, y_{i1} > 0;\right\} = \text{Min}\left\{\frac{3}{3}\ \frac{2}{1}\right\} = 1 \text{ for } r = 1$$

So α_6 **is departing**. Pivot value $y_{11} = 3$

Performing $R_1 \to \frac{R_1}{R_{11}} = \frac{1}{3} R_1$

$$R_2 \to R_2 - \frac{y_{12}}{y_{11}} R_1 = R_2 - \frac{1}{3} R_1$$

			$c =$	0	0	0	0	0	−1	1
			$\vec{b}$	α_1	α_2	α_3	α_4	α_5	α_7	α_6 is dropped from table being artificial vector which has been removed from basis.
0	α_1	x_1	$\frac{3}{3} = 1$	1	$-\frac{1}{3}$	$-\frac{1}{3}$	$-\frac{1}{3}$	0	0	
7	α_7	x_7	$2-1$ $= 1$	$1-1$ $= 0$	$-1+\frac{1}{3}$ $= -\frac{2}{3}$	$1+\frac{1}{3}$ $= \frac{4}{3}$	$0+\frac{1}{3}$ $= \frac{1}{3}$	-1 $= -1$	$1 = 1$	
			$z_i - c_i =$	0	$0+\frac{2}{3}$	$-\frac{4}{3}$	$-\frac{1}{3}1$	0		

↑ α_1 entering

$z_i - c_i$ is most negative $\left(= -\frac{4}{3}\right)$ for $i = 3$.

So α_3 **is the entering vector.** For choosing the departing vector, we find

$$\text{Min}\left\{\frac{\vec{b}}{y_{i3}}, y_{i3} > 0\right\} = \text{Min}\left\{\frac{1}{-\text{ive}}\ \frac{1}{4/3}\right\} = \frac{3}{4}, \text{ for } r = 2$$

So α_7 **is departing** pivot value $= y_{23} = \frac{4}{3}$

Performing $\quad R_2 \to \dfrac{R_2}{y_{23}} = \dfrac{3}{4} R_2$

$$R_1 \to R_1 - \left(\frac{-1}{3}\right)\left(\frac{3}{4} R_2\right) = R_1 + \frac{R_2}{4}$$

We have

Phase I

Table 3

			$\vec{b}$	0	0	0	0	0
0	α_1	x_1	$1 + \frac{1}{3}\left(\frac{3}{4}\right) = \frac{5}{4}$	$1 + \frac{1}{3} \times 0 = 1$	$-\frac{1}{3} + \frac{1}{3}\left(\frac{-1}{2}\right) - \frac{1}{2}$	$-\frac{1}{3} + \frac{1}{3} \times 1 = 0$	$-\frac{1}{3} + \frac{1}{3 \times 4} = -\frac{1}{4}$	$0 + \frac{1}{3}\left(\frac{-3}{4}\right) = -\frac{1}{4}$
0	α_3	x_3	$\frac{3}{4}$	0	$-\frac{1}{2}$	1	$\frac{1}{4}$	$-\frac{3}{4}$
			$z_i - c_i =$	0	0	0	0	0

As all $z_i - c_i \geq 0$. So the solution of 1st phase is optimal with $x_1 = \frac{5}{4}$, $x_3 = \frac{3}{4}$, α_3 the basis. Considering the solution of original problem with α_1, α_3 in basis.

Phase II

Table 1

				-7.5	3	0	0	0
c_B	α_B	X_B	$\vec{b}$	α_1	α_2	α_3	α_4	α_5
-7.5	α_1	x_1	$\frac{5}{4}$	1	$-\frac{1}{2}$	0	$-\frac{1}{4}$	$-\frac{1}{4}$
0	α_3	x_3	$\frac{3}{4}$	0	$-\frac{1}{2}$	1	$\frac{1}{4}$	$-\frac{3}{4}$
			$z_i - c_i$	0	$\frac{15}{4} - 3 = \frac{3}{4}$	0	$\frac{7}{8}$	$\frac{7}{4}$

As all $z_i - c_i \geq 0$, so the solution is optimal.

Ans. $x_1 = \frac{5}{4}$, $x_2 = 0$, $x_3 = \frac{3}{4}$,

$$z'_{\max} = -\frac{15}{2}\left(\frac{5}{4}\right) + 0 = -\frac{75}{8},$$

$$z_{\min} = -\frac{1}{z} = \frac{75}{8}.$$

PROBLEM SET 4.6

Use the phase method to solve the following L.P. problems.

1. Minimize $z = 2x_1 + 9x_2 + x_3$
   subject to $x_1 + 4x_2 + 2x_3$, 7, 5
   $3x_1 + x_2 + 2x_3 \geq 4,\ x_1, x_2, x_3 \geq 0$
   Ans. $x_1 = x_2 = 0,\ x_3 = 5/2,$
2. Maximize $z = 2x_1 + 3x_2 + 2x_3 - x_4 + x_5$
   subject to $3x_1 - 3x_2 + 4x_3 + 2x_4 - x_5 = 0$
   $x_1 + x_2 + x_3 + 3x_4 + x_5 = 2,\ x_i \geq 0$
   for $i = 1, 5$
   Ans. $x_1 = x_2 = x_3 = 0,\ x_4 = \frac{2}{5},\ x_5 = \frac{4}{5},\ z_{min} = \frac{2}{5}.$ *(Raj 2003)*
3. Minimize $z = 4x_1 + x_2$
   subject to $3x_1 + x_2 = 3;$
   $x_1 + 2x_2 \leq 4;$
   $4x_1 + 3x_2 \geq 6,$
   $x_1, x_2 \geq 0$
   Ans. $x_1 = \frac{3}{5},\ x_2 = \frac{6}{5},\ x_3 = x_4 = 0,\ z_{min} = \frac{18}{5}$
4. Maximize $z = 5x_1 + 3x_2$
   subject to $2x_1 + x_2 \leq 1;$
   $x_1 + 4x_2 \geq 6,$
   $x_1, x_2 \geq 0$
   Ans. No solution.
5. Maximize $z = 5x_1 - 4x_2 + 3x_3$
   subject to $2x_1 + 2x_2 - x_3 \geq 2;$
   $3x_1 - 4x_3 \leq 3;$
   $x_2 + x_3 \leq 5,$
   $x_1, x_2, x_3 \geq 0.$
   Ans. $x_1 = \frac{23}{3},\ x_2 = 5,\ x_3 = 0,\ z_{max} = \frac{55}{3}.$
6. Maximize $z = 2x_1 + 3x_2 + 10x_3$
   subject to $x_1 + 2x_3 = 0$
   $x_2 + x_3 = 1$
   $x_1, x_2, x_3 \geq 0$
   Degenerate solution
   Ans. $x_1 = 0$ **(non basic)** $x_2 = 1, x_3 = 1,\ z_{max} = 3.$

7. Maximize $z = 9x_1 + 3x_2$
subject to $4x_1 + x_2 \le 8$
$2x_1 + x_2 \le 4,$
$x_1, x_2 \ge 0$
Ans. $x_1 = 2,\ x_2 = 0,\ z_{max} = 18$

8. $z = 3x_1 - x_2$
subject to $2x_1 + x_2 \ge 2;$
$x_1 + 3x_2 \le 2;$
$x_2 \le 4,$
$x_1, x_2 \ge 0$ *(Meerut 98)*
Ans. $x_1 = 3,\ x_2 = 0;\ z_{max} = 9$

9. Minimize $z = x_1 + x_2 + x_3$
subject to
$x_1 - 3x_2 + 4x_3 = 5;$
$x_1 - 2x_2 \le 3,$
$2x_2 + x_3 \ge 4$
$x_1, x_2, \ge 0,$
x_3 unrestricted.
Ans. $z_{min} \dfrac{43}{5},\ x_1 = 0,\ x_2 = \dfrac{21}{5},\ x_3 = \dfrac{22}{5}$

4.28 DUALITY

Consider two linear programming problems

(i) $$\textbf{Max } z_p = c_1x_1 + \ldots + c_n x_n = c_x$$

$$\text{Subject to } \sum_{j=1}^{n} a_{ij} x_j \le b_i,$$

$i = 1, 2, \ldots m$ or $AX \le B$

$x_i \ge 0$ for all $i = 1, \ldots m$, which has n variables and m constraints and

(ii) $$\textbf{Min } z_D = b_1 \omega_1 + \ldots v_m w_m = b^T W$$

$$\sum_{i=1}^{m} a_{ji} w_i \ge c_j,$$

$j = 1, 2, \ldots m$, all $w_i \ge 0$ or $A^T W \ge c^T$

which has m variables and n constraints. The two problems both have matrices A, C, B. So they are related. They can be written in the matrix form as

$$\text{Max } z_P = CX, \quad AX \le b, \quad X \ge 0 \qquad \ldots(1)$$

and

$$\text{Min. } z_D = b^T W,\ A^T W \ge c^T,\ W \ge 0 \qquad \ldots(2)$$

The same matrix A and vectors b and c are involved in the two problems, they are related problems.

If the **first problem be called the primal, the second is called its dual**. If we write the dual of (2), we have

$$\text{Max } z_{DD} = (c^T)^T V,\ (A^T)^T V \le (b^T)^T,\ V \ge 0 \qquad \text{...(3)}$$

But (3) is the same as (1) with $z_{DD} = z_P$ and $V = X$.

Hence if **second be the primal**, the **first is its dual**. So **Dual of the dual is primal.**

The most important thing about the primal and dual L.P. problems is **that the optimal values of their respective objective functions comes out to be equal,** *i.e.*,

$$\textbf{Optimal } z_P = \textbf{optimal } z_D \qquad \text{...(4)}$$

Another important property of them is that the solution of one can be read from the final simplex table of the solution of other.

4.29 SIMPLEX TABLE OF THE DUAL

So if the primal has 4 variables and 10 constraints whose computation is difficult to handle because of so many constraints, we can have its solution by solving its dual which will have **only 4 constraints.** Based on the various theorems, we have the following rules for writing the dual of a given primal L.P. problem.

4.30 RULES FOR WRITING THE DUAL OF A PRIMAL L.P. PROBLEM

1. Symmetrical Dual-Primal pair

Primal Maximize $z_P = CX$

Subject to $A_X \le b$

$X \ge 0$

then Dual is minimize $z_D = b^T W$

$A^T W \ge C^T$

$W \ge 0.$

To note here

(1) In maximization all the constraints are in the form of ($\le$)

(2) In its dual all constraints are in the form of ($\ge$).

(3) All primal and dual variables are non-negative.

2. Unsymmetrical Dual-Primal

Here the constraints in one are in the form of equation and those in the other in the form of inequality.

(i) Primal

Max $z_P = CX$

s.t. $AX = b$

$X \ge 0$

Dual

Minimize $z_D = b^T W$

$A^T W \ge C^T$

W is unrestricted

If not all but only any of the constraints in the primal (dual) be in the form of an equation, the corresponding dual (primal) variable will be unrestriction.

(ii) Primal

Max $z_P = CX$

$AX \le b$

X unrestricted

Dual

Minimize $z_D = b^T W$

$A^T W = C^T$

$W \ge 0.$

If not all but only some are primal (dual) variable be unrestricted the corresponding dual (primal) constraint will be in the form of an equation.

So if not all but only th i^{th} primal (dual) variable is unrestricted, the ith dual (primal) constraint will be an equation with $W_i \geq 0$, $(x_i \geq 0)$.

If the jth primal constrant be an equation the jth dual variable will be unrestricted.

To note : Number of variables in primal $= n =$ Number of constraints in the dual

Number of constraints is primal $= m =$ **Number of variables in the dual.**

4.31 OTHER IMPORTANT RESULTS ON DUALITY

(1) If X_0 be a feasible solution of the maximization problem

$$\text{Max } z_P = CX$$

$$\text{subject to } AX \leq b,\ X \geq 0$$

and W_0 is any feasible solution of the dual Min $z_D = b^T W$,

$$A^T W \geq C^T, W \geq 0,$$

then $z_0 = CX_0 \leq (z_D)_0 = b^T W_0$

Principal of Duality

But when $(z_p)_0$ becomes $= (z_D)_0$ **oprimal** with X_0 as the **optimal solution of the maximization Problem** and W_0 **is the optimal solution of the minimization** dual problem, and then (they) become equal

or
$$CX_0 = b^T W_0$$

Otherwise in general the set of **solution of maximization < the solutions of minimization.** It is only at optimal condition that the two solutions give equal values of Z_p and Z_D.

Unbounded Solution

(2) If either one of the two (primal or its dual) has an unbounded solution, the other has no solution.

4.32 RELATION BETWEEN VARIABLES OF PRIMAL AND DUAL AT OPTIMALITY

Let $(x_1)_0, (x_2)_0 \ldots (x_n)_0$ be the values of the primal at optimality and $(x_{n+1})_0 \cdots (x_{n+m})_0$, the values of its slack variables then dual in this case may have more equations but which can be changed in the first form after combining some of them.

Example 4.32. Write the dual of the L.P. Problem :

Maximize $z = 5x_1 + 3x_2$

Subject to $3x_1 + 5x_2 \leq 15$ ...(1)

$5x_1 + 2x_2 \leq 10$ ...(2)

$x_1 \geq 0, x_2 \geq 0$

The dual as per rules of dual writing is

Min $z_D = b^T W$, Minimize $15W_1 + 10W_2$, subject to

$$A^T W \geq C^T \Rightarrow \begin{cases} 3W_1 + 5W_2 \geq 5 \\ 5W_1 + 2W_2 \geq 3' \end{cases} W_1, W_2 \geq 0$$

(Meerut 91)

Aliter. Changing the given problem is **standard from** (by changing in equations) by adding slack variables the problem is

$$\text{Max } z = 5x_1 + 3x_2 + 0x_3 + 0x_4$$

subject to $3x_1 + 5x_2 + 1x_3 + 0 = 15$

$$5x_1 + 2x_2 + 0 + 1x_4 = 10,\ X_1, X_2, X_3, X_4 \geq 0$$

Dual is minimize $Z_D = 15W_1 + 10W_2$

Subject to $3W_1 + 5W_2 \geq 5$, $\quad 5W_1 + 2W_2 \geq 3$

$$\left.\begin{array}{l} 1W_1 + 0 \geq 0 \\ 0 + 1W_2 \geq 0 \end{array}\right\} \Rightarrow W_1 \geq 0, W_2 \geq 0.$$

W_1, W_2 (unrestricted, it is rebundant in virtue of above two. So both methods give the same dual.

Example 4.27. Write the dual of L.P. Problem

Minimize $z = 4x_1 + 6x_2 + 18x_3$

Subject to $x_1 + 3x_2 \geq 3$

$x_2 + 2x_3 \geq 5$, $x_1, x_2, x_3 \geq 0$

Solution : According to rules of writing the dual, we have the dual as

Maximize $z_D = 3W_1 + 5W_2$

Subject to
$$\left.\begin{array}{r} 1W_1 + 0W_2 \leq 4 \\ 3W_1 + 1W_2 \leq 6 \\ 0 + 2W_3 \leq 18 \end{array}\right\} \text{ or } \begin{array}{r} W_1 \leq 4 \\ 3W_1 + W_2 \leq 6 \\ 2W_3 \leq 18 \\ W_1, W_2, W_3 \geq 0 \end{array}$$

Example 4.28. Write the dual of the L.P. Problem

Minimize $\quad z = 1x_1 - 3x_2 - 2x_3$

subject to $\quad 3x_1 - 1x_2 + 2x_3 \leq 7 \quad$ **...(1)**

$\quad 2x_1 - 4x_2 + 0 \geq 12 \quad$ **...(2)**

$\quad -4x_1 + 3x_2 + 8x_3 = 10 \quad$ **...(3)**

$x_1, x_2 \geq 0$, x_3 unrestricted

After changing (1) in the form (≥), $-3x_1 + 1x_2 - 2x_3 \geq -7$, the dual is.

(Delhi 95, Madurai 92)

Solution : Dual is Maximize $\quad z_D = -7W_1 + 12W_2 + 10W_3$

subject to $\quad 3W_1 + 2W_2 - 4W_3 \leq 1$

$\quad -1W_1 - 4W_2 + 3W_3 \leq -3$

$\quad 2W_1 + 0 + 8W_3 = -2.$

As the first primal constraint is given in the form (≤ 7) instead of ($\ge$) form so first dual variable will be negative instead of positive, if we do not change it in $\ge$ form.

$$W_1 \le 0,\ W_2 \ge 0,\ W_3 \text{ unrestricted.}$$

x_3 was unrestricted so as per rules, the third constraints of the dual is an equation. Third constraints of primal was an equation so W_3 in the dual is unrestricted.

Example 4.29. Write the dual of the L.P. Problem.

Maximize $z = 2x_1 + 3x_2 + 4x_3$

Subject to $2x_1 + 3x_2 + 5x_3 \ge 2]$

or $-2x_1 - 3x_2 - 5x_3 \le -2$ ...(1)

$3x_1 + 1x_2 + 7x_3 = 3$ ...(2)

$x_1 + 4x_2 + 6x_3 \le 5$ ...(3)

$x_1, x_2 \ge 0, x_3$ unrestricted. *(Madras 96)*

Solution : The given problem is a maximization problem, so the constraints inequalities should be in the form of ($\le$). So (1) should be changed by muiltiplying by a negative sign or W_1 will be ≤ 0 if we do not change the inequality.

By the rules of dual-writing the second dual variable will be unrestricted as the second primal constraint is in the form of equation. The third primal varible is unrestricted so the third dual constraint will be in the form of equation. Following these, the dual is

Min $z_D = 2W_1 + 3W_2 + 5W_3$

$-2W_1 + 3W_2 + 1W_3 \ge 2$

$-3W_1 + 1W_2 + 4W_3 \ge 2$

$-5W_1 + 7W_2 + 6W_3 = 4$

$W_1 > 0,\ W_2$ unrestricted, $W_3 \ge 0$.

Example 4.30. Obtain the dual of the following L.P. problem.

Maximize $z = 2x_1 + 5x_2 + 6x_3$

Subject to $5x_1 + 6x_2 - x_3 \le 3$

$-2x_1 + 1x_2 + 4x_3 \le 4$

$x_1 - 5x_2 + 3x_3 \le 1$

$-3x_1 - 3x_2 + 7x_3 \le 6,\ x_1, x_2, x_3 \ge 0$ *(Madras 91S)*

Solution : The problem is given in the symmetrical form. By rules of writing the dual, it is

Minimize $z_D = 3W_1 + 4W_2 + 1W_3 + 6W_4$

subject to $5W_1 - 2W_2 + W_3 - 3W_4 \ge 2$

$6W_1 + 1W_2 - 5W_3 - 3W_4 \ge 5$

$-1W_1 + 4W_2 + 3W_3 + 7W_4 \ge 6$

$W_1, W_2, W_3, W_4 \ge 0.$

Example 4.31. **Write the dual of the following problem**

Min $z_P = 1x_1 + 4x_2 - 2x_3$

subject to $2x_1 - x_2 + 3x_3 \leq 10$

$3x_1 - 5x_2 \geq 12$

$-5x_1 + 2x_2 + 7x_3 = 15, \quad x_1, x_2 \geq 0, x_3$ **unrestricted**

Solution : It is a minimization problem, so first constraint should be changed in sign as

$-2x_1 + 1x_2 - 3x_3 \geq -10$ ...(1)

kept as it is $3x_1 - 5x_2 \geq 12$ ...(2)

kept as it is $-5x_1 + 2x_2 + 7x_3 = 15$ ...(3)

$x_1, x_2 \geq 0, x_3$ unrestricted

3rd constraint is an equation so W_3 in the dual will be unrestricted x_3 is unrestricted so third constraint in the dual will be an equation. The Dual is

$$-2W_1 + 3W_2 - 5W_3 \leq 1$$

$$1W_1 - 5W_2 + 2W_3 \leq 4$$

$$-3W_1 + 0W_2 + 7W_3 = -2$$

$W_1 \geq 0$, $W_2 \geq 0$, W_3 unrestricted. (Note : If the first constraint is not changed as above then $W_1 \leq 0$ instead of greater than or equal to).

PROBLEM SET 4.7

Write the dual of the following L.P. problems :

1. Max $z = 2x + 3y$

subject to $3x + 5y \leq 10$,

$5x + 2y \leq 12$,

$x, y \geq 0$

Ans. Min $z_D = 10W_1 + 12W_2$

subject to $3W_1 + 5W_2 \geq 2$,

$5W_1 + 2W_2 \geq 3$,

$W_1, W_2 \geq 0$.

2. Minimize $z_P = 1x_1 + 4x_2 - 2x_3$;

subject to $2x_1 - x_2 + 3x_3 \leq 10$

$3x_1 - 5x_2 \geq 12$,

$-5x_1 + 2x_2 + 7x_3 = 15$; $\quad x_1, x_2 \geq 0$, x_3 unrestricted.

Ans. Max $z_D = 10W_1 + 12W_2 + 15W_3$

subject to $-2W_1 + 3W_2 - 5W_3 \leq 1$

$-W_1 - 5W_2 + 2W_3 \leq 4$

$3W_1 + 0W_2 + 7W_3 \leq -2$; $\quad w_1 \leq 0, w_2 \geq 0, w_3$ unrestricted

3. Minimize $z = 2x_1 + 2x_2 + 4x_3$
subject to
$$2x_1 + 3x_2 + 5x_3 \geq 2$$
$$3x_1 + 1x_2 + 7x_3 \geq 3$$
$$1x_1 + 4x_2 + 6x_3 \leq 5, \quad x_1\, x_2\, x_3 \geq 0$$
Ans. Max $z = 2W_1 + 3W_2 - 5W_3$
subject to $2W_1 + 3W_2 - W_3 \leq 2$
$$3W_1 + 1W_2 - 4W_3 \leq 2$$
$$5W_1 + 7W_2 - 6W_3 \leq 4, \quad W_1, W_2, W_3 \geq 0$$

4. Minimize $z = 1x_1 - 3x_2 - 2x_3$
subject to $-3x_1 + 1x_2 - 2x_3 \geq -7$
$$2x_1 - 4x_2 \geq 12$$
$$-4x_1 + 3x_2 + 8x_3 = 10$$
$x_1, x_2 \geq 0$, x_3 unrestricted
Ans. Max $z_D = -7W_1 + 12W_2 + 10W_3$
subject to $-3W_1 + 2W_2 - 4W_3 \leq 1$
$$1W_1 - 4W_2 + 3W_3 \leq -3$$
$-2W_1 + 0W_2 - 8W_3 = -2$, $W_1\, W_2 \geq 0$ W_3 unrestricted

5. Minimize $z = 2x_1 + 3x_2 + 4x_3$
subject to $3x_1 + 4x_2 + x_3 = 11$
$$+2x_1 + 3x_2 - 2x_3 \geq 7$$
$$-x_1 + 2x_2 + 3x_3 \geq 1,$$
$3x_1 + 2x_2 + 2x_3 = 5$, $x_1, x_2 \geq 0$, x_3 unrestricted
Ans. Maximize $z_D = 11W_1 + 7W_2 + 1W_3 + 5W_4$
subject to $3W_1 + 2W_2 - W_3 + 3W_4 \leq 2$
$$4W_1 + 3W_2 + 2W_3 + 2W_4 \leq 3$$
$$1W_1 - 2W_2 + 3W_3 + 2W_4 = 4$$
W_1, W_3 unrestricted, $W_4, W_2 \geq 0$.

4.33 SOLUTION OF A L.P. PROBLEM USING THE CONCEPT OF DUALITY

We know when the L.P. problem has a finite optimal value, the optimal values of primal and its dual are equal. Further the solution of one can be read from the final simplex table of the ther. We illustrate it by the exampels solved below :

Example 4.32. Use duality to solve the L.P. problem

$$\text{Minimize} \quad z = 3x_1 + x_2$$
$$\text{subject to} \quad x_1 + x_2 \geq 1,$$
$$2x_1 + 3x_2 \geq 2;$$
$$x_1, x_2 \geq 0.$$

Solution : The dual of the above problem is
$$\text{Maximize} \quad z_D = 1W_1 + 2W_2,$$

subject to $1W_1 + 2W_2 \le 3,$

$1W_1 + 3W_2 \le 1,$

$W_1, W_2 \ge 0$

Adding the slack variables W_3 and W_4, the problem in standard form becomes

Maximize $z_D = 1W_1 + 2W_2 + 1W_3 + 0 = 3$

$1W_1 + 3W_2 + 0 + 1W_4 = 1$

1st Simplex Table

			$c =$	1	2	0	0
C_B	α_B	W_B	$\vec{b}$	α_1	α_2	α_3	α_4
0	α_3	W_3	3	1	2	1	0
0	α_4	W_4	1	1	$\boxed{3}$	0	1
			$z_i - c_i$	$0 \times 1 + 0 \times 1 - 1 = -1$	$0 - 2 = -2$	0	0

↑ entering ↑ diparting
vector $= \alpha_2$

$z_i - c_i$ is most negative for $i = 2$, so α_2 **is entering** vector for basis.

Min $\left\{\frac{\vec{b}}{y_{i2}}, y_{i2} \ge 0\right\} = \left\{\frac{3}{2}\ \frac{1}{3}\right\} = \frac{1}{3}$ for $r = 2$, so W_4 **is departing.** Pivot element $y_{22} = 3$.

Performing $R_2 \to \frac{R_2}{y_{22}} = \frac{1}{3} R_2$

$R_1 \to R_1 - \frac{y_{12}}{y_{22}} R_2 = R_1 - \frac{2}{3} R_2$, we have

Table 2

			c_i	1	2	0	0
			$\vec{b}\ \alpha_i$	α_1	α_2	α_3	α_4
0	α_3	W_3	$3 - \frac{1}{3} = \frac{7}{3}$	$1 - 2/3 = 1/3$	$2 - 2 = 0$	$1 - 0 = 1$	$0 - \frac{1}{3} \times 2 = -2/3$
2	α_2	W_2	$\frac{1}{3}$	$\boxed{\frac{1}{3}}$	1	0	$\frac{1}{3}$
			$z_i - c_i =$	$2\frac{1}{3} + 0 - 1 = -\frac{1}{3}$	$0 + 2 - 2 = 0$	$0 - 0 = 0$	$\frac{2}{3} - 0 = \frac{2}{3}$

↑ entering ↓ α_2 diparting

$z_i - c_i =$ most negative for $i = 1$, so α_1 **is the entering vector**

$$\text{Min}\left\{\frac{\vec{b}}{y_{i1}}\right\} = \left\{\frac{7/3}{1/3}, \frac{1/3}{1/3}\right\} = 1$$

So α_2 **is departing**

$$\text{pivot element} = y_{21} = \frac{1}{3}.$$

Performing $R_2 \to \frac{R_2}{y_{21}} = 3R_2$

$$R_1 \to R_1 - \frac{3}{3}R_2 = R_1 - R_2.$$

Table 2

		c_i	1	2	0	0
		$\vec{b}$	α_1	α_2	α_3	α_4
0	α_3	W_3 $\frac{7}{3}-\frac{1}{3}=2$	$\frac{1}{3}-\frac{1}{3}=0$	$0-1=-1$	$1-0=1$	$\frac{-2}{3}-\frac{1}{3}$ $=-1$
1	α_1	W_1 1	1	3	0	1
		$z_i - c_i$	$1-1=0$	$3-2=+1$	0	1

As all $z_i - c_i \geq 0$. So **the solution of the dual is optimal** with max $z_D = 1 \times 1 + 0 + 0$ and the solution is

$$\mathbf{W_1 = 1,\ W_2 = 0,\ W_3 = 2}$$

From the last two columns, $z_3 - c_3 = 0 = x_1$, $z_4 - c_4 = 1 = x_2$

Solution of Primal is $x_1 = 0, x_2 = 1$, $\boldsymbol{z_P}$ **Min = 0 + 1 = 1.**

Example 4.33. **Use duality to solve the L.P. Problem :**
Maximize $z = 4x_1 + 3x_2$
subject to $x_1 \leq 6,\ x_2 = 8,\ x_1 + x_2 \leq 7,\ 3x_1 + x_2 \leq 15$
$-x_2 \leq 1,\ x_1\ x_2 \geq 0.$

Solution : The dual of the given problem is

$$\text{Minimize } z_D = 6W_1 + 8W_2 + 7W_3 + 15W_4 + 1W_5$$

Let $z'_D = -z_D$ or Maximize $z'_D = -6W_1 - 8W_2 - 7W_3 - 15W_4 - W_5$

subject to $1W_1 + 0W_2 + 1W_3 + 3W_4 + 0W_5 \geq 4$

$$0W_1 + 1W_2 + 1W_3 + 1W_4 - 1W_5 \geq 3,\ W_1, \ldots, W_5 \geq 0$$

After subtracting slack variables, we have

$$1W_1 + 0W_2 + 1W_3 + 3W_4 + 0W_5 - W_6 + 0 = 4$$
$$0W_1 + 1W_2 + 1W_3 + 1W_4 - 1W_5 + 0 - W_7 = 3$$

Writing it as $\alpha_1 W + \alpha_2 W_2 + \alpha_3 W_3 + \alpha_4 W_4 + \alpha_5 W_5 + \alpha_6 W_6 + \alpha_7 W_7 = b$

$\alpha_1 = \begin{pmatrix}1\\0\end{pmatrix}$, $\alpha_2 = \begin{pmatrix}0\\1\end{pmatrix}$. So they provide us an initial basis for operation of the simplex method.

			$c_i =$	−6	−8	−7	−15	−1	0	0
C_B	α_B	X_B	$\vec{b}\ \alpha_i =$	α_1	α_2	α_3	α_4	α_5	α_6	α_7
−6	α_1	W_1	4	1	0	1	[3]	0	−1	0
−8	α_2	W_2	3	0	1	1	1	−1	0	−1
			$z_i - c_i =$	$-6\times 1+8 \times 0+6=0$	$-8+8 = 0$	$-6-8 +7=-7$	$-18+87 +15=-11$	$+8+1 =9$	$=+6$	$=+8$

↑ α_4 is **the entering vector**

$z_i - c_i$ is most negative $= -11$, for $i = 4$ for so α_4 **is entering.**

Min $\left\{\frac{\bar{b}}{y_{i4}}, y_{i4} > 0\right\} = \left\{\frac{4}{3}\ \frac{3}{1}\right\} = \frac{4}{3}$ for $r = 1$. So 1st row vector α_1 **is departing.**

The pivot value $= y_{14} = 3$.

Performing $$R_1 \to \frac{R_1}{y_{14}} = \frac{1}{3} R_1$$

$$R_2 \to R_2 - 1\,\frac{R_1}{3}$$

			c	−6	−8	−7	−15	−1	0	0
C_B	α_B	X_B	$\vec{b}$	α_1	α_2	α_3	α_4	α_5	α_6	α_7
−15	α_4	W_4	$\frac{4}{3}$	$\frac{1}{3}$	0	$\frac{1}{3}$	1	0	$-\frac{1}{3}$	0
−8	α_2	W_2	$3-\frac{4}{3} = \frac{5}{3}$	$0-\frac{1}{3} = -\frac{1}{3}$	$1-0 = 1$	$1-\frac{1}{3} = \frac{2}{3}$	$1-1 = 0$	$-1-0 = -1$	$0+\frac{1}{3} = \frac{1}{3}$	$-1-0 = -1$
			$z_i - c_i =$	$-\frac{15}{3}+\frac{8}{3} +6 = \frac{11}{3}$	$-8+8 = 0$	$-\frac{15}{13}-\frac{16}{3} +7 = \frac{10}{3}$	$-15+15 = 0$	$+8+1 = 9$	$-\frac{8}{3}+\frac{15}{3} = \frac{7}{3}$	$+8=8$

↓ α_2 ↑ α_3 entering

The most negative value $z_i - c_i = -\frac{10}{3}$ for $i = 3$. So α_3 is the entering vector

$$\text{Min}\left\{\frac{\vec{b}}{y_{i3}}, y_{i3} > 0\right\} = \left\{\frac{4/3}{1/3}\ \frac{5/3}{2/3}\right\} = \frac{5}{2} \text{ for } \boldsymbol{r = 2}$$

So α_2 is departing.

Key element $= \boldsymbol{y_{23} = 2/3}$

Performing $R_2 \to \frac{R_2}{y_{23}} = \frac{3}{2} R_2$

$$R_1 \to R_1 - \frac{1}{3} \times \frac{3}{2} R_2 = \frac{R_2}{2}$$

			$c_i =$	−6	−8	−7	−15	−1	0	0
C_B	α_B	X_B	$\vec{b}$ $\alpha_i =$	α_1	α_2	α_3	α_4	α_5	α_6	α_7
−15	α_4	W_4	$\frac{4}{3} - \frac{1}{3} \times \frac{5}{2} = \frac{1}{2}$	$\frac{1}{3} - \frac{1}{3}\left(-\frac{1}{2}\right) = \frac{1}{2}$	$0 - \frac{1}{3}\left(\frac{3}{2}\right) = -\frac{1}{2}$	$\frac{1}{3} - \left(\frac{1}{3}\right) = 0$	$1 - 0 = 1$	$0 + \frac{1}{2} = \frac{1}{2}$	$\frac{1}{3} - \frac{1}{6} = -\frac{1}{2}$	$0 + \frac{1}{2} = \frac{1}{2}$
−7	α_3	W_3	$\frac{5}{2} = \frac{5}{2}$	$-\frac{1}{2}$	$\frac{3}{2}$	1	0	$-\frac{3}{2}$	$\frac{1}{2}$	$-\frac{3}{2}$
			$z_i - c_i =$	$\frac{-15+7}{2} + 6 = 2$	$\frac{15-21}{2} + 8 = 5$	$-7 + 7 = 0$	$-15 + 15 = 0$	$\frac{-15+21}{2} + 1 = 4$	$\frac{15-7}{2} = 4$	$\frac{-15+21}{2} = 3$

As $z_i - c_i \geq 0$, the solution of the dual is optimal, with $W_3 = \frac{5}{4}$, $W_4 = \frac{1}{2}$, $W_1 = W_2 = W_5 = 0$. For solution of primal the last two values of $z_i - c_i$ are $z_6 - c_6 = 4 = \boldsymbol{x_1}$, $z_7 - c_7 = 3 = \boldsymbol{x_2}$ primal solution is $x_1 = 4, x_2 = 3$, $(\boldsymbol{z_P})_{\mathbf{max}} = \mathbf{25}$ **Ans.**

We have $(\boldsymbol{z_D})_{\mathbf{min}} = 0 + 0 + 7\left(\frac{5}{2}\right) + 15\left(\frac{1}{2}\right) = \mathbf{25}$

$$(\boldsymbol{z_P})_{\mathbf{max}} = (4x_1 + 3x_2)_{x_1 = 4,\, x_2 = 3} = 16 + 9 = \mathbf{25}.$$

Example 4.34. Solve the L.P. problem

Maximize $z_P = 5x + 9y$

subject to $2x + 3y \leq 16$;

$1x + 2y \leq 10$,

$x, y \geq 0$.

Solution : The dual problem is Minimize $z_D = 16w_1 + 10w_2$,

subject to $2w_1 + 1w_2 \geq 5$, $3w_1 + 2w_2 \geq 9$, $w_1, w_2 \geq 0$

Let $z_D = -2D$, So max $z'_D = -16w_1 - 10w_2$. To bring the problem is standard form subtracting surplus variables w_3, w_4 and adding artificial variables w_5, w_6 with large negative costs $-M, -M$ in

Maximize $\quad z' = -16w_1 - 10w_2 + 0w_3 + 0w_4 - Mw_5 - Mw_6 \quad$ ...(1)

subject to $\quad 2w_1 + 1w_2 - w_3 + 0w_4 + w_5 + 0w_6 = 5 \quad$ ...(2)

$\quad 3w_1 + 2w_2 + 0w_3 - 1w_4 + 0w_5 + 1w_6 = 9 \quad$ ...(3)

All $w_i \geq 0$.

The primal of problem (1) then is

$$\text{Subject to} \quad \left.\begin{aligned} \text{Min } z_P = 5x_1 + 9x_2 \\ 2x + 3x_2 \geq -16 \\ 1x_1 + 2x_2 \geq -10 \\ -x_1 \geq 0 \\ -x_2 \geq 0 \\ x_1 \geq -M \\ x_2 \geq -M \end{aligned}\right\} \quad \ldots(4)$$

Solution Table

			$c_i =$	-16	-10	0	0	$-M$	$-M$
C_B	α_B	w_B	$\vec{b}$	α_1	α_2	α_3	α_4	α_5	α_6
$-M$	α_5	w_5	5	$\boxed{2}$	1	-1	0	1	0
$-M$	α_6	w_6	9	3	2	0	-1	0	1
			$z_i - c_i =$	$-2M - 3M + 16$	$-M - 2M + 10$	$M - 0$	$M - 0$	$-M + M$	$-M + M$

↑ α_1 entering ↓

Most negative $z_i - c_i = -5M + 16$, for $i = 1$, so α_1 is the entering vector in the basis.

$$\text{Min}\left\{\frac{\vec{b}}{y_{i1}}, y_{i1} \geq 0\right\} = \left\{\frac{5}{2}, \frac{9}{3}\right\} = \frac{5}{2}, \text{ for 1st row.}$$

So 1st row vector α_5 is departing. Key element $= y_{11} = 2$

Performing $R_1 \to \dfrac{R_1}{y_{11}} = \dfrac{R_1}{2}$; $R_2 \to R_2 - \dfrac{3}{2}R_1$

		$c =$	-16	-10	0	0	$-M$	$-M$
		$\vec{b}$	α_1	α_2	α_3	α_4	α_5	α_6
-16	α_1 w_1	$\frac{5}{2}$	1	$\frac{1}{2}$	$-\frac{1}{2}$	0	$\frac{1}{2}$	0
$-M$	α_6 w_6	$9 - 3 \times \frac{5}{2} = \frac{3}{2}$	$3 - 3 = 0$	$2 - \frac{3}{2} = \frac{1}{2}$	$0 - 3\left(-\frac{1}{2}\right) = \frac{3}{2}$	$-1 - 3 \times 0 = -1$	$0 - \frac{3}{2} = -\frac{3}{2}$	$1 - 3 \times 0 = 1$
		$z_i - c_i =$	$-16 + 16 = 0$	$-8 - \frac{M}{2} + 10$	$8 - \frac{3}{2}M$	$+M$	$\frac{3}{2}M + M$	$-M + M$

↑ entering

$z_i - c_i$ is most negative for $i = 3$. So α_3 is the entering vector

Min $\left\{\frac{\vec{b}}{y_{i3}}, y_{i3} \geq 0\right\} = \left\{\frac{5/2}{-\text{ive}}, \frac{3/2}{3/2}\right\} = 1$ for $r = 2$, so α_6 is departing, key element

$$= y_{23} = \frac{3}{2}$$

Performing $R_2 = \frac{2R_2}{3}$, $R_1 \to R_1 - \left(-\frac{1}{2}\right)\left(\frac{2}{3}R_2\right)$

		c_i	-16	-10	0	0	$-M$	$-M$
		$\vec{b}$	α_1	α_2	α_3	α_4	α_5	α_6
-16	$\alpha_1\ w_1$	$\frac{5}{2} + \frac{1}{2} \times 1 = 3$	$1 + \frac{1}{2} \times 0 = 1$	$\frac{1}{2} + \frac{1}{2} \times \frac{1}{3} = \frac{2}{3}$	$-\frac{1}{2} + \frac{1}{2} \times 1 = 0$	$0 - \frac{1}{2} \times \frac{2}{3} = -\frac{1}{3}$	$\frac{1}{2} + \left(-\frac{1}{2}\right) = 0$	$0 + \left(\frac{1}{2}\right) \times \frac{4}{3} = \frac{1}{3}$
0	$\alpha_3\ w_3$	1	0	$\boxed{\frac{1}{3}}$	1	$-\frac{2}{3}$	-1	$\frac{2}{3}$
		$z_i - c_i =$	$-16 + 16 = 0$	$-\frac{32}{3} + 10 = -\frac{2}{3}$ ↑	0	$\frac{16}{3}$ ↓	M	M

$z_i - c_i = -2/3 < 0$ for $i = 2$, so α_2 is entering

$$\text{Min}\left\{\frac{3}{2/3}, \frac{1}{1/3}\right\} = \text{Min}\left\{\frac{9}{2}, 3\right\} = 3 \text{ for } r = 2$$

So α_3 is departing. Key element = 1/3

Performing $R_2 \to \frac{R_2}{y_{22}} = 3R_2$, $R_1 \to R_1 - \frac{2}{3} \times 3R_2$

		c_i	-16	-10	0	0	$-M$	$-M$
		$\vec{b}$	α_1	α_2	α_3	α_4	α_5	α_6
-16	$\alpha_1\ w_1$	$3 - \frac{2}{3} \times 3 = 1$	$1 - \frac{2}{3} \times 0 = 1$	$\frac{2}{3} - \frac{2}{3} \times 1 = 0$	$0 - \frac{2}{3} \times 3 = -2$	$-\frac{1}{3} + \frac{4}{3} = 1$	$0 - \frac{2}{3}(-3) = 2$	$\frac{1}{3} - \left(\frac{2}{3}\right)2$ $-3/3 = -1$
-10	$\alpha_2\ w_2$	3	0	1	3	-2	-3	2
		$z_i - c_i =$	0	0	$32 - 30 = 2 = x_1$	$-16 + 20 = 4 = x_2$	$-32 + 30 + M = M - 2$	$16 - 20 + M = M - 4$

The solution is optimal with $w_1 = 1$, $w_2 = 3$, $w_3 = w_4 = w_5 = w_6 = 0$

Max $z'_D = -16 \times 1 - 10 \times 3 = -46$,

Min $z_D = +46$ Ans.

The first two $z_i - c_i$ values corresponds to the dual variables w_3, w_4 and other two for x_1 and x_2 leaving those corresponding to the artifician variables.

So $x_1 = 2,\ x_2 = 4,\ (z_P)_{\max} = 5x_1 + 9x_2 = 46$.

PROBLEM SET 4.8

Solve the following L.P. Problems, using duality

1. Maximize $z = 2x_1 + x_2$,
s.t. $x_1 + 2x_2 \le 10,\ x_1 + x_2 \le 6$,
$x_1 - x_2 \le 2,\ x_1 - 2x_2 \le 1;\ x_1, x_2 \ge 0$ ***(Karnataka 92)***

Ans. Dual $w_3 = \frac{1}{2},\ w_2 = \frac{3}{2}$

Primal $x_1 = 4,\ x_2 = 2,\ z_{\text{Max}} = 10$

Min $z_D = 10w_1 + 6w_2 + 2w_3 + w_4 = 0 + 9 + 1 = 10$

Primal sol. $x_1 = 4,\ x_2 = 2,\ z_{\max} = 10$.

2. Maximize $z_P = 2x_1 + 4x_2 + 4x_3 - 3x_4$
subject to $x_1 + x_2 + x_3 = 4$,
$x_1 + 4x_2 + x_4 = 8$,
$x_1, x_2, x_3, x_4 \ge 0,\ W_1 = 4,\ W_2 = 0$

Ans. Dual Sol. Min $z_D = 16,\ x_1 = 0,\ x_2 = 2,\ x_3 = 2,\ x_4 = 0$

3. Minimize $z = 15x_1 + 10x_2$,
subject to $3x_1 + 5x_2 \ge 5,\ 5x_1 + 2x_2 \ge 3,\ x_1, x_2 \ge 0$ ***(Meerut 91)***

Ans. $x_1 = \frac{5}{19},\ x_2 = \frac{16}{29},\ z_{\min} = \frac{235}{19}$.

4. Maximize $z = x_1 + 5x_2 + 3x_3$
subject to $x_1 + 2x_2 + x_3 = 3,\ 2x_1 - x_2 = 4$,
$x_1, x_2, x_3 \ge 0$

Ans. Dual Min $z_D = 3w_1 + 4w_2$
subject to $w_1 + 2w_2 >- 1,\ 2w_1 - w_2 \ge 5,\ w_1, \ge 3$,
w_2 unrestricted
$w_1 = 3,\ w_2 = -1,\ z_{\min} = 5$.

5. Maximize $z = 30x_1 + 23x_2 + 29x_3$
subject to $6x_1 + 5x_2 + 3x_3 \le 26$,
$4x_1 + 2x_2 + 5x_3 \le 7$,
$x_1, x_2, x_3 \ge 0$,

Ans. $x_1 = x_3 = 0,\ x_2 = \frac{7}{2},\ z_{\max} = \frac{161}{2}$

Dual Min $z_D = 26w_1 + 7w_2$

Ans. $w_1 = 0,\ w_2 = \frac{23}{}$

6. Maximize $z_P = 3x_1 - 2x_2$,
subject to $x_1 \le 4,\ x_2 \le 6,\ x_1 + x_2 \le 5,\ -x_2 \le -1,\ x_1, x_2 \ge 0$.

Ans. Min $z_D = 4w_1 + 6w_2 + 5w_3 - w_4$

Ans. $w_1 = 3,\ w_2 = w_3 = 0,\ w_4 = 2$, Min $z_D = 10$.

7. Min $z = x_1 - x_2$,
subject to $2x_1 + x_2 \ge 2,\ -x_1 - x_2 \ge 1,\ x_1, x_2 \ge 0$.

Ans. Sol. unbounded.

8. Minimize $z = 10x_1 + 6x_2 + 2x_3$;
subject to $-x_1 + x_2 + x_3 \ge 1,\ 3x_1 + x_2 - x_3 \ge 2$,
$x_1, x_2, x_3 \ge 0$.

Ans. Dual Max $z_D = 1w_1 + 2w_2,\ w_1 = 2,\ w_2 = 4,\ w_3 = w_4 = 0,\ w_5 = 4,\ z_{max} = 10$.

Primal sol. $x_1 = \frac{1}{4},\ x_2 = \frac{5}{4},\ x_3 = 0$.

4.34 DUAL SIMPLEX METHOD

As like the simplex method of solving a L.P. problem it is another method having many similarities and dissimilarities with the simplex method, stated below :

1. It operates when the problem is put in the maximization form as like the simplex method.

2. As in the simplex method, it also requires a basic solution of start with.

3. The first difference between this method and the simplex method is that the starting basic solution need not be a feasible solution (all basic variables need not have a non negative value). This is because no artificial variables are employed in this method. If any constraints is given in the form of (>= 0), then it is brought to the less than form (≤ 0) by multiplyingit by (–1). The value b_i becomes $-b_i <= 0$.

4. For this method to work, the initial basic solution should be optimal *i.e.*, all the evaluations $z_i - c_i \ge 0$.

As all slack variables have coefficients zero in the value of the objective function and they form the initial basis so we have $z_i = 0$ so this method can work only when $0 - c_i \ge 0$ or all $c_i \le 0$.

5. As will be seen in the working procedure, in this method for improving the value of the objective function first the departing variable is chosen and then the incoming one, it is just the opposite of what is done in the simplex method.

4.35 WORKING PROCEDURE OF DUAL SIMPLEX METHOD

Step 1. Bring the problem **in the maximization form** if it is not so.

Step 2. Bring **all constraint in the less than form**. For doing so, the constraints given in the form of ≥ 0, be multiplied by –1. Then bring the problem in the standard form by adding slack variables in all the cosntraints.

Step 3. Check that all c_{ij} in **the value of objective function to be maximized are as $c_{ij} \le 0$ or not. If it is not so this method cannot be applied**. When this is so all net evaluations $z_i - c_i \geq 0$ and the initial solution optimal through need not be feasible. If it is also feasible it provides the answer. So some b_i will bear negative sign.

Step 3. When some b_i are negative. Choose the largest among them. **This will be give the outgoing vector**. A feasible solution will exist only when some of the coefficients in this row are negative.

Step 4. Outgoing Vector

Let b_i be the largest negative value occurring in the ith row. Then the vector α_i will be the departing out of the m vectors $\alpha_{n+1}, \alpha_{n+2}, \ldots \alpha_{n+m}$, n denoting the number of variables and m, the number of constraints.

Step 5. Incoming Vector

Out of the coefficients $y_{i1}, y_{i2} \cdots y_{i,(n+m)}$ some will be negative, if a feasible solution to the problem exists. For all negative coefficients of this i^{th} row Find $\text{Min}\left\{-\frac{(z_j - c_j)}{y_{ij}}, y_{ij} = -\text{ive} < 0\right\}$ If this is true for the kth column then α_k will be the entering vector.

Step 6. Divide this row by y_{ik} then perform for all other rows $R_j \to R_j - \frac{y_{jk}}{y_{ik}} R_k$, so that all elements of this k^{th} column except y_{ik} becomes zero.

Step 7. Form new dual simplex table and repeat the above steps till all b_i becomes non negative.

Example 4.35. Use Dual simplex method to solve the L.P. Problem. Maximize

$$z = -3x_1 - x_2$$

subject to $x_1 + x_2 \geq 1$

$$2x_1 + 3x_2 \geq 2,$$

$$x_1, x_2 \geq 0.$$

Solution : The constraints on multiplying each with (–1) becomes

$$-x_1 - x_2 \leq -1 \quad \text{...(1)}$$

$$-2x_1 - 3x_2 \leq -2 \quad \text{...(2)}$$

The problem is given in the maximization form with both $c_1, c_2 \leq 0$ so the essential conditions for application of this method are satisfied. Then slack variables x_3, x_4, the problem becomes

$$\text{Max } z = -3x_1 - 1x_2 + 0x_3 + 0x_4 \quad \text{...(3)}$$

subject to $-1x_1 - 1x_2 + 1x_3 + 1x_4 = -1$ ...(4)

$$-2x_1 - 3x_2 + 0x_3 + 1x_4 = -2 \quad \text{...(5)}$$

or $\begin{pmatrix} -1 \\ -1 \end{pmatrix} x_1 + \begin{pmatrix} -1 \\ -3 \end{pmatrix} x_2 + \begin{pmatrix} 1 \\ 0 \end{pmatrix} x_3 + \begin{pmatrix} 0 \\ 1 \end{pmatrix} x_4 \begin{pmatrix} 1 \\ -2 \end{pmatrix}$

$x_1, x_2 \geq 0.$

$$\alpha_1 x_1 - \alpha_2 x_2 + \alpha_3 x_3 + \alpha_4 x_4 = b$$

We have $b_1 = -1$, $b_2 = -2$. So most negative value is $\boldsymbol{b_2 = -2}$. So vector α_4 of the slack variable in second row α_4 will be departing vector.

Table

			c_i	-3	-1	0	0
C_B	α_B	X_B	$\vec{b}$	α_1	α_2	α_3	α_4
0	α_3	x_3	-1	-1	-1	1	0
0	α_4	x_4	-2	-2	-3	0	1
			$(z_i - c_i) =$	$0 + 3$	$0 + 1$	0	0

Min $\left\{-\dfrac{3}{-2}, -\dfrac{1}{-3}\right\} = \dfrac{1}{3}$, for vector α_2 so α_2 will be the entering vector, key element $= -3 = y_{22}$

Performing $R_2 \to \dfrac{R_2}{-3}$, $R_1 \to R_1 - (-1)\dfrac{R_2}{-3}$.

			c_i	-3	-1	0	0
			$\vec{b}$	α_1	α_2	α_3	α_4
0	α_3	x_3	$-1 + 2/3$ $= -\dfrac{1}{3}$	$-1 + 2/3$ $= -1/3$	$-1 + 1 = 0$	$1 + 0 = 1$	$0 - \dfrac{1}{3}$ $= -\dfrac{1}{3}$
-1	α_2	x_2	$\dfrac{2}{3}$	$\dfrac{2}{3}$	1	0	$-\dfrac{1}{3}$
			$z_i - c_i$	$-\dfrac{2}{3} + 3$	$-1 + 1$	0	$\dfrac{1}{3}$

All $z_i - c_i \geq 0$ and all $b_i \geq 0$. So the solution is not optimal feasible.

Now $b_1 \leq 0$ so α_3 will be departing.

Min $\left\{-\dfrac{7/3}{-1/3}, -\dfrac{1/3}{-1/3}\right\} = 1$. So α_4 will be entering. Key element $= y_{14} = -1/3$.

Performing $R_1 \to \dfrac{R_1}{y_{14}} = -3R_1$; $R_2 \to R_2 - \dfrac{-1/3}{-1/3} R_1$

			c_i	-3	-1	0	0
			$\vec{b}\,\alpha_i$	α_1	α_2	α_3	α_4
0	α_4	x_4	1	1	0	-3	1
-1	α_2	x_2	$\dfrac{2}{3} + \dfrac{1}{3} \times 1$ $= 1$	$\dfrac{2}{3} + \dfrac{1}{3} = 1$	$1 + 0 = 1$	$0 + \dfrac{1}{3}(-3)$ $= -1$	$-\dfrac{1}{3} + \dfrac{1}{3} \times 1$ $= 0$
			$z_i - c_i$	$-1 + 3$	$-1 + 1$	1	0

As all $z_i - c_i \geq 0$, the solution $x_4 = 1, x_2 = 1, x_1 = 0, x_3 = 0$ is optimal with $z_{\max} = -3(0) - 1 = -1$ **Ans.**

Example 4.36. **Use dual simplex method to solve the following L.P. problem**

Min $z = 2x_1 + x_2$

Subject to $3x_1 + x_2 \geq 3$

$4x_1 + 3x_2 \geq 6$

$x_1 + 2x_2 \geq 3,$

$x_1, x_2 \geq 0$

Solution. Changing it into a maximization problem, it becomes

Max $z' = -2x_1 - x_2$ where $z' = -z$ As both the coeffs. $c_1 = -2$, $c_2 = -1$ are negative, the essential condition for applying this method is satisfied multiplying each constraint by (–1) to bring it in the form $\leq$ and adding slack variables x_3, x_4, x_5, finally the problem becomes

$$\text{Max } z' = -2x_1 - x_2 + 0x_3 + 0x_4 + 0x_5 \quad \text{...(1)}$$

Subject to
$$-3x_1 - x_2 + x_3 + 0 + 0 = -3 \quad \text{...(2)}$$
$$-4x_1 - 3x_2 + 0 + x_4 + 0 = -6 \quad \text{...(3)}$$
$$-x_1 - 2x_2 + 0 + 0 + x_5 = -3 \quad \text{...(4)}$$

$$x_1, x_2 \geq 0 \text{ or } \begin{pmatrix} -3 \\ -4 \\ -1 \end{pmatrix} x_1 + \begin{pmatrix} -1 \\ -3 \\ -2 \end{pmatrix} x_2 + \begin{pmatrix} 1 \\ 0 \\ 0 \end{pmatrix} x_3 + \begin{pmatrix} 0 \\ 1 \\ 0 \end{pmatrix} x_4 + \begin{pmatrix} 0 \\ 0 \\ 1 \end{pmatrix} x_5 = \begin{pmatrix} -3 \\ -6 \\ -3 \end{pmatrix}$$

or
$$\alpha_1 x_1 + \alpha_2 x_2 + \alpha_3 x_3 + \alpha_4 x_4 + \alpha_5 x_5 = \vec{b}$$

The largest negative = $b_2 = -6$ so α_4 will be the departing variable.

			c_i	-2	-1	0	0	0
C_B			$\vec{b}$	α_1	α_2	α_3	α_4	α_5
0	x_3	α_3	-3	-3	-1	1	0	0
0	x_4	α_4	-6	-4	-3	0	1	0
0	x_5	α_5	-3	-1	-2	0	0	1
			$z_i - c_i$	$0 + 2$	$0 + 1$	0	0	0

All $z_i - c_i \geq$ so solution is optimal.

Min $\left\{\frac{-(z_j - c_j)}{y_{2j} \leq 0}\right\} = \left\{-\frac{2}{-4}, \frac{-1}{-3}\right\} = \frac{1}{3}$, so 2nd column vector α_2 is entering. Key element

$$= y_{22} = -3$$

Performing
$$R_2 \to \frac{R_2}{y_{22}} = \frac{R_2}{-3},$$
$$R_1 \to R_1 - (-1)\frac{R_2}{-3},$$
$$R_3 \to R_3 - (-2)\frac{R_2}{-3}$$

		c_i	-2	-1	0	0	0
		$\vec{b}$	α_1	α_2	α_3	α_4	α_5
0	x_3 α_3	$-3+1$ $=-1$	$-3+\frac{4}{3}$ $=-\frac{5}{3}$	$-1+1=0$	$1+0=1$	$0+-\frac{1}{3}$ $=-\frac{1}{3}$	$0+0=0$
-1	x_2 α_2	$\frac{-6}{-3}=2$	$\frac{-4}{-3}=\frac{4}{3}$	$\frac{-3}{-3}=1$	0	$-\frac{1}{3}$	0
0	x_5 α_5	$-3+2\times 2$ $=1$	$-1+2\times\frac{4}{3}$ $=\frac{5}{3}$	$-2+2\times 1$ $=0$	$0+2\times 0$ $=0$	$0+2\left(\frac{-1}{3}\right)$ $=-\frac{2}{3}$	$1+2\times 0$ $=1$
		z_i-c_i	$-\frac{4}{3}+2$	$-1+1$	0	$\frac{1}{3}$	0

All $z_i - c_i \geq 0$. The solution is optimal but $b_2 < 0$, so not yet feasible. So α_3 is the departing vector. For the incoming choice

$$\text{Min}\left\{-\frac{z_k - c_k}{y_{1k}}, y_{1k} < 0\right\} = \left\{\frac{-2/3}{-5/3}, \frac{-1/3}{-1/3}\right\} = \frac{2}{5}$$

For $k = 1$. So 1st row vector α_1 is the entering vector. Pivot element $= y_{11} = -5/3$.

Performing $\quad R_1 \to \dfrac{R_1}{y_{11}} = -\dfrac{3}{5} R_1,$

$$R_2 \to R_2 - 4/3\,\frac{R_1}{y_{11}} = R_2 + \frac{4}{5} R_1$$

$$R_3 \to R_3 - \frac{5}{3} \times \left(-\frac{3}{5}\right) R_{211} = R_3 + R_1, \text{ we have}$$

			c_i	-2	-1	0	0	0
				α_1	α_2	α_3	α_4	α_5
-2	x_1	α_1	$\frac{3}{5}$	1	0	$-\frac{3}{5}$	$+\frac{1}{5}$	0
-1	x_2	α_2	$2-\frac{4}{3}\left(\frac{3}{5}\right)$ $=\frac{6}{5}$	$\frac{4}{3}-\frac{4}{3}\times 1$ $=0$	$1-0=1$	$0-\frac{4}{3}\left(\frac{-3}{5}\right)$ $=\frac{4}{5}$	$-\frac{1}{3}-\frac{4}{5}\left(\frac{-3}{5}\right)=\frac{-3}{5}$	$0-0=0$
0	x_5	α_5	$1-\frac{5}{3}\times\frac{3}{5}$ $=0$	$\frac{5}{3}-\frac{5}{3}\times 1$ $=0$	$0-\frac{5}{3}\times 0$ $=0$	$0-\frac{5}{3}\left(\frac{-3}{5}\right)$ $=1$	$\frac{-2}{3}-\frac{5}{3}\times\frac{1}{5}=-1$	$1-\frac{5}{3}\times 0$ $=1$
			$(z_i-c_i)=$	$-2+2$	$-1+1$	$\frac{6}{5}-\frac{4}{5}+0$	$\frac{-2}{5}+\frac{3}{5}+0$	0

As all $z_i - c_i \geq 0$, the solution is optimal. Further all $b_i \geq 0$. So it is feasible also.

Ans. $x_1 = 3/5,\ x_2 = 6/5,\ x_5 = 0,\ x_3 = 0,\ x_4 = 0$

$$z'_{max} = -2\left(\frac{3}{5}\right) - 1\left(\frac{6}{5}\right) = -\frac{12}{5}.\ \text{So } z_{min} = \frac{12}{5}.$$

PROBLEM SET 4.9

Solve the following L.P. problems, using dual simplex method :

1. Maximize $z = -3x_1 - 2x_2$
subject to $x_1 + x_2 \geq 1;\ x_1 + x_2 \geq 7;$
$x_1 + 2x_2 \geq 10;\ x_2 \geq 3;\ x_1, x_2 \geq 0.$
Ans. $x_1 = 4,\ x_2 = 3,\ z_{max} = -18$

2. Maximize $z = -2x_1 - x_2,$
subject to $x_1 + x_2 - x_3 \geq 5;\ x_1 - 2x_2 + 4x_3 \geq 8,$
$x_1, x_2, x_3 \geq 0$
Ans. $x_1 = 0,\ x_2 = 14,\ x_3 = 9,\ z_{max} = -14$

3. Maximize $z = 4x_1 - 6x_2 - 18x_3$
subject to $x_1 + 3x_3 \geq 3,\ x_2 + 2x_3 \geq 5,$
$x_1, x_1, x_3 \geq 0.$
Ans. $x_1 = 0, x_2 = 3, x_3 = 1,\ z_{max} = -36.$

4. Minimize $z = 10x_1 + 6x_2 + 2x_3$
subject to $-x_1 + x_2 + x_3 \geq 1$
$3x_1 + x_2 - x_3 \geq 2,$
$x_1, x_2, x_3 \geq 0.$
Ans. $x_1 = 1/4, x_2 = 5/4, x_3 = 0, z_{min} = 10$

5. Minimize $z = 2x_1 + 2x_2 + 4x_3$
subject to $2x_1 + 3x_2 + 5x_3 \geq 2$
$3x_1 + x_2 + 7x_3 \leq 3$
$x_1 + 4x_2 + 6x_3 \leq 5,$
$x_1, x_2, x_3 \geq 0.$
Ans. $x_1 = 0,\ x_2 = 2/3,\ x_3 = 0,\ z_{min} = 4/3.$

6. Minimize $z = x_1 + 2x_2 + x_3 + 4x_4$
subject to $2x_1 + 4x_2 + 5x_3 + x_4 \geq 10$
$3x_1 - x_2 + 7x_3 - 2x_4 \geq 2$
$5x_1 + 2x_2 + x_3 + 6x_4 \geq 15,$
$x_1, x_2, x_3, x_4 \geq 0$ ***(Madras 92S)***
Ans. $x_1 = \frac{65}{23},\ x_2 = 0,\ x_3 = \frac{20}{23},\ x_4 = 0.$

TUTORIALS

AMITY SCHOOL OF ENGINEERING & TECHNOLOGY
AMITY UNIVERSITY UTTAR PRADESH
B.TECH (3rd Semester)

APPLIED MATHEMATICS - III

TUTORIAL SHEET-1

1. Form partial differential equations from the following equations by eliminating the arbitrary constants:

(i) $z = (x + a)(y + b)$

(ii) $z = ax + a^2y^2 + b$

(iii) $z = ax + by + ab$

(iv) $z = ax + ay + b$

(v) $2z = (ax + y)^2 + b$

(vi) $az + b = a^2x + y$

(vii) $z = axe^y + a^2e^{2y} + b$

(viii) $ax^2 + by^2 + z^2 = 1$

(ix) $x^2 + y^2 = (2 - c)^2 \tan^2 \alpha$

(x) $2z = \frac{x^2}{a^2} + \frac{y^2}{b^2}$

(xi) $x^2 + y^2 + (z - c)^2 = a^2$

(xii) $\frac{x^2}{a^2} + \frac{y^2}{b^2} + \frac{z^2}{c^2} = 1$

(xiii) $(x - h)^2 + (y - k)^2 + z^2 = 4$

2. Form partial differential equations from the following equations by eliminating the arbitrary functions:

(i) $z = y^2 + 2f\left(\frac{1}{x} + \log y\right)$

(ii) $z = f\left(\frac{y}{x}\right)$

(iii) $z = F(x^2 + y^2)$

(iv) $z = e^{my}\, \phi\, (x - y)$

(v) $z = f(x + iy) + g(x - iy)$

(vi) $z = f(x + ay) + g(x - ay)$

(vii) $f(x + y + z,\ x^2 + y^2 - z^2) = 0$

(viii) $lx + my + nz = \phi(x^2 + y^2 + z^2)$

(ix) $z = xf(x + y) + g(x + y)$

3. Solve the following partial differential equations:

(i) $xys = 1$

(ii) $xr + p = 9x^2y^3$

(iii) $s = 2x + 2y$

(iv) $t - xq = x^2$

(v) $r = 2y^2$

(vi) $t = \sin xy$

(vii) $\log s = x + y$

(viii) $yt - q = xy$

(ix) $s = \left(\frac{x}{y}\right) + a$

(x) $rx = (n - 1)p$

(xi) $ys + p = \cos(x + y) - y \sin(x + y)$

(xii) $r = 6x$

(xiii) $s = 0$

(xiv) $xr = p$

(xv) $ar = xy$

(xvi) $xs + q = 4x + 2y + 2$

(xvii) $2yq + y^2t = 1$

(xviii) $\frac{\partial^3 z}{\partial x^2 \partial y} = \cos(2x + 3y)$

(xix) $\frac{\partial^2 z}{\partial x \partial y} = xy^2$

(xx) $\frac{\partial^2 z}{\partial x \partial y} = e^y \cos x$

4. Solve the following partial differential equations by using the given conditions:

(i) $s = \sin x \sin y$; given $q = -2 \sin y$ when $x = 0$ and $z = 0$ when y is an odd multiple of $\frac{\pi}{2}$.

(ii) $r + z = 0$, given that when $x = 0, z = e^y$ and $p = 1$.

(iii) $s = x^2y$ subject to the conditions $z(x, 0) = x^2$ and $x(1, y) = \cos y$.

(iv) $t = z$, if $y = 0, z = e^x$ and $q = e^{-x}$.

(v) $r = a^2z$, when $x = 0, p = a \sin y$ and $q = 0$.

5. Find the surface passing through the parabolas $z = 0$, $y^2 = 4ax$ and $z = 1$, $y^2 = -4ax$ and satisfying the equation $xr + 2p = 0$.

6. Find the surface satisfying the equation $t = 5x^3y$, containing two lines $y = 0 = z$, $y = 1 = z$.

Answers

1. (i) $z = pq$; (ii) $q = 2p^2y$; (iii) $z = px + qy + pq$; (iv) $p = q$; (v) $px + qy = q^2$; (vi) $pq = 1$; (vii) $q = px + 2p^2$; (viii) $z(px + qy) = z^2 - 1$; (ix) $yp - xq = 0$; (x) $2z = xp + yq$; (xi) $yp - xq = 0$; (xii) $-zq + yq^2 + yzt = 0$; (xiii) $z^2(p^2 + q^2 + 1) = 4$

2. (i) $x^2p + yq = 2y^2$; (ii) $px + qy = 0$; (iii) $yp - xq = 0$; (iv) $p + q = mz$; (v) $r + t = 0$; (vi) $t = a^2r$; (vii) $(y + z)p - (z + x)q = x - y$;
(viii) $(l + np)y + z(lq - pm) = (m + nq)x$
(ix) $r + t - 2s = 0$

3. (i) $z = \log x \log y + f(x) + g(y)$; (ii) $z = x^3y^3 + f(y) \log x + g(y)$;
(iii) $z = x^2y + y^2x + f(x) + g(y)$; (iv) $z = -xy + f(x)e^{xy} + g(x)$
(v) $z = x^2y + xf(y) + g(y)$; (vi) $z = -\dfrac{(\sin xy)}{x^2} + yf(x) + g(x)$
(vii) $z = e^{x+y} + h(y) + g(x)$; (viii) $z = \dfrac{(xy^2 \log y)}{2} - \dfrac{xy^2}{4} + \left(\dfrac{y^2}{2}\right) f(x) + g(x)$;
(ix) $z = \left(\dfrac{x^2 \log y}{2}\right) + axy + f(y) + g(x)$; (x) $z = \left(\dfrac{x^n f(y)}{n}\right) + g(y)$
(xi) $yz = y \sin(x + y) + f(y) + g(x)$; (xii) $z = x^2 + xf(y) + F(y)$; (xiii) $z = f(x) + g(y)$;
(xiv) $z = x^2f(y)/2 + F(y)$; (xv) $az = x^3 y/6 + xf(y) + g(y)$;
(xvi) $zx = 2x^2y + y^2x + 2xy + f(y) + g(x)$; (xvii) $yz = y \log y - f(x) + yg(x)$;
(xviii) $z = -\sin(2x + 3y)/12 + xf(y) + g(y)$; (xix) $z = x^2y^3/6 + f(y) + g(x)$;
(xx) $z = e^y \sin x + f(y) + g(x)$

4. (i) $z = (1 + \cos x) \cos y$; (ii) $z = e^y \cos x + \sin x$; (iii) $z = x^3y^2/6 + \cos y - y^2/6 - 1 + x^2$
(iv) $z = e^y \cosh x + e^{-y} \sinh x$; (v) $z = \sin y \sinh ax$.

5. $8axz = 4ax - y^2$

6. $z = x^3y^3 + y(1 - x^3)$

AMITY SCHOOL OF ENGINEERING & TECHNOLOGY
AMITY UNIVERSITY UTTAR PRADESH
B.TECH (3rd Semester)

APPLIED MATHEMATICS - III

TUTORIAL SHEET-2

1. Solve the following Lagrange's linear equations:

(i) $xp + yq = 3z$

(ii) $yzp - xzq = xy$

(iii) $p - q = \log(x + y)$

(iv) $z(z^2 + xy)(px - qy) = x^4$

(v) $xzp + yzq = xy$

(vi) $(z - y)p + (x - z)q = y - x$

(vii) $(y + zx)p - (x + yz)q = x^2 - y^2$

(viii) $(y^2 + z^2)p - xyq + zx = 0$

(ix) $px((x + y) = qy(x + y) - (2x + 2y + z)(x - y)$

(x) $(x^2 - y^2 - yz)p + (x^2 - y^2 - xz)q = z(x - y)$

(xi) $p + 3q = 5z - \tan(y - 3x)$

(xii) $(mz - ny)p + (nx - lz)q = ly - mx$

(xiii) $(x^2 - yz)p + (y^2 - xz)q = z^2 - xy$

(xiv) $(2x^2 + y^2 + z^2 - 2yz - zx - xy)p + (x^2 + 2y^2 + z^2 - yz - 2zx - xy)q$
$= (x^2 + y^2 + 2z^2 - yz - zx - 2xy)$

(xv) $z(xp - yq) = y^2 - x^2$

(xvi) $x^2p + y^2q = z^2$

(xvii) $x(y^2 - z^2)p + y(z^2 - x^2)q = z(x^2 - y^2)$

(xviii) $(y - z)p + (x - y)q = z - x$

(xix) $(x + 2z)p + (4zx - y)q = 2x^2 + y$

(xx) $(y + z)p + (x + z)q = (y + x)$

Answers

(i) $x^3 = zf\left(\frac{x}{y}\right)$ or $F\left(\frac{x^3}{z}, \frac{x}{y}\right) = 0$

(ii) $F(x^2 + y^2, x^2 - z^2) = 0,$

(iii) $F[x + y, x\log(x + y) - z] = 0$

(iv) $F(xy, x^4 - z^4 - 2xyz^2) = 0$

(v) $F\left(\frac{x}{y}, xy - z^2\right) = 0$

(vi) $F(x+y+z,\ x^2+y^2+z^2)=0$

(vii) $F(x^2+y^2-z^2,\ xy+z)=0$

(viii) $F\left(\frac{y}{z},\ x^2+y^2+z^2\right)=0$

(ix) $F\ [xy,\ (x+y)\ (x+y+z)]=0$

(x) $F\left[x-y-z,\ \frac{(x^2-y^2)}{z^2}\right]=0$

(xi) $F\ [y-3x,\ e^{-5x}\ \{5z+\tan\ (y-3x)\}]=0$

(xii) $F\ (lx+my+nz,\ x^2+y^2+z^2)=0$

(xiii) $F\left[\frac{(x-y)}{(y-z)},\ \frac{(y-z)}{z-x}\right]=0$

(xiv) $F\left[\frac{(x-y)}{(y-z)},\ \frac{(z-x)}{y-z}\right]=0$

(xv) $F(xy,\ x^2+y^2+z^2)=0$

(xvi) $F\left[\left(\frac{1}{x}\right)-\left(\frac{1}{y}\right),\ \left(\frac{1}{y}\right)-\left(\frac{1}{z}\right)\right]=0$

(xvii) $F(xyz,\ x^2+y^2+z^2)=0$

(xviii) $F\left[x+y+z,\ \left(\frac{x^2}{2}\right)+yz\right]=0$

(xix) $F(xy-z^2,\ x^2-y-z)=0$

(xx) $F\left[\left(\frac{(x-y)}{(y-z)}\right),\ (y-z)\ (x+y+z)^{1/2}\right]=0$

AMITY SCHOOL OF ENGINEERING & TECHNOLOGY
AMITY UNIVERSITY UTTAR PRADESH
B.TECH (3rd Semester)

APPLIED MATHEMATICS - III

TUTORIAL SHEET-3

1. Solve the following Non-linear equations using standard forms I, II, III, IV (Clairaut's equation) :
   (i) $p^3 - q^3 = 0$
   (ii) $p^2 + q^2 = npq$
   (iii) $(x + y)(p + q)^2 + (x - y)(p - q)^2 = 1$
   (iv) $(x - y)(px - qy) = (p - q)^2$
   (v) $zpq = p + q$
   (vi) $(pz)^2 + q^2 = p^2 q$
   (vii) $(xp)^2 = z(z - qy)$
   (viii) $yp + xq + pq = 0$
   (ix) $(pq)^2 + (xy)^2 = (xq)^2 (x^2 + y^2)$
   (x) $zpy^2 = x(y^2 + z^2 q^2)$
   (xi) $z = px + qy + \log pq$
   (xii) $(p - q)(z - px - qy) = 1$
   (xiii) $pq = x^m y^n z^l$
   (xiv) $q^2 = z^2 p^2 (1 - p^2)$
   (xv) $(pz)^2 + q^2 = 1$
2. Use Charpit's Method to solve the following equations:
   (i) $z^2 = pqxy$
   (ii) $2(z + xp + yq) = yp^2$
   (iii) $qz - p^2 y - q^2 y = 0$
   (iv) $yz - p(xy + q) - qy = 0$
   (v) $z - q^2 y - p^2 x = 0$

Answers

(i) $z = ax + ay + c$

(ii) $z = ax + by + c, a^2 + b^2 = nab$

(iii) $z = a(x + y)^{1/2} + (1 - a^2)^{1/2} (x - y)^{1/2} + c$

(iv) $z = b^2(x + y) + bxy + c$

(v) $\frac{az^2}{2} = (1+a)(x+ay) + b$

(vi) $z = a\tan(x+ay) + b$

(vii) $z^{1/k} = xy^a b, \; k = \frac{\{-a \pm (a^2+4)^{1/2}\}}{2}$

(viii) $z = \frac{x^2}{2(a-1)} - \frac{y^2}{2a+b}$

(ix) $z = \left\{\frac{(x^2+a^2)^{3/2}}{3}\right\} + (y^2-a^2)^{1/2} + b$

(x) $z^2 = ax^2 + (a-1)^{1/2}y^2 + b$

(xi) $z = ax + by + \log ab$

(xii) $z = ax + by + \frac{1}{(a-b)}$

(xiii) $z^{1-l/2} = \left(1-\frac{l}{2}\right)\left[\frac{ax^{m+1}}{m+1} + \frac{y^{n+1}}{a(n+1)} + c\right]$

(xiv) $z^2 = a^2 + (x+ay+b)^2$

(xv) $z\sqrt{z^2+a^2} + a^2\log\{z+\sqrt{z^2+a^2}\} = 2(x+ay+b)$

2. (i) $z = bx^a y^{1/a}$

(ii) $z = \left(\frac{ax}{y^2}\right) - \left(\frac{a^2}{4y^3}\right) + \frac{b}{y}$

(iii) $z^2 = a^2y^2 + (ax+b)^2$

(iv) $(z-ax)(y+a)^a = be^y$

(v) $\{(1+a)z\}^{1/2} = (ax)^{1/2} + y^{1/2} + b$

AMITY SCHOOL OF ENGINEERING & TECHNOLOGY
AMITY UNIVERSITY UTTAR PRADESH
B.TECH (3rd Semester)

APPLIED MATHEMATICS - III

TUTORIAL SHEET-4

1. Solve the following Homogeneous linear equations with constant coefficients:

(1) $4r + 12s + 9t = e^{3x - 2y}$

(2) $r - 2s + t = \sin x$

(3) $p - 2q = \sin (x + 2y)$

(4) $2r - 5s + 2t = 5 \sin (2x + y)$

(5) $r - 2s = \sin x \cos 2y$

(6) $r + 5s + 6t = e^{x - y}$

(7) $r + t = x^2 y^2$

(8) $z_{xx} - z_{xy} - 2z_{yy} = (y - 1)e^x$

(9) $(2D_x + D_y + 1)(D_x^2 + 3D_xD_y - 3D_x)z = 0$

(10) $(2D_x + D_y + 5)(D_x - 2D_y + 1)^2 z = 0$

(11) $(2D_x + 3D_y - 1)^2 (D_x - 3D_y + 3)^3 z = 0$

(12) $(D_x^4 + D_y^4 - 2D_x^2 D_y^2)z = 0$

(13) $r + 3s + p + 2t - 2z = e^{3x + 4y} + y(1 - 2x)$

(14) $3s - 2t - q = \cos (3y + 2x)$

(15) $6r + 5s - 6t = 132 \log (x + 3y)$

(16) $r - t = x - y$

(17) $r + t = \cos mx \cos ny$

(18) $r + s - 6t = y \cos x$

(19) $p - 2q = (y + 1) e^{3x}$

(20) $p + 3q = \cos (2x + 3y)$

(21) $(D^2 - 2DD' + D'^2)z = e^{x + 2y} + x^3$

(22) $4r - 4s + t = 16 \log (x + 2y)$

(23) $(D^3 - 3DD' + D' + 1)z = e^{2x + 3y}$

(24) $(D - 2D' - 1)(D - 2D'^2 - 1)z = 0$

(25) $(x^2D^2 - 4xyDD' + 4y^2D'^2 + 6yD')\, z = x^3y^4$

(26) $x^2r - 3xys + 2y^2t + px + 2qy = x + 2y$

(27) $r - t = \tan^3 x \tan y - \tan x \tan^3 y$

(28) $\dfrac{\partial^2 z}{\partial x^2} + \dfrac{\partial^2 z}{\partial x \partial y} - 6\dfrac{\partial^2 z}{\partial y^2} = x^2 \sin (x + y)$

Answers

(1) $z = f(2y - 3x) + xg(2y - 3x) + \left(\frac{x^2 e^{3x - 2y}}{8}\right)$, **(2)** $z = f(y + x) + xg(y + x) - \sin x$

(3) $z = f(y + 2x) + \frac{\{\cos(x + 2y)\}}{3}$, **(4)** $z = f(2y + x) + g(y + 2x) - \left(\frac{5}{3}\right) x \cos(y + 2x)$

(5) $z = f(y) + g(y + 2x) + \left(\frac{1}{15}\right)(\sin x \cos 2y + 4 \sin 2y \cos x)$

(6) $z = f(y - 2x) + g(y - 3x) + \left(\frac{e^{x - y}}{2}\right)$, **(7)** $z = f(y + ix) + g(y - ix) + \frac{(15x^4y^2 - x^6)}{180}$

(8) $z = f(y - x) + g(y + 2x) + ye^x$, **(9)** $z = f(y) + e^{-x/2} g(2y - x) + e^{3x} h(y - 3x)$

(10) $z = e^{-5x/2} f(2y - x) + e^{-x}\{g(y + 2x) + xh(y + 2x)\}$

(11) $z = e^{x/2}\{f(2y - 3x) + xg(2y - 3x)\} + e^y\{h(y + 3x) + yi(y + 3x) + y^2 j(y + 3x)\}$

(12) $z = xf(x - y) + g(x - y) + xh(x + y) + i(x + y)$

(13) $z = e^x f(y - x) + e^{-y} g(y - 2x) + \left(\frac{1}{78}\right) e^{3x + 4y} + xy + \frac{3}{2}$

(14) $z = f(x) + e^{y/2} g(3y + 2x) - \left\{\frac{\sin(3y + 2x)}{3}\right\}$

(15) $z = f(2x + 3y) + g(3y - 2x) + (x + 3y)^2 \{3 - 2\log(3y + x)\}$

(16) $z = f(y + x) + g(x - y) + \left\{\frac{x(x - y)^2}{4}\right\}$, **(17)** $z = f(y + ix) + g(y - ix) - \left\{\frac{\cos mx \cos ny}{(m^2 + n^2)}\right\}$

(18) $z = f(y + 2x) + g(y - 3x) + \sin x - y \cos x$

(19) $z = f(y + 2x) + \left(\frac{1}{3}\right)\left\{y + \left(\frac{5}{3}\right)\right\} e^{3x}$

(20) $z = f(y - 3x) + \left(\frac{1}{5}\right) \sin(2x + y)$

(21) $z = f(y + x) + xg(y + x)\, e^{x + 2y} + \frac{x^5}{20}$

(22) $z = f(2y + x) + xg(2y + x) + 2x^2 \log(x + 2y)$

(23) $z = \frac{-e^{2x + 3y}}{7} + \Sigma A e^{hx + ky}$, where $h^2 - 2hk + k + 1 = 0$

(24) $z = e^x f(y + 2x) + \Sigma A e^{ky + (2k^2 + 1)x}$

(25) $z = f(yx^2) + xg(yx^2) + \frac{x^3 y^4}{30}$

(26) $z = f(xy) + g(x^2 y) + x + y$

(27) $z = f(y + x) + g(y - x) + \frac{\{\tan x \tan y\}}{2}$

(28) $z = f(y + 2x) + g(y - 3x) + \frac{\left\{\left(x^2 - \frac{13}{8}\right) \sin(x + y)\right\}}{4} - \frac{\{3x \cos(x + y)\}}{8}$

AMITY SCHOOL OF ENGINEERING & TECHNOLOGY
AMITY UNIVERSITY UTTAR PRADESH
B.TECH (3rd Semester)

APPLIED MATHEMATICS - III

TUTORIAL SHEET-5

1. Expand $f(x) = x \sin x,\ 0 < x < 2\pi$ in Fourier series.
2. Find the Fourier series for $f(x) = \pi + x$ in $(-\pi, \pi)$.
3. Obtain the Fourier series for the following functions:
   (I) $f(x) = -5x + 2$ in the interval $[-\pi, \pi]$.
   (II) $f(x) = x - \frac{1}{2}$ in the interval $[-\pi, \pi]$.
   (III) $f(x) = 2x^2 - 3$ in the interval $[0, 2\pi]$.
   (IV) $f(x) = -x^2 + \frac{1}{3}$ in the interval $[0, 2\pi]$.
   (V) $f(x) = x - x^2$ in the interval $[-\pi, \pi]$.
   (VI) $f(x) = x$ in the interval $0 < x < 2\pi$.
4. Using the Fourier series of e^{-ax} over the interval $(-\pi, \pi)$ find the value of the series $\frac{1}{2^2+1} - \frac{1}{3^2+1} + \frac{1}{4^2+1}$ ....
5. Obtain the Fourier series of $f(x) = x + x^2$ in the interval $(-\pi, \pi)$. Hence prove that $\sum_1^\infty \frac{1}{n^2} = \frac{\pi^2}{6}$.
6. Obtain the Fourier series to represent $f(x) = \frac{1}{4}(\pi - x)^2,\ 0 < x < 2\pi$. Hence obtain the following relations:
   (I) $\frac{1}{1^2} + \frac{1}{2^2} + \frac{1}{3^2} + \frac{1}{4^2} + \ldots.. = \frac{\pi^2}{6}$.
   (II) $\frac{1}{1^2} - \frac{1}{2^2} + \frac{1}{3^2} - \frac{1}{4^2} + \ldots.. = \frac{\pi^2}{12}$.
   (III) $\frac{1}{1^2} + \frac{1}{3^2} + \frac{1}{5^2} + \ldots.. = \frac{\pi^2}{8}$.
7. Obtain the Fourier series to represent $f(x) = e^{-x},\ 0 < x < 2\pi$.

8. Express, $f(x) = |x|$, $-\pi < x < \pi$, as Fourier series. Hence show that

$$\frac{1}{1^2} + \frac{1}{3^2} + \frac{1}{5^2} + \ldots.. = \frac{\pi^2}{8}.$$

9. Obtain the Fourier series of $f(x) = x^2$ in the interval $-\pi \le x \le \pi$. Hence prove that

$$\frac{1}{1^2} + \frac{1}{2^2} + \frac{1}{3^2} + \frac{1}{4^2} + \ldots.. = \frac{\pi^2}{6}.$$

10. Obtain the Fourier series for the function $f(x)$ given by

$$f(x) = \begin{cases} 1 + \frac{2x}{\pi}, & -\pi \le x \le 0 \\ 1 - \frac{2x}{\pi}, & 0 \le x \le \pi \end{cases}$$

Hence deduce that $\frac{1}{1^2} + \frac{1}{3^2} + \frac{1}{5^2} + \ldots.. = \frac{\pi^2}{8}$.

Answers

1. $x \sin x = -1 + \pi \sin x - \frac{1}{2}\cos x + 2\sum_{2}^{\infty} \frac{1}{n^2 - 1}\cos nx.$

2. $\pi + x = \frac{\pi}{2} - 2\sum_{1}^{\infty} \frac{(-1)^n}{n} \sin nx$

3. (I) $f(x) = 2 + 10\sum_{1}^{\infty} \frac{(-1)^n}{n} \sin nx$

(II) $f(x) = -\frac{1}{2} - 2\sum_{1}^{\infty} \frac{(-1)^n}{n} \sin nx$

(III) $f(x) = \frac{8\pi^2 - 9}{3} + 8\sum_{1}^{\infty} \left[\frac{\cos nx}{n} - \frac{\pi}{n}\sin nx\right]$

(IV) $f(x) = \frac{1 - 4\pi^2}{3} - 4\sum_{1}^{\infty} \left[\frac{\cos nx}{n} - \frac{\pi}{n}\sin nx\right]$

(V) $f(x) = \frac{-\pi^2}{3} + \sum_{1}^{\infty} \left[\frac{4(-1)^{n+1}}{n}\cos nx + \frac{2(-1)^{n+1}}{n}\sin nx\right]$

(VI) $f(x) = \pi - 2\sum_{1}^{\infty} \frac{\sin nx}{n}$

4. $\dfrac{\pi}{(2\sinh \pi)}$

5. $\dfrac{\pi^2}{3} + 4\sum_{1}^{\infty} \dfrac{(-1)^n}{n^2}\cos nx - 2\sum_{1}^{\infty}\dfrac{(-1)^n}{n}\sin nx$

6. $\dfrac{\pi^2}{12} + \sum_{1}^{\infty}\dfrac{\cos nx}{n^2}$

7. $\dfrac{1-e^{-2\pi}}{\pi}$

$$\left[\frac{1}{2} + \left(\frac{1}{2}\cos x + \frac{1}{5}\cos 2x + \frac{1}{10}\cos 3x + \ldots\right) + \left(\frac{1}{2}\sin x + \frac{2}{5}\sin 2x + \frac{3}{10}\sin 3x + \ldots\right)\right]$$

8. $\dfrac{\pi}{2} - \dfrac{4}{\pi}\left(\cos x + \dfrac{\cos 3x}{3^2} + \dfrac{\cos 5x}{5^2} + \ldots\right)$

9. $\dfrac{\pi^2}{3} - 4\left(\dfrac{\cos x}{1^2} - \dfrac{\cos 2x}{2^2} + \dfrac{\cos 3x}{3^2} - \dfrac{\cos 4x}{4^2} + \ldots\right)$

10. $\dfrac{8}{\pi^2}\left(\dfrac{\cos x}{1^2} + \dfrac{\cos 3x}{3^2} + \dfrac{\cos 5x}{5^2} + \ldots\right)$

AMITY SCHOOL OF ENGINEERING & TECHNOLOGY
AMITY UNIVERSITY UTTAR PRADESH
B.TECH (3rd Semester)

APPLIED MATHEMATICS - III

TUTORIAL SHEET-6

1. Find Fourier expansion for the following functions:

I. $f(x) = x - x^2, -1 < x < 1$

II. $f(x) = x^2 - 2$, in the interval $-2 \le x \le 2$.

III. $f(x) = e^{-x}$, in the interval $-l < x < l$

IV. $f(x) = 1 - x^2$ in the interval $-1 < x < 1$.

V. $f(x) = \begin{cases} \pi x, & 0 \le x \le 1 \\ \pi(2 - x), & 1 \le x \le 2 \end{cases}$

VI. $f(x) = x - x^3$ in the interval $-1 < x < 1$.

VII. $f(x) = \pi x$, in the interval $-c < x < c$.

VIII. $f(x) = \begin{cases} 0, & -2 < x < 0 \\ 1, & 0 < x < 2 \end{cases}$ in the interval $(-2, 2)$.

IX. $f(x) = \begin{cases} x, & 0 < x < 1 \\ 0, & 1 < x < 2 \end{cases}$ in the interval $(0, 2)$.

X. $f(x) = \begin{cases} x, & 0 < x < 1 \\ 1 - x, & 1 < x < 2 \end{cases}$ in the interval $(0, 2)$.

XI. $f(x) = \begin{cases} 0, & -2 < x < -1 \\ k, & -2 < x < 1 \\ 0, & 1 < x < 2 \end{cases}$ in the interval $(-2, 2)$.

2. A sinusoidal voltage $E \sin \omega t$ is passed through a half wave rectifier, which clips the negative portion of the wave. Expand the resulting periodic function in a Fourier series where

$$f(t) = \begin{cases} 0, & \frac{-T}{2} < t < 0 \\ E \sin \omega t, & 0 < t < \frac{T}{2} \end{cases}$$

and $$T = \frac{2\pi}{\omega}.$$

3. Find the Fourier coefficients corresponding to the function

$$f(x) = \begin{cases} 0, & -5 < t < 0 \\ 3, & 0 < t < 5 \end{cases}$$

Answers

1. I. $\frac{-1}{3}+\frac{4}{\pi^2}\left(\frac{\cos\pi x}{1^2}-\frac{\cos 2\pi x}{2^2}+\frac{\cos 3\pi x}{3^2}-\ldots\right)+\frac{2}{\pi}\left(\frac{\sin\pi x}{1}-\frac{\sin 2\pi x}{2}+\frac{\sin 3\pi x}{3}-\ldots\right)$

II. $\frac{-2}{3}-\frac{16}{\pi^2}\left(\cos\frac{\pi x}{2}-\frac{1}{4}\cos\pi x+\frac{1}{9}\cos\frac{3\pi x}{2}-\ldots\right)$

III. $\sinh l\left[\frac{1}{l}+2l\sum_{n=1}^{\infty}\frac{(-1)^n}{l^2+n^2\pi^2}\cos\frac{n\pi x}{l}+2\pi\sum_{n=1}^{\infty}\frac{n(-1)^n}{l^2+n^2\pi^2}\sin\frac{n\pi x}{l}\right]$

IV. $\frac{2}{3}+\frac{4}{\pi^2}\left(\cos\pi x-\frac{\cos 2\pi x}{2^2}+\frac{\cos 3\pi x}{e^2}-\ldots\right)$

V. $\frac{\pi}{2}-\frac{4}{\pi}\left(\frac{\cos\pi x}{1^2}+\frac{\cos 3\pi x}{3^2}+\frac{\cos 5\pi x}{5^2}+\ldots\right)$,

VI. $\frac{12}{\pi^3}\left(\sin\pi x-\frac{\cos 2\pi x}{2^3}+\frac{\sin 3\pi x}{e^3}-\ldots\right)$

VII. $2c\left[\sin\frac{\pi x}{c}-\frac{1}{2}\sin\frac{2\pi x}{c}+\frac{1}{3}\sin\frac{3\pi x}{c}-\ldots\right]$

VIII. $\frac{1}{2}+\frac{2}{\pi^2}\left(\sin\frac{\pi x}{2}+\frac{1}{3}\sin\frac{3\pi x}{2}+\frac{1}{5}\sin\frac{5\pi x}{2}+\ldots\right)$

IX. $\frac{1}{4}-\frac{2}{\pi^2}\left(\cos\pi x\,\frac{\cos 3\pi x}{3^2}+\frac{\cos 5\pi x}{5^2}+\ldots\right)+\frac{1}{\pi}\left(\sin\pi x-\frac{\sin 2\pi x}{2}+\frac{\sin 3\pi x}{3}+\ldots\right)$

X. $\frac{-4}{\pi^2}\left(\cos\pi x+\frac{\cos 3\pi x}{3^2}+\frac{\cos 5\pi x}{5^2}+\ldots\right)+\frac{2}{\pi}\left(\sin\pi x+\frac{\sin 3\pi x}{3}+\ldots\right)$

XI. $\frac{k}{2}+\frac{2k}{\pi}\left(\cos\frac{\pi x}{2}-\frac{1}{3}\cos\frac{3\pi x}{2}+\frac{1}{5}\cos\frac{5\pi x}{2}+\ldots\right)$

2. $\frac{E}{\pi}+\frac{E}{2}\sin\omega t-\frac{2E}{\pi}\left(\cos\frac{2wt}{1.3}+\frac{\cos 4wt}{3.5}+\ldots\right)$

3. $a_0=3,\ a_n=0,\ b_n=\begin{cases}0, & \text{if } n \text{ is even}\\ \frac{6}{n\pi}, & \text{if } n \text{ is odd}\end{cases}$

AMITY SCHOOL OF ENGINEERING & TECHNOLOGY
AMITY UNIVERSITY UTTAR PRADESH
B.TECH (3rd Semester)

APPLIED MATHEMATICS - III

TUTORIAL SHEET-7

1. Express $f(x) = x$ as a sine series in $0 < x < \pi$.

2. Find the Fourier sine series expansion of the following functions:

I. $f(x) = \begin{cases} x, & 0 < x < \frac{\pi}{2} \\ \frac{\pi}{2}, & \frac{\pi}{2} < x < \pi \end{cases}$

II. $f(x) = a^{ax}$ for $0 < x < \pi$

III. $f(x) = 2x - 1$ for $0 < x < 1$.

3. Represent the following function by a Fourier cosine series:

I. $f(x) = \begin{cases} 1, & 0 < x < \frac{\pi}{2} \\ 0, & \frac{\pi}{2} < x < \pi \end{cases}$

II. $f(x) = \sin \frac{\pi x}{l}, \ 0 < x < l$

III. $f(x) = e^x$ in the interval (0, 1).

IV. $f(x) = \begin{cases} 2x, & 0 < x < 1 \\ 2(2 - x), & 1 < x < 2 \end{cases}$

V. $f(x) = \pi - x$ in $(0, \pi)$

VI. $f(x) = x^2$ in $(0, \pi)$

VII. $f(x) = \cos(sx), \ -\pi \le x \le \pi$.

VIII. $f(x) = e^x$ in the interval $0 < x < \pi$.

4. Find a half range even expansion of the function

$$f(x) = \left(\frac{-x}{l}\right) + 1, \ 0 \le x \le l.$$

5. Find a series of cosine of multiples of x which will represent $f(x)$ in $(0, \pi)$ where

$f(x) = \begin{cases} 0, & 0 < x < \frac{\pi}{2} \\ \frac{\pi}{2}, & \frac{\pi}{2} < x < \pi \end{cases}$ and deduce that $1 - \frac{1}{3} + \frac{1}{5} - \frac{1}{7} + \ldots = \frac{\pi}{4}$.

6. Show that if :

$$f(x) = \begin{cases} 2, & 0 < x < \dfrac{\pi}{2} \\ \pi - x, & \dfrac{\pi}{2} < x < \pi \end{cases}$$

I. $f(x) = \dfrac{4}{\pi}\left(\sin x - \dfrac{1}{3^2}\sin 3x + \dfrac{1}{5^2}\sin 5x - \ldots\right)$

II. $f(x) = \dfrac{\pi}{4} - \dfrac{2}{\pi}\left(\dfrac{1}{1^2}\cos 2x + \dfrac{1}{3^2}\cos 6x + \dfrac{1}{5^2}\cos 10x + \ldots\right)$

7. If $f(x) = x + 1$ for, $0 < x < \pi$, find its Fourier sine series and Fourier cosine series. Hence deduce that

I. $1 - \dfrac{1}{3} + \dfrac{1}{5} - \dfrac{1}{7} + \ldots = \dfrac{\pi}{4}$

II. $1 + \dfrac{1}{3^2} + \dfrac{1}{5^2} + \dfrac{1}{7^2} + \ldots = \dfrac{\pi^2}{8}$

Answers

1. $2\left[\sin x - \dfrac{1}{2}\sin 2x + \dfrac{1}{3}\sin 3x - \ldots\right]$

2. I. $\left(\dfrac{2}{\pi} + 1\right)\sin x - \dfrac{1}{2}\sin 2x + \left(\dfrac{-2}{9\pi} + \dfrac{1}{3}\right)\sin 3x + \ldots$

II. $\dfrac{2}{\pi}\left[\dfrac{1 + e^{a\pi}}{a^2 + 1}\sin x + \dfrac{2(1 - e^{a\pi})}{a^2 + 2^2}\sin 2x + \ldots\right]$

III. $\dfrac{-2}{\pi}\left[\sin 2\pi x + \dfrac{1}{2}\sin 4\pi x + \dfrac{1}{3}\sin 6\pi x + \ldots\right]$

3. I. $\dfrac{1}{2} + \dfrac{2}{\pi}\left[\cos x - \dfrac{1}{3}\cos 3x + \dfrac{1}{5}\cos 5x - \ldots\right]$

II. $\dfrac{2}{\pi} - \dfrac{4}{\pi}\left[\dfrac{1}{3}\cos\dfrac{2\pi x}{l} + \dfrac{1}{15}\cos\dfrac{4\pi x}{l} + \dfrac{1}{35}\cos\dfrac{6\pi x}{l} + \ldots\right]$

III. $e - 1 + 2\left[\dfrac{-e-1}{\pi^2 + 1}\cos \pi x + \dfrac{e-1}{4\pi^2 + 1}\cos 2\pi x + \dfrac{-e-1}{9\pi^2 + 1}\cos 3\pi x + \ldots\right]$

IV. $1 - \left(\dfrac{8}{\pi^2} + \dfrac{4}{\pi}\right)\cos\dfrac{\pi x}{2} - \dfrac{4}{\pi^2}\cos\dfrac{2\pi x}{2} + \left(\dfrac{-8}{9\pi^2} + \dfrac{4}{3\pi}\right)\cos\dfrac{3\pi x}{2} + \ldots$

V. $\frac{\pi}{2}+\frac{4}{\pi}\left(\cos x+\frac{\cos 3x}{3^2}+\frac{\cos 5x}{5^2}+\ldots\right)$

VI. $\frac{\pi^2}{3}-\frac{4}{\pi}\left(\cos x-\frac{1}{2^2}\cos 2x+\frac{1}{3^2}\cos 3x-\ldots\right)$

VII. $\frac{\sin \pi x}{\pi s}+\frac{1}{\pi}\sum\left[\frac{\sin (s\pi+n\pi)}{s+n}+\frac{\sin (s\pi-n\pi)}{s-n}\right]\cos nx$

VIII. $\frac{e^{\pi}-1}{\pi}-\frac{2}{\pi}\sum_{1}^{\infty}\frac{1-(-1)^n e^{\pi}}{n^2+1}\cos nx$

4. $\frac{1}{2}+\frac{4}{\pi^2}\left[\cos\frac{\pi x}{l}+\frac{1}{3^2}\cos\frac{3\pi x}{l}+\frac{1}{5^2}\cos\frac{5\pi x}{l}+\ldots\right]$

5. $\frac{\pi}{4}-\cos x+\frac{1}{3}\cos 3x-\frac{1}{5}\cos 5x+\ldots$

AMITY SCHOOL OF ENGINEERING & TECHNOLOGY
AMITY UNIVERSITY UTTAR PRADESH
B.TECH (3rd Semester)

APPLIED MATHEMATICS - III

TUTORIAL SHEET-8

1. Find the complex form of the Fourier series of the following functions:

   (a) $f(x) = e^{2x},\ 0 < x < 2$

   (b) $f(x) = x^2 + x,\ -\pi < x < \pi$

   (c) $f(x) = \begin{cases} -x, & -\pi < x < 0 \\ x, & 0 < x < \pi \end{cases}$

   (d) $f(x) = \sin x,\ 0 < x < \pi$

   (e) $f(x) = \cos ax,\ -\pi < x < \pi$

   (f) $f(x) = \begin{cases} 0, & -\pi \le x \le 0 \\ 1, & 0 \le x \le \pi \end{cases}$

2. Use Parseval's identity to prove the following:

   (a) $\sum_{n=1}^{\infty} \frac{1}{(2n-1)^4} = \frac{\pi^4}{96}$

   (b) $\sum_{n=1}^{\infty} \frac{1}{n^4} = \frac{\pi^4}{90}$ for $f(x) = |x|$ in $(-\pi, \pi)$.

3. Expand $f(x) = x - \frac{x^2}{2}$ in (0, 2) as Fourier series and hence find the value of $\sum_{n=1}^{\infty} \frac{1}{(2n-1)^6}$ (use Parseval's identity only).

4. Using the half range cosine series for $f(x) = x$ in $0 < x < 1$, find the value of $\sum_{n=1}^{\infty} \frac{1}{(2n-1)^4}$ (use Parseval's identity only).

5. Obtain the first three coefficients in the Fourier cosine series for y, where y is given in the following table :

x	0	1	2	3	4	5
y	4	8	15	7	6	2

6. For the rotation in degrees (x) of the flywheel of a certain machine part the following values of displacement (y) are obtained :

x	0	30	60	90	120	150	180	210	240	270	300	330
y	1.8	1.1	0.3	0.16	1.5	1.3	2.16	1.25	1.30	1.52	1.76	2.00

Calculate the fundamental harmonic.

7. The turning moment T on the crank-shaft of a steam engine for the crank angle θ degree is given as follows:

θ	0	30	60	90	120	150	180
T	0	6.1	8.2	7.9	5.5	2.5	0

Find the coefficient of 2θ if T is expanded in a series of sines.

8. Obtain the Fourier series of y for the given values of x neglecting the harmonics above the second

x	0	1	2	3	4	5
y	9	18	24	28	26	20

9. Express the function $f(x) = \begin{cases} 1, & |x| \le 1 \\ 0, & |x| > 1 \end{cases}$ as a Fourier Integral. Hence evaluate

$$\int_0^\infty \frac{\sin\lambda \cos\lambda x}{\lambda}\, d\lambda.$$

10. Find the Fourier transform of $f(x) = \begin{cases} 1 - x^2, & |x| \le 1 \\ 0, & |x| > 1 \end{cases}$ and hence evaluate

$$\int_0^\infty \left(\frac{x \cos x - \sin x}{x^2}\right) \cos\frac{x}{2}\, dx.$$

11. Find the Fourier transform of $f(x) = \begin{cases} 1, & |x| < a \\ 0, & |x| > a \end{cases}$ and hence evaluate

(i) $\int_{-\infty}^{\infty} \frac{\sin sa \cos sx}{s}\, ds$

(ii) $\int_0^\infty \frac{\sin s}{s}\, ds$

12. Find the Fourier sine transform of

(i) $\frac{e^{-ax}}{x}$

(ii) $f(x) = \begin{cases} x, & 0 < x < 1 \\ 2 - x, & 1 < x < 2 \\ 0, & x > 2 \end{cases}$

13. Find the Fourier cosine transform of

(i) $f(x) = \begin{cases} \cos x, & 0 < x < a \\ 0, & x \geq a \end{cases}$

(ii) $f(x) = \begin{cases} x, & 0 < x < \frac{1}{2} \\ 1 - x, & \frac{1}{2} < x < 1 \\ 0, & x > 1 \end{cases}$

Answers

1. (a) $e^{2x} = (e^4 - 1) \sum_{n=-\infty}^{\infty} \frac{4 + 2in\pi}{16 + 4n^2\pi^2} e^{in\pi x}$ (b) $f(x) = \sum_{n=-\infty}^{\infty} \frac{(-1)^n}{n}\left[\frac{2}{n} + i\right] e^{inx}$

(c) $f(x) = \frac{1}{\pi} \sum_{n=-\infty}^{\infty} \left[\frac{(-1)^n - 1}{n^2}\right] e^{inx}$

(d) $f(x) = \frac{2}{\pi}\left[1 - \frac{(e^{2ix} + e^{-2ix})}{1.3} - \frac{(e^{4ix} + e^{-4ix})}{3.5} - \ldots\right]$

(e) $f(x) = \frac{a}{\pi} \sin a\pi \sum_{-\infty}^{\infty} \frac{(-1)^n e^{inx}}{a^2 - n^2}$

(f) $f(x) = \frac{1}{2} - \frac{1}{i\pi}\left[(e^{ix} - e^{-ix}) + \frac{1}{3}(e^{3ix} - e^{-3ix}) + \frac{1}{5}(e^{5ix} - e^{-5ix}) + \ldots\right]$

3. $\frac{16}{\pi^2} \sum_{n=1}^{\infty} \frac{1}{(2n-1)^3} \sin \frac{(2n-1)\pi x}{2}$ **4.** $\frac{\pi^4}{960}$

5. $y = 7 - 2.83 \cos \frac{\pi x}{3} - 1.5 \cos \frac{2\pi x}{3}$

6. $0.04 \cos x - 0.63 \sin x$ **7.** 1.56

8. $20.84 - 8.33 \cos \frac{\pi x}{3} - 2.33 \cos \frac{2\pi x}{3} - 1.16 \sin \frac{\pi x}{3}$

9. $\frac{\pi}{4}$ **10.** $\frac{3\pi}{16}$ **11.** (i) $\begin{cases} \pi, & |x| < a \\ 0, & |x| > a \end{cases}$ (ii) $\frac{\pi}{2}$

12. (i) $\tan^{-1} \frac{s}{a}$ (ii) $\frac{2(1 - \cos s) \sin s}{s^2}$

13. (i) $\frac{1}{2}\left\{\frac{\sin (1+s)a}{1+s} + \frac{\sin (1-s)a}{1-s}\right\}$ (ii) $\left\{-\frac{\cos s}{s^2} + \frac{2 \cos\left(\frac{s}{2}\right)}{s^2} - \frac{1}{s^2}\right\}$

AMITY SCHOOL OF ENGINEERING & TECHNOLOGY
AMITY UNIVERSITY UTTAR PRADESH
B.TECH (3rd Semester)

APPLIED MATHEMATICS - III

TUTORIAL SHEET-9

Find the Laplace transform of the functions given below (1 to 5) :

1. (i) $7e^{2t} + 9e^{-2t} + 5\cos t + 7t^3 + 5\sin 3t + 2$
   (ii) $(1 + te^{-t})^3$

2. (i) $\left(\sqrt{t} + \frac{1}{\sqrt{t}}\right)^3$
   (ii) $e^{-3t}(2\cos 5t - 3\sin 5t)$

3. (i) $\sinh \frac{t}{2} \sin \frac{\sqrt{3}}{2} t$
   (ii) $te^{-4t} \sin 3t$

4. $$f(t) = \begin{cases} \cos\left(t - \frac{2\pi}{3}\right), & t > \frac{2\pi}{3} \\ 0, & t < \frac{2\pi}{3} \end{cases}$$

5. $$f(t) = \begin{cases} 1, & 0 \le t < 1 \\ t, & 1 \le t < 2 \\ t^2, & 2 \le t < \infty \end{cases}$$

6. Find the Laplace transform of $F(t)$ defined as $F(t) = |t - 1| + |t + 1|, t \ge 0$.

7. (i) If $L\{J_0(t)\} = \frac{1}{\sqrt{1 + p^2}}$, find $L\{J_0(at)\}$.
   (ii) If $L\{F(t)\} = \frac{p^2 - p + 1}{(2p + 1)^2 (p - 1)}$ show that $L\{F(2t)\} = \frac{p^2 - 2p + 4}{4(p + 1)^2 (p - 2)}$.

8. Define functions of exponential order and a function of class 'A' and show that e^{t^2} is not of exponential order.

9. State existence theorem for Laplace transform and verify that $e^{at} \sin bt$ and $t^3 \cos bt$ are of exponential orders with $b > a$ and $b > 0$ respectively.

10. Find the Laplace transform of $\frac{\sin at}{t}$. Does the Laplace transform of $\frac{\cos at}{t}$ exits?

11. If, $F(t) = \frac{e^{at} - \cos bt}{t}$, find the Laplace transform of $F(t)$.

12. Find the Laplace transform of

(i) $t^n e^{at}$, $p > a$; n is a positive integer

(ii) $t^2 e^t \sin 4t$.

13. Evaluate :

(i) $\int_0^\infty \frac{\sin^2 t}{t^2}\, dt$

(ii) $\int_0^\infty \frac{\cos 6t - \cos 4t}{t}\, dt.$

14. Find the Laplace transform of :

(i) $\int_0^t \frac{e^{-at} - e^{-bt}}{t}\, dt$

(ii) $\int_0^t e^{-t} \frac{\sin t}{t}\, dt.$

15. Find the Laplace transform of :

(i) $\sin\sqrt{t}$; hence find $L\left(\frac{\cos\sqrt{t}}{\sqrt{t}}\right)$

(ii) $\int_0^{t/2} \frac{1 - e^{-2x}}{x}\, dx.$

Answers

1. (i) $\frac{7}{p-2} + \frac{9}{p+2} + \frac{5p}{p^2+1} + \frac{42}{p^4} + \frac{15}{p^2+9} + \frac{2}{p}.$ (ii) $\frac{1}{p} + \frac{6}{(p+3)^4} + \frac{3}{(p+1)^2} + \frac{6}{(p+2)^3}$

2. (i) $\sqrt{\pi}\left[\frac{3}{4p^{5/2}} - 2\sqrt{p} + \frac{3}{2p^{3/2}} + \frac{3}{\sqrt{p}}\right]$ (ii) $\frac{2p-9}{p^2+6p+34}$

3. (i) $\frac{\sqrt{3}p}{2(p^4+p^2+1)}$ (ii) $\frac{6(p+4)}{[(p+4)^2+9]^2}$ **4.** $e^{-(2\pi/3)p}\frac{p}{p^2+1}$

5. $\frac{1}{p} + \frac{2}{p}e^{-2p} + \frac{e^{-p}}{p^2} + \frac{3}{p^2}e^{-2p} + \frac{2}{p^3}e^{-2p}$ **6.** $\frac{2}{p}\left(1 + \frac{e^{-p}}{p}\right)$ **7.** (i) $\frac{1}{\sqrt{p^2+a^2}}$

10. $\tan^{-1}\left(\frac{a}{p}\right)$ **11.** $\frac{1}{2}\log\left(\frac{p^2+b^2}{(p-a)^2}\right)$ **12.** (i) $\frac{n!}{(p-a)^{n+1}}$ (ii) $\frac{8(3p^2-6p-13)}{(p^2-2p+17)^3}$

13. (i) $\frac{\pi}{2}$ (ii) $\log\frac{2}{3}$ **14.** (i) $\frac{1}{p}\log\left(\frac{p+b}{p+a}\right)$ (ii) $\frac{1}{p}\cot^{-1}(p+1)$

15. (i) $\frac{\sqrt{\pi}}{2p^{3/2}}e^{-(1/4p)}$; $\sqrt{\frac{\pi}{p}}\, e^{-\left(\frac{1}{4p}\right)}$ (ii) $\frac{1}{p}\log\left(1+\frac{1}{p}\right)$

AMITY SCHOOL OF ENGINEERING & TECHNOLOGY
AMITY UNIVERSITY UTTAR PRADESH
B.TECH (3rd Semester)

APPLIED MATHEMATICS - III

TUTORIAL SHEET-10

1. Find $L\,(erf\,\sqrt{t})$ and hence prove that $L(t.erf\,2\sqrt{t}) = \dfrac{3p+8}{p^2\,(p+4)^{3/2}}$.

2. Find, $L\{J_0(t)\}$ where $J_0(t)$ is the Bessel function of order zero. Hence or otherwise obtain $L\{J_1(t)\}$.

3. Evaluate: $L\{L_n(t)\}$, where $L_n(t)$ is Laguerre polynomial and n is a positive integer.

4. Find the Laplace transform of the following integrals:
   (i) $\int_0^t C_i(t)dt$, where $\int_t^\infty \dfrac{\cos u}{u}\,du$ (ii) $\int_0^t e^{2t}\,erf\,(\sqrt{t}\,)dt$.

5. Find the Laplace transforms of
   (i) $e^{t-2}\,u(t-2)$ (ii) $\sin 2t\;u(t-\pi)$.

6. Express $f(t)$ in terms of unit step function and find its Laplace transform, where
$$f(t) = \begin{cases} 1, & 0 \le t \le a \\ 2, & a \le t \le 2a \\ 3, & 2a \le t \le 3a \end{cases} \text{ and so on.}$$

7. Find the Laplace transform of the rectified semi-wave function defined by: .
$$f(t) = \begin{cases} \sin \omega t, & 0 < t < \dfrac{\pi}{\omega} \\ 0, & \dfrac{\pi}{\omega} < t < \dfrac{2\pi}{\omega} \end{cases}$$

8. Find the inverse Laplace transforms of:
   (i) $\dfrac{e^{-\pi p}}{p^2+1}$
   (ii) $\dfrac{e^{-\pi p}}{p^2}$

9. Find the inverse Laplace transforms of:
   (i) $\dfrac{pe^{-2p}}{p^2-1}$
   (ii) $\dfrac{e^{-cp}}{p^2(p+a)}$, $c > 0$.

10. (i) If $L^{-1}\left\{\dfrac{p}{(p^2+1)^2}\right\} = \dfrac{1}{2}\,t\sin t$, find $L^{-1}\left\{\dfrac{32p}{(16p^2+1)^2}\right\}$.

(ii) If $L^{-1}\left\{\frac{e^{-\sqrt{p}}}{\sqrt{p}}\right\} = \frac{e^{-1/4t}}{\sqrt{\pi t}}$, find $L^{-1}\left\{\frac{e^{-K\sqrt{p}}}{\sqrt{p}}\right\}$.

11. Find the inverse Laplace transforms of :

(i) $\frac{3p+1}{(p+1)^4}$

(ii) $\frac{72}{p^5} - \frac{3\sqrt{\pi}}{2p^{5/2}} + \frac{6}{p}$.

12. Find the inverse Laplace transform of :

$$\frac{2p^3 + 2p^2 + 4p + 1}{(p^2+1)(p^2+p+1)}.$$

13. Show that :

$$L^{-1}\left(\frac{p}{p^4+p^2+1}\right) = \frac{2}{\sqrt{3}} \sinh \frac{t}{2} \sin \frac{\sqrt{3}}{2} t.$$

14. Find the inverse Laplace transform of :

$$\frac{p}{(p+1)^2 (p^2+1)}.$$

Answers

1. $\frac{1}{p\sqrt{p+1}}$ **2.** $\frac{1}{\sqrt{p^2+1}}$, $1 - \frac{p}{\sqrt{p^2+1}}$ **3.** $\frac{(p-1)^n}{p^{n+1}}$; $p > 1$.

4. (i) $\frac{1}{2p^2} \log (p^2+1)$ (ii) $\frac{1}{p(p-2)\sqrt{p-1}}$ **5.** (i) $\frac{e^{-2p}}{p-1}$ (ii) $\frac{e^{-p} - 2e^{-2p} + e^{-3p}}{p^2}$

6. $\frac{1}{p}$ $1 - e^{-ap})$ **7.** $\frac{\omega}{\left(1 - e^{-\frac{\pi p}{\omega}}\right)(p^2+\omega^2)}$ **8.** (i) $-\sin t \,.\, u(t-\pi)$ (ii) $(t-\pi)\,.\,u(t-\pi)$

9. (i) $\cosh (t-2)\, u(t-2)$ (ii) $\frac{1}{a^2}\,[a(t-c) - 1 + e^{-a(t-c)}]\, u(t-c)$

10. (i) $\frac{t}{4} \sin \frac{t}{4}$ (ii) $\frac{e^{-K^2/4t}}{\sqrt{\pi t}}$

11. (i) $e^{-t}\left(\frac{3}{2}t^2 - \frac{1}{3}t^3\right)$ (ii) $3t^4 - 2t^{3/2} + 6$

12. $\cos t + 2 \sin t + e^{-t/2}\left(\cos \frac{\sqrt{3}}{2} t - \frac{1}{\sqrt{3}} \sin \frac{\sqrt{3}}{2} t\right)$ **14.** $\frac{1}{2}(\sin t - te^{-t})$

AMITY SCHOOL OF ENGINEERING & TECHNOLOGY
AMITY UNIVERSITY UTTAR PRADESH
B.TECH (3rd Semester)

APPLIED MATHEMATICS - III

TUTORIAL SHEET-11

1. Find the inverse Laplace transforms of :

(i) $\log \frac{p(p+1)}{p^2+4}$

(ii) $\cot^{-1}\left(\frac{p+3}{2}\right)$

(iii) $\frac{1}{2}\log\left(\frac{p^2+b^2}{p^2+a^2}\right)$

2. Find the inverse Laplace transforms of :

(i) $\frac{1}{p^3(p^2+a^2)}$

(ii) $\frac{1}{p\sqrt{p+4}}$

3. Find the inverse Laplace transforms of :

(i) $\frac{p^2-a^2}{(p^2+a^2)^2}$

(ii) $\frac{2ap}{(p^2+a^2)^2}$

(iii) $\frac{1}{(p^2+a^2)^2}$.

4. Show that :

(i) $L^{-1}\left(\frac{1}{p}\sin\frac{1}{p}\right) = t - \frac{t^3}{(3!)} + \frac{t^5}{(5!)} - \frac{t^7}{(7!)} + \ldots$

(ii) $L^{-1}\left(\frac{1}{p}\cos\frac{1}{p}\right) = 1 - \frac{t^2}{(2!)} + \frac{t^4}{(4!)} - \frac{t^6}{(6!)} + \ldots$

Apply Heaviside's expansion formula to evaluate : (5 to 8)

5. $L^{-1}\left\{\frac{3p+16}{p^2-p-6}\right\}$.

6. $L^{-1}\left\{\frac{2(p^2-2)}{(p+1)(p-2)(p-3)}\right\}$

7. $L^{-1}\left\{\dfrac{2p^2+5p-4}{p^3+p^2-2p}\right\}$

8. $L^{-1}\left\{\dfrac{p^2-6}{p(p+1)(p+3)}\right\}$

9. Show that :

$$L^{-1}\left\{\frac{1}{p^3+1}\right\}=\frac{1}{3}\left[e^{-t}-e^{t/2}\left(\cos\frac{\sqrt{3}}{2}t-\sqrt{3}\sin\frac{\sqrt{3}}{2}t\right)\right]$$

10. Prove that :

$$L^{-1}\left\{\frac{1}{p^{3/2}(p-1)}\right\}=e^t\, erf(\sqrt{t})-2\sqrt{\frac{t}{\pi}}$$

11. Evaluate :

(i) $\int_0^\infty x\cos x^3 dx$

(ii) $\int_0^\infty \dfrac{x\sin tx}{1+x^2}dx,\ t>0.$

12. Using convolution theorem, prove that :

$$L^{-1}\left\{\frac{1}{p^3(p^2+1)}\right\}=\frac{t^2}{2}+\cos t-1$$

13. Using convolution theorem, evaluate :

$$L^{-1}\left\{\frac{1}{p(p+1)^3}\right\}\text{ and } L^{-1}\left\{\frac{1}{p^4(p^2+1)}\right\}.$$

14. Prove that :

$$\beta(m,n)=\int_0^1 x^{m-1}(1-x)^{n-1}dx=\frac{\Gamma(m)\Gamma(n)}{\Gamma(m+n)};\ m,n>0.$$

15. Show that :

$$1*1*1=\frac{t^2}{2}\text{ hence evaluate } 1*1*1*\ldots*1\ (n\text{ times}).$$

16. Apply convolution theorem to show that

(i) $\int_0^t J_0(u)J_1(t-u)du=J_0(t)-\cos t$

(ii) $\int_0^t J_0(u)\sin(t-u)du=tJ_1(t).$

17. Find $L^{-1}\{e^{-\sqrt{p}}\}$. Hence or otherwise show that :

$$L^{-1}\left\{\frac{e^{-k\sqrt{p}}}{p}\right\}=erf_c\left(\frac{k}{2\sqrt{t}}\right).$$

Answers

1. (i) $\dfrac{2\cos 2t - e^{-t} - 1}{t}$ (ii) $\dfrac{e^{-3t}\sin 2t}{t}$ (iii) $\dfrac{\cos at - \cos bt}{t}$

2. (i) $\dfrac{1}{a^2}\left[\dfrac{t^2}{2} + \dfrac{\cos at}{a^2} - \dfrac{1}{a^2}\right]$ (ii) $\dfrac{1}{2}\, erf(2\sqrt{t}\,)$

3. (i) $t\cos at$ (ii) $t\sin at$ (iii) $\dfrac{\sin at - at\cos at}{2a^3}$

5. $5e^{3t} - 2e^{-2t}$ **6.** $-\dfrac{1}{6}e^{-t} - \dfrac{4}{3}e^{2t} + \dfrac{7}{2}e^{3t}$ **7.** $2 + e^{t} - e^{-2t}$ **8.** $-2 + \dfrac{5}{2}e^{-t} + \dfrac{1}{2}e^{-3t}$

11. (i) $\dfrac{\pi}{3\sqrt{3}\,\Gamma(1/3)}$ (ii) $\dfrac{\pi}{2}e^{-t}$ **13.** $1 - e^{-t}\left(1 + t + \dfrac{t^2}{2}\right)$ and $\dfrac{t^3}{6} + \sin t - t$.

15. $\dfrac{t^{n-1}}{(n-1)!}$ **17.** $\dfrac{t^{-3/2}}{2\sqrt{\pi}}e^{-1/4t}$

AMITY SCHOOL OF ENGINEERING & TECHNOLOGY
AMITY UNIVERSITY UTTAR PRADESH
B.TECH (3rd Semester)

APPLIED MATHEMATICS - III

TUTORIAL SHEET-12

Solve the following equations by Laplace transform (1 to 5) :

1. $(D^2 + 5D + 6)x = 5e^t$, $x(0) = 2$, $x'(t) = 1$
2. $(D^2 - 1)x = a \cosh t$, $x(0) = x'(0) = 0$
3. $(D^3 - D^2 + 4D - 4)x = 68e^t \sin 2t$; $x = 1$, $Dx = -19$, $D^2x = -37$ at $t = 0$
4. $(D^3 - 3D^2 + 3D - 1)y = t^2e^{2t}$; $y = 1$, $Dy = 0$, $D^2y = -2$ at $t = 0$
5. $(D^2 + 1)x = t \cos 2t$ given that $x(0) = x'(0) = 0$

Solve the following simultaneous equations by using Laplace transform (6 to 9) :

6. $(D^2 - D)y + z = 0$, $(D - 1)y + Dz = 0$ given that for $t = 0$, $y = 0$, $z = 1$ and $Dy = 0$.
7. $D^2x + y = -5 \cos 2t$, $D^2y + x = t \cos 2t$, where $x(0) = x'(0) = y'(0) = 1$ and $y(0) = -1$.
8. $Dx - Dy - 2x + 2y = 1 - 2t$, $D^2x + 2Dy + x = 0$; given that $x = Dx = y = 0$ at $t = 0$.
9. $(D - 2)x - (D + 1)y = 6e^{3t}$, $(2D - 3)x - (D - 3)y = 6e^{3t}$; given : $x = 3$, $y = 0$ when $t = 0$.
10. The currents i_1 and i_2 in mesh are given by the differential equations : $Di_1 - \omega i_2 = a \cos pt$, $Di_2 - \omega i_1 = a \sin pt$. Find the currents i_1 and i_2 by Laplace transform, if $i_1 = i_2 = 0$ at $t = 0$.

Solve the following equations with variable coefficients by using Laplace transform (11 to 13):

11. $[tD^2 + (1 - 2t)D - 2]y = 0$, if $y(0) = 1$, $y'(0) = 2$.
12. $y''(t) + at\, y'(t) - 2a\, y(t) = 1$; $y(00 = y'(0) = 0$, $a > 0$.
13. $[tD^2 + D + 4t]y = 0]$ if $y(0) = 3$, $y'(0) = 0$.

Solve the following integral equations by using Laplace transform (14 to 16):

14. $y(t) = t^2 + \int_0^t y(u) . \sin(t - u)\, du.$
15. $\int_0^t \frac{y(u)}{\sqrt{t - u}}\, du = 1 + t + t^2.$
16. $\int_0^t y(u) . y(t - u)du = 16 \sin 4t.$

Answers

1. $x = \frac{5}{12} e^{t} + \frac{16}{3} e^{-2t} - \frac{15}{4} e^{-3t}$ 2. $x = \frac{1}{2} at \sinh t$

3. $x = \frac{1}{5} (e^t + 14 \cos 2t - 3 \sin 2t) - 2e^t(\cos 2t + 4 \sin 2t)$

4. $y = (t^2 - 6t + 12)e^{2t} - \left(\frac{3}{2} t^2 + 7t + 11\right) e^t$ 5. $x = \frac{1}{9} (4 \sin 2t - 5 \sin t - 3t \cos 2t)$

6. $y = \frac{1}{2} (\sinh t - te^t), z = \cosh t$ 7. $x = \sin t + \cos 2t,\ y = \sin t - \cos 2t$

8. $x = 2(1 - e^{-t} - te^{-t}), y = -t(1 + 2e^t) + 2(1 - e^{-t})$

9. $y = \sinh t + \cosh t - e^{-3t} - te^t;\ x = e^t + 2t\, e^t + 2e^{3t}$

10. $i_1 = \frac{a}{p + \omega} (\sin \omega t + \sin pt)$ and $i_2 = \frac{a}{p + \omega} (\cos \omega t + \cos pt)$

11. $y = e^{2t}$ 12. $y = \frac{1}{2} t^2$ 13. $y = 3J_0(2t)$ 14. $y = t^2 + \frac{t^4}{12}$

15. $y = \frac{t^{-1/2}}{3\pi} (3 + 6t + 8t^2)$ 16. $y = \pm 8 J_0 (4t)$

AMITY SCHOOL OF ENGINEERING & TECHNOLOGY
AMITY UNIVERSITY UTTAR PRADESH
B.TECH (3rd Semester)

APPLIED MATHEMATICS - III

TUTORIAL SHEET-13

Formulate the following four problems as linear programming problems :

1. A manufacturer of a line of patent medicines is preparing a production plan on medicines A and B. There are sufficient ingredients available to make 20,000 bottles of A and 40,000 bottles of B but there are only 45,000 bottles into which either of the medicines can be put. Further more it takes 3 hours to prepare enough material to fill 1,000 bottles of A and it takes one hour to prepare enough material to fill 1,000 bottles of B and there are 66 hours available for this operation. The profit is Rs. 8/- per bottle for A and Rs.7/- per bottle for B. How the manufacturer schedule his production in order to maximize profit.

2. A resourceful home decorator manufactures two types of lamps say A and B. Both lamps go through two technicians, first a cutter, second a finisher. Lamp A requires 2 hours of the cutter's time and 1 hour of the finisher's time. Lamp B requires 1 hour of the cutter's time and 2 hours of the finisher's time. The cutter has 104 hours and finisher 76 hours of time available each month. Profit on one lamp A is Rs. 6.00 and on one lamp B is Rs. 11.00. Assuming that he can sale all that, he produces, how many of each type lamps should he manufacture to obtain the best return.

3. A firm can produce three types of cloths say A, B and C. Three kinds of wool are required for it, say red wool, green wool and blue wool. One unit length of type A cloth needs 2 yards of red wool and 3 yards of blue wool; one unit length of type B cloth needs 3 yards of red wool, 2 yards of green wool and 2 yards of blue wool, and one unit length of type C cloth needs 5 yards of green wool and 4 yards of blue wool. The firm has only a stock of 8 yards of red wool, 10 yards of green wool and 15 yards of blue wool. It is assumed that the income obtained from one unit length of type A cloth is Rs. 3.00, of type B cloth is Rs. 5.00, and of type C cloth is Rs. 4.00. Determine how the firm should use the available material, so as to maximize the income from the finished cloth.

4. Old hens can be bought for Rs. 2.00 each but young ones cost Rs. 5.00 each. The old hens lay 3 eggs per week and the young ones 5 eggs per week. Each egg being worth 30 paise. A hen costs Rs.1.00 per week to feed. If I have only Rs. 80.00 to spend for hens, how many of each kind should I buy to give a profit of more than Rs. 6.00 per week assuming that I cannot house more than 20 hens?

5. Find all the basic solutions of the following systems :
$x_1 + 2x_2 + x_3 = 4$, $2x_1 + x_2 + 5x_3 = 5$ and prove that they are non-degenerate.

6. If $a_1 = \begin{bmatrix} 3 \\ 4 \end{bmatrix}$, $a_2 = \begin{bmatrix} -1 \\ 2 \end{bmatrix}$, $a_3 = \begin{bmatrix} 1 \\ 4 \end{bmatrix}$ and $b = \begin{bmatrix} 1 \\ 4 \end{bmatrix}$ then determine whether all possible basic solutions exist for the following set of equations : $[a_1 \quad a_2 \quad a_3]x = b$.

7. Show that the feasible solution $x_1 = 1, x_2 = 0, x_3 = 1$ and $Z = 6$ to the system of equations $x_1 + x_2 + x_3 = 2,\ x_1 - x_2 + x_3 = 2,\ x_j \le 0, j = 1, 2, 3$ which minimize $Z = 2x_1 + 3x_2 + 4x_3$ is not basic.

8. Define a basic feasible solution to a linear programming problem and find all the B.F.S. of following system of equations :
$8x_1 + 6x_2 + 13x_3 + x_4 + x_5 = 6,\ 9x_1 + x_2 + 2x_3 + 6_4 + 10x_5 = 10.$

9. Is $x_1 = 1, x_2 = \frac{1}{2}$, $x_3 = x_4 = x_5 = 0$ a basic solution to the following equations :

$x_1 + 2x_2 + x_3 + x_4 = 2,\ x_1 + 2x_2 + \frac{1}{2}x_3 + x_5 = 2$?

10. Mark the feasible region represented by the constraint equations $x_1 + x_2 \le 1$, $3x_1 + x_2 \le 3,\ x_1 \ge 0,\ x_2 \ge 0$ of a linear optimizing function $Z = x_1 + x_2$.

Answers

1. If x_1 and x_2 bottles of medicines A and B respectively, are produced then L.P.P. is Max. $Z = 8x_1 + 7x_2$ s.t. $3x_1 + x_2 \le 66{,}000,\ x_1 + x_2 \le 45{,}000,\ x_1 \le 20{,}000,\ x_2 \le 40{,}000$.

2. If x_1 and x_2 lamps of types A and B respectively, are manufactured then L.P.P. is Max. $Z = 6x_1 + 11x_2$ s.t. $2x_1 + x_2 \le 104,\ x_1 + x_2 \le 76,\ x_1 \ge 0,\ x_2 \ge 0$.

3. If the firm produces x_1, x_2, x_3 yards of three types of cloths A, B and C respectively, then L.P.P. is Max. $Z = 3x_1 + 5x_2 + 4x_3$ s.t. $2x_1 + 3x_2 \le 8,\ 2x_2 + 5x_3 \le 10$, $3x_1 + 2x_2 + 4x_3 \le 15,\ x_1, x_2, x_3 \ge 0$.

4. If x_1 and x_2 are the old hens and young hens respectively then L.P.P. is Max. $Z = 0.50x_2 - 0.10x_1$ s.t. $2x_1 + 5x_2 \le 80,\ x_1 + x_2 \le 20,\ x_1, x_2 \ge 0$.

5. $(2, 1, 0),\ (5, 0, -1),\ \left(0, \frac{5}{3}, \frac{2}{3}\right)$.

6. Yes.

8. $\left(\frac{2}{3}, 0, 0, \frac{2}{3}, 0\right),\ \left(\frac{50}{71}, 0, 0, 0, \frac{26}{71}\right),\ \left(0, \frac{26}{35}, 0, \frac{54}{35}, 0\right),\ \left(0, \frac{50}{59}, 0, 0, \frac{54}{59}\right),$

$\left(0, 0, \frac{13}{38}, \frac{59}{38}, 0\right),\ \left(0, 0, \frac{25}{64}, 0, \frac{59}{64}\right).$

9. No.

AMITY SCHOOL OF ENGINEERING & TECHNOLOGY
AMITY UNIVERSITY UTTAR PRADESH
B.TECH (3rd Semester)

APPLIED MATHEMATICS - III

TUTORIAL SHEET-14

1. Solve graphically the following L.P. Problems:
(i) Max. $Z = 8x_1 + 7x_2$ s.t. $3x_1 + x_2 \le 66{,}000$, $x_1 + x_2 \le 45{,}000$, $x_1 \le 20{,}000$, $x_2 \le 40{,}000$ and $x_1 \ge 0, x_2 \ge 0$.
(ii) Max. $Z = 5x_1 + 7x_2$ s.t. $x_1 + x_2 \le 4$, $3x_1 + 8x_2 \le 24$, $10x_1 + 7x_2 \le 35$, $x_1, x_2 => 0$.
(iii) Max. $Z = 6x_1 - 2x_2$ s.t. $2x_1 - x_2 \le 2$, $x_1 \le 3$ and $x_1, x_2 \ge 0$
(iv) Max. $Z = 3x_1 + 4x_2$ s.t. $x_1 - x_2 \le -1$, $-x_1 + 8x_2 \le 0$ and $x_1 \ge 0, x_2 \ge 0$.
(v) Max. $Z = 3x_1 + 2x_2$ s.t. $-2x_1 + 3x_2 \le 9$, $x_1 - 5x_2 \le -20$ and $x_1 \ge 0, x_2 \ge 0$.
(vi) Max. $Z = x_1 + x_2$ s.t. $-2x_1 + x_2 \le 1$, $x_1 \le 2$, $x_1 + x_2 \le 3$ and $x_1, x_2 \ge 0$.
(vii) Max. $Z = 4x_1 + 5x_2$ s.t. $x_1 + x_2 \le 1$, $-2x_1 + x_2 \le 1$, $4x_1 - 2x_2 \le 1$ and $x_1, x_2 \ge 0$.
(viii) Max. $Z = 0.75x_1 + x_2$ s.t. $x_1 - x_2 \ge 0$, $-0.5x_1 + x_2 \le 1$ and $x_1, x_2 \ge 0$.
(ix) Max. $Z = 3x_1 + 5x_2$ s.t. $-3x_1 + 4x_2 \ge 12$, $2x_1 - x_2 \ge -2$, $2x_1 + 3x_2 \le 12$, $x_1 \le 4$, $x_2 \ge 2$ and $x_1, x_2 \ge 0$.
(x) Max. $Z = 4x_1 + 2x_2$ s.t. $x_1 + 2x_2 \ge 2$, $3x_1 + x_2 \ge 3$, $4x_1 + 3x_2 \le 6$ and $x_1, x_2 \ge 0$.
(xi) Max. $Z = -x_1 + 2x_2$ s.t. $-x_1 + 3x_2 \le 10$, $x_1 + x_2 \le 6$, $x_1 - 3x_2 \le 2$ and $x_1, x_2 \ge 0$.
(xii) Max. $Z = x_1 + x_2$ s.t. $5x_1 + 10x_2 \le 50$, $x_1 + x_2 \ge 1$, $x_1 \le 4$ and $x_1, x_2 \ge 0$.

2. Determine $x \ge 0$ and $y \ge 0$, so as to maximize $Z = 2x + 3y$ subject to the constraints : $x + y \le 30$, $y \le 12$, $x \le 20$, $y \ge 3$, $x - y \ge 0$.

3. Does the L.P.P. Max. $Z = x_1 + x_2$ s.t. $x_1 - x_2 \ge 0$, $3x_1 - x_2 \le -3$ and $x_1, x_2 \ge 0$ have a feasible solution? Show with the help of a graph.

4. Define a general linear programming problem and obtain the conditions under which solution of L.P.P. by graphical method exists.

5. A firm manufactures two types of products A and B and sells them at a profit of Rs. 2.00 on type A and Rs.3.00 on type B. Each product is processed on two machines M_1 and M_2.Type A requires one minute of processing time on M_1 and two minutes on M_2; type B requires one minute on M_1 and one minute on M_2. The machine M_1 is available for not more than 6 hours 40 minutes while machine M_2 is available for 10 hours during any working day. Find how many products of each type should the firm produce each day in order to get maximum profit.

6. Consider two different types of foodstuffs, say F_1 and F_2. Assume that these foodstuffs contain vitamins V_1, V_2 and V_3 respectively. Minimum daily requirement of three vitamins are 1 mg. of V_1, 50 mg. of V_2 and 10 mg. of V_3. Suppose that the foodstuff F_1 contains 1 mg. of V_1, 100 mg. of V_2 and 10 mg. of V_3; whereas the foodstuff F_2 contains 1 mg. of V_1, 10 mg. of V_2 and 100 mg. of V_3. Cost of one unit of foodstuff

F_1 is Re. 1 and that of F_2 is Rs. 1.5. Find the minimum cost diet that would supply the body at least the minimum requirements of each vitamin.

7. A soft drink plant has two bottling machines A and B. It produces and sells 8 ounce and 16 ounce bottles. The following data is available.

Machine	8 Ounce	16 Ounce
A	100/minute	40/minute
B	60/minute	75/minute

The machines can be run 8 hrs. per day, 5 days per week. Weekly production of the drinks cannot exceed 3,00,000 ounces and the market can absorb 25,000 eight ounce bottles and 7,000 sixteen ounce bottles per week. Profit on these bottles is 15 paise and 25 paise per bottle respectively. The planner wishes to maximize his profit subject to all the production and marketing restrictions. Formulate it as a linear programming problem and solve.

8. Convert the following L.P. Problems in standard forms:
(i) Max. $Z = x_1 - x_2 + 3x_3$ s.t. $x_1 + x_2 + x_3 \leq 10$, $-2x_1 + x_3 \geq -2$, $-2x_1 + 2x_2 - 3x_3 \leq 0$ and $x_1, x_2, x_3 \geq 0$.
(ii) Max. $Z = x_1 - 2x_2 + x_3$ s.t. $2x_1 + 3x_2 + 4x_3 \geq -4$, $3x_1 + 5x_2 + 2x_3 \geq 7$, $x_1 \geq 0$, $x_2 \geq 0$, x_3 is unrestricted in sign.

Answers

1. (i) $x_1 = 10{,}500$, $x_2 = 34{,}500$, Max. $Z = 3{,}25{,}500$ (ii) $x_1 = 1.6$, $x_2 = 2.4$, Max. $Z = 24.8$
(iii) $x_1 = 3$, $x_2 = 4$, Max. $Z = 10$ (iv) No Solution (v) Unbounded solution
(vi) Infinite number of solutions (vii) Unbounded solution (viii) Unbounded solution
(ix) $x_1 = 3$, $x_2 = 2$, Max. $Z = 19$ (x) $x_1 = 0.6$, $x_2 = 1.2$, Max. $Z = 4.8$
(xi) $x_1 = 2$, $x_2 = 0$, Max. $Z = -2$ (xii) Infinite number of solutions.

2. $x = 18$, $y = 12$, $z = 72$ 3. No. 5. Type $A = 0$, Type $B = 400$, Profit = 1200.

6. $F_1 = 1$ unit, $F_2 = 0$ unit, Cost = Re. 1

7. If x_1 and x_2 bottles of 8 and 16 ounces respectively, are produced then L.P.P. is

Max. $Z = 0.15x_1 + 0.25x_2$ s.t. $8x_1 + 16x_2 \leq 3{,}00{,}000$, $\dfrac{x_1}{100} + \dfrac{x_2}{40} \leq 2400$,

$\dfrac{x_1}{60} + \dfrac{x_2}{75} \leq 2400$, $0 \leq x_1 \leq 25{,}000$, $0 \leq x_2 \leq 7000$,

$\dfrac{x_1}{60} + \dfrac{x_2}{75} \leq 2400$, $0 \leq x_1 \leq 25{,}000$, $0 \leq x_2 \leq 7000$

$x_1 = 25{,}000$, $x_2 = 6250$, Max. Z = Rs. 5312.50.

8. (i) Max $Z = x_1 - x_2 + 3x_3$ s.t. $x_1 + x_2 + x_3 + x_4 = 10$, $2x_1 - x_3 + x_5 = 2$, $-2x_1 + 2x_2 - 3x_3 + x_6 = 0$ and $x_1, x_2, x_3, x_4, x_5, x_6 \geq 0$.
(ii) Max. $Z = -x_1 + 2x_2 - (x'_3 - x''_3)$ s.t. $-2x_2 - 3x_2 - 4(x'_3 - x''_3) - x_4 = 4$, $3x_1 + 5x_2 + 2(x'_3 - x''_3) - x_5 = 7$, $x_1, x_2, x'_3, x''_3, x_4, x_5 \geq 0$ where $Z' = -Z$.

AMITY SCHOOL OF ENGINEERING & TECHNOLOGY
AMITY UNIVERSITY UTTAR PRADESH
B.TECH (3rd Semester)

APPLIED MATHEMATICS - III

TUTORIAL SHEET-15

1. Solve the following problems by simplex method :
   (i) Max. $Z = 2x_1 + 4x_2$ s.t. $2x_1 + 3x_2 \leq 48, x_1 + 3x_2 \leq 42, x_1 + x_2 \leq 21, x_1, x_2 \geq 0$.
   (ii) Max. $Z = 2x_1 + x_2$ s.t. $x_1 - x_2 \leq 10, 2x_1 - x_2 \leq 40, x_1, x_2 \geq 0$.
   (iii) Max. $Z = 4x_1 + 10x_2$ s.t. $2x_1 + x_2 \leq 50, 2x_1 + 5x_2 \leq 100, 2x_1 + 3x_2 \leq 90, x_1, x_2 \geq 0$.
   (iv) Max. $Z = 4x_1 + 8x_2$ s.t. $x_1 + x_2 \geq 2, 2x_1 + x_3 \geq 5, x_1, x_2, x_3 \geq 0$.
   (v) Max. $Z = 2x_1 + 3x_2$ s.t. $2x_1 - 2x_2 \leq 2, -3x_1 + 3x_2 \leq 6, x_1, x_2 \geq 0$.
   (vi) Max. $Z = 2x_1 + 3x_2$ s.t. $-x_1 + 2x_2 \leq 4, x_1 + x_2 \leq 6, x_1 + 3x_2 \leq 9, x_1, x_2$ unrestricted.

2. Use two phase simplex method to solve the following L.P.P.
   (i) Max. $Z = 5x_1 + 8x_2$ s.t. $3x_1 + 2x_2 \geq 3, x_1 + 4x_2 \geq 4, x_1 + x_2 \leq 5, x_1, x_2 \geq 0$.
   (ii) Max. $Z = 3x_1 - x_2$ s.t. $2x_1 + x_2 \geq 2, x_1 + x_2 \leq 2, x_2 \leq 4, x_1, x_2 \geq 0$.
   (iii) Max. $Z = x_1 + x_2$ s.t. $2x_1 + x_2 \geq 4, x_1 + 7x_2 \leq 7, x_1, x_2 \geq 0$.

3. Solve the following problems by 'Big M' method :
   (i) Max. $Z = 2x_1 - x_2 + x_3$ s.t. $x_1 + x_2 - 3x_3 \leq 8, 4x_1 - x_2 + x_3 \geq 2, 2x_1 + 3x_2 - x_3 \geq 4$ and $x_1, x_2, x_3 \geq 0$.
   (ii) Max. $Z = 2x_1 + 9x_2 + x_3$ s.t. $x_1 + 4x_2 + 2x_3 \geq 5, 3x_1 + x_2 + 2x_3 \geq 4, x_1, x_2, x_3 \geq 0$
   (iii) Max. $Z = x_1 + 2x_2 + 3x_3 - x_4$ s.t. $x_1 + 2x_2 + 3x_3 = 15, 2x_1 + x_2 + 5x_3 = 20,$
   $x_1 + 2x_2 + x_3 + x_4 = 10$ and $x_1, x_2, x_3, x_4 \geq 0$.
   (iv) Max. $Z = -x_1 - x_2$ s.t. $3x_1 + 2x_2 \geq 30, -2x_1 + 3x_2 \leq -30, x_1 + x_2 \leq 5, x_1, x_2 \geq 0$.

4. Solve the following problems by appropriate methods :
   (i) Min. $Z = x_1 + x_2 + 3x_3$ s.t. $3x_1 + 2x_2 + x_3 \leq 3, 2x_1 + x_2 + 2x_3 \leq 2, x_1, x_2, x_3 \geq 0$.
   (ii) Min. $Z = -2x_1 - x_2$ s.t. $3x_1 + x_2 = 3, 4x_1 + 3x_2 \geq 6, x_1 + 2x_2 \leq 4, x_1, x_2 \geq 0$.
   (iii) Min. $Z = x_1 + x_2 + x_3$ s.t. $x_1 - x_4 - 2x_6 = 5, x_2 + 2x_4 - 3x_5 + x_6 = 3,$
   $x_3 + 2x_4 - 5x_5 + 6x_6 = 5$ and $x_i \geq 0$ $(i = 1, 2, ..., 6)$
   (iv) Min. $Z = 3x_1 + 2x_2 + x_3$ s.t. $2x_1 + 5x_2 + x_3 = 12, 3x_1 + 4x_2 = 11, x_2, x_3 \geq 3$
   (v) Min. $Z = 3x_1 + 2.5x_2 + x_3$ s.t. $2x_1 + 4x_2 \geq 40, 3x_1 + 2x_2 \geq 50, x_1, x_2 \geq 0$
   (vi) Min. $Z = 3x_1 + 2x_2$ s.t. $2x_1 + x_2 \leq 2, 3x_1 + 4x_2 \geq 12, x_1, x_2 \geq 0$

5. A company produces three types of leather belts A, B and C, which are processed on three machines M_1, M_2 and M_3. Belt A requires 2 hours on machine M_1 and 3 hours on machine M_3. Belt B requires 3 hours on machine M_1, 2 hours on machine M_2 and 2 hours on machine M_3 and belt C requires 5 hours on machine M_2 and 4 hours on machine M_3. There are 8 hours of time per day available on machine M_1, 10 hours of time per day available on machine M_2 and 15 hours of time per day available on machine M_3. The profit gained from belt A is Rs. 3.00 per unit, from belt B is

Rs. 5.00 per unit and from belt C is Rs. 4.00 per unit. What should be the daily production of each type of belt so that the profit is maximum?

6. Solve the following system of simultaneous linear equations by using simplex method:
(i) $x_1 + x_2 = 1,\ 2x_1 + x_2 = 3.$
(ii) $x_1 - x_3 + 4x_4 = 3,\ 2x_1 - x_2 = 3,\ 3x_1 - 2x_2 - x_4 = 1,\ x_1, x_2, x_3, x_4 \geq 0.$

7. Use simplex method to obtain the inverse of the matrix $A = \begin{bmatrix} 3 & 2 \\ 4 & -1 \end{bmatrix}$.

Answers

1. (i) $x_1 = 6, x_2 = 12$, Max $Z = 60$ (ii) Unbounded
(iii) $x_1 = 0, x_2 = 20$ or $x_1 = \frac{75}{4},\ x_2 = \frac{25}{2}$, Max. $Z = 200$. (iv) $x_1 = \frac{5}{2},\ x_2 = 0, x_3 = 0$ and Max. $X = 10$ (v) Unbounded (vi) $x_1 = \frac{9}{2},\ x_2 = \frac{3}{2}$, Max. $Z = \frac{27}{2}$

2. (i) $x_1 = 0, x_2 = 5$, Max. $Z = 40$ (ii) $x_2 = 2, x_2 = 0$, Max. $Z = 6$.
(iii) $x_1 = \frac{21}{13},\ x_2 = \frac{10}{13}$, Max. $Z = \frac{31}{13}$

3. (i) Unbounded (ii) $x_1 = 0 = x_2, x_3 = \frac{5}{2}$, Max. $Z = \frac{5}{2}$
(iii) $x_1 = x_2 = x_3 = \frac{5}{2} x_4 = 0$, Max. $Z = 15$ (iv) No feasible solution.

4. (i) $x_1 = 0 = x_2 = x_3$, Min. $Z = 0$ (ii) $x_1 = \frac{3}{5},\ x_2 = \frac{6}{5}$, Max. $Z = -\frac{12}{5}$
(iii) $x_1 = \frac{213}{30},\ x_2 = 0 = x_3 = x_5, x_4 = \frac{13}{10},\ x_6 = \frac{2}{5}$, Max. $Z = \frac{213}{30}$
(iv) $x_1 = \frac{11}{3},\ x_2 = 0, x_3 = \frac{14}{3}$, Max. $Z = \frac{47}{3}$ (v) Unbounded
(vi) No feasible solution.

5. $A = \frac{89}{41},\ B = \frac{50}{41},\ C = \frac{62}{41}$, Max. Profit = Rs. $\frac{765}{41}$

6. (i) $x_1 = 2, x_2 = -1$ (ii) $x_1 = 5, x_2 = 7, x_3 = 2$ and $x_4 = 0$

7. $A^{-1} = \begin{bmatrix} \frac{1}{11} & \frac{2}{11} \\ \frac{4}{11} & -\frac{3}{11} \end{bmatrix}$.

AMITY SCHOOL OF ENGINEERING & TECHNOLOGY
AMITY UNIVERSITY UTTAR PRADESH
B.TECH (3rd Semester)

APPLIED MATHEMATICS - III

TUTORIAL SHEET-16

1. What is degeneracy? Discuss a method to resolve degeneracy in L.P.P.
2. Solve the following L.P. Problems by resolving the degeneracy in the problems:
   (i) Max. $Z = 3x_1 + 9x_2$ s.t. $x_1 + 4x_2 \le 8, x_1 + 2x_2 \le x_1, x_2 \ge 0$.
   (ii) Max. $Z = 3x_1 + 5x_2$ s.t. $x_1 + x_3 = 4, x_2 + x_4 = 6, 3x_1 + 2x_2 + x_5 = 12$ and $x_i \ge 0$ $i = 1, 2, ..., 5$.
   (iii) Max. $Z = 2x_1 + 3x_2 + 10x_3$ s.t. $x_1 + 2x_3 = 0, x_2 + x_3 = 1\ x_1, x_2, x_3 \ge 0$
3. Write the dual of the following L.P. Problems
   (i) Min. $Z = 3x_1 + x_2$ s.t. $2x_1 + 3x_2 \ge 2, x_1 + x_2 \ge 1$ and $x_1, x_2 \ge 0$
   (ii) Max. $Z = x_1 + 2x_2$ s.t. $2x_1 - 3x_2 \le 3, 4x_1 + x_2 \ge -4$ and $x_1, x_2 \ge 0$
   (iii) Max. $Z = 2x_1 + 3x_2 + x_3$ s.t. $4x_1 + 3x_2 + x_3 = 6, x_1 + 2x_2 + 5x_3 = 4$ and $x_1, x_2, x_3 \ge 0$
   (iv) Min. $Z = x_1 + x_2 + x_3$ s.t. $x_1 - 3x_2 + 4x_3 = 5, x_1 - 2x_2 \le 3, 2x_2 - x_3 \ge 4, x_1, x_2, x_3 \ge 0$, s_3 is unrestricted in sign.
   (v) Min. $Z = 2x_2 + 5x_3$ s.t. $x_1 + x_2 \ge 2, 2x_1 + x_2 + 6x_3 \le 6, x_1 - x_2 + 3x_3 = 4, x_1, x_2, x_3 \ge 0$
   (vi) Max. $Z = 6x_1 + 4x_2 + x_3 + 7x_4 + 5x_5$ s.t. $3x_1 + 7x_2 + 8x_3 + 5x_4 + x_5 = 2$, $2x_1 + x_2 + 3x_3 + 2x_4 + 9x_5 = 6$ and $x_1, x_2, x_3, x_4 \ge 0, x_5 = 2$ is unrestricted in sign.
4. Solve the following L.P.P. by the dual simplex algorithm.
   (i) Min. $Z = 3x_1 + x_2$ s.t. $x_1 + x_2 \ge 1, 2x_1 + 3x_2 \ge 2$ and $x_1, x_2 \ge 0$.
   (ii) Min. $Z = 3x_1 + 2x_2 + x_3 + 4x_4$ s.t. $2x_1 + 4x_2 + 5x_3 + x_4 \ge 10$, $3x_1 - x_2 + 7x_3 - 2x_4 \ge 2$, $5x_1 + 2x_2 + x_3 + 6x_4 \ge 15$ and $x_1, x_2, x_3, x_4 \ge 0$
   (iii) Max. $Z = -6x_1 - 7x_2 - 3x_3 - 5x_4$ s.t. $5x_1 + 6x_2 - 3x_3 + 4x_4 \ge 12$, $x_2 + 5x_3 - 6x_4 \ge 10$, $2x_1 + 5x_2 + x_3 + x_4 \ge 8$ and $x_1, x_2, x_3, x_4 \ge 0$.
   (iv) Max. $Z = -2x_1 - 3x_3$ s.t. $x_1 - 2x_2 + 4x_3 \ge 8, x_1 + x_2 - x_3 \ge 5$ and $x_1, x_2, x_3 \ge 0$
5. Use duality to solve the following L.P. Problems :
   (i) Max. $Z = 3x_1 + x_2$ s.t. $x_1 + x_2 \le 1, 2x_1 + 3x_2 \ge 2$ and $x_1, x_2 \ge 0$
   (ii) Min. $Z = 2x_1 + 2x_2$ s.t. $2x_1 + 4x_2 \ge 1, x_1 + 2x_2 \ge 1\ 2x_1 + x_2 \ge 1$ and $x_1, x_2 \ge 0$

Answers

2. (i) $x_1 = 0, x_2 = 2, Z = 18$ (ii) $x_1 = 0, x_2 = 6, x_3 = 4, x_4 = 0, x_5 = 0, Z = 30$
   (iii) $x_1 = 2, x_2 = 0, x_3 = 1, Z = 14$
3. (i) Max. $Z_D = 2w_1 + w_2$ s.t. $2w_1 + w_2 \le 3, 3w_1 + w_2 \le 1$ and $w_1, w_2 \ge 0$
   (ii) Min. $Z_D = 3w_1 - 4w_2$ s.t. $2w_1 + 4w_2 \ge 1, -3w_1 + w_2 \ge 2$ and $w_1, w_2 \ge 0$
   (iii) Min. $Z_D = 6w_1 + 4w_2$ s.t. $4w_1 + w_2 \ge 2, 3w_1 + 2w_2 \ge 3, w_1 + 5w_2 \ge 1$ and w_1, w_2 both are unrestricted in sign.

(iv) Max. $Z_D = 5w_1 - 3w_2 + 4w_3$ s.t. $w_1 - w_2 \le 1, -3w_1 + 2w_2 + 2w_3 \le 1, 4w_1 - w_3 = 1$
w_1, w_2, w_3 is unrestricted in sign.

(v) Max. $Z_D = 2w_1 - 6w_2 - 4w_3$ s.t. $w_1 - 2w_2 - w_3 \le 0, w_1 - w_2 + w_3 \le 2, -6w_2 - 3w_3 \le 5$ and $w_1, w_2 \ge 0, w_3$ is unrestricted in sign.

(vi) Min. $Z_D = 2w_1 + 6w_2$ s.t. $3w_1 + 2w_2 \ge 6, 7w_1 + w_2 \ge 4, 8w_1 + 3w_2 \ge 1,$
$5w_1 + 2w_2 \ge 7,\ w_1 + 9w_2 = 5$ and w_1, w_2 unrestricted in sign.

4. (i) $x_1 = 0, x_2 = 1, Z = 1$

(ii) $x_1 = \frac{65}{23},\ x_2 = 0, x_3 = \frac{20}{23},\ x_4 = 0, Z = \frac{215}{23}.$

(iii) $x_1 = 0,\ x_2 = \frac{30}{11},\ x_3 = \frac{16}{11},\ x_4 = 0, Z = -\frac{258}{11}.$

(iv) $x_1 = 0, x_2 = 14, x_3 = 9, Z = -9$

5. (i) $x_1 = x_2 = 0, Z = 3$

(ii) $x_1 = \frac{1}{3},\ x_2 = \frac{1}{3}, Z = \frac{4}{3}.$

EXAMINATION PAPER

B.TECH (COMPUTER SCIENCE AND ENGINEERING, ELECTRONICS AND COMMUNICATION ENGINEERING)

THIRD SEMESTER END TERM EXAMINATIONS, JANUARY, 2007

APPLIED MATHEMATICS-III

Time : 3 Hours *Maximum Marks* : 60

Note : Attempt any six questions.
All questions carry equal marks

1. (a) Solve $xp + yq = 3z$ **(5)**

(b) Define Clairaut's form and then solve $(p - q)(z - px - qy) = 1$. **(2+3)**

2. (a) Solve $(3D^2 - 2D'^2 + D - 1)z = 4e^{x+y} . \cos(x + y)$ **(5)**

(b) Solve $(D^2 + 2DD' + D'^2)z = 2\cos y - x\sin y$ **(5)**

3. (a) A firm manufactures 3 products A, B, C. The profits are Rs. 3, Rs. 2, Rs. 4. The firm has 2 machines.

Machines	Products		
	A	*B*	*C*
G	4	3	5
H	2	2	4

Machines G, H have 2000 and 2500 machine minutes. The first machine must manufacture 100 A's, 200 B's and 50 C's but not more than 150 A's. Setup L.P.P. to maximise profit. **(4)**

(b) Use simplex method to solve the following system of linear equation :

$$x_1 - x_3 + 4x_4 = 3, \quad 2x_1 - x_2 = 3,$$
$$3x_1 - 2x_2 - x_4 = 1, \quad x_1, x_2, x_3, x_4 \geq 0$$ **(6)**

4. (a) Solve Max $Z = 4x_1 + 5x_2 - 3x_3$,

Subject to $x_1 + x_2 + x_3 = 10$

$x_1 - x_2 \geq 1$

$2x_1 + 3x_2 + x_3 \leq 40$

$x_1, x_2, x_3 \geq 0$ **(7)**

(b) Define the conditions under which solution of L.P.P. by graphical method exists **(3)**

5. (a) Find the complex form of the Fourier Series of $f(x) = e^{-x}$ in $-1 \le x \le 1$. **(5)**

(b) Obtain the first three coefficients in Fourier Cosine Series for y where y is **(5)**

x:	0	1	2	3	4	5
y:	4	8	15	7	6	2

6. (a) Obtain Fourier Series for the function $f(x)$ given by

$$f(x) = \begin{cases} 1 + \frac{2x}{\pi}, & -\pi \le x \le 0 \\ 1 - \frac{2x}{\pi}, & 0 \le x \le \pi \end{cases}$$

(5)

(b) Express $f(x) = x$ as half range sine series in $0 < x < 2$. **(5)**

7. (a) Find Laplace transform of $\frac{\cos at - \cos bt}{t}$. **(5)**

(b) Find the inverse transform of $\frac{S}{S^4 + 4a^4}$. **(5)**

8. (a) Apply Convolution theorem to evaluate

$$L^{-1}\left(\frac{S^2}{(S^2 + a^2)(S^2 + b^2)}\right)$$

(4)

(b) Solve $ty'' + 2y' + ty = \cos t$ given $y(0) = 1$.

9. (a) Find

$$L^{-1}\left(\frac{Se^{-S/2} + \pi e^{-S}}{S^2 + \pi^2}\right)$$

(5)

(b) If $f(x) = |\cos x|$, then $f(x)$ as a Fourier Sereis in interval $(-\pi, \pi)$ is a function of $\sin nx$ or $\cos nx$. Explain. **(2)**

(c) Derive partial differential equation of

$$2z = \frac{x^2}{a^2} + \frac{y^2}{b^2}.$$

(3)

B.TECH (CSE, IT ECE, E&TC)

THIRD SEMESTER END TERM EXAMINATIONS DECEMBER, 2008

APPLIED MATHEMATICS-III

Time : 3 Hours

Maximum Marks : 60

SECTION - A

(24 marks)

Note : Attempt any **4** out of **5** questions.
Each question carries **6** marks

1. Solve the following differential equation :

$$(x^2 - y^2 - z^2)p + 2xyq = 2xz$$

2. Find the Fourier series for the function

$$f(x) = x + x^2, \quad -\pi < x < \pi$$

Hence show that

(i) $\dfrac{\pi^2}{6} = 1 + \dfrac{1}{2^2} + \dfrac{1}{3^2} + \dfrac{1}{4^2} + \ldots$

(ii) $\dfrac{\pi^2}{12} = \dfrac{1}{1^2} - \dfrac{1}{2^2} + \dfrac{1}{3^2} - \dfrac{1}{4^2} + \ldots$

3. Find the Laplace transform of the following functions :

(i) $\dfrac{e^{-t}\sin t}{t}$

(ii) $\dfrac{1 - \cos t}{t^2}$ **(3+3)**

4. (a) Solve : $(D - 3D' - 2)^2 z = ze^{2x} \tan(y + 3x)$.

(b) Solve $\dfrac{\partial^3 z}{\partial x^3} - \dfrac{\partial^3 z}{\partial y^3} = x^3 y^3$. **(3+3)**

5. Maximize $Z = 3x_1 + 2x_2$

Subject to $2x_1 + x_2 \le 5$

$x_1 + x_2 \le 3$

and $x_1, x_2 \ge 0$

SECTION - B

(20 Marks)

Note : Attempt any **2** out of **3** questions.
Each question carries **10** marks

6. (a) Solve the following non-linear Partial differential equation

$$(x+y)(p+2)^2 + (x-y)(p-q)^2 = 1$$

(5)

(b) Obtain the first three co-efficients in the Fourier cosine series for y, where y is given in the following table :

(5)

x :	0	1	2	3	4	5
y :	4	8	15	7	6	2

7. (a) Solve $(p^2 + q^2)y = qz$ by Charpits method. **(5)**

(b) State and prove the convolution theorem. **(5)**

8. (a) Solve the linear Partial differential equation

$$\frac{\partial^2 z}{\partial x^2} + \frac{\partial^2 z}{\partial x \partial y} - 6\frac{\partial^2 z}{\partial y^2} = y \cos x$$

(5)

(b) Obtain Fourier series for the function $f(x)$ given by

$$f(x) = \begin{cases} 1 + \dfrac{2x}{\pi}, & -\pi \le x \le 0 \\ 1 - \dfrac{2x}{\pi}, & 0 \le x \le \pi \end{cases}$$

Hence, deduce that $\frac{1}{1^2} + \frac{1}{3^2} + \frac{1}{5^2} + \ldots = \frac{\pi^2}{8}$

(5)

SECTION-C *(Compulsory)*

(16 Marks)

(a) Maximize $Z = 4x_1 + 5x_2 - 3x_3$

Subject to $x_1 + x_2 + 3 = 10$

$x_1 - x_2 \ge 1$

$2x_1 + 3x_2 + x_3 = 40$

and $x_1, x_2, x_3 \ge 0$

(8)

(b) Using Laplace transform solve the following differential equation :

$$\frac{d^2x}{dt^2} + 2\frac{dx}{dt} + 5x = e^{-t} \sin t$$

where $x(0) = 0$ and $x'(0) = 1$

(5)

(b) If $L^{-1}\left(\frac{e^{-1/p}}{\sqrt{p}}\right) = \frac{\cos 2\sqrt{t}}{\sqrt{\pi t}}$, find $L^{-1}\left\{\frac{e^{-a/p}}{\sqrt{p}}\right\}$.

(3)